G000109722

First published in 2012
This edition published in 2019:
Britain's Next Bestseller
An imprint of Live It Ventures LTD
126 Kirkleatham Lane,
Redcar. Cleveland. TS10 5DD
www.bnbsbooks.co.uk

ISBN 978-1-906954-41-3
Cover designed by Peter O'Toole

Dressing and messing at the match and more.
As told by the lads that were there

Northern Monkeys

Britain's Next
BESTSELLER

William Routledge

This book is dedicated to:

Freedom of speech and expression.
Nonconformists and pioneers.
Those that seek and don't follow.
Those who were there.
And most all,
my fellow Northern Monkeys.

ACKNOWLEDGMENTS

To Mick – for Keeping the Faith and not giving up on me. Because there were times that I thought this book wouldn't see the light of day and that my incoherent ramblings wouldn't be worthy of putting to print. There was a period while putting the book together when I was walking a very dark, lengthy and lonely road. Many thanks.

To Cuey – what a diamond geezer – *gives me 'ead a wobble. I mean, what a sound lad he is. Without his help and attention with my last book, that too might not have seen the light of day. I know you had your hands full and your head was all over the shop. Cheers pal. (Diamond geezer, that's nearly as bad as telling someone to be lucky)

To Lucan – my son, and mate. I love you; always have, always will do and I'll always be there – just pay me in kind.

To Jackie – the missus. I'm sorry that for over three years I've not done any D.I.Y. or 'owt around the home. Also, I'm sorry for the seemingly lack of concern I showed to your updates on the X Factor, Big Brother and all the soaps. And, I'm sorry for reciting my fables to you while I was typing them up. From the blank expression on your face, I knew you didn't/don't have a shred of interest in the subjects I bleated on about. The looks I received had 'ask me again if I would marry such a basket case if I had my time over again' written all over them. I suppose that's why opposites attract, isn't it? Jackie, you are my *Tellus, Ventus et Ignis* for an infinite of reasons.

And finally – thank you to all you Northern Monkeys, and the southerners too, too numerous to mention for contributing and for keeping it real. Also for being full of wit, grit and innumerable facts and knowledge and, for pulling my head out of the clouds and keeping my feet well and truly planted on terrafirma in the north-west of England.

BIG THANKS to each and every one of you.

PROLOGUE

Born in the North. Return to the North. Exist in the North. Die in the North.

So, just what is it about the north then that makes Northerners quietly brim with pride of coming from the north and also, being Northern? Being brought into the world in the north? Always wanting to come back to the north? Living in the north? And departing this world in the North? Also, why do southerners hate everything about the north and northerners too? It's plain and simple, really. The north is where it's at and happening and it always has been, hasn't it? Well read on then and you'll find out!

When I decided to put pen to paper on the period of my existence and events that have moulded who I am today, for this book, I'd had quite a few occurrences and experiences during my time on planet earth.

I also wanted to gleam some light on an obsession of mine, clobber, in abundance, and the casual/dresser culture. Only once I began turning my memories on such incidents, encounters and episodes of adventure, and schmutter, into facts and figures and print, nine-times-out-of-ten these circumstances involved fellow northerners. Fellow Northern Monkeys, that is. And I didn't want the book to be all about me, myself and I too.

With that in mind I proceeded to ask the lads, mates and associates to chip in and add their tuppence-worth towards the fable. They did, with characteristic quality tales and seasoned knowledge that was forthcoming in copious amounts. Also, due the diversity of these folk, they acquainted me to their friends, contacts and main men in certain aspects which I would never have had the pleasure of ever having being introduced to. I salute you one and all – even the southerners who contributed to the findings between these bindings. Because of the combined wealth of expertise, au fait and clued-upness of these good eggs, the formula found in the pages that follow is a right good 'un. Well I think so. But then again, who am I to cast judgement on such matters?

Southerners have seemingly 'always' looked down their bent, Roman noses at proletariat, downtrodden scowling northerners, who reside in back-to-back cardboard boxes with disdain and dismissive self-righteousness even though Northern Monkeys take an age grooming their hair. Why can't we all just get along with each other? It's beyond me.

The myth is that southerners are the dogs' bollocks, the bee's knees, the cream and everything of worth begins, is established, and ends, in the epicentre of the universe, that is, London. I want to dispel these myths; because myths are just what they are and the north oozes creativity. Only we like to keep these happenings between ourselves, and not shout them from the roofs of our caves, and the tops of our trees for all and sundry to hear. Until now that is – we're not loudmouths, though.

And one of these spearheads is the rise of the casual/dresser cult. But we – we being us Northern Monkeys – have also had a lot more say on style, cultures and music genres that have emerged in the UK than any southerner would give us credit for when credit is due.

The fundamental, spinal column of the factual tales in this book are based in and around the north-west; and a stereotypical, run of the mill backwater/backward northern town called, Preston. A town where the inhabitants wear donkey jackets, half-mast jeans and DMs, and head bang to Status Quo while drinking bitter in the Rovers Return after they've scranned their tea swimming in gravy (or so southerners would have you believe).

To back all of this up there are heaps of questionable chronicles from sources and fable tellers other than those from the grim, north-west of England. There are even a couple of urban yarns from deepest bandit country too! Also, some of the stories have within them northern dialect and the raconteurs use localism, jargon and slang – for those who come from south of Stoke, I hope you can get your swede round 'em.

So without further ado, let's get down to business then. And if you take this book seriously and its contents as unquestionable fact, you're either a southerner or you haven't a sense of humour. Or worse still, both!

'The North is invisible. Who is to say where the North begins and ends? And yet, we 'feel' northern. It's something in the water, in the blood, in the bricks, in the soil, in the soul; northern soul. Regardless of abstract notions of race, ethnicity or nationality, somewhere deep in our DNA we are northern and we long to be in northern climes. We fear the sun, despise the summer, we cherish the dark, worship the rain; we are built for the cold. From our red brick reservations we funnel out to the hills and the streams and the forests. This is not quaint tourism or hippy ecology; it's an elemental need to be atone with the wind, to feel the icy breath of Woden on our faces. Like salmon, we migrate from shore to shore, sea to sea but we are drawn back to whence we came; back to our spawning grounds. Back to the Magnetic North'

Phil Thornton, author, Casuals.

THE EVOLUTION OF THE NORTHERN MONKEY

If most of us are ashamed of shabby clothes and shoddy furniture, let us be more ashamed of shabby ideas and shoddy philosophies... it would be a sad situation if the wrapper were better than the meat wrapped inside it.

Albert Einstein.

The evolution of the Northern Monkey and the birth of the catalytic northern casual/dresser: To define the true substance of Casual, that can have many meanings, let's try to make sense of the tag that lads who have, and still do, live-a-lifestyle that culture has been labelled with – those who live the lifestyle, don't dub themselves as casuals, though.

Denotation of a single locution for a wide spectrum of individuals can be very damning. Firstly I'll run through the misinterpretations of what a casual/dresser is not, for those who didn't know, so they might just grasp a designer thread or two of the implications, and the significance, of being a northern casual/dresser. For those who do know, skip the next cross-references.

Casual/dresser:

1. Something that happened by accident or chance.

2. A shallow or superficial culture.
3. An individual with a careless, nonchalant lackadaisical outlook and approach to life.
4. Someone who attends football matches with the sole purpose of starting fights.
5. A word and culture that is somewhat of a cliché nowadays.

What does define and epitomise a Northern Monkey, casual/dresser then?

I can't articulate for a culture that has survived four decades single-handedly, I'm no guru. So with the help, values and the wealth of knowledge of fellow Northern Monkeys – and the odd southerner I will try to shed a little illumination on occurrences that moulded the species. Along the way I'll hopefully enlighten the world of their attachments, passions, and witty anecdotes that are connected to all things northern.

Really, what makes them tick. A subject that I've chewed the fat over many a time, while having an ale or two with pedigreed, dapper dressed lads. Because it can be argued that within subcultures how individuals dress, their presence, and the aura they give off, is an indicator of an underground mysterious identity.

No more so than with the Northern Monkey. Subcultures and youth styles have improvised in their development over periods of time, which in itself is casualism/dresserism to the core. The non-narrow mindedness and innovative casual/dresser trends changed weekly, never mind seasonally, in the Eighties. These Northern Monkeys camouflaged themselves from mainstream media attention for many a year. And when the press finally twigged onto the then unwritten-about phenomenon that was sweeping the terraces of every decrepit football ground in Britain, and analysed it, they got their facts all wrong, again. The casual/dresser culture had been a virtually media-free stained movement until the mid-Eighties. The cult was then contaminated by mass media and two-bob lazy journalistic misrepresentation. They gave casual the epithet identification of, 'it's a hooligan thing.'

Over the years, extensive study and research trying to evaluate casuals/dressers has been undertaken without much real success. Features and articles alike in lads' mags have filled the racks of newsagents too. But the only way to really get to the roots and ancestry of the culture is from the lads who were there at the start – it requires a Darwinian examination.

This was a time of existence filled with happiness (apart from that Maggie

T squatting in Downing Street, and mass unemployment), prosperity (before security tags) and innocence (no CCTV evidence) for those who emerged in the pivotal years – the golden age.

Since the turn of the century books were written and were published by lads that were there, on casual/the dressing front. And if you've read these factual accounts you will know there has been an ongoing bitching-war (albeit a friendly one?) about who were the first casuals/dressers.

Dave Hewitson in The Liverpool Boys are in Town claims that they, the scousers, were first in, best dressed. When Liverpool played Manchester United in the Charity Shield at Wembley in August 1977, a new creation shone out from amidst the hordes of scarfers. A complete contrast to the 'normal' Red follower. The Liverpool boys seen that day outside the stadium were a group of teenagers wearing straight leg jeans and cords amongst a sea of flares. But most of all, they had charisma and emitted confidence by the bucket-load.

Within six months the scouse scally uniform became the staple Adidas all-black range or Kick, Lois jeans and an ST2 Adidas navy blue cagoule. Their barnets shaped in a girl style wedge – very debonair indeed. Only what whetted their appetites the most was footwear, more widely known in scouse circles as trainees, and, "Where d'ya get em from la?" By hook, or by crook, these scallies from Anfield, Goodison Park and from all districts in and around Merseyside, obtained sport shoes from far and wide, including the continent. And Dave Hewitson emphasises this in his excellent pictorial, nostalgic afterglow book.

Ian Hough in Perry Boys, creates a chronology of the emergence of a newly, naturally selected life-form: The Manc perry boy. From their humble origins of high-rise tenant blocks and Victorian terrace houses in Manchester, Salford and surrounding areas they caused, created and pushed the boundaries of an explosive phenomenon. He would have you believe Mancs have vastly superior, elite DNA (a tongue-in-cheek proclamation he informed me!) which can never be begged, stolen or borrowed. 'It' was the Manc, tribal Nameless Thing. Between 1976-78, a hybrid species emerged which attracted the title of the "perry", the Fred Perry laurel wreath their symbol of choice. The look was carried off by wearing slim-fit cords, slip-on boat shoes and topped with a classic wedge hairstyle cut to geometrical, perfect precision. This was a somewhat transitional cross over period. Or, the interchange of sections between pairing chromosomes during meiosis that produces variations in inherited characteristics by rearranging genes. I think this is how Houghie would describe the methodology in his flamboyant, familiar writing style.

And what do the southern shandy drinking fairies, or more so cockney chaps, born within the sound of the bells of St Mary-le-Bow church, bring to the table from the same era? MA-1 flight jackets, Lonsdale sweatshirts, half-mast Levi jeans and 16-hole Dr. Martens Airwair. The mod revival in 1979. Smart old-boy blazers, Gabicci V-neck jumpers, some boasting suede patches, white polo-necks, Farah slacks with comb in the back sky-rocket, and cream colour crocodile skin loafers, complemented with a silver buckle, on their plates of meat. Also, you'd to be dripping in Tom Foolery. And, the big southern-based soulboy wedge haircut. This being the Sticksman Look. They would also have you know they wore this raiment long before the Germans bombed our chippies.

Wherein, Phil Thornton recounts such get-ups with the aid of southerners in his cracking book Casuals, an account of football, fighting and fashion plus the north/south divide and the whole origination and advancement of the casual/dresser.

Whereas, Mick Mahoney states in The Soul Stylists, without hesitation, and an uncompromising dyed-in-the-wool attitude, south-east Londoners were 100 per cent, the maiden casuals.

Whereupon, Andy Nicholls in Scally puts it down to a simple mathematical equation as to who 'were' the first casuals/dressers. Even though he hates to admit it, 'the Red shite' were rampant on the field of play in the Seventies, winning many a League title and FA Cup trophy. Whereby, their achievements on the domestic front ensued that Liverpool forayed into Europe, with mass hordes of scouse apostles in tow. An overseas alien city full of scallywags, sportswear and designer shops with no security tags attached to the clobber, and training shoes in pairs on racks, equates to the first football casual/dresser.

Fullstop. No back answers.

All the above are seemingly contradictory statements, but nonetheless they all may be true. Yes, they are all very paradoxical facts and books, indeed. In fact, though, the roots to all these declarations deem that we delve deeper into social history and see what there is to unearth...

Know, first, who you are; and then adorn yourself accordingly.

Epictetus

Well, Ian Hough may be right on his theory that the Mancs were the forerunners in the dresser stakes.

Let's rewind some one hundred years or so to the warrens of cobbled back streets and alleyways of Manchester's then, rundown slum areas.

These deprived working-class neighbourhoods in the early 1870s saw the uprising of gangs of youths who named themselves after the main street that ran through their manor. Names such as the Hope Street Gang in Salford, Forty Row in Ancoats, and the Holland Street Gang in Miles Platting; to name just three of many. Cobblestone, trawling guttersnipes got branded with the name 'scuttlers', who scuttled with each other. Scuttling meaning different gangs getting it on while armed to the teeth with various weapons; lumps of wood, iron bars, knives and massive, weighted buckled belts. In the scuttle/fight the main aim was to leave your mark on an opponent, be it a slash across the face (copied in the early Eighties with craft knives at the football, and still dished out in Scotland to this day) or to take an eye out with their favourite embellished, brass belt buckle.

The buckle would usually display an engraving and grace their love of their lives name or a mythical creature. And at one stage there were more young offenders housed in Strangeways Prison for being involved in scuttling than any other crime. The Screws would have had their hands full if they'd have kicked-off and taken to the roofs back then, wouldn't they?

Now the mythomania, of the mythology, of who were the first to hatch out onto plant earth as a casual/dresser in the Mesozoic era, and finally rubber stamping the Diophantine equation, may just stem from how the scuttlers dressed. And the cut of their hair: scuttlers had a traditional short back and sides only they left the fringe to grow to a considerable length, usually grown longer on the left hand side and known as a donkey fringe – the first flick 'ead even before David Bowie brought it to mainstream attention. Peaked caps were also pulled over to the left of the head to emphasise the fringe. Sometimes the hair was greased down with beef dripping out of the chip-pan, so the myth goes. Their clobber consisted of heavy carved wooden clogs, which were brass-tipped and often sharpened for sticking the boot in the balls. Bell-bottomed naval fustian trousers, which flared out from the knee downwards. Topping the look off was a dapper shirt, dandy waistcoat, a luxurious fine silk scarf, neckerchief or cravat and tailored jacket too.

Yes, they were possibly the earliest, casual / dresser.

I suppose this was a vast advancement on the naked shin-kickers of Lancashire not too many years before.

Clog fighting, or to be more technical, 'purring', occurred between coal miners and feuding locals to settle disputes. Wearing nothing more than a pair of metal trimmed clogs, and a cloth cap, they kicked the shit out of each other bollock naked. They booted their opponent on their shins until one of them keeled over and hit the deck with either a fractured tibia or lumps of flesh and bone missing from their shinbones. The horizontal geezer would then be throttled by the vertical bloke while knelt on the challenger's chest, this before he followed up the stranglehold with a volley to chops this being known affectionately as a timber kiss! The man left standing would then be declared the winner by the stickler – the umpire. There's nothing as queer as Lanky folk, I tell thee.

Meanwhile 35 miles due west in Liverpool, a notorious violent gang, the High Rip, were setting their own standards, of a sort. This scruffy bunch of toe rags and urchins had a noticeable uniform of dark blue jacket, filthy stained kecks and hats with huge front mufflers. Caps were prized processions and 'bonneting' – whacking off and slagging of someone else's hat – would take place and a duel would ensue.

―――――――――

"Clog fighting, or to be more technical, 'purring', occurred between coal miners and feuding locals to settle disputes. Wearing nothing more than a pair of metal trimmed clogs, and a cloth cap, they kicked the shit out of each other bollock naked. They booted their opponent on their shins until one of them keeled over and hit the deck with either a fractured tibia or lumps of flesh and bone missing from their shinbones."

―――――――――

Down south; in the City of Westminster, round the same epoch, the term 'hooligan' was used for the first time to describe, and be connected to, a gang of youths from Lambeth (I wonder if they did the walk as well with their thumbs behind their braces?), the Hooligan Boys. These ruffians would emulate, while also mimicking, London Town's upper-class toffs. And when they steamed into battle, the war cry of "boot 'em" went up.

These boys would don spruce threads often obtained in street robberies or thieving. The cockneys adopted their own urban flair by supplementing cloth caps with velvet or plaid ones. Get them.

Coming out of the Victorian age and with the dawn of the 20th century – including the next 50 years – styles and fashions changed, though nothing too dramatically. No real spearheading subculture came to the forefront in dress, at all, perhaps because of the two World Wars and the Great Depression. A very bleak aeon for who lived through this stage of British, and worldwide, existence. These were bulldog spirit times.

During this period frock coats were replaced by sack coats and three-piece suits in heavy cotton and tweed. Trousers sprouted turn-ups. Cravats became key. Flannel suits and knickerbockers in bright fabrics became conventional. Then textiles toned down in appearance with darker shades of plaid patterning, herringbone and houndstooth.

Hugo Boss's company wanted to take the world on; his company manufactured uniforms for German military personal, including the SS. Only the British War Office commissioned Thomas Burberry to adapt his yarned water and tear proof, yet breathable, gabardine overcoat for warfare, to counteract such actions. Thus, his company produced, by adding shoulder straps and D-rings, the trench coat. It is said the D-rings were added for attaching map cases or swords. Others say that hand grenades were hung from the D-rings.

Materialism sprang back into the forte in the Forties; spivs materialised from the murky shadows of Blitzed London. These spivvly dressed wide boys wore flashy American-look zoot/dapper suits, camp shirts and lurid wide-knotted kipper ties complete with fool's-gold tiepin. A greased back DA hairstyle, whisperer 'tash and a glint in the eye added to their 'ducker and diver' appeal. Only the spiv was a sartorial cipher, a Flash Harry to most youth of the day, and the younger element distanced themselves from them. Specifically because an older age range assumed spiv, and that they were in the main, technically, petty criminals. Spivs lived on their wits supplying much sought after black market goods such as ration coupons, nylon stockings and bananas.

But it was Cecil Gee who was instrumental in introducing a re-vamped

American gangster associated image to Blighty from his outfitters in The Smoke. All extremely butch, bold and rakish, without doubt. Cecil Gee suits are still available across the UK to this day, and casuals/dressers, over the years, have frequented his shops for other items that they stocked.

This peacockery didn't catch on in the northern towns and cities, though. Because it was quoted 'northern males were too busy surviving to give fashion a thought?' Only a similar guise of spiv could be clocked selling his wares in the Lancashire seaside resort of Blackpool. The fraternity were referred to in the local press as 'the illicit sand and street traders' that targeted day-trippers and holidaymakers. They primarily sold candy floss, rock and sunglasses along the Golden Mile.

To this day you can still see these bobbers and weavers punting cheap, snide gear to pissed-up stag and hen dos in England's holiday capital – 'avoid the glare, a pound a pair.'

Goodness gracious, great balls of fire: The term 'teenagers' had never been coined until the Fifties, only with near peace achieved in Europe, and calm descending on the rest of the world, a kick-start in the economy was needed.

The media played a big part in this mechanism as numerous magazines, adverts broadcast on TV and at cinemas, and especially music, targeted the adolescent market. And all things American influenced British teens in a colossal way from then on – and still do. Yes, the parturition of fashion conscious Brit teenagers. Youth activism.

A Voice Of The Youth.

There were less than 100 juke boxes in Britain when the Second World War ended; this increased to thousands like grease lighting over the next 10 years. There was an explosion of coffee bars and cafés where these new gadgets, juke-boxes, belted out tunes from across the Pond. The good old U S of A gave us jazz and rock 'n' roll. And in 1953, the teenagers who listened to rock 'n' roll had begun dressing the part in Edwardian inspired styles and were nicknamed the teddy boys. Edwardian – Edward – Teddy – Ted – the teddy boys.

This new breed developed their own style in the East End and north London: dark contrast drape jackets, some complemented by a black velvet collar, a brocade waistcoat with pockets galore, including one for their watch, and drainpipe trousers with turn-ups. Plus the obligatory flick-knife slipped in the back pocket. Suits were bespoke and paid for on the 'tick'. A white high neck, loose collared shirt commonly known as a Mr. B, was worn with a Slim Jim tie or bootlace held together by a lucky silver horseshoe or skull 'n' cross bone toggle. A fist-full of knuckleduster size brass rings were slid onto fingers too. Brightly coloured socks and chunky brothel shoes usually in black suede with a full ribbed crêpe-sole on their feet (these were first worn by World War Two officers in the desert to stop their feet getting burnt on the hot sand). And the hairstyle: a moulded quiff formed on the forehead with a ton of pomade, usually Brylcreem, with the rest of the hair swept back in a DA – duck's arse – or a square-neck or Boston finish. The hairstyle was finished off with big sideburns, sideboards or diggers – their greatest glory. The stereotypical haircut shouted 'I'm a rebel from head to toe.' The style and ebullience of an iconic subculture; the first real national manifestation of youth; a social revolt for the youth.

Only this élan was seemingly stolen from London's gay community. So, the Edwardian dandy style had sprinklings of middle and upper-class, English Savile Row, a large slice of American pie, and a dash of homosexual overtones! Suits you sir. Some teds modified their appearance by wearing ratter caps, others wore duffel coats.

Teds got their 'kicks' hanging out in caffs, arcades and the flicks. Only the media being the media associated the cult with trouble and crime, making them out to be a real threat to society. This was grossly exaggerated, because they wouldn't have wanted to ruin their outfits in a ruck. But when the US film Blackboard Jungle was shown in south London the Teds lived up to the press' reputation; slashing seats and lawless actions were witnessed. This set a watershed for wherever the movie was viewed – mass disorder. This led to rival gangs of teds clashing. Also, many London teds held racist tendencies, and in the summer of 1958, racially-motivated riots took place in the capital under the banner 'Keep Britain White', this against the newly arrived West Indian population.

The ted look soon spilled out of the metropolis to south coastal seaside resorts before sweeping the rest of the country by ponderous, slow-moving ripples. Each region adopted certain elements of teddy boy, but not the full on London package, adding their own twist, which diluted the London look. Northern peasants couldn't afford tailored habiliment due to lack of funds while just about keeping their heads above water, though.

The same-old, same-old story.

While on the reference of water, I think it's only right that Preston cercopithecoids make an appearance into the ongoing equation.

Because, A: I was born in Preston, and now reside just outside the town/city boundaries. And B: Preston could be classed as somewhat archetypal Northern town/city. Only I don't know what super family we Prestonians equate to from the Dryopithecus period? We may be either a Pongidae or, maybe a Hommidae? I don't know. But what I do know is we Prestonians live in a cold and damp climate, up north, a somewhat Oligocene. So, we could be Aegyptopitecus! Books by Charlie Darwin on The Expression of the Emotions in Man and Animals, and more so, The Effects of Cross and Self Fertilisation in the Vegetable Kingdom maybe key to giving us northerners some sort of substance, and balance? If anyone has come up with the answer, please let me know.

Preston: a pretty town with an abundance of gentry living in it.

Priest Town, or Preston as it's more commonly known, like Liverpool, is sat on the base level of a river (Liverpool on the mouth of the Mersey, Preston the Ribble) that flows into the Irish Sea, and both had thriving docks in the Fifties.

The Albert Edward Dock in Preston was once claimed to be the largest single dock basin in the world when it was constructed. And we Prestonians can also boost that Preston had the first roll-on roll-off ferries. But during the port's 90 year working history it only made a profit in 17 of those years! Cargoes from around the world came, and other materials left; timber, china clay, cotton, cattle, coal, wheat and fruit and vegetables arrived, and on the main, cloth, yarn and sewing thread departed the quayside.

There are stories still doing the rounds of families in Preston, especially those near the docks, sitting down for Sunday dinner at a solid oak table, in front of a roaring open fire, for a meal of roast beef and veg on fine porcelain plates accompanied with freshly baked bread, and bananas and cream for afters.

Whether they wore smart threads is somewhat clouded in smog and mystery.

Aside from all the goodies that had fallen off the back of a boat that were available at a price, kids would slip the docks security and make a beeline for the Geest & Fyffes warehouse. Here would be bananas by the boat load and workers stacking railway wagons with fruit and veg day and night while having a crafty swig of grog – Day-O, work all night on a drink of rum. Workers would turn a blind eye to the youngsters and let them eat all the yellow bananas they could until they made themselves sick. Also pets could be found hidden in the tropical fruits; giant spiders, scorpions and snakes.

Bundles of cotton would be heading out to sea from the port because Preston had a booming spinning and weaving industry producing cotton for going on 180 years. But in the Fifties, mills began shutting down with new methods of production having been invented. There was a glut of cotton mills at one stage and 80% of the population almost totally depended on the trade in Preston/'Coketown.'

Charles Dickens had once visited Preston for research purposes for his book Hard Times. And later when he wrote the novel, that as a classical tripartite structure, he based his fictional town, Coketown, on what he'd observed in the time that he'd spent in town and with Prestonians. In 2002 Preston was granted city status, but I can vouch it still has strong connections with 'Coketown' in more ways than one.

The only boat I've ever had the pleasure of boarding at the docks was the Manx Man, but it didn't set sail for sea. This old ship had been turned into a nightclub in the Eighties and there's many a fisherman tale from its time moored in the docks as well. There was always a distinct smell of fish onboard the gaff and I'm sure the DJ was an ex-sailor called Seaman Stains.

Like any town or city Preston has had its local characters, prize fighters and seamen. My Dad, Tom, boxed in the ring – Queensberry rules – between the World Wars nearly every week, sometimes twice; he boxed just to put food on the table for his family. If he fought twice within seven days he would use a pseudonym or crack on he was a brother of Tom's. But he was a quiet, gentle man once out of the ring.

Oh how he would laugh at modern day boxers who only fought two or three times a year that said they'd trained hard for their fight and made major sacrifices in the process leading up to the bout. Nevertheless, win or lose, a big fat cheque is always waiting for them. And a backhander if they've taken a dive too. Foreign, visiting seamen and dockers brought their own cosmopolitan styles and prevailing tastes of fashion in clothes from different spheres of the world in to the public houses and the cobbled streets of Preston. Most had one-upmanship in the macrocosm.

street culture: the liverpool – new york connection

Down the coastline, heading south from Preston's docks, Dave Hewitson's father was a seaman during the Fifties, who would sail to far off shores and bring back pieces of treasure home to his city of birth, Liverpool. Dave's dad was commonly known locally as, along with other seamen, a 'Cunard Yank.'

Dave Hewitson: *I was born in Liverpool, that place that seems to stand alone at the end of the M62 looking out towards the ocean and far horizons with its back to the country. Its accent is quite rightly described as 'exceedingly rare', and its culture certainly seems to take on a course of its own at times.*

Liverpool has been a great port since the 17th century. At that time Liverpool merchants developed a trade with America mainly due to its position on the Mersey which gave it an overwhelming advantage for trading with the new world. By the 1800s Liverpool was the main European port and was known as the second city of the Empire.

Its close links with the Atlantic slave trade was incontrovertible to the expansion and prosperity of the city. Profits from the trade were used on buildings of a grand scale and Liverpool was even known as "The New York of Europe" due to its wealth and the grandeur of many of these buildings. Outside of London, Liverpool has more Grade I and II listed buildings than any other British city.

Throughout the centuries it is safe to assume that many scousers would have been employed in the sea trade. Travel was in the blood.

My father was a merchant seaman, travelling all over the world on numerous ships in the late Fifties. He would regale me with tales of jumping ship in Australia, being deported from Italy, and bringing back rock 'n' roll records from the United States. At the age of 15 most school leavers longed to join 'the merch' and set sail into the unknown. He would become one of many, all with tales to tell, but until recently kept mainly to close family and friends. No wonder I wanted to travel when I got older. My chance would arrive with ventures to far off lands with the mighty Reds, but more of that later, because my father's words are not just a passing tale. He, and others like him, have their own adventures to tell. Tales that could only be told in Liverpool, similar to my own of following Liverpool FC In terms of youth cultures his and those like him developed their own inimitable style and culture.

The Fifties is famous for teddy boys becoming the first youth movement. But at a similar time and possibly a bit earlier the Cunard Yanks were the fore-runners of a teenage explosion yet to come. From the late Forties through to the early Sixties, 25,000 seamen (mainly scousers) sailed from Liverpool across the Atlantic working as catering staff, waiters, cooks and stewards. They worked for the Cunard shipping line and became affectionately known as the Cunard Yanks due to the ships' main ports of call being New York, Boston, and further up the North coast, Halifax and Montréal.

The prime focus of any culture is its fashion, style and music. These guys had all three ingredients in abundance. Comparisons with the Liverpool fans travelling around Europe collecting exciting European sportswear and designer wear run parallel with the Cunard Yanks' trips to New York. They became pioneers, just like ourselves a generation later. In the early Fifties Liverpool was scarred from war and the fashions were drab to say the least. A mix of black, brown and greys. Fashion was most definitely in a rut. New York on the other hand had a magnetic pull, its interior of bright lights inspiring many.

In 1851 Bankers Magazine described Liverpool as the New York of Europe and vice versa, New York being described as the Liverpool of the Americas. How apt that a century later these teenage styles would be described as similar to those New York stars of the big screen Frank Sinatra and Tony Curtis. Their parents' ambitions, dress and attitude was rejected in favour of Americana. Bringing back pieces of America unavailable back home. If it wasn't available in New York it wasn't available anywhere, and we're not just talking clothes here. Consumer goods including washing machines and fridge freezers were loaded on to the ship for the ship's electrician to convert the current for UK use.

Stepping from the ship in New York harbour was like stepping into another world. It was so easy to be sucked into this cultural explosion. One Cunard Yank described Britain as being in Black & White while the Big Apple was in Technicolor. It's an analogy I sometimes use myself to describe our visits to Europe in the late Seventies and early Eighties when Britain was blighted with recession with three million unemployed. To us, Britain was still in Black & White, the clothing and footwear was drab, yet Europe seemed to be like a glorious Technicolor TV with a hue of vibrant polo shirts, tracksuits and multi-coloured trainers.

Suits were the order of the day in the Fifties and the Sinatra style three button suits were unheard of in the U.K. Lightweight materials and lighter in colour than anything back home, the styles were 15 years ahead of their time.

It wasn't only suits though; hats, ox-blood moccasins, ties, cufflinks, even aftershave, anything really that made them standout. When they returned the *girls would says 'the ships are in'; their style was so unique. The hairstyle was Tony Curtis. The look was American.*

My dad would bring back jeans; Levi and Wrangler, another sure-fire way of distinguishing a seaman. A craze for denim was about to begin.

Demand for such clothing attire began to grow throughout the Fifties in Liverpool. Seamen returned to Liverpool laden with black market goods to sell to family and friends. American magazines were also brought back so that local tailors could copy the American styles. Entrepreneurism was encouraged, and was to become a tradition within the city.

Besides the usual clothes, anything from double-door fridge freezers to record players had a market value. One guy had to leave his fridge freezer in the back-yard plugged in through the window because it was too big to fit through an English width doorway. The Salvation Army thrift store in Manhattan was often the first port of call on docking to stock up on white goods at a knockdown price. These household goods were something the middle-classes of Britain had not even seen as yet. But here was the working class youth of Liverpool living the high-life. Dressing better, and living a more comfortable lifestyle than many of their elders.

The Cunard Yanks would also have you believe they had a hand in the Beatles sound. George Harrison purchased a second hand electric guitar from one seaman. Apparently it was one of only two electric guitars in Liverpool at the time. The guy still has a signed £20 IOU because George didn't have the full £90 cash on him at the time. I suspect this is now worth more than the original £20 he was owed. John Lennon was also believed to have purchased American records from returning sailors.

Music raced through their veins: New sounds first heard in the jazz clubs plus local radio stations playing doo-wop, blues and country and western meant the seaman's musical tastes knew no boundaries. I remember as a kid playing my dad's old 45's purchased from the US, and even Australia, long before they were released in the UK. He purchased a record player in Australia whilst on a sojourn during a 14-month trip. The self-made entertainment on the ships often included nights sitting around a record player.

By 1961 the grand ocean liners were giving way to air travel. The quicker way of crossing the Atlantic meant the liners demand diminished, also meaning employment on such vessels became less frequent. My father disembarked one last time to take up a job with Ford, but his tales had planted a seed; the draw and pull of New York would once again have an impact on the youth of this city during the Nineties. The place would again be the centre of attraction for the Liverpool fashionistas of the day.

A generation on from my father's adventures at sea, Liverpool FC are conquering Europe and together we embark on a journey by train to see our beloved team pick up the first of many European Cups. Two days by train via Belgium, Germany and Switzerland to the final destination of Rome in 1977 has this 14 year-old observing another new world for the first time. A world with such an extreme palette of colour, and style, in comparison with the restrained look of Blighty; colours and styles that I would hunger for so much.

Over the next eight years we would be spoilt as Liverpool enjoyed the most productive period in its history with trips to Europe happening on a frequent scale. Holland, Germany, Switzerland, Belgium, Portugal, Italy and Spain were all stamped into the passport as myself and a new generation of travellers began an insatiable quest for the 'new'. As everyone should already know this period would lead to a new youth culture being born, that of the 'casual'. Fila, Tacchini, Adidas, to name a few became wardrobe staples during this time of Transalpino trips to the continent to obtain such brands unavailable in the UK.

This amazing sense of personal style was running through our veins and this story has now been told on numerous occasions, but what the 'casual' did do, was, change the British high street forever. Sportswear became everyday wear. Designer goods aimed at the upper-classes are now so popular it verges on ubiquity. Every town is now saturated with sports stores while designer has become mainstream. Now that the internet has made the world a tiny place it is easier today to pick up the latest trainers fresh off the third world production line without leaving the house. Was the Eighties casual the last great period of travel for the youth of Liverpool? Did the stores of this city stock all of the latest labels and brands that anyone would ever need? Well the answer to both of these questions is a resounding... No!

In early 1998, to much furore, Tommy Hilfiger opened his first flagship store in Europe, London being his capital of choice. But what significance does this hold with Liverpool and its band of travelling protagonists? Three years earlier New York once again became the destination of choice as the youth of our city once again needed to quench their appetite for stylistic pedantry.

The Nineties had also saw Florida become the number one travel destination for Brits. With the dollar at a good rate of $1.65 to the £1, and air fares at a very reasonable price, suitcases would be filled with Calvin Klein, Timberland, Gant, Bass Weejuns and Ralph Lauren at almost half the cost of the stores back home. A new concept on us Brits was the outlet malls with prices even more reduced than the department stores. This influx of Americana cast its spell on Britain, not least the acolytes of this city.

The draw of the USA was there for all to see. Florida may have been the place for a once-in-a-lifetime family holiday but New York had a certain je ne sais quoi about it. A good friend of mine was one of only a few to jet out for a weekend in early '95. One guy owned a small store and knew he could stock up on Lacoste as well as Hilfiger. They went to Macy's and Bloomingdales and stocked upon Hilfiger jackets, jumpers and polos. They had paid £180 for flights, stayed at cheap digs and spent the least they could on expenses. Tommy Hilfiger was about to explode on to the Liverpool fashion scene. The jackets cost £80 in New York but back home could command a fee of £160/£180 depending on the style.

The closest outlet mall to Manhattan is Woodbury Common, and it was here, besides a Hilfiger store, there was a Lacoste store too. Lacoste became massive in Liverpool over the next 10 years and they would eventually open its largest independent UK store adjoining Wade Smith in the city centre. Wade Smith would sell that much Lacoste over the years that the president and owner of the brand Monsieur Lemaire came for the opening of its new store and stated "Liverpool's a bit like the Lacoste capital of the world and shows no sign of waning."It could be said that he should have thanked the entrepreneurs who made these trips to New York for starting a trend.

It wasn't long before my wife and I were flying across the Atlantic and touching down at JFK, half empty suitcases in hand, in readiness for some serious shopping. There wasn't enough supply to deal with the demand, so even before we left home we had a large shopping list of Hilfiger jackets and Lacoste tracksuits. The profits made covered the weekend trip and we had a bit over to put towards the next trip a few months later. That's how it was for a couple of years. New York would be paid a visit two or three time during the year, and Florida for the summer. For us it was about the New York experience as well as the product. Our enthusiasm for travel borders on fanaticism.

Liverpool's obsession with fashion and style has always been the foundation of its wardrobe; from those seamen of the Fifties, through to the Eighties casuals, and then the New York trips of the Nineties, it still continues to this day.

Forever in blue jeans

Youths in the UK would much rather be, forever in blue jeans. Levi's, Lee, Wrangler and dozens of other jeans manufacturers never looked back when British youths went all cockamamie for denim.

Only the early history of blue jeans (indigo dye is added to make the fabric blue), or more so denim, was tarred with visions of African slave labour wearing denim dungarees while working on cotton plantations picking cotton, from the boll, in sweltering conditions in deep south USA. Gold miners and cowboys wore the rugged, hard-wearing jeans too, though.

The twill-weave fabric jeans and chambray shirts were also prison issue, regulation dress. Maybe jeans had the 'rebel appeal' and that's why they caught on with the need-to-have youth. It's more likely to be the American soldiers based in the UK during the Second World War who introduced jeans to Brits by wearing them while off-duty on civvy-street. Bamber Bridge, a village on the outskirts of Preston, had an American army base, and local lads lauded the Yanks jeans, begging them to trade wares so they could get their hands/legs in them.

Britons had never had it so good: and two other subdivisions were also in a state of development during the Fifties; these subordinates were the Ton-up Boys; later on Sixties rockers, and beatniks; later on Sixties Hippies. The 'Ton-up' came from a time-honoured initiation, that was, to ride your bike at, or over and above, 100mph. The motorcycle was as much as part of the image as the leathers they wore. They were influenced and inspired by the characters portrayed in the films The Wild One, Johnny Strabler/Marlon Brando, and Rebel Without a Cause, Jim Stark/ James Dean. The British greasers statement was completed by black leather bikers' jacket, white T-shirt, Levi 501s and long woolly socks with the tops pulled over engineer boots. Hints of the Royal Air Force were also present while out cruising looking for chicks: jet helmets, aviator goggles and white silk scarves would bellow in their slipstream.

Maybe the beatniks were the initial ingredient for the cauldron that served-up the juicy, sumptuous casual/dresser stock? Or they were merely just a condiment? The beat generation were a more-or-less horizontal laid-back US progenies, that bore bohemian, ecstatic epicureans and purred evocate desegregation. The beatnik theme would shape things to come – BIG TIME. Beatniks were a profound youthful culture, with philosophical analysed minds of their own.

Nothing like this cult had, at any time, ever been acknowledged. They were a direct scion of teenagers from San Fran and the Big Apple. These beatnik coffee bar cats had a fundamental soul-searching ethos and proclaimed in their own hip jargon; 'cool man', 'love 'n' peace' and 'ban the bomb.' Beatniks were mainly confined to swanky London cafés and coffee houses and they drank proper coffee while reciting poetry from the Lost Generation. They also appreciated fine wines and narcotics: they took Benzedrine soaked papers out of inhalers and dropped them into their infused, roasted coffee. They also smoked marijuana, to 'chill.'

Their clothes varied from turtle/polo neck tops, black strides and shoes, to the stereotypical French Look; loose fitting hooped T-shirt, beret, shades and open toe sandals only minus the onions hung round the neck. Facial hair became fashionable as well; they sprouted tufts of whiskers on the chin and goatee beards, plus locks were grown longer. Beatnik was a cross-fusion of later countercultures; mod, hippy and rappers toasting.

The Fab Four even took their name from the era, only originally they wanted to call themselves the Beetles.

2

THE SOUL SEARCHING SWINGING SIXTIES

If you can remember anything about the Sixties, then you weren't really there

Paul Kantner

The consumerist modern Sixties started with the abolishment of National Service, and ended in a hippy, psychedelic haze. Many experts in 'the powers that be' cited by the latter years of decade, that with teenagers not being called up for compulsory military service, a systematic breakdown in society had occurred; this in turn formed a general lack of respect for authority too, which produced manifestations of anarchy in the UK! Mods and rockers fought running battles on the beaches by the mid-Sixties. And by the conclusion of the decade, hooliganism had also spread in epidemic proportions on the terraces of football grounds nationwide.

If exchanging blows in a row didn't float your boat, recreational drugs, casual sex and flower power might have. Only if you chose the aforementioned, being a hipster, that grew their hair long and preached love and peace, a big lump of a skinhead may have taken an aversion and antipathy towards you, which would then cause him to boot the crap out of you for no reason other than he wanted to for the fun of it.

One youth of the early Sixties who I know all too well, and who was to ditch the denim for a spanking new style of dress, is my brother, Frank –

there's a 21 year age gap between us. Frank was a war baby, and our Dad didn't see him until he was touching three years-old. These early, developing years could never be replaced. And we think we've got it hard in today's environment. Without further ado, take it away, Bro'.

Frank Routledge: *I was born in the year 1944, in Preston, Lancashire, and lived with Mum and Grandma over a hairdressers that my gran owned. My dad served in the Royal Navy during the Second World War and also the Russian Arctic Convoys, so he didn't return home until I was nearly three. The first recollection I have of us all being together is when we went to look for a house. I remember walking down a road surrounded by tin houses, and one of these prefabs, as they were called, became our home for the next nine years.(These prefabricated houses were meant to be a quick solution to provide homes for families after the war, which were meant to have a life span of no more than 10 to 20 years. This short term housing scheme, and the houses that were erected, are still standing today and lived in!)*

I've many fond memories of living on Grange Estate; Tin Town, as it was nicknamed back then, was a safe environment to play out in and you could walk to school on your own, crossing a main road to get there because there weren't that many cars around. You could even leave your front door open without the fear of being burgled – all there was to steal was the coal and the scuttle that contained it. One day I heard my dad cheer loudly and found out he'd won £50 on Spot The Ball – a small fortune in those days. With his winnings he bought the first car on our street, a 'shooting brake' as my dad called it – its make and model I can't recall. And when he pulled up outside our house in the car, he pomped the horn and most of the neighbours came out, gathering round to admire the vehicle. Well the glamour of having a car soon wore off when the cold winters came that we had back then. My dad had to put the spark plugs from the jalopy in the grill pan under the grill to warm them up and my Mum and me – I was only seven at the time – had to push-start the car down a slight, inclined road. And if it didn't start first time, we'd to push the damn thing back up the hill and try again.

Luxuries during the Fifties were few and far between. Living in a prefab did have its advantages though; we'd a bathroom with a bath and an inside toilet. Only toilet paper was usually old newspapers or comics hung on the back of the door stuffed through a wire coat hanger, so you'd something to read while on the throne too. This being a step forward from having to have a weekly scrub in an old tin bath in front of the fire and a trek through the backyard to the outside loo in the middle of the night.

On Saturdays our treat would be a trip to the town's swimming baths, and then afterwards the rest of the morning was spent watching the morning matinee at the GB Cinema. After dinner it was onto another cinema, the Star, for the afternoon matinee. Football, hide and seek and jumping across a local brook was our amusements during the summer. Boring winter months were spent listening to Dan Dare on the wireless – we'd no telly – while keeping an eye out for the Parched Pea Man. On hearing his bell ring, front doors would open and there would be a dash to his cart to obtain a warm bag of parched peas. (There weren't any sweets available due to them still being rationed.) With not having central heating I'd to make do with a large, brown pot sarsaparilla bottle to warm my bed. I dread to think what would have happened if it had ever rolled out of the bed, the pot was that heavy. The only other two events that would brighten up the winter months were a trip to the illuminations in Blackpool and Bonfire Night. On the 5th November we would sit round the local fire on deckchairs watching dangerous fireworks lit by dads while eating jacket potatoes and homemade treacle toffee.

At the age of 12 we moved to a bigger home on a newly built estate nearby, Brookfield, a spanking new, red rustic brick council house. By this time I was really into my football both playing and watching Preston North End.

The mates and I would even go on reserves matches as the reserve team in those days had some quality players who could have slotted straight into the first team if they had any injuries.

Getting back on track: we would turn up for first team games before 2pm, because many a time fans flocking to Deepdale in their droves would be locked out due the sheer volume of fans attending – crowds of 30,000 plus would be the norm. I remember being passed overhead on the Spion Kop at Preston's Deepdale ground, then over the hoardings and onto the cinder track that ran round the pitch so I could see the game. I can still visualise, when looking back, the crammed in crowd behind me, especially at night matches. Plumes of blue smoke would rise upwards into the floodlight beam while the red glow of uncapped cigarettes hanging from the corner of every bloke's mouth would be a common sight. All the men wore overcoats and flat caps, slightly tilted to one side which were thrown in the air when Preston scored, this followed by raucous cries and rapid applause. Back then North End were in the old First Division and we would have the likes of Arsenal, Man Utd, Wolves and Chelsea visiting Deepdale. I can remember when we played Chelsea once and Tommy Thompson for Preston scored a hat-trick only to be out done by a certain Jimmy Greaves in a blue shirt for Chelsea who bagged five – Preston lost 4-5.

On the way home, after the game, everyone talked about how well Preston had played. There was no criticism of the team; we were all true fans.

Then the Sixties arrived – the best decade of the century in my eyes – and our social lives were 'buzzing.' There were a few teddy boys still knocking about in their dated Edwardian jackets, drainpipe trousers and crêpe soled shoes though. Only us boys wore razor-sharp suits either a nice bespoke tailored number that you paid for in instalments/on the drip/the never never or, bought off the peg from Burtons – because you get bags more buzz at Burtons. The suit would be slim fitting with narrow lapels, three buttons and trouser buttons so braces could be attached to them. Suits bore an Italian feel with a British twist. Underneath the suit was a crisp, starched white shirt complemented by a narrow tie. And winklepicker shoes adorned our feet. You'd to size up with winklepickers, sometimes two sizes, as such was the desire for excessive narrowness of the shoes. Dressing the part wasn't just saved for Saturday best; you went to great lengths to look smart if you were just going down the pub to play darts with your mates.

We'd notice changes in styles and fashions by catching music programmes, recorded in London, at whoever's house that could afford a TV, since the late Fifties. We huddled round the telly open-mouthed and wide-eyed watching groups perform over the years on; Cool For Cats, Six-Five Special, Oh Boy! and Juke Box Jury, coming out of the Fifties. Later on; Thank Your Lucky Stars, Ready Steady Go! and Top Of The Pops followed in the Sixties.

After either playing football on Saturdays or watching PNE, I'd have a bath, and then meet my mates to go 'bopping.' The place to be seen and to pick up girls was the AD Dancehall in town only it didn't serve ale. So, the lads and I went for a few pints of northern bitter with a decent head and a game of arrows in a nearby pub, The Spindlemakers, before heading to the AD.

A good night was usually had by all although the club closed at 11 o'clock. Outside the venue there might be the odd bit of trouble but on the whole it was just a occasional one-on-one fight over who was walking a girl home.

I think one of the main reasons is because no-one wanted to ruin their neat, expensive clothes. There weren't any mass battles that would occur on the scale of when the mods and rockers fought in the mid-to-late Sixties in town. Unlike in today's diverse society, where bottles, baseball bats or guns are common place, and more often than not, used. Also I saw many a live band play the towns Public Hall. Groups like the Beatles, Rolling Stones, The Searchers, The Fortunes and Freddie & the Dreamers to name but a few.

By 1964 Preston had reached the FA Cup Final at Wembley Stadium and would face the team of the moment West Ham United, after defeating Swansea Town in the semis at Villa Park. However, these are stories of their own...

'WE ARE THE MODS, WE ARE THE MODS,
WE-ARE WE-ARE THE MODERNISTS.'

Out of the depths of jazz and blues clubs in Soho London, in the very late Fifties/early-Sixties, emerged smart, clean-cut young men, and what well turned-out chaps they were. These teenage prophets not only tore the stagnant scene of the monochromatic Fifties to shreds, they blazed into the Sixties forming a cult that not only set new standards of the time, but a hedonistic cult that would resurface twice in the next 50 years, such was its benchmark. Noted for their clothes-consciousness, the mods strutted their stuff in the West End, Kings Road and Carnaby Street in London.

They could walk-the-walk in sharp whistle & flutes , because they were the first generation of working class kids to have a substantial disposable income since the end of World War II. A legendary phenomena, if ever there was one.

Mod mavericks had snappy suits tailor-made to high specifications by traditional English tailors, many at Savile Row, Mayfair, in bespoken, striking quality cloth and each suit was individualised for the individual.

Suits were a fusion of French, Italian and American Ivy League styles in tonik, mohair or Prince of Wales dark coloured fabrics. Modifications would be made to already small lapels; the size and amount of buttons were either added to or taken off; side or back vents were cut and tucked; cuffs, waistbands, sewn-in seams and other factors of the suit would be modified before the customer would be totally satisfied the suit was unique. Extravagance and self-indulgence to the extreme for these freethinkers wasn't seen as anything out of the ordinary, it was expected and upheld. Shirt collar lengths would vary but they always had an inch gap at the front for a slim knitted tie with suit sleeves fused together by cufflinks. Trousers were narrow and cut at the ankle on the angle to show their shinny shoes. Sometimes the strides had minor slits to the side, and years later casuals/dressers would cut their Lois jeans in the same vein. And winklepickers, tassel loafers or brogues that you could see your face in executed the exhibiting mien.

A dressing down dilution for an everyday look could be a Harrington jacket or boating blazer, or a Ben Sherman paisley or polka dot shirt. Also, a Fred Perry polo would be worn, this being the first sportswear label seen as a fashion label. Shrink-to-fit Levi's ensured to hug your sparrow legs were achieved by sitting in a cold bath for at 'least' 24 hours, or Sta-Prest pants were pulled on. And bowling shoes or Clarks desert, Chelsea or Hush Puppies boots rounded things off.

Hairstyles ranged from camp back combed, centre parted barnets of wannabe popstars, to a classic, sculptured neat cut that glided over the ears with a short fringe and slight parting. Mods began entering women's hair salons for their locks to be washed, chopped and a full-bodied blow-dry, all unheard of and scorned by young men until now.

Most still chose spinning red and white barbers poll shops to get their mops cropped in a refined razor and taper style with a side or centre part French look, though.

The hysteria surrounding mods, and their aurora, wasn't solely about the polished clothes they wore but other accompanying elements too. Clubs, music and dancing, plus associated mind alerting substances that kept you an on-the-ball and Italian motor-scooters were also recognised as a super cool representation of oneself.

Lambrettas and Vespas (wasps) scooters were favoured by mods for getting about on because, smelly grease-ball rockers rode motorbikes so it wasn't creditable to been seen riding a bike at all. Also scooter stockist arranged finance payments and insurance which most teenagers couldn't obtain from high street brokers. Scooters were sleek and stylish; they had enclosed leg panels and you could add optional fly-shields to protect your lower leg attire from the elements that your US Army fishtail parka couldn't fend off.

Customising your scooter became commonplace by enhancing the standard look with spotlights, mirrors, mud-flaps, chrome panels, two-tone paint spray jobs and many more multitudinous accessories. Or even cutting back side panelling for a more minimalist statement was done. Each scooter was personalised to the owner's taste, giving the scooter refinement and the rider distinctiveness.

With a need to be with-it, and on-the-ball, at bop-till-you-drop allnighter clubs, mods popped pills for fun to stay focused on the job in hand. Getting tanked-up or off-your-'ead was a no-no, and frowned upon. So, the drugs of choice, for staying awake and in control, were amphetamines, the most sought after being Drinamyl, more commonly known as purple hearts. These 'uppers' were legal until 1964, so what harm could they do? And when such drugs became illegal, did it stop clubbers using them? Did it balls. I bet bubblegum sales soared through the roof too. Amph' was essential kit for either dancing the night away or to give you bottle to chat to the stunning modette on the dancefloor that you'd been showing off all your best moves to – more often than not they'd end up chewing her ear off. These 24-hour party people also necked cocktails of Benzedrine, Dexedrine, Methedrine and Durophet in whichever way or form. Chemist shops would be rifled and looted for prescribed medication, or doctors would be tapped to issue iffy prescriptions for their needs . And quite a few practitioners got busted when the Feds cottoned on to such activities. Whizzing-their-tits-off mods would trip the light fantastic till dawn and then toddle off to a coffee shop. Mods even had a certain way of walking, a certain way of standing, 10-to-2, and holding a pose (I believe there's a book that has been published on How to be a Mod, or similarly titled). Wearing dark shades to protect their eyes from sunlight, like vampires, and to hide their dilated pupils from the squares, mods would try and chill while rehydrating parched mouths and would stimulate rapid heart rates with a strong, brewed bean.

Conversations would be of more adjustments to a new suit they were having made or extreme talkativeness and excitability of which club they'd be hitting that night.

Up north, Northern Monkeys were still hanging round the woodlands and forests while tutting on banana skins, with their feet.

In clubs frequented by the mods, DJs would spin sounds from across the Pond of young, black American artists in the form of Motown, early soul and R & B. Jazz began to be played less and less. British acts wanted a slice of the action too, with groups such as The Small Faces, The Kinks, The Stones, The Yardbirds and The Who trying to break onto the scene dominated by the Yankee stranglehold of the underground vibe. Only most mods didn't take to British bands and their music much. So, Brit pop groups adopted gimmicks to try and win over teenagers and captivate their audiences.

Apart from their different style of music, band members began wearing Union Jack suits and RAF roundel target symbol patches sewn on jackets. Also, eye-catching adorned LP album covers would have adroit pop art splashed across them by such hip artists as Peter Blake, Roy Lichtenstein and Andy Warhol in an attempt to swing sceptical mods and hold their attention for more than a nanosecond so they would at least take a look at home-grown British bands' approach to music while they browsed through vinyl in their the local record store.

Anyway, let's climb onboard a Frank Sanderson SCOMDI 250cc Lambretta and burn some rubber to the present day and hear what one young man's take is on mod, and just what mod means to him. His views may seem full of contemptuousness and uppishness, but hey, he's still only in the springtime of life. I think in the main, he's having a swipe at modern-day cults and the non-existence of cults to be precise, not so much an arrogant view. His views are more a cunning way of thought with ironical intent. He's a very artistic chap too; here's Jonny.

My Generation

Jonny: *Although I'm a very young chap, at the tender age of 20 in 2012, I feel that I was truly born in the wrong era. The Nineties and Noughties were all well and good, but it completely cheapened and debased the classic look that I am so fond of. I'm talking about the mod look and the era I wasn't born in, the early Sixties – more specifically, 1959-1963.*

My passion for the era is the clothes. Not the scooters, nor the clubs, or even the music, as such, but the clothes. Pure and simple, I love everything about that early mod look. Well I say I mean everything but, I can't stand these middle aged men you see in a patch ridden parka and stone wash denim nowadays – dossers. That's not mod, that's a mid-life crisis. Anyway, I love the perfectly fitted suits (not to be confused for skinny suits), I love the big collared shirts, and I love the slick and almost nonchalantly styled haircuts. I mean, why would you walk down the street looking like all these other little subcultures, the indie kids, the chavs, the emos (goth lite), the skater lot, or even the trendy Topman 'geezer' when you could swagger in a tasty mid-brown tonic suit with your best suede shoes on and a mustard yellow slim knitted tie! Looking down on people is all part of 'it' – being one above. Untouchable. I mean who are the girls going to be looking at, them, or me? Certainly not young Rob hanging about in his ripped jeans and skin tight cardigan, are they? I'm sure he doesn't know about the classic concept of combining Ivy League with English tailoring and continental details, not dressed like that, does he? Good. Keep it that way.

Mod is a different thing to everyone. To some, it's about wearing Fred Perry, Levi's and desert boots whilst hopping about to The Jam. Fun as this may be, you'll look like a fool to some. And not a very dapper one at that. To others, it's Northern soul and showing off your best moves. Mod, to me, is about making an effort, only not making it too apparent. If you leave the house, looking absolutely sharp as fuck, but do it without looking like you've spent hours preparing to go out, then you've done the job properly. That seems illogical to some who have spent hundreds on clothes to not be noticed. But who's cooler at the end of the night? The loud chap jumping around like a moron on the dancefloor, getting the attention of everyone in the room? Or, the overlooked lad casually leaning against the doorway at the back, hand in pocket, wearing a pair of shades and gently tapping his foot to a groovy soul number? That's my excuse anyway for not being out on the floor, I'm not much of a mover. I'm not even a self-confident type of person. However, pulling on that meticulously prepared outfit feels like pulling on a cloak of arrogance. You're the best dressed person in that club, and everyone knows it. Few people talk to you in fear of you just staring back through those night black Wayfarers and not saying a word. Cool is quite intimidating, you know. It's also not uncommon to put together a tasty outfit two nights before going out, taking it all down the dry cleaners, and come two minutes before heading off out on the town, you change your outfit into something completely different – twice. Sometimes the better looking things in life come spontaneously.

All these other modern day subcultures, they might have fashion, something that everyone will latch onto for a bit, but they don't have style. They don't have substance. And yes, there is a difference. Style is about looking the Don; it's about walking around like you own the place with an unmatchable swagger. Today fashions are merely looking like every other little personality-less clone that wanders down the local high street overlooking the cool independent boutiques in favour of River Island and the likes.

I suppose you're expecting me to say I got into mod after watching Quadrophenia and put Green Onions on my phone as my ring tone because of this. But that wasn't really the case. I don't even like The Who, The Jam or mod bands that much. It was evolution. I was originally into the terrace casual look, good and proper. I loved the look that the Gallagher brothers of Oasis rocked in the Nineties, baggy cagoules, bootcut jeans and Adidas trainers. However, when you realise that baggy stuff doesn't look good on someone as skinny as me, you look elsewhere for inspiration. At first it was the latter Oasis look, where they all went all silk scarved and tailored denimed-up, even a suede shoe here and there. But what really pushed it out was seeing Franz Ferdinand play on the telly, probably one of them late night Channel 4 things, I can't exactly remember. Only I do recall exactly what he was wearing; a cream coloured polo neck jumper, a black one-button school type blazer with the white piping, some very slim Prince of Wales check trousers and narrow, pointed Chelsea boots with orange socks. This I thought was a look that I could definitely associate with. All very fitted, all very smart, yet looking very laid back. I loved it! It also helped that I have a passing resemblance to the lead singer. Soon the mop top became a side parting, cagoules became blazers, jeans became tailored kecks, Adidas trainers became suede goatskin loafers. It was quite a drastic, almost instant transformation, but one that I could truly identify with and suited my tidy-minded personality. As with the clobber, the tunes also evolved. Britpop became British Invasion R&B, the very genre that influenced it so clearly. I don't like jazz though – Jonny hates jazz!

Refinement of tastes soon gave way to an appreciation of things I would've previously not given a second glance. Where before I was mad for a big budget film or two, particularly The Italian Job and The Great Escape , I became accustomed to a bit of lo-fi, low budget independent British cinema. Yes, Quadrophenia did help shape that, leading me onto more modern day cult hits such as Dead Man's Shoes, This Is England, Trainspotting and Layer Cake too. I grasped that a good film didn't need two million quid's worth of special effects, one liners and big names. Just damn fine acting and an incredible story, and there you have a marvellous film. Of course, after clothes, music and cinema, there comes art. Now I've never seen paintings as interesting, and I can't even see the tragedy and fury in Picasso's Guernica , but it's there. I know, because I've read it on Wikipedia as I type this very paragraph. However, I've always had a passion for photography. Particularly the more experimental, arty farty, dynamic stuff. And this idea of mod constantly trying to make yourself more cultured led me to research it more thoroughly, and deeply, to better my knowledge. As a result I had plenty of sleepless nights, lots of filled notepads and scrapbooks too, I've now had several images published by large corporations and I've selected photography as my chosen career. Strangely, I'm not into the 'retro' style of photography but, as mentioned, the more quirky, arty style, expressing more personality into something as opposed to creating a Sixties' throwback cliché photo. And this style now happens to be an interesting trademark of mine that I'm fairly well known for on certain internet sites and is quite rapidly growing. So thanks to this little group of kids that fought on Brighton beach one May Bank Holiday weekend, I've now shaped myself a decent occupation which will hopefully make me unfeasibly rich in the near future.

I was unsure of how to end this little ditto as I'm not a journalist, writer, or indeed thinker (I'm only 20 for Christ's sake, give me a chance). I'll just leave you with some words of advice; it might take a brave bloke to leave the house naked, but it takes an even braver bloke to leave the house in some suede brogues in the rain.

The Mersey Beat

Returning to the northern vibe; unthinkable events had been happening far, far away from London since the year of 1958. And, all of a sudden, northern chic was en vogue . The north had begun to conquer the world on the music front; Liverpudlians had given beat music a rejuvenated twist. Yes, out of the depths of Liverpool, and surrounding Merseyside's countless clubs, the city gave listening ears of planet earth the sounds of Mersey Beat .

The man who baptised the beat scene Mersey Beat was Bill Harry. He also published a newspaper that went in to circulation under the same banner in the Sixties round Merseyside on the topics of music, local bands and

Liverpool's 300-plus club venues. He stole/borrowed the sobriquet from an Old Bill's round/beat.

These scallywag bands broke the myth that all modernists were effeminate snobs too. It seemed that 'all' social backgrounds of a society had moved into the modern age, and the melting pot of Liverpool's inhabitants, plus those who'd recently put down roots in the city from far-flung, and nearby shores, added their takes on new music sounds.

Included in this melodic vessel was a established black community following the abolition of the slave trade in Britain in 1807, and an even bigger Irish population that had crossed the Irish Sea subsequently because of the Irish Famine in 1740-41, as well as the Great/Irish Potato Famine in 1845-52. Liverpool began to make their unique mark on the beat scene.

The integration of creeds and nationalities of all societies, along with globetrotting Cunard Yanks, blended their wealth of knowledge on music and musical talents together, produced harmonious euphonies. Just like the pronunciation peculiarity of Liverpudlians – and their fosterage and name changing of a certain meat stew, labskause/skause/scouse, that was brought to Merseyside docks by northern European sailors – they created, but also included, other genres of music. Scousers intermingled and combined, attributes of doo wop, R&B, folk, rock 'n' roll, skiffle and soul – thus, Mersey Beat. And out of the depths of a dungeon/cave-like club, The Cavern, the first recognised boy band set foot on the road to worldwide stardom in 1962; the Beatles.

Formed in 1960, the Beatles achieved prevailing success in 1962 and rocked the universe by 1963. What was Beatlemania, then? Girls screamed hysterically wherever the Beatles appeared and performed, many a teenager passing out. These girls went wild not just for the music the cheeky boys strummed, but for their looks and their spruce sense of dress too. Unafraid of conformity, in the year 1961 they wore black leather jackets, and sometimes matching strides. By 1963, they were styled by manager Brain Epstein. He commissioned four Edwardian/copied French designer Pierre Cardin collarless grey suits, and Cuban- heeled Chelsea boots with either elasticised or zipped sides. They boys also had mop-top haircuts, known as an *Arthur* chop to their besotted fans. The cut was collar length at the back, trimmed over the ears with a *bang-on* level fringe. A US wig manufacture even applied for a license on authentic styled Beatle syrups! However, the band weren't afraid of change on their long and winding road career. The morphogenesis went from the early clean-cut fresh-faced young men style, to being bewhiskered hippies draped in psychedelic, tie-dyed dashikis, rejecting conventional values while seeking revolution and hedonism by the end of the Sixties.

But way before *the* biggest band in the world ever dramatically split in 1970, London record companies disputed that bands, and record labels from outside the perimeter of London could challenge their asphyxiation and controlling on how the music industry was run/manipulated. The southerners slammed the door well and truly shut on the north and its intuition, because they wanted nothing other from the metropolis setting the ideals and setting the pace.

You Can't Reinvent The Wheel

Meanwhile, elsewhere in the north-west, a steady flow of teenagers were heading in another particular direction around 1963, this being a venue in the heart – and soul – of Manchester. A club called the *Twisted Wheel* commenced to fill to the brim with ultra hip, subterranean dwellers come twilight, and right through the night too. The Manc master-plan had begun.

200 miles due north from the capital of England lies Manchester, a city whose streets are paved in sandstone cobble sets, not gold, as cockneys would have you believe London's are. In the centre of the city, encompassing these streets, are domineering Collyhurst sandstone historical buildings, some nowadays transformed into grand hotels. Also, mammoth red clay brick former cotton mills, of an erstwhile age, have been converted into luxury apartments that fringe the crux. These pitted facade structures have seen and housed the growth, the rise, and the fall of the textile trade – include in this the Industrial Revolution – when Manchester was dubbed 'Cottonopolis.' Manchester had the perfect, moist climate and waterway links for the cotton industry's Richard Arkwright's spinning frames. There's even an entry in the *Domesday Book* noting that Manchester was a 'wool-town.' Some even say the trigger point of the English Civil War began in the city. Riots also took place on the damp, slippery cobbles during the 18th Century recession over the lack of available food – this saw soup kitchens set up.

The blazing of a trail from the banks of the River Mersey to Salford Quays, which is more commonly known as the Manchester Ship Canal, began in the late 19th century. This broad canal was dug because the Mersey and connecting rivers to Manchester narrowed to shallow depths and couldn't accommodate large enough vessels that would be laden with inter-continental goods, for the city's needs. Plus, the Port of Liverpool hammered any cargo that had to be unloaded there, and then transported by train to Manchester, with tolls, fees and taxes (nothing ever changes on the taxing front). Liverpool, 30 miles west of Manchester, had a stranglehold on the movement of commodities and held the upper hand; a somewhat commercial monopoly. So that's why the canal was entrenched. And during the World War II Blitz, bombing raids saw the destruction of several dominant, masterpiece architectural buildings in the city; this also hit Manchester hard.

Manchester also carries a myth, a myth that many wrongly quote, that it's the wettest place in England because of 24/7 cloudbursts of the wet stuff. National weather records and meteorology facts state that it is a myth, and Manchester sees less than below average rainfall. This myth has never deterred drifters, travellers and migrants though, from coming to the city to live or doss, even if it meant sleeping rough on the streets. Only during the early Sixties there was an emerging group of youths who seemingly chose to doss-down in shop doorways and back alleys or just about anywhere really they could rest their weary heads even if it was lashing cats and dogs.

Lingering in the shadows, with stealth, an evolving movement was becoming increasing popular and was establishing itself amongst teens in Manchester. Resting in the arms of *Morpheus*, beneath flattened cardboard boxes staring at a sky filled with the blaze of shooting stars and hazy moonlight, through rainclouds, became a modernistic fad for some. These reprobates who sought shuteye anywhere they could were to be known as the 'dossers.' Their motto, 'I'm on the road.' Probably this way of life, dossing, was truly the *Numero Uno* northern cult?

These nomads had amongst their ranks real and weekend dossers – the aforementioned despised by the serious kind. There was a large contingent of Scottish wayfarers present too, chiefly Glaswegians. Dressing the part consisted of a kind of unkempt-beatnik/dishevelled-army/pre-hippie/bedraggled/down-and-out look. Not hard to achieve when you're living a lifestyle of kipping rough. These hoboes wore ex-army combat jackets out of Army & Navy stores or leather jackets. Leathers would have names of their favourite bands depicted across them in white paint. And because the jackets were never washed, the writing would be a lasting tribute to their musical tastes. To accomplish the package, fray-legged bell-bottomed jeans or tight-fit ice blue ones were their choice along with suitable light footwear for walking the streets. These were in the form of laced up, camel colourised suede leather boots – desert boots. Jesus Boots, a type of leather sandal, were also popular in milder, none rainy conditions.

Heaven And Hell: Manchester Clubland Tales

Quite a lot of these dosser types frequented a nightspot called *Heaven & Hell Beat Club,* on Chorlton Street, of a night. This after drinking in select public houses that landlords would let them drink in due to the way they dressed and conducted themselves, plus the trouble they caused with regulars. The dive of a gaff, *Heaven & Hell,* had a reputation for its notorious clientele of undesirables: scruffs, deadbeats and dossers. The former office building consisted of two levels: Heaven on the ground-floor, and Hell in the basement, furnished with old bus seats. Dossers would try and bum money for drink off 'normal' folk in attendance or try and swap tins of soup or baked beans for ale, or even pills.

Peter, a club goer in and around Manchester in the early Sixties, whom only ever went to *Heaven & Hell* a mere three times, has memories of the club etched in his mind forever, as well the Scottish dossers who haunted the club too.

Peter: *Most of the real dossers that I met were Scottish lads, most of whom were OK, and really just an early breed of migrant part-time workers.*

There were, however, a hardcore of Glaswegian gang members who usually travelled in pairs, or groups. You could always tell where they had dossed as they left their gang names written on the gents' toilet walls in the clubs. You would stand at the piss stones and read in front of you "Fleet Ya Bas" or "Tongs Ya Bas, etc. I only went to the Heaven & Hell *Club three times because, on the last occasion, I accidentally tripped over one lad dossing in his sleeping bag on the floor. I apologised but he and his mate got up, and grabbed me. His mate pinned my arms behind my back whilst the lad I tripped over flashed a knife repeatedly in front of my face shouting a torrent of abuse. He flicked the blade across my right eye and either by accident or design, the tip of his blade sliced through my right eyebrow. They let me go and I ran as fast as I could to Ancoats Hospital where I got it stitched. I've still got a small scar to this day. You didn't mess with those lads.*

"About two years later, I was having a drink in a city centre pub called The York, with a girlfriend, before going on to a club, when I saw three lads walk in the pub. 'Oh fuck no', I thought, 'it couldn't be.' "We're going now." I said to my girlfriend, "And don't look at those lads that came in, just look the other way. Get

out quick as you can, and I'll explain once we're outside." With our backs to the lads we walked out of the pub.

As I was passing through the door I could hear that they had picked on another lad sat with his girlfriend. "You're sitting in our seats" I heard. We hurried out of the door and stopped about 30 yards up the road. We then turned round to witness that the three lads had dragged the unfortunate lad in question, outside and were beating the crap out of him. One thing had changed though; they were no longer in dossin' gear, but in smart mohair suits.

Across town, in Manchester, a former leftwing Coffee House, where duffel coat wearing avant-garde mavericks used to hangout, and where the Manchester Fenian Society occasionally held meetings, had had a lick of paint and knackered, buckled and twisted cart, wagon and bike wheels nailed to its walls. The café had a change of name too, to the *Twisted Wheel*, and the building now became a beat club for both dancing to the latest hits in the charts and to watch live music. Manchester Beat embarked. And when the Twisted Wheel on Brazennose Street introduced all-nighters, dossers would get their heads down in the opulence of arid side rooms using their duffel bags as pillows. But the Wheel also attracted the 'in' crowd. Barry, a local lad, began putting in appearances at the club at weekends with his mates and joined the clubs' membership scheme. Also, a few years later when the club moved to Whitworth Street(the *new* Twisted Wheel) a chap called Derek got wind of the new sensation that was the talk of the town. The Wheels' growing reputation had begun spreading further afield by word of mouth with even southerners trapping up north to have a nose at what all the fuss was about. To some Wheel goers, the club would become the epicentre of the world.

Derek, at 18 years of age, made his first ever visit to this Mecca he had heard so much about in 1966 from where he lived, Stockton Heath. And from that day forward his life would never be the same ever again. When he crossed the threshold of the Twisted Wheel's doors, which had an illuminated, orangey pink glowing sign overhead of the clubs name, he had seemingly stepped into another world. He never really let on to locals in the small village where he was from of this sanctuary, though. He would just think to himself 'they don't know what they're missing' when he returned home the following day from his many visits to the Wheel, while he quietly laughed to himself.

He has tales galore of events and incidents that happened on nights out round Manchester, this before flashing his membership card at door staff on the Wheel's door to gain entry later in the evening or in the wee hours. Plus the goings-on once inside the club too. Such accounts like, being stopped and searched for drugs by the 'Feds.' Also, observing clubbers being taxed for sixpence off a non-soulful, West Indian gang at the foot of the stairway that led to the toilets. And once, when a guy dressed in a roaring Twenties suit complete with shoulder holster, discharged a starting pistol that resembled a Colt 45! The bloke in question drew his pistol and let loose at the end of the first line of a track called *Mr Bang*

Bang by Little Hank. This action triggered clubbers to dive to the floor as a sound not too dissimilar to an atomic bomb bounced and echoed off the clubs solid, cellar walls. When the now deaf, bewildered faux-mobster gunslinger was shown the door by two of the management, Derek went on to witness lads returning to the dance floor with dust and talc covering their strides. Some lads even had holes in their trouser knees but, true to form, they carried on dancing while wiggling their fingers in their ears. Talk about a new dance craze.

Only these anecdotes will be saved for another day and chronicled into a book that Derek is working on at the present and hopefully put to print very soon. But one thing Derek is willing to do is give a knowledgeable acumen on both the Twisted Wheel's venues in the Sixties (and up until the Wheel sadly closed its doors in 1971) and also when the world famous club reopened its iconic doors once again.

Both Derek and Barry will give an insight into their nights at the Wheel: Barry at Brazennose Street, and Derek a brief history on the old Wheel, and also the Whitworth Street venue.

ONE HELL OF A RIDE
The Twisted Wheel Club, Manchester – Brazennose Street 1963-1965 & Whitworth Street, 1965 – 1971

Derek: *Clubs are clubs. But anybody who went on, or even near, this particular journey would certainly never ever forget it!*

The Twisted Wheel was a rarity in the fact that it didn't just open and then run. Oh no. It evolved, it seeded, it grew, it discovered and it merged, and it melded into a bedrock of soul, discovery, innovation, dancing, fashion and astounding music. And what makes it even more unusual is that it wasn't just the management that progressed this phenomenon. It was also the members and the dancers and the DJs and the groups. All of them had a massive part to play in the gradual yet unstoppable formulation of not a club, but to the members, a pure temple of beating brotherhood soul that lasted inside you for a lifetime.

The Twisted Wheel Club was opened on the 27th January 1963 by the Abadi brothers, a pair of businessmen who had a feeling that they could make something tick. Their first site, in Brazennose Street, was formerly the residence of the Left Wing Coffee House *which was a type of heavy folk and student dive that had lost its street cred. The Abadi brothers moved in and bought it.*

Manchester, at that time, was rife with clubs and teenbeat coffee bars but the Abadi brothers had a feeling that with their talent they could make the Wheel work, even in the midst of the many high class and long established rock and pop emporiums that abounded in the city.

The club started slightly hippyish, but thanks to the brothers it soon began featuring innovative soul beat groups and attracted the mod type soul tempo fans. These new energetic teenagers were commandeering the dancing and the fashion, and also were dictating what sort of music was acceptable. If they didn't like the group or the songs on stage, the floor would empty and the crowd would move to another part of the club and continue dancing to their beloved record tracks much to the consternation of the singer. There wasn't a hope in hell that they would listen to slower tempo! Their music ruled the roost and that was that. The stage act had to humbly finish their piece and shuffle off the stage.

One of the Abadi brother's acquisitions at Brazennose Street was a DJ called Roger Eagle who favoured rhythm & blues. And boy did the new breed like it. So much so, that Roger could expand his disc selection and try out new sounds he thought were suitable and different. Roger's ability to hit the spot with his newly discovered tracks kept the soul boys thinking, dancing and wanting more, so much so that the club now began to open more often through the week. And then in what proved to be a masterstroke, the infamous all-nighters were introduced. This simple move cemented the name of the club in musical history forever. The reputation of the club and Roger grew and grew and it became a top venue. DJs, soon to be famous groups, and soul boys, were clamouring to get there. The Wheel's soul-dancing and music fame had spread all over the country and the now kaleidoscopic mix was further enriched by another element. The clientele were starting to be fuelled by pills that would keep them going all night in the ethereal pulsating atmosphere.

"the twisted wheel was a rarity
in the fact that it didn't just open
and then run. oh no. it evolved,

it seeded, it grew, it discovered and it merged,
and it melded into a bedrock of soul,
discovery, innovation, dancing, fashion
and astounding music."

Barry: *My recollections of nights at the Twisted Wheel from 1964 to 1966 are plentiful but, none-to-vivid due to the passage of time, and age.*

The Wheel didn't open its doors before 10:30pm on a Saturday night, and the queues to enter the place would form stretching along Brazennose Street, twisting and turning along the pavement and also on the cobbled street. We would be dressed to impress; starched white, small stiff collared shirts, which we would pick up on the way home from work on Friday from the local Chinese launderette, and neat narrow ties were worn that would sit snugly under the collar too. Suits were mohair, bespoke to your spec, by an Italian tailor in Manchester. Our shoes would reflect the street lamps' glow after hours of shining them with spit and polish. And, un-tipped cigarettes would hang to the side of our mouths while we coolly chatted and eyed-up the talent in the queue.

I can remember once we arrived pretty late on Saturday night and saying to my friend "There's no way we will get in for some considerable time tonight with the amount of people queuing. It might be even full by the time we get anywhere near the front" whilst we waited for the doors to open. Then one of the policemen on duty keeping order came talking to my friend (the copper was a friend of his family). When the copper left I said to my mate "I've an idea! Why don't we go along the line telling everyone that police will be carrying out searches for Purple Hearts and Bombers, plus any other drugs that kept everyone on the dance floor all night." This we did. The queue halved in size in no time so we more or less guaranteed our entry within the next hour. You didn't want to miss a much looked forward to night in The Wheel, no matter what you'd to resort to.

In my day there was never any thought given to health and safety, or how many could enter the building, it was a case of once it was full, the doors would close. Apart from the resident DJs playing tunes of the time and black American imported sounds, different groups would play on a Saturdays. The one group that really stood out, and who I still listen to today are The Moody Blues. They went on to play bigger venues and have successful chart hits over the years. I can also remember John, 'Long John', Baldry playing at The Wheel on many an occasion. The problem for John was he was 6' 7", and the stage was 2ft off the floor, so he always had to do his set on the dance floor. This would create another problem; he would get knocked about by people dancing while on 'uppers.' The ceilings were low, the crowd were packed in, and the music was of the time, so you could imagine the sight of 'Long John' being moved along the floor as he tried to sing.

Blues or soul music had begun to be played more and more, all night long, and into the early hours of the morning, nearing the end of the Brazennose Street days. The biggest song played at The Wheel became '1-2-3' by Len Barry. You only went to the Twisted Wheel to dance, watch up and coming bands, and for the sweet, sweet music, not to drink. The girls would bring talcum powder to put on the dance floor so that dancing was a lot easier and faster for the more upbeat sounds. And if there was a clear run along the dance floor to the toilets, which were few and far between, lads would run and the slide right into the gents. When it got to about 4:30am, people would start to crash out in the tiny rooms scattered about the place when the Purple Hearts began wearing off. Then when the last 45" had been spun, it was the norm for everyone to head into town and call in the coffee bars and cafés near Piccadilly to grab breakfast or a strong coffee before heading off home on the first bus of the day out of Manchester.

Times like these will never be seen again.

Derek: *The Twisted Wheel moved to its new home in Whitworth Street and opened in September 1965. And if the scene at Brazennose Street had been changing at a heady pace, then, when the club moved to Whitworth Street, it became positively supercharged.*

Roger Eagle had moved across the city with them and carried on there in the same vein. He was still cock of the walk and still in magisterial control; or so he thought. Roger had not realised that the club was still evolving and although his searching and playing of freshly unearthed tracks was to be admired, he was getting a bit too deep and way out for the soul boys. The now famous dancing was moving on apace and needed powerful beats and hooks in the music so that they could hammer in their stylish moves and turns. That and the amphetamine factor, led to groups of dancers going down to the DJs' cage to request their favourites. If a poor track went on they would march back down and bang and rattle on the steel DJs' cage until Roger caved in and did as requested. He realised he couldn't play what he wanted so he decided to go. He left the Wheel around 1965 for the Blue Note Club around the corner.

The new DJs were soul boys, just like the dancers, and knew exactly what they wanted and this in turn led to another building block in the Wheels history being laid. The dance floor was always full, but if an unpopular track was put on the deck and the dance floor emptied the DJ would drop one step down the DJ status ladder so the DJs were constantly searching for, and discovering, the right sounds to keep dancers on the floor. Tracks were fervently sourced from shops and warehouses in Britain that bought tracks from America. DJs would ask around the dockyards and US air bases, and search through the record shops deleted bins and even beg them from American sailors, all in the quest for better and better sounds. The music was 'King' but was very much controlled by the dancers needs and so the pioneering DJs were pushed to find and uncover even more and increasingly rarer tracks that fitted the dancers' requirements and kept them on the floor. Early records with their personalised and colourful labels from tiny recording studios in American towns and backwoods began to be sought and uncovered by guys actually going over the Pond (not an easy thing in those days) to find label names like Stateside, Island, Capitol, Sue, O'Keh, Stax, Beacon, Atlantic, Cameo, Ric-tic, Tamla and many more.

A DJ unearthing a particularly good dancing track would sometimes cover the label or disguise it with a false title and artist to throw rival DJs off the scent and so keep that top sound for himself for as long as possible in his effort to be the dancers' 'top dog' of the tables. In short, the DJs and the dancers were fuelling off each other which then spun off on to the record collectors who then tried to find and buy or swap the best tracks for, sometimes, quite large sums of money. As dancing got more and more stylish and athletic, so the music grew and developed and the Wheel became the groundbreaking venue that every soul minded person must visit, and many thousands of real soul boys and girls from all over the country did just that.

After a myriad of the usual, and unusual, legal, and illegal modes of transport, Saturday nights started for most people by rendezvousing up at a mixture of coffee bars and dark pubs around the centre of Manchester, all within easy reach of the Wheel but out of obvious sight of wandering thugs and the Feds. At these places records and other items would be discussed and the journey to the Wheel would be timed such that they could go straight there and straight in or, sometimes to arrive a half hour earlier which enabled them to go into the White Hart pub (now Monroes, and still used by the soul boys before going in to the dancing temple).

At the magic hour of eleven o'clock the atmosphere would change and become electric as the shuffle towards the club door and the apparently mile long queue would begin to form.

Dry-mouthed and chewing gum, the dancers entered the upstairs coffee bar which was already filled by record collectors with their shoe boxes full of tracks and buyers haggling to get the best deal. From these dealings came some of the most sought after tracks in soul music (and very often unknowingly so).

Further in, a set of stairs led downwards into a whirlpool of pure pulsating dancing soul, initially with the different regional groups dancing in circles, but gradually as the Wheel dance steps evolved and as soul boys and girls from different countrywide areas got to know each other, they would dance solo, picking up steps and moves from each other and evolving until the soul style of dancing that is now clearly recognisable throughout the land.

Using a base of the Latin American, Boogaloo and Shing-a-ling dances, further steps and styles came from such places as, Scotland, London, Sheffield, Stoke, Stafford, Liverpool, Warrington, Bradford, and within Manchester and Moss Side itself. We got many steps and moves from the Jamaican guys and black Americans who loved the ska music and were great friends of ours. The whole lot was mixed together and plunged into a melting pot of fast cellar dancing soul.

It is still with much pride I can say that back in the Sixties, racism just didn't exist at the Wheel, we were all soul boys and that was that!

The many famous, and soon to become famous, groups that appeared on stage just had to be right on their game as the eyes of the soul world were on them. The lightning tom tom drums of the music world would rapidly transmit your sad message if you 'lost' the dance floor at the Wheel and the dancers went off into the other room to listen to the records instead.

Fashion, which just had to be kept up with, also owed a lot to the Wheel and its followers. Italian-style lightweight mohair suits with the almost week by-week slight variances of numbers of buttons or pocket flaps or size and number of back vents, ruled the roost for a long time. Other trends included yellow shirts, button-down collars, Crombie coats, Ben Sherman shirts, pot hats, brogue shoes, dancing shoes, tank tops, black and white and patent leather shoes. The roaring Twenties look complete with gangster trilby and shoulder holster (sometimes complete with a real starting pistol) reigned for a while. Many more fine styles came and went including the wearing of one black glove on a clenched fist held high in the air which became one of the endearing and everlasting symbols of dancing soul music.

At Brazennose and Whitworth Street clubs, stars like The Stones, Rod Stewart, Hendrix, Long John Baldry and Clapton called in, and allegedly Elton John once said "If you wanted to make it as an R&B band in England, you had to be accepted at the Wheel in Manchester first."

Some of the Wheel acts were, Edwin Starr and Geno Washington, John Mayall, Yardbirds, Ike and Tina, Alvin Cash (who started the famous dancing Backdrop) James and Bobby Purify, Ben E King, Alan Bown, Amboy Dukes, Robert Parker and many many others too numerous to mention. All of them loved it, especially as their music just bounced back off the cellar walls and into your very psyche. The famous stage room pulsated with top innovative dancing soul sounds and groups, who, in their hearts, wanted to play there and not just turn up for the money.

The story goes on and on: friendship, camaraderie, like-mindedness, soul, essence, oneness: these words were never mentioned, they were just there inside you.

Even when the Wheel was closed down by the police efforts in January 1971, it was fortuitous that it was closed at the very top of its game and thus thousands of soul dance fans were all left wanting, and begging, for more with only the best memories of the Wheel left ingrained in their minds.

This can only be the reason that when Pete Roberts and John Green re-opened the Twisted Wheel doors many moons later, playing the exact same sounds, it once again became very popular and was once again visited by fans and former Wheel-goers from the Sixties from all over; not just this country, but the world. Even university students use the Wheel people and its history for research into music, dance and the scene for their exams.

Speak to any ex–Twisted Wheel-goer and once the dreamy faraway mist of a wonderful past disappears from his eyes you will hear the same clichés heard time and time again, 'Tingles down my spine!'...'Superb dancing'...'Wonderful, no, incredible music'... 'Top superstar groups you stood next to on the floor'...'Pulsating tracks'...'World of discovery'...' Couldn't get off the dance floor, it was just too good to miss'...'Best time of my life'... The plaudits go on and on and on.

It was where it all began and it became known eventually to some as Northern Soul, and luckily moved on to other clubs who carried it on and furthered it in their own way. The Twisted Wheel, especially from 1965, developed the true beginnings and depth of dancing soul and its music that touched the lives of so many people of its time and beyond – not just at the teenage stage, but for the rest of their lives.

*The Twisted Wheel opened again in the original Whitworth Street venue playing strictly original Wheel music. But for how long? Who knows? Some of the above extracts have been kindly forwarded and used from the article 'From Stockton Heath to the Twisted Wheel'.

From Mods To Boot Boys

By the time the mods and rockers fought on the beaches in Brighton, Bournemouth, Clacton and Margate in 1964, it was the beginning of the end of mod. The pioneers in youth rebellion, mods, bedecked in their finest fighting gear with razor blades hid behind their jacket lapels, just in case the enemy got a grip of them, kicked sand in rockers' faces, while others threw pebbles at the bikers and pummelled the greaseballs over the head with deckchairs. The media declared that mods weren't nice boys, but thugs, and were an enemy within that showed little or no respect for law and order!

If mods hung their mohair suits up in the closet for the quieter life, the 'smooth' mods amongst them might have chosen to morph into a flower power loving hippies. The 'harder' mods though shaved off their impeccable hairstyles and became skinheads.

More on these two offshoots of mod, shortly.

———

1965 was an evocation year in more ways than one – it was the year of my birth too. There was a dangerous, but also exciting, culture sweeping Britain, namely, football hooliganism. Bovver boys in *de rigueur* steel toecap boots, surplus army kit, and either a bush or donkey jacket (or maybe such combat gear was only worn in the north?) were taking the law into the own hands, and feet, up and down Britain, and inside football grounds. The media and tabloids hadn't the foggiest on this new activity though, yet. And one teenage boy, Ronnie Sharpe, saw firsthand on the terraces of Bramall Lane, and various other grounds, the emergence of scalping of scarves, the shredding of banners with teams names painted on them and, the Kings' of the Kops' taking issue with who was king for the day.

Ronnie hails from Dronfield, a town of some twenty-odd thousand lost souls which lies in a valley on the banks of the stream Drone, near the north east Derbyshire / south Yorkshire border. The *steel city* of Sheffield stands six miles to the north. The market town famous for its crooked spire, Chesterfield, is six miles to the south. Many a well-to-do Sheffield family moved to Dronfield in the Sixties, and it was seen as a step-up-the-ladder moving from Yorkshire to the more tranquil and up market county of Derbyshire. Sheffield folk trying to be posh, eh? Impossible! Ronnie the youngest of five children, was born in a back-to-back, one up one down, crumbling, bed bug riddled, rat infested dwelling. But as he grew up, he never complained, he just got on with it – life moulding adventures were to be had. Ronnie recently self-published two books titled *Sharpe as a Blade*, and *Sharpe as a Blade 2*, both are humorous, evocative and honest accounts of working-class life in the post-war years. His wit is razor Sharpe, and the books are littered with dry humour.

Below is a brief introduction to his roots and passions.

Cammells Row: The close proximity of the houses kept families on the Row community tight. There was always activity, someone coming up, or coming down the gennels. Men arriving home from, or setting off to, work. Women gossiped as they hung out the washing or emptied the piss-pot. Other housewives were either donkey-stoning the front step or making trips to the dustbin to pour in the ashes. Herds of threadbare, infants and toddlers, dressed in hand-me-down grey shirts with frayed collars and short trousers hanging below their knees held up by snake belts, laughed, screamed and dashed from yard-to-yard. Gangs of teenagers and adolescents sat chatting on the dividing walls or banged balls against the slime green painted shithouse door. They lived from day to day and from hand to mouth. Kids were sent round to the neighbours to borrow all manners of things.

Local characters: The Lockets, who had too many kids to count, lived in one of the semis directly opposite Ronnie's. They kept a strange pet in the form of a donkey. Nowt wrong with that I suppose? But the beast was part of the family. Like a giant dog the donkey lived in the front room where nippers would ride it around the house. And it slept by the side of the fire at night.

Football: Team, Sheffield United, a diehard Unitedite, and Blades man of the highest order too.

Hooliganism: Football violence really started to take off in 1965. Why 1965? I don't know. Seemingly, it just begun overnight, so to speak. Was it the scrapping of National Service? (This where lads from all parts of the country had bonded and got on so well together for two years out of their young lives.) Was it the lack of wars? (There hadn't been a war for some considerable time, but if the lads involved would have been born thirty years earlier they'd have bounced up the beach of Dunkirk.) It was obviously territorial, and it all began to happen in 1965.

The Stones: Like a rolling stone, Ronnie gathered no moss. Ronnie fell in love with the group, The Stones (later they changed their name to The Rolling Stones), after watching them perform on *Thank Your Lucky Stars*. A band whose music and image would have an everlasting effect on the rest of Ronnie's life. He even started to grow his hair in 1963! Long hair, now there's a thing. So, Ronnie's 13 years of age and his hair is just covering his ears, but even that was considered outrageous. The older age group couldn't quite grasp it. Elderly ladies who he passed in the street turned their heads and tutted, some screamed in horror, others fainted. Grown men huffed and puffed while mumbling, "I've never seen anything like it, bloody disgusting." Building site workers shouted to him hilarious comments like "Is it a boy? Or a girl? Tha can't tell 'em apart these days." Or, "Where's ya handbag darling?" They then fell about laughing. He just flobbed on the floor and went on his merry way. Some folk had scientific theories on the subject. Someone, who no doubt had a university degree in the hair maintenance and management, told him that by being a boy and growing his hair, it would become weak and break. And by the time he reached twenty-one, it would all have fallen out. His reply, "Wow-ee, pretty scary. Because by the time I reach 21 I would be an old man, and wouldn't give a fuck."

Rising To Occasions

I wish I could take full recognition for the above context and milieu, but I can't. In a nutshell the majority are Ronnie's waxing lyrics – I've adapted them to suit. Ronnie has also kindly donated extracts from both his books towards the explanation, the rise and the adaptation of the Northern Monkey in a southern based 'they are superior' development theory in Britain.

So, here's an anthology off Ronnie, on the music and club scene in Sheffield and the surrounding towns in the mid-Sixties.

Ronnie Sharpe: *An old disused flourmill on Leadmill Road, Sheffield, housed The Esquire club. (It's nowadays the site of Leadmill nightclub). The three-storey building had a small doorway at street level which led up a steep narrow staircase to the first floor. Past the admission desk to the right was the TV room, where a television that nobody watched sat flickering in the corner. We also used this area as an early form of 'chill-out' room away from the roar of the music where we could doss down for a while at all-nighters. Courting couples snogged and groped in the corners. The toilets had strange, foreign toilety type names stuck on the doors, one of which was 'lavabobo'; we used this name for the bogs for years after, "I'm just nipping to the lavabobo for a shit." Another narrow flight of stairs led to the dance floor. At the far end was a stage, made from, so the rumour went, the tops of two grand pianos with the legs sawn off. In the centre of the stage, a graffiti covered wooden pole held up the ceiling.*

Yet another narrow staircase gave access to the snack bar on the upper floor. Also a rectangular hole in the floor surrounded by three-foot high wooden balcony railings allowed punters a birds-eye view onto the dance floor and the stage. The walls and ceilings were decorated with fishing nets, ancient blunderbusses, steel-rimmed wagon wheels, tribal masks, a large stuffed crocodile and other paraphernalia. A skeleton wearing a top hat and a pair of wellies hung from the roof; the seats and the tables were different sized barrels.

The Esquire, what a place; smoke filled, dark, damp and dangerous; tremendous pounding, roaring beat music, a fourteen-year-old boy's dream come true. There were no dress restrictions, and as far as I knew, no age restrictions too – I always got in anyway. No alcohol was sold on the premises, just Coke and other fizzy drinks.

The Esquire was in direct competition with Peter Stringfellow's (whatever happened to him?) Mojo Club. The Mojo stood in the mainly black, Pittsmoor area of the city. The clientele there were pure mod, whereas the punters of the Esquire were a mixture of mods, beatniks and young lads and lasses from all walks of life. The DJ at The Esquire always slagged off the Mojo, and vice-versa.

At 14, Kek Keeble and me were the youngest of the Dronny lads who went to the club most Friday and Saturday nights. The other lads (Ansh, Rocket, Andy Ellis, Simmo, Wuss, Steve Buckley, Hodgy, Don Keeble and Tiny) were all a year older, with Gig Ellis and Piggy Bacon the oldest at 17.

Tiny was well into the soul and Tamla music, and the mod scene, but he went to both clubs. I was more into the beat groups. I only went to the Mojo once (with Tiny) to see Wilson Pickett at an all-nighter. We queued for ages along with hundreds of others, only the club was packed out and we couldn't get in. We sat outside for an hour or so then walked off round the corner down Pilgrim Street where Tiny's auntie lived. We planned to knock her up and stay the night. On our way we saw an old-ish West Indian guy dressed in a baggy zoot suit, trilby hat and the loudest tie I'd ever seen, wobbling from side-to-side outside a blues party on the street. He had obviously been thrown out and stood shouting threats in a marvellous Jamaican accent at the building. "Bastard house. Shithouse. Ya not a house. Ya a fucking shithouse". He staggered up the path then fell backwards disappearing over a wall. He reappeared minus his hat and shouted "Bastard, fucking shithouse" again. Tiny and me were laughing so much we had to hold each other up.

All the up and coming beat groups played The Esquire; The Kinks, Small Faces, The Who, The Pretty Things, plus American Rhythm & Blues legends including Howling Wolf, John Lee Hooker and Screaming Jay Hawkins. There were also regular appearances from local Sheffield acts such as Dave Berry and the Cruisers, Joe (The Blade) Cocker and The Frank White Band.

New Years Eve 1965: The Pretty Things (singer Phil May had the longest hair of all the new bands) headlined the all-nighter. We went to the first session at The Esquire, which finished at 11 o'clock, and then went outside to join the queue for the nighter that started just before 12 o'clock. I was a "midnight to six man". In the queue I got talking to a young mod girl from Barnsley who was stood near me. She was 16 (I told her I was 16 as well) and it was her first visit to the club. With a 'horn', that nearly burst through my hipsters' zip, I promised to show her around.

Pass-outs, in the form of a piece of wallpaper ripped off a full roll, were available at the pay-in counter if you needed to nip out at any stage. After an hour or so, hand-in-hand, we took our pieces of wood-chip and went for a walk around the deserted back streets.

Although I'd been close on several occasions, I still hadn't lost my cherry. We stopped, snogged, groped, fumbled, and mauled each other at the back of a derelict house for a good 10 minutes but I was too scared to actually 'do it'. This happened on two more occasions during the night. I'd the horn on for so long I was beginning to feel badly so I left the girl for a while and found my mates. When they found out I hadn't actually 'done it' they started taking the piss. I said I'd got gut ache.

"I know what's up with you Ron." Wuss said, "She gave ya a 'Blow Back', dint she?"

"What's a blow back?" I said,

"Well." Wuss said, "When you're ready to shoot your load, she puts her thumb over your Jap's eye and it shoots back down and nearly blows your bollocks off". Everybody cracked up.

The dance floor heaved with sweaty bodies as The Pretty Things took to the stage. I swayed and surged trying to reach the front. It's like the Shoreham End I thought, but with music, and birds. Sweet-smelling older girls gave me New Year kisses too. What could be better than this?

We left the club at six o'clock in the morning and were on too much of a high to go home so three of us decided to hitchhike somewhere. We managed to thumb a lift to Mansfield where we walked round the town for half an hour or so. Then we thumbed it back home again, grabbed a few hours kip, then it was off to The Lane to see the Blades play Northampton.

The highlight of my Esquire days was a concert by The Who (on a par with The Stones as my favourite ever bands) in February 1966. The tickets cost seven shillings (35p). My lasting memory is of Keith Moon bouncing his sticks off the bass drum into the audience, where the punters fought each other trying to grab them.

The weekend starts here: Home from school to a roaring coal fire with the 'damper' down to heat the water for the Friday teatime weekly bath. Hair, sleek and shining courtesy of a sachet of Silvikrin egg and lemon shampoo. Best mod togs washed, ironed and laid out on the bed. Black Watch, tartan tab collared shirt (my favourite ever shirt) that hung to perfection.

Checked Rupert Bear hipsters, which itched like fuck due to me not wearing undercrackers. These were held up with a thick leather brass buckled belt (stolen from the Boy Scout cupboard in the church hall youth club). And for the finishing touch, Cherry Blossomed, black Cuban heeled, Chelsea boots with blue satin lining. 10 bob (50p) scrounged from my unk's brown paper wage packet. Switch on the TV to hear Manfred Mann's 5-4-3-2-1 introduce **Ready Steady Go***, hosted by the gorgeous Cathy McGowan. Ooh Cathy, every red-blooded teenage boy's fantasy and dream. Then the bus into town. The Esquire. Magic. This became the weekend routine in late 1965, early 1966.*

On Saturdays we sometimes stayed in Sheffield after the Blades' home games and went straight in the club when it opened at seven o'clock. It closed at 11 o'clock, and most nights we even stopped trying to get the last bus home – we didn't want the night to end. We walked around town shouting and laughing at ancient 30-year-old suities, (too drunk and too old to chase us) until midnight. Then the streets were all but deserted, we walked or hitched-hiked the six miles back home, completely sober and drug-free. But, nevertheless, flying.

As well as the trips to The Esquire, we started attending the Saturday all-nighters at the Victoria Ballroom in Chesterfield. The Vic was a massive dancehall housed on the top floor in a Tudor style building on Knifesmithgate, in the centre of town.

On my first visit to the club half-a-dozen Dronny lads were stretched out on the top deck of the number 12 Chesterfield bus, taking up a seat each, and engaging in a bit of ruthless teenage banter. Paddy O'Brien's two sizes too big, and four years out of fashion, battered winkle-pickers dangled over one of the seats.

"Nar-then Pad" one of the lads shouted, "I bet your big-un's had to stay in tonight hasn't he?"

"I don't know" Paddy answered "Why?"

"Well you've only got one pair of shoes between ya and you've got the fuckers on."

The nighters were again 12am till 6am with no alcohol on sale. Some of the older lads had been before and told me how 'easy' the Chesterfield birds were.

To the latest pop sounds the girls filled the dance floor performing The Frug, The

Shake, The Watutsy and The Boogaloo. Older tarts still did the Twist, the Jive and the Locomotion. Hardly any lads, and certainly none of the Dronny lot, ever danced, it was considered 'puffy'. The lads walked in circles round-and-round trying to pluck up courage to talk to the lasses. I got talking to a girl and now having lost my cherry (a story in itself) and being a man of the world, my usual strategy was to say "hello" and go straight for the tit. It saved messing about and you knew where you stood if the girls didn't object too much. But remembering what my mates had said about the Chezzy birds being easy, after about 30 seconds or so I stuck my hand straight up her mini-skirt. She gave me a slap that made my cheek burn and stormed off.

We also used the Vic on Mondays for the 7-till-11 on soul and Tamla Motown nights, frequented mostly by local mods. Hodgy, a small 16-year-old, red-haired fireball with a permanent grin, was as hard as a mongoose. His idea of fun was to walk round Dronny (or Chesterfield) swigging a bottle of whiskey, looking for people to fight.

When we arrived in Chesterfield for the Monday Vic nights, he would nip off on his own to a pub, somewhere or other, to purchase a few Black Bombers (Dexedrine pills). I think he paid about half a crown each for them. None of the rest of us had seen, or even heard of the speed tablets. Hodgy was very secretive about the whole thing and wouldn't even tell us which boozer he visited to pick up the gear.

The first time we went to the club – on the invitation from the Chesterfield Blades we knew – I could feel the tension. Groups of mods eyed us up and gave us the stares. We were strangers and I could tell that they took exception to us being there. And a group came over and stood close to the five or six of us, making comments.

"Who's these cunts?" one of them said, loud enough for us to hear.

"Get ready" Hodgy said.

We didn't have to as he calmly stepped forward and with one swift punch, put one of the lads on his arse. The rest of the Chezzy lads moved off after picking up their mate.

Our Chezzy Blade mates arrived later and knew the lads who had tried it on with us and calmed things down a bit. They had Mario, the main Chesterfield lad of the time, who came from a large, rough family of Italian descent. We had Gig Ellis aboard, the 'cock' of Dronny. Gig and Mario knew of, and had mutual respect for, each other. They met and spoke for the first time that night and got to know each other. Mario and his crew even came down to The Esquire one night in a joint venture with the Dronny mob after we had some trouble with a group of Sheffield lads in the club.

Later that night, Hodgy and me pulled two birds. I say birds, but mine was a fuckin' old woman, at least 21 years old. This little cracker left nothing to the imagination. She wore a white see-through blouse with a black bra underneath and a six-inch mini-skirt. She had a foot high, circa 1960, beehive hairstyle and eyelashes like a camel too. We left the club and went down an alley at the back of the club. Marge Simpson leaned back against the wall and hitched her skirt and girdle up over her hips saying, "Come on hurry up. I haven't got all night, I'm on the early shift at Robbo's in the morning (every bird in Chezzy worked at Robinson's jam-rag factory back then).

"Yeah" I replied undoing my zip, "I've got to be up early myself for school".

"School." she said "Fucking school. What ya talking about? You're still at school?"

"Yeah." I said "But I leave in a few weeks".

"Fuck-off" she shouted pulling her skirt back down. She stormed off and grabbed her mate who stood a few yards further down with Hodgy, saying "Come on, they're both still at fucking school",

"I'm not at fucking school." Hodgy said, "I left ages ago." The other girl pulled away from Hodgy.

The last we heard from the two trollops was the scraping and echo of stiletto heels as they wobbled across the cobbles and disappeared out of the end of the alley. Hodgy cracked up saying, "Still at fucking school. I can't believe you said you were still at school. Fuck me, you do me in Ron". We stood and rocked with laughter as Hodgy, whizzing off his head kept shouting "I'm still at fucking school" at passers-by.

We'd missed the last bus home and had to walk the six miles back. I dossed on Hodgy's settee that night. He rose at the crack of dawn and went off to the farm where he worked. I went back to sleep and was late for fucking school that morning.

Spirit Of A Skinhead

Returning to the by-products of mod: I've no need to go extensively into what hard mods went on to be, or what influenced the next generation of northern council/latchkey kids of the late Sixties on the music front, or what garb they wore, because who better to give you a smack in the kisser representation of skinhead and a detailed and thorough account, than none other than an old skinhead himself – Nobby. He will also elucidate the interchange of skinhead to suedehead, suedehead to smoothie, and smoothie to flares, platform shoes and feathercuts in quick succession and what they aligned themselves to.

Nobby: *Some things seem to have been around forever and were destined to go together; bacon & eggs, fish & chips, gin & tonic, Wallace & Gromit, you get my drift, don't you? For a certain generation of people you can add to that list football and fashion – not everyone will make this connection but there are plenty out there who will know exactly what I'm on about. What follows are ramblings from yours truly on an era that seems like yesterday to those who were there, and, I believe one that made a great impact on football fashion to the present-day. Also, a certain kind of dressing as mob mentality that has been around football lads for many years. In the main, I focus on ever changing prevailing tastes, and styles, in Preston, and an even smaller northern town, Leyland.*

The first Preston game I attended was in our 1963/64 West Ham FA Cup Final season: As a young lad of nine, obviously, nothing registered in the fashion sense at such a tender age, though. However, as you reach your teens and start going to games with your mates things like clobber start standing out – in the trouser department too – so I'm going to attempt a brief run down, in the main, on the skinhead era, and what styles followed. I'm bound to miss some stuff out and almost certain to get a couple of facts and dates slightly awry, so I'll apologise now. But, in my defence, a lot of this is now shrouded in the mists of time.

I bet it's hard for most to imagine in today's multicultural fashion society what the impact of seeing the first skinheads was like. You've got to know it was all long hair, flares, and love and peace, man. The first skinheads were akin to Joe Public as an appearance of the anti-Christ and likened to species from a different planet! There was already a gang mentality for young lads at football matches, and I can clearly remember both mods and greasers knocking about on the Kop at Deepdale – though for the life of me I can't remember, or picture in the grey matter, a decent hippy firm ever roaming the terraces. In the coming years though, in the era that followed skinhead and suedehead, I must admit we must have looked pretty similar to these long haired lovers – as you will gather later on.

If you've read up on the start of the skinhead it usually ascribes to the theory that the cult evolved from the 'hard mods' which in my opinion, when I think back to how the original mod look changed, is probably right. Sometime in the mid-Sixties a lot of mods started leaning towards more of a hippy sort of look, or they'd settled down by then. But there were also lads around who preferred to stick to the Fred Perry and jeans look and these are what were classed as the 'hard mods' in my book. Hard mods often lived in the same economically depressed areas of south London as West Indian immigrants and they began to emulate the 'rude boy' attire of pork-pie hats and short Levi jeans. So again, a lot of the original skinhead look also stems from working class roots. Cord and denim jackets with button down shirts became staple too.

I can actually remember going on my first shopping trip to Preston in late 1969 when I'd decided to be a skinhead. I bought my first Ben Sherman (who by the way wasn't actually British but lived in the UK) from a small hippy type boutique situated in Miller Arcade, in town. It was a blue and yellow candy stripe button down Oxford style, with sewn in pleats and a higher collar than the types churned out nowadays. I also obtained pair of Levis and a genuine US Army parka from a Army & Navy store. To complement my transformation, from your average teenager of the time, I purchased a couple of Tamla Motown Chartbusters albums and several Trojan Tighten Up compilations from Brady's on Market Square. So what more do you need? A skinhead haircut! I climbed into the barber's chair and asked for a number three – not a number one, or shaved, which is associated with the late Seventies/early Eighties skins. Spirit of a skinhead, complete.

I still recollect Leicester turning up at a home game at ours in 1969, and that the skinheads were all togged up smartly. I'm not saying they were the first skinheads I'd come across, only they were the first really well dressed skinhead mob of any size I ever witnessed. They were all wearing Dr. Martens Airwair (actually made fairly near Leicester – the boots were originally designed for factory workers), half-mast Sta-Prest pants or jeans, checked shirts, braces and V-neck jumpers. The skinheads prior to these had wore a more working class uniform; hobnail (steel toe-capped) boots, three-buttoned granddad vests, half-mast jeans, collarless union striped shirts, thin braces, near shaven heads with a razor cut side parting and sideburns if they were able to grow them.

The problem at the time was where to purchase all the smart skinhead gear, especially in Preston and the surrounding areas; compared to nowadays, clothes were in a much more limited stock and supply. I picked up my first pair of Docs, which were the seven hole version with the yellow band around the top, from a farmers trade shop at the local cattle market. There were only two places in town that you could buy them, the cattle market and a small shoe shop halfway down New Hall Lane on the way to the Preston By-pass when leaving town. They cost just over £7 and what a feeling it was when you got hold of your first pair. I shined them in oxblood polish once back home. And on leaving the house, I felt like I was walking on air – literally – with my Levi's turned up just above the top of the DMs. Later on everyone started wearing the classic 'Astronaut' 1460 eight-eyelet Dr Martens. The more highly shined you could get 'em, the better they looked. In the main I used Tuxan red polish and you could see your reflection in them. All the younger lads and the girls used to wear monkey boots, from Tommy Balls down Glovers Court, a budget shoe shop, because Docs were unobtainable in smaller sizes. Saying that, the skinhead girls always looked tasty with their feather cut hair (Chelsea cut), short skirts or fitted two-tone suits with patterned tights and tight fitting check shirts or Fred Perrys.

Jeans were always half-mast; and Levis 501s or Wranglers were the mainstay, sometimes bleached, and for a spell worn with sewn on patches. However, if you wanted to be a cut above, Lee Riders were a more expensive pair of jeans and I always thought the better looking denim.

Other trousers that were always popular in the north were half-mast white bakers' pants which were worn at the football. Smarter trousers were Levi Sta-Prest, with or without turn-ups, and made to measure 19, 20, 21 or 22" parallels, normally with a turn-up and usually with sewn-in creases. Shops like Harry Fenton and Burtons sold them off the peg too.

I remember taking a length of Prince of Wales check material to an Italian tailors down near Preston Railway Station and getting measured for a pair of parallels once. The tailor didn't have a problem with the 22" parallels, the waistband or the 1/2 inch turn-ups. But trying to get through to him that I wanted them four inches above my ankle was like trying to tell him to make 'em with just one leg or summat. After he finally cottoned on what I wanted I departed. I returned about two weeks later for a final fitting and adjustment only the poor guy was distraught and kept saying "I told you they would be too short!" I thought they were perfect. And not long later I left with my bespoke Prince of Wales parallels as happy as Larry and the Italian, tape around his neck, shaking his head and totally nonplussed.

"the look was evolving all the time and it's difficult to say when skinhead evolved into suedehead, but suffice to say it was a gradual change rather than a sudden change into another look. in fact, i would go so far as to say it was just another name that was adopted and the hair was worn a little longer, as most of the same clothes were still worn with slight tweaks added to the new look all the time."

Some people may look back on that period of time, the late 1960s/early 1970s, as having only one particular style. Well it wasn't, there were three different styles. Skinhead to suedehead to smoothie happened in a relative short spell of about three to four years – the look was constantly changing.

Preston was a bit of a desert when it came to keeping up with all the latest stuff coming out, especially if you wanted to be the first wearing whatever was 'in'. And there was a certain street-cred-snobbery attached to being ahead of the crowd just like the Eighties' casuals 10 or so years later. Erik Pass, a small shop situated on the higher level of St George's Shopping Centre, just to the left at the Friargate end of town, was the number one place for Ben Shermans. Strangely, the shop was run by a camp looking guy and his mother with her poodle, that had ribbon on its head, usually in attendance. It couldn't have been run by a couple more detached from the main clientele the shop attracted. The only other shop that catered for the skinhead and suedehead crowd was Stone Dri on Fishergate, run by a genial old bloke and his wife. There was also a shop called Patches which opened on the outside of Miller Arcade a little later that had a few decent bits in.

As an apprentice at Leyland Motors I once travelled down on the Friday overnight train to a shop in Aldgate East near Petticoat Lane, London, with a load of orders off the lads at work. I'd a pocket full of money and a long list of clothes that you couldn't get up here in the north. I was completely barmy and clobber obsessed at the time. The alternative to Preston was a trip to Manchester on the train where there were plenty of shops on New Brown Street, before it was bulldozed for the Arndale Centre. This old street was full of warehouses, and almost everyone of them was brimming with tons of skinhead and suedehead gear. Also two other shops to visit were Justins and Ivors which faced each other upstairs in the Market Centre. It was always dodgy if you were carrying a wad of cash as there were always gangs of white and black lads hanging about – you definitely had to keep a wary eye open and be on your guard.

The look was evolving all the time and it's difficult to say when skinhead evolved into suedehead, but suffice to say it was a gradual change rather than a sudden change into another look. In fact, I would go so far as to say it was just another name that was adopted and the hair was worn a little longer, as most of the same clothes were still worn with slight tweaks added to the new look all the time. The word suedehead refers to a grown-out short crop but their attitude and clothing were very similar to the skinhead. The suedehead of the early Seventies wasn't so much a separate entity more a continuation of the smart skinhead who had always worn his hair slightly longer than the shaved-in parting number one of 1969.

Therefore, the hairstyle and clothes had gone full circle, because skinhead had metamorphosed from mod in the first place, so it had headed back to where it all began in a fashion. Suedehead incorporated smarter and more expensive clothes, and maybe a little of that came about as boots were outlawed at some football grounds. And the smarter look wasn't as much of a giveaway as the original boot boy/skinhead look had been. In much the same vein as certain casual looks, amongst other things that came to be – avoiding the attentions of the Old Bill, to an extent.

The original check shirt worn by the skinhead was a Ben Sherman and usually square dance or gingham check. The shirts mutated into many different types of check over time and the search for the one that nobody else had was upper most. Slightly cheaper shirts were Jaytex and Brutus Trimfit. I personally thought Brutus looked the smarter shirt as they did the best tartan checks.

Smart shoes were always worn aside from the boots; royals (brogues), penny or tassled loafers, squires, plaincaps (Gibsons), Oxfords and weavers (Norwegians) to name a few. They were pretty expensive and leather soled. The best shop in town for royals and such was Manfield on Fishergate. The craze at one point was to have metal segs in the heel and front under tip, and they sounded dogs as you walked down the street. But I can tell you they could be pretty deadly if you were involved in a pursuit or in flight from a bigger mob at a match – you could soon go arse over tit.

Apart from denims, Sta-Prest pants in the colours of stone, black, bottle green or navy and parallels would adorn skinny legs. Two-tone tonik trousers and suits by Trevira made an appearance, as did Rupert (Sylvesters) checked trousers along with Prince of Wales strides and suits. Suits were almost always made to measure and this must have been a nightmare for the tailor as everything had to be just so: five or more buttons on the sleeve, multiple rows of ticket pockets on both sides, exact width of lapels, three or four button up fronts and a single vent at the back – in some cases the longer the better. I even saw some about two inches off the collar with a button half way down to stop it from flapping in the wind. Barrathea blazers were also worn for the evening. And another popular touch around here was the Lancashire red rose embroidered onto the pocket.

A Crombie overcoat (almost always a snide) was worn in winter months with a tie pin and silk hankie in the top pocket – red to match your red socks, and then various colours from bright yellow to orange to fluorescent green followed. Quite often the Crombie was teamed up with a black umbrella – not for keeping you dry but being quite handy at certain games. Another mainstay was the Harrington jacket with an essential tartan lining, the originals made by Baracutta, but once again mostly copies were worn. Harringtons, to this day, still make a comeback every now and then. On the main they were black but I also remember them in Prince of Wales check, maroon, green and navy blue. A lot of lads at one stage wore stone or beige fly-fronted gabardine macs. Total oneupmanship as far as outerwear was concerned, in my eyes, was the full length sheepskin coat in slightly different styles. I bought mine, along with a mate, from Louis Gross warehouse in Manchester at £35 each and he knocked us a fiver off for buying two. Paying £35 for a coat was a fortune at the time and way over a week's wage, though it turned out to be one of my best investments in clobber ever as they stayed en vogue for years to come on the terraces. It's still hanging in the back of my wardrobe as I can't bear to throw it out after it has travelled all over the country with me and brings back a flood of memories every time it catches my eye.

Fred Perry polo shirts never went out of style all through the mod, skinhead, suedehead (even with soul boys and early casuals later) and are still popular today. Classic style never dates. Slazenger V-neck pullovers were also very popular in the suedehead period along with chunky knit cardigans with brown leather covered, football-like, buttons in some shade of mustard or brown.

Woollen polo necks started to come in just prior to the cult changing to what was named the smoothie look. Another 'in' item that time were skinners; a type of baggy denim jeans bought in Manchester which only the younger end wore amongst us. There was a similar style you could buy from one shop on Scotty Road in Liverpool called Flemings which could be obtained in any width. It always brought a smile to your face on Euston Station in London when you saw some scouser turn up in about 36" wide Flemings trying to outdo everyone else but he looked like an extra from Billy Smart's Circus.

Mentioning Euston station, it brings back memories of how many away games in London we used to go to the night before and doss on the platforms or Victoria coach station. Or we would catch the midnight National Express from Preston which always had a few on annoying the normal passengers heading for The Smoke with classics songs like "I'm a knock-kneed chicken, I'm a bow-legged hen..." after being on the pop all evening. There was even a chip machine on Victoria for a bite to eat, the only one I've ever seen in my life. And there always seemed to be one of the scouse teams playing in London when PNE did. Friendly chat would have them asking "Hey la. I like your shoes la. Can I try 'em on la?"

"Aye, reet. As if!"

The start of the smoothie era heralded some pretty smart attire. But as it developed everyone was trying to go a bit further and it all ended up going a bit too far and merged with the glam rock, in my opinion. Shirt collars became half or penny round followed by long pointed collars. Simon shirts were popular around this time too. Knitwear was varied with such things as what were called football jumpers or cardigans, patchwork jumpers, anything made by South Sea Bubble and slightly later, three star jumpers. Falmers slightly flared brush denim jeans then came in. Trousers were longer and Levi's needle-cords were popular worn with wedge heeled shoes. The most popular were clumpy crêpe-soled, maroon leather pairs and suede affairs whose name escapes me. Toppers springs to mind, but I could be wrong.

Hair was getting longer all the time, the ultimate goal being a feather cut, the longer the better and short on top. As I mentioned it all started getting mixed up around 1973. Trousers were worn slightly flared, and then baggier, developing into 'Bags'. Birmingham and Oxford Bags had wide sewn-on pockets half way down the leg. Not much cop if you were a short-arse and needed to get 'em taking up as the pockets were liable to end up resting on your ankles. Pants began to get baggier and baggier. Then came really wide flares in a canvas type material, usually in pretty bright hues, that came with a two-inch turn up. I had a pair of vivid blue ones. And when you walked in the pub in pants that wide you certainly stood out from the crowd. I'm sure you would have taken off if high winds had swept under them.

All sorts of stuff started being worn such as velvet flares, loons and a hybrid of those two called loggers which were available from an exclusive shop down Cannon Street in Preston called Dan Kerrs, for those with a bit more cash to spare. Shoes got higher as trousers got longer – ending up with nearly six inch heeled platforms. The smaller you were the better platforms looked. The opposite for someone who was over six-feet tall lumbering around in high platform shoes looking like Herman Munster. Starsky & Hutch dense wool belted cardigans, trench coats with the belt tied at the back, long leathers, Mickey Mouse T-shirts, Budgie jackets, satin jackets, slip on clogs – great for dancing in – all came and went. A lot of the latter attire was inspired by Adam Faith in the ITV programme Budgie, *so he'd a lot to answer for, I can tell you.*

It became the silk scarf era on the terrace too; firstly knotted around the neck, then the wrist, and occasionally round the head at away games. Denim bib and braces were seen at the football as well as army or jungle greens (old style combat trousers) often still worn with Docs. There was also a brief period when lads painted their Docs, and I clocked quite a few psychedelic versions amidst the battling on the terraces. Peace and love man. Not.

It would take till the mid-to-late 1970s, 1977 I reckon, when those in the know went straight back to narrow Levi's with moccasins. Once again you looked a million light years ahead from everyone else – a strange irony was that to be at the forefront of fashion in those days everyone else thought you were very, very strange.

Then came the first trainers; and I remember buying a pair of Dunlop Green Flash. How odd that through all the aforementioned eras trainers, so standard nowadays, (unless you count the short-lived basketball boot late in skinhead) never became a real fashionable item till the birth of the casual.

On the terraces: As I've said football and fashion seemed to go together, only that's not to say all skinheads and suedeheads followed football. But, I would say almost exclusively they went hand-in-hand and most involved in the scene would go to the match with their mates even if they weren't into off field events. In bygone days, with no internet, or TV coverage on what was in, going the match is how the fashions caught on and developed so quickly. You would travel away and see someone wearing something one week and by the next match you had to have it, by hook or by crook!

I vividly remember the rockers and greasers on the terraces at one stage. They seemed to be the majority at places like Blackburn, Bolton and Derby. Only there was also a disparate group on the Kop at Deepdale; Donkey jacketed skins, in steel toe cap boots, leather clad greasers in drain pipe jeans and fish tailed parka wearing mods. If a scarf was worn it was the old woollen blue and white knitted one by a kindly auntie or gran. You'd get chanting against each other, usually skinheads and greasers, and a few half-hearted battles between the two if there was nobody else to fight with.

One short lived fashion I haven't mentioned is the 'Clockwork Orange' look; white jeans, painters white bib and brace or boiler suit and white smocks. This topped off with a bowler hat and black eye makeup. You wouldn't have got away with that get-up anywhere else but on the terraces.

The two biggest groups at Deepdale in those days were of course the Preston lads and the Leyland lads who always got along well with each other and always mixed at games. The Leyland lads started a fad for having a stitched 'A' (aggro) in a circle on denim jackets, they were always at the forefront of fashion and had pretty good numbers too. In the 1970/71 season the late Alan Ball christened PNE's following 'The Gentry' and the fans took up the roll sporting Crombies, bowler hats, royals or brogues and carrying black brollies en masse. This conjured a surreal vision of a mob of city gents ready to battle it out on the terraces. The bowler hat look pre-dated the Clockwork Orange *one by a number of years though.*

As anyone will testify from the early days of travelling down to The Smoke, *it wasn't like today when you can buy any sort of beer almost anywhere.*

Away trips down there where always scary and that was just the ale.

"... the 'Clockwork orange' look;
white jeans, painters white bib &
brace or boiler suit and white smocks.

> This topped off with a bowler hat and
> black eye makeup. you wouldn't have
> got away with that get-up anywhere
> else but on the terraces."

Flat, warm and insipid were about the only choices you had. And as for Courage, you bloody needed it to tackle the stuff that they called bitter.

The early skinheads were always into reggae, especially Trojan. And of course, Northern Soul – before the name Northern Soul was actually coined. The term so-called to differentiate between the top music listened to from the Midlands upwards as opposed to the shite jazz/funk disco which became the norm 'Dahn Sahf!' Thank God for the north/south divide, eh?

Vinyl wise: There was Brady's record shop on Market Square which was great for picking up Motown or Trojan compilation albums which I still own 40-odd years on. Desmond Dekker, Jimmy Cliff, Bob & Marcia, Dave & Ansel Collins, Horace Faith, Derrick Morgan, Max Romeo – Wet Dream (had a few in those days too), Harry J Allstar – Liquidator, Al Capone – One Step Beyond and of course Symarip, with the anthem skinhead Moonstomp. Each and every one of them when played can take me straight back in time. The best place for picking up northern imports was Spin-A-Disc, a small record booth on Preston bus station. I can still recall the first Northern 45's I purchased: Mitch Ryder - You Get Your Kicks, Human Beinz – Nobody But Me, Gladys Knight – Just Walk in My Shoes, Archie Bell – Here I Go Again. Once I got into Northern, I was hooked for life. In fact, I still collect vinyl, it's a real passion. And as far as the music goes, like the Isley Brothers sang, I Guess I'll Always Love You.

Obviously mentioning the music brings me onto the clubs around in those days. Prior to Wigan Casino there was a group of lads who went to the Twisted Wheel in Manchester, who were all older lads and a lot of the younger lads referred to them as the 'Big-Time.' As for Preston, there was of course the Top Rank which has had many guises over the years from Clouds to Tokyo Joes. It had a main room playing mainly chart music and as in those days the obligatory resident band – something to do with the Musicians Union, I believe. However, down a small passageway and in the far corner was another small open disco which played mainly soul sounds. Just before you got to it, there was a hot dog stand which looked like the proprietor had absent mindly wandered in off Friargate – strange days!

Another strange little room was to the left at the top of the steps as you entered the Top Rank – a TV lounge. This room always used to fill up with lads when Match of the Day started. You watched the trouble on the terraces as much as the football, as they always showed any aggro in those days.

The other club in town that was frequented by skinheads was the Stax Club, down a little alley off Fishergate, just around the corner from the Rank. It was in reality a dingy joint but played plenty of Northern Soul and reggae. I particularly remember the walls all being painted black and it had those purple lights that made all the bits of fluff and dust on your clothes luminous (whatever happened to them, they were brilliant if you were having a bit of a boring night and hadn't pulled. But then again, maybe you hadn't pulled because you looked like a luminous walking ball of fluff). Scamps opened slightly later about '73, and if my memory serves me right, it was always a good place for a bit of decent soul music.

There were numerous other discos and clubs out of town which seem to have all disappeared, possibly due to the fact that it never seemed to bother anyone if they'd had 10 pints or not before they drove. There was the Barred Gate at Samlesbury (now a hotel), the Lodestar on the outskirts of Ribchester, the Beechwood, near Blackburn, and the Howard Arms, Whittle-le-Woods. Memories come flooding back of a night out at the Howard Arms with a load of apprentices from Leyland Motors – it all kicked off big style with a mob of lads from Preston. Tables went over, bottles and glasses thrown, total mayhem ensued. You could also hear one of Sweets early hits belting out in the background as people were slugging it out. Everyone came through the blitz that night to fight another. The fucking Ballroom Blitz, that is!

Another odd spot I used to frequent was the Cranberry Fayre on top of the moors in Darwen, of all places. It was all done out like a fairground with mirrors everywhere. You actually thought there were about ten times more punters in than there were. In fact, I nearly had a fight with myself a couple of times when I'd had one over the eight. Another strange thing in there was a small pool between the dance floor and bar area. Every Saturday night a bouncer used to escort a female employee from the back room and she used to swim around in the pool topless. The pool was surrounded by blokes from about 10 minutes before the allotted time all hoping to do a bit of the old breast stroke themselves. Lads easily pleased in the days before DVDs or even videos. For most it was the nearest some would come to sex all night.

Anyone wanting to travel further afield was catered for by free buses from Preston bus station to Blackpool Mecca, which played shite in the Main Ballroom, though it was always packed out so you had a good chance of pulling. However, up a set of escalators, there was a smaller disco, namely the famed Highland Room. Suffice to say the music in there was all Northern Soul and was brilliant compared to downstairs. The only drawback in the old days, which may be hard to imagine now, was that you had to be suited and booted to gain entry. No tie. No entry.

Simple as that. We were a couple of ties short one night for some reason, and duly made our way in wearing velvet tie backs from a certain pubs curtains. There was also a free bus to Blackburn Mecca, aka The Golden Palms, which didn't have a soul room but did have a much better reputation as a spot for picking up a willing bird. Decisions, decisions.

There were plenty of all-nighters about in those days catering for Northern Soul, as I mentioned earlier the Twisted Wheel. But there was also Va-Vas at Bolton, the Golden Torch in Hanley, and of course, Wigan Casino, which opened in 1973. These clubs had always been places that the skinhead and suedehead fraternity frequented. A lot of the old skinheads morphed quite naturally into soul boys and the fashions often crossed over. Fred Perry's for example were always popular and early Northern Soul fashion included button-down Ben Sherman shirts, bowling shirts, Barrathea blazers with centre vents and complemented with red rose badges, brogue leather-soled shoes and baggy trousers, all perfect to dance in.

I could go on forever, which I nearly have, only I've a bid on eBay for an original Trojan track that needs my attention as it's coming to an end. I'd just like to add; the spirit of 1969 lives on forever.

The Hippy Hippy Shake

No grass? Right we've got a problem, man

Dylan (The floppy eared, buck-toothed rabbit from the *Magic Roundabout*)

My earliest recollections and awareness of anything hippified, was watching the dopey looking 'spacey' rabbit called Dylan (allegedly after Bob Dylan) in *Magic Roundabout*, strumming his guitar while rambling on incoherently to the rest of the gang. Even at an impressionable age I just knew that Dylan grew plants and fungi in his vegetable patch at the allotment other than just carrots. Yes, Dylan was a hippy. And I'm sure the rest of cast were on some sort of narcotics too?

The etymology of 'hippy' stems from the mellowed-out, free-and-easy loosely chilled jargon hip, hep and hipster. Hippy meaning 'one who is aware'. Really? I severely doubt it! Because hippies were either out of their heads on a 'Bicycle Day' from Lysergic Acid Diethylamide (LSD) and making love to a tree while partaking in the sexual revolution; off their faces on psilocybin cubensis's (magic mushies); stroking a refrigerator or, totally stoned and floating by on a nebulous cloud of marijuana smoke without a care in the world. (Weed; Little Weed being another of children's TV puppet characters, only I don't think she were on any form of hard drugs). Come on. One who is aware? I think that naming of a culture was way, way off the mark.

Hippy was another American Dream ideology purloined from across the Atlantic Ocean, the focal point being Haight-Ashbury, San Francisco. Forming from major beatnik morals, the USA youth had begun growing their hair and beards long, as well as finding their 'inner peace.' British *smooth* mods also took the plunge and set in motion enriching their lives.

If these guys weren't 'sky clad' ('cause they loved naturism) aside from love beads, headbands and flowers behind their ears while sat cross-legged meditating holding a joss stick in one hand and giving a two-finger peace gesture with the other, they wore loose, spirited/earthy clothing. Desired items were cheesecloth kurtas, frayed bellbottom jeans (again), sandals and intricately embroidered afghan coats, suede outer, sheepskin inner.

New Age hippies also lived off the land, nomadically travelled the countryside in VW camper vans and sometimes danced *bollocko* around a circular collection of immense, upright antediluvian stones – Stonehenge. Their preferred music held references to their spiritual and political emotions in euphonious psychedelic rock, folk and hymns.

Xtrabop

A smooth mod, Phil Eaves, recalls the transition in cults, music and groups through the Sixties and Seventies, along with his involvement in the noteworthy milestones. These events weren't viewed through rose-tinted penny round shades, though.

Phil Eaves: *It was a Saturday afternoon in July 1984, when I called in Greenwoods musical instrument store in Preston to see how sales of my book,* Xtrabop, *the first edition, were going. I was followed into the premises by a couple of youths dressed in bondage trousers and black bikers leather jackets, daubed in various cult slogans, their hair dyed in vivid colours and sculpted into amazing art-forms. The youths approached the counter, picked up a copy of* Xtrabop *from the display stand and spent around 30 seconds flicking through its pages. "You're right," said one lad "it's just about a load of boring old farts". They then replaced the copy in the stand and left the shop.*

In only 30 seconds they had written off over 30 years of local rock music, and at least three generations of rebellious youth culture, including their own! But that's rock for you.

Since rock 'n' roll first made inroads into the established dance band scene in the 1950s, much as happened musically. Although one generation's music is often ridiculed by another, rock in all its guises still lives on with each generation bringing something new to the table whilst adapting much of what has gone before.

My earliest recollection of sitting behind a drum kit, of sorts, was around 1952. I was five years old and I recall performing on stage with my father at a number of parochial events over the following couple of years. This brief flirtation with music soon passed, however, and I was soon pursuing the greater joys that trainspotting and football had to offer.

Then in the early Sixties, my father escorted me to several pop/rock concerts ranging from local outfits to the likes of Adam Faith and The John Barry Seven. I watched in awe as they stormed through jumping sets and the seeds of rock were well and truly sown in my soul. This led to me and three close friends watching in envy, and admiration, bands from the local Beat Group scene playing youth clubs in Preston. And by 1962 our dreams and aspirations as four young hopefuls were eventually achieved in the form of The Centurions. The old drum kit was resurrected from beneath the stairs and with an assortment of loud speakers extracted from broken radio sets, kit-built Linear amplifiers, (which my father had spent many hours cursing while assembling), The Centurions set out to take the world by storm.

Over the next couple of years The Centurions, and many other second generation groups, established themselves in and around Preston. One of the lads left the band in '65 to team up with two other lads doing the circuit to form The System, leaving us to be a three piece. We considered both the lads he joined to be seasoned pros and I remember once when one of the said lads sat in on the drums with us for a song or two. He was a wild character but a very good drummer has I watched in horror as he demolished my kit to the strains of Louie Louie. He showed me how it should be done and taught me the value of substantial hardware. My father was now faced with a bill for a new drum kit.

The Sunday night 'teen-scene' at the newly opened Top Rank Ballroom in town provided many local groups with an opportunity to play a prestigious venue. Strict dress restrictions applied; collar and tie, jacket (not leather) and no long hair. The bouncer's inspections were always thorough. 'Up Town Top Ranking' and on its famous, if somewhat erratic revolving stage, the resident Johnny Wollatson Dance Band would slowly disappear stage left whilst The Centurions appeared stage right. Through 'Hippy Hippy Shake', 'Talking 'bout You' and 'House of the Rising Sun', enthusiastic young girls would react encouragingly as Watkins Dominator amplifiers strained to project our sound from the stage and beyond the first few rows of eager female fans. The blokes present were somewhat less keen on local lads playing to their girls and you'd to keep an eye out for those who might be getting just a little jealous or trouble could ensue – even though your assailant wore regulation dress.

With discos, (as we have come to know them nowadays) still some years away, the early Sixties were the times when live music ruled supreme. Rock music, however, was only just emerging from its infancy and many groups, including ours, were serving their apprenticeships. Some bands carried on making their mark years later, many faded from the scene completely, but it was certainly to be many years before Preston saw such an abundance of groups and a healthy live music scene.

By the second half of the Sixties, new and important developments were beginning to stir and the past several years of essentially innocent pop music was about to be challenged by a new and more aggressive, visual and improvised sound force. Rock music itself was entering its rebellious youthful years and the stage was set for The Stones, The Who, Jimi Hendrix, Cream and Pink Floyd to make their mark. Most of these groups had evolved out of the early British R & B bands and while some (i.e. John Mayall and Fleetwood Mac, amongst many) continued to sustain and develop the blues theme, others presented totally new unheard before musical horizons.

The 'pop art, underground, psychedelic era had arrived, and while mod fought with rocker, hippies made love, dropped out, got stoned and fought all of society's established values.

Many ignored these new directions and a marked split developed in the ranks of music fans. Dance fanatics turned to the sound of soul and Tamla Motown thus heralding the start of 'disco'. Lovers of rock created the 'Supergroups' who would become the spokesmen of a new rock generation.

The Centurions by '66 had changed their name to 'Left, Right & Centre' and adopted a mod image. Fortunately for the band, very few, if any, other local outfits on the circuit at the time had picked up on the image and we were able to capitalise with great success. With a growing reputation, and gruelling work schedule of 250 or so gigs in two years, it wouldn't be long before we made the 'big-time' we told ourselves. We even supported our mentors The Small Faces in Southport and David John & the Mood in Preston. We had a large following throughout the north-west and with Union Jack shirts, exploding drums and smashed guitars we emulated our heroes. Hectic days to say the least!

Once we played Blackpool Winter Gardens supporting a popular soul outfit – The

Reg James Experience – to a sell out audience. As we apprehensively took the stage to open the evening's entertainment our lead singer grasped the microphone stand and was thrown across the stage after an electric shock. We hadn't played a note, but the incident was met with rapturous applause. Our mate was stretched unconscious from the building and spent the night in the hospital.

In the press the next day we learnt that the rowdy crowd hadn't thought too much of Reg James either and had wrecked the joint. The rest of the lads and I thanked the mate for helping us escape with our lives.

In 1967 Left, Right & Centre became Cats Squirrel, the band's direction becoming bluesier, and as the name implies, heavily influenced by Cream. Only some 12 months later, and with the growing increase of disco clubs, we were told, "You play the wrong sort of music" and, "You ain't playing that shite here."

Whilst there was still a huge demand for progressive rock music on record, rock fans had become ever more selective and critical in their choice. Since the mid-Sixties the music had continued to diversify, artistes became pigeonholed into specific categories and musicians took themselves, and their work, some would say, far too seriously. The age of the carefully constructed concept album was upon us, and higher standards of musicianship, lengthy virtuoso solos and political and social comment became ever increasingly important. From this background had grown the University concert circuit. And it was at these venues, which as well as being large enough to present these supergroups, also held a captive, intellectual, liberally-minded and musically aware audience, which suited the current direction of rock.

We continued to gig with endless motorway trips undertaken too. This was until we established our own progressive/blues venue in Preston in 1969, firstly in a 'disco' premises, before moving to a larger licensed club. And on Thursday nights the Amethyst Club opened its doors.

I approached the police soon after opening the Amethyst Club as we were getting a bit of dope smoking and probably a little bit of dealing. Not to inform the police of the goings on because I was relatively open minded about such things though. Only I'd realised that if we were seen to openly condone the use of drugs on the premises we would soon be raided and no doubt closed down. The local drug squad certainly knew where most of what was actually quite a minor number of users would be on Thursday nights – Amethyst!

I don't know whether the Detective Sergeant from the drug squad was a little disappointed that I had volunteered this information (I think he might have quite enjoyed a dramatic drug bust of a load of long haired hippies) but he thanked me and assured me he would pay regular unannounced visits to the club to keep an eye on things. The Amethyst Club members were made aware of the situation;

'take whatever you like before entering the club but do not use or carry anything on the premises or you will lose a great venue.'

The DS did visit Amethyst every few weeks and usually he would just chat to our girlfriends, who looked after the door as 'bouncers' to give the clubs entrance a more calming effect. He would frisk the occasional user who was known to him and then return to his complimentary drink. There were only a small percentage of the members who ever took anything other than alcohol anyway, I bet. We never even had any trouble, just hugely enjoyable nights with a friendly atmosphere and great music.

By contrast outside The Top Rank Ballroom, a 100 yards away in Avenham Street (the place where you had to wear a collar, tie and have short hair to get in) was the scene of many a street battle as we passed on our way home after closing up the club at 11.30pm. And I don't think things have changed much over the years, even to this day!

Over the club's period of live music, and at its zenith, membership for the club at one stage stood at almost 2,000. There were many memorable spaced out evenings which included techno/flash rock from the likes of Genesis, Barclay James Harvest, Caravan, Renaissance, Van der Graaf Generator, Supertramp, top British blues outfits and Irish band Skid Row, featuring a very young Gary Moore. This set the scene for some hot and steamy sessions. UFO, Hawkwind and others supplied nonsense quality rock. Lindisfarne, Mike Chapman and John Martyn, who were leading exponents of folk/rock won many devotees at the club too.

Clark Hutchinson was in fact the only act who almost emptied the club on their one and only visit. The evening began quite strangely and ended up becoming very weird indeed. The band arrived having apparently ingested considerable amounts of hallucinogenic substances, one member convinced he was a fly! Things had not improved by the time they were guided onto the stage, completely out of it. Very little was forthcoming except a microphone stand launched into the audience which almost decapitated a girl. A halt was brought to proceedings, the band packed into their van and they departed Preston for who knows where. Forerunners of punk? Maybe. But Amethyst wasn't quite ready for such things yet.

Like they say, all good things come to an end, and less than four years on from when the club opened its doors, they shut for the last time in September 1973 – all very sad and traumatic it was too. It was part of our social history, and I am proud to have been part of it. I wouldn't have missed it for the world.

I still play in three bands 40 years later and enjoy every minute. So, forget the hype, get out there. Enjoy it. And let the good times roll.

3

SOUL OF THE NORTH

Northern Soul is music that originates from Detroit and Chicago by lesser known, somewhat underground, black American artists. It also seemed the more obscure and rarer the record or demo, to a greater degree, the better the track – making it a must have. The rhythm is deep beat fast tempo and meaningful: soulful.

The venues which became famously associated in the north for playing such Northern Soul sounds right through the night in the mid-Sixties and into the Seventies were: the Twisted Wheel, Manchester (as you may have already read earlier on in the book). King Mojo Club, Sheffield (run by Peter Stringfellow and his brothers, which were decorated in a pop-art style). The Golden Torch, Tunstall, Stoke-on-Trent (originally a church, soul worshippers danced to Motown tracks in black and white painted surroundings). Blackpool Mecca, Blackpool (where folk *shuffled* to 'controversial' modern soul in the Highland Room, sometimes). And, Wigan Casino, Wigan, which was once voted *The Best Disco in the World*. The Casino was a former Victorian theatre, and this is where the nice-to-be-nice 'chosen few' attendees in the Mr M's room would hear the same three songs traditionally end the night every week. These three songs became known as the *3 before 8*: *Time Will Pass You By*, by Tobi Legend, *Long After Tonight Is Over*, by Jimmy Radcliffe, and *I'm On My Way*, by Dean Parrish.

These clubs held nights that would go under the moniker of "all-nighters". And the moves displayed from lads and lasses at all-nighters were rond de jambes, treble saltos, coin drops, helicopters, side summys, double back flip in tucks and suicide rubberbands. These manoeuvres were demonstrated as lads made their way back to the Johnson's Baby powder-coated dance floor to commence stomping in a pair of clogs. This after changing their bowling shirt for a fresh one in the lavs and following a good splashing with either *Brut 33* or *Hai Karate* aftershave under their armpits. Northern Soul stomping is a sort of contortioned/gymnastic/ballerina/high-kicking-ninja outré blend performed and beheld at least 10 years before b-boying *crews* did *battle* on street corners to looped, rhythmic *breaks* of dance records blaring out from a boombox/ghetto blaster. Lads tried to outsmart each other too, with off-the-wall *moves*. Necking a handful of barbs might also have helped, though...

Dave Godin, a journalist and overseer of a record shop called Soul City in Covent Garden, London, gave genesis to the term Northern Soul in 1968. He briefed his staff that if any northern footy fans graced the shop with their presence before a game in *The Smoke* and inquired, "Eh up, luv. As thee getten any of that slow soul stuff by them black Yankee fellas?" to point them towards a section where urbane, Motown or homogeneous sounding soul vinyl were – Northern Soul. You see, the south had gone all... ' *funky!*' Only woe betide any cockney rabbiting fly a kite at the match later on, he might get a copy of Frank Wilson's, *Do I Love You, Indeed I Do*, pebble dashed over their loaf of bread. This is when the real meaning of funk would have been observed from Londoners. The term Northern Soul was first documented in Godin's weekly column in *Blues and Soul* magazine in June 1970.

Gum chewing, bag carrying, nocturnal sojourners, from every nook and cranny of the British Isles, pulled on their patch covered vests, Oxford strides and preferred dancing shoes come weekend and flocked to all-nighters held at northern clubs. And who better to elucidate on these clubs? None other than the club goers themselves – '*right on now!*

Too Darn Soulful

David Nowell, the author of the excellent and informative book *Too Darn Soulful* and co-author of *Soul Survivors – The Wigan Casino Story*, has kindly let me use extracts from both books to add clout to the Soul of the North.

David: *Northern Soul has been described as the longest running ' fad' in the history of British music culture. What began as an underground Sixties mod scene in unlicensed, no-frills clubs in the north-west of England became 'the'* *youth craze of the mid-Seventies. Northern Soul has confounded its critics by surviving, and endlessly growing into a dance scene whose followers share a passion for the music of black America unrivalled anywhere else in the world. Frequently misunderstood and often mocked, Northern Soul devotees have cocked a snook at convention for nearly 50 years.*

So what on earth is Northern Soul, and how did it get its peculiar name? The short answer is that the term was original coined to describe 'rare soul of the type enjoyed in the north of England.' But what used to be called Northern Soul spread so far and wide, throughout Britain and on to the Continent, that the term is nowadays somewhat misleading. Rare soul is probably a more accurate phase now, because the music that has spanned six decades has become truly international. Even so, Northern Soul, or rare soul, has its roots in the mod scene in Britain in the Sixties.

Motown was enormous in Britain through consolidated recordings for the most part on the Tamla Motown label. For many soul fans, those recordings of the mid-Sixties were the epitome of soul music. Music dripping with emotion and powerful vocals. Although ballads were part and parcel of soul music, the British club-goer demanded soul with an up-tempo dance beat, a stomping beat. And during a period of change to 'softer' soul music coming out of America in the late Sixties and early Seventies northern DJs started to look back in time for more obscure labels for their 'new' material.

DJs often made trips to the US to hunt down such sounds in second-hand shops and the vaults of defunct labels. But expense was more than worth it if the DJ unearthed a handful of classic tunes. Their value could soon be ten, twenty or a hundred times what the DJ paid for it if the record proved popular in the clubs back home in the north of England. David Godin, a columnist with 'Blues and Soul' magazine, is credited with coining the phrase Northern Soul, to differentiate between the music enjoyed by northern and southern club-goers in the mid-to-late Sixties. Clubs like the Twisted Wheel in Manchester and Blackpool Mecca were the forerunners, followed by the Golden Torch in Stoke-on-Trent and Wigan Casino, plus many other venues in the north. There was even a difference in dance style and clothes between the north and south scene too.

And so the seeds of the Northern Soul scene were sown. 'Soullies' would travel miles to a venue by car, hitchhike or endure interminable train and bus journeys that would became part of the scene and Northern Soul fans' lifestyle. All-night venues were alcohol-free and trouble-free.

Dancers packed holdalls with several changes of clothes to stay fresh during the mammoth dance sessions of six hours or more. The Northern Soul explosion had arrived, changing and influencing the musical tastes of a Northern generation of youngsters, and would do so for years to come!

Wigan Casino

I was about 15 and still at school in Chorley when I first heard of Wigan Casino. If someone had told me then what an influence that the club would have on the rest of my life I would never have believed them.

"soullies' would travel miles to a venue by car, hitchhike or endure interminable train and bus journeys that would became part of the scene and northern soul fans' lifestyle. All-night venues were alcohol-free and trouble-free. Dancers packed holdalls with several changes of clothes to stay fresh during the mammoth dance sessions of six hours or more. The northern soul explosion had arrived, changing and influencing the musical tastes of a northern generation of youngsters, and would do so for years to come!"

I was a fairly late convert to soul music in some respects, having grown up listening to the Beatles, heavy rock groups like Deep Purple and Uriah Heep, and later David Bowie. Then in about 1973-4 I started to get more into commercial soul music like the Detroit Emeralds' 'Feel the Need in Me' and Barry White stuff.

The guys at school were by this time wandering around talking about Northern Soul instruments like 'Sliced Tomatoes' (Just Brothers) and 'Cigarette Ashes' (Jimmy Conwell). I wondered what the hell they were on about and showed no interest in Wigan Casino until early 1975. By then I had left school and there were various characters in the Chorley area already going to the all-nighters. Me and my mate, Dave from Burnley were by then going to the odd soul night in Burnley (the Rose Room and the Circulation Club), and elsewhere.

By the spring of 1975 I could not resist it any longer and asked my parents if I could go to the Casino all-nighter. The place already had a dubious reputation and so my dad asked a detective who lived nearby for his opinion of this strange club which was always in the newspapers and on the TV. The policeman described it as a 'den of iniquity' and I immediately thought, 'this sounds like my kind of place.' But my parents were having none of it and refused to let me go. A couple of months later, however, when I turned 17, they reluctantly agreed.

So Dave and I found ourselves on the last bus from Chorley to Wigan to await the doors opening at 2am for our first Casino all-nighter. That first visit was awe-inspiring. The heat, the atmosphere and the crowd were incredible. The music was weird and wonderful and totally unknown to us and the whole experience seemed unreal.

Betty White was on live that night and she took the roof off the place with her performance. From that night on, my whole social life and music tastes changed, and over the next seven years I gained lifelong friends, great memories and a passion for the music that lives with me to this day.

The magic of the Casino was a combination of experiences: the anticipation on a Saturday morning, knowing that you wouldn't see your bed until maybe the next afternoon: phoning round friends to make arrangements; making an excuse to the girlfriend to take her home at 11pm instead of going to a nightclub; driving through the dark country lanes to Wigan with the cassette on and the car full of excited chatter; pulling into a packed car park and going in search of mates you perhaps hadn't seen for weeks or months.

It was the buzz you got from walking into the seething club and seeing the already-packed dance floor; shouting so much over the music that come morning you were almost hoarse; feeling an incredible sensation of belonging when you hit the dance floor; realising that the hours were flying by and the rest of the world was asleep. Then there was the sense of shellshock when the lights went on at 8am and you had to re-enter the outside world: sitting muttering over a brew at Charnock Richard services or going back to a mate's house for several more hours of soul music or perhaps a lunchtime pint. It was having your head full of records, some that you couldn't name, which haunted you for the whole day afterwards; lying in bed in the afternoon reliving the all-nighter and finding that sleep wouldn't come.

It was all these things and more. The Casino's friendliness was amazing. It was the only disco I ever went to alone without knowing that anyone I knew would be there. It literally did not matter if you wandered about the place all night on your own, chatting to various groups of people. Strangers would quite often come up to you and ask for a fag or a swig of Coke and they were rarely refused. It was easy to get chatting to strangers and many firm friendships were formed. All the Casino-goers in Chorley, Leyland and Preston got to know one another and buses, cars and trains would be shared. The Burnley crowd would know the Blackburn crowd, who knew the Bolton lot, who had friends among the Dundee crowd, who knew the Edinburgh and Falkirk mob, and so it went on.

The regular Saturday all-nighters became the focal point of my week, and were replaced some years later by the monthly oldies all-nighters, when other commitments made it difficult to attend more often. The best times for me were the late Seventies and early Eighties, when I had money to throw around in the record bar, a car and some great mates.

The final nights at the Casino and the emotion as dancers refused to move from the floor when the last records had been spun will live with me forever. I remember looking up at Russ Winstanley as he played 'Do I Love You?' over and over again, and I swear he was crying. A Scots bloke I was standing with suddenly filled up and said: "I can't stand it" and walked out for the final time. Thanks, Wigan Casino, for a great youth.

Soul is something that transcends music, race and age. It's also a feeling that starts deep within you and builds up to create warmth and happiness, or misery and despair. Soul is the humanity and emotion in all of us.

My Mecca

Ste Ellison: *After going to local clubs in and around Darwen from the age of 16, we decided to join the throngs going on the free coach to Blackpool Mecca. So dressed in our finest, we waited for the coach to arrive at the car park behind the Fleece pub in Blackburn town centre. Most were Northern Soul fans but also there was a few goons going for the night to Blackpool, and possibly the main room at the Mecca which played cheesy chart music. But most of us were there for the magical Highland Room.*

On arrival at Central Drive we all disembarked to join the large queue to enter the Mecca. As the queue got nearer to the doors the burly bouncers screamed out "No tie. No admission." You can imagine the look on mine and my mate Tony's faces – wounded. What do we do with nothing resembled a tie between us? A quick decision was made that we would knock on a few locals doors. The first bloke that answered the door told us to 'do one' in no uncertain terms. Next door an old guy came to the door and we explained our problem. And bingo! He came back with a selection, of sorts. The top bloke didn't even want any payment either – what a winner. So off we went to join the queue once again.

We were in. Up the escalators we went, to the top of the building, down the short corridor and finally we were at the doors to the room of our Holy Grail for Northern Soul. (Many things happened in that room to change my life over the coming years, and I still look back now with a big smile. The people I met, the music I heard and the top DJs that spun the tunes; Ian Levine and Colin Curtis, who also formed my love of soul music to this day.) As we burst through the doors into the Highland Room, a sight and scene erupted before our eyes. The music was the tops. To the left were Kev Roberts and Francis Tee with record boxes bursting with a variety of top tunes. Also the bar ran nearly the length of the club, which made getting served a beer very easy. There was a food bar to the right, and opposite the bar was a small stage which is where the DJs were. Wow, we'd made it in. It was a scene we would encounter for many weeks, and months, to come.

We started going week-in, week-out, and met other groups from other towns and some notable individuals too. One of the largest groups was from Preston. And a lad who I met through another mate, then introduced us to the rest of the Preston crew. Some good times were had with these 'guys and gals!' The other large mob who attended were from Bolton (I got to know them through my girlfriend, who was from Harwood, a suburb of the said town). Now I got to know all the 'main men' at the nighters through her brother. These guys were older and wiser than me and part of the Wanderers mob of the time. But they were also involved with knocking out the illegal substances too, which, like a fool, I embraced with both hands and mouth. Some of the Mecca days are a complete blur because of this...

One good time which I still smile about today is when I think back is: I happened to be propping up the bar one night – the bar was stopping me sliding to the floor – when all of a sudden in through the doors burst a mob of lads from the downstairs 'stiffs room' who were intent on bashing any Northern Soul lad who got in their way. Big mistake. A uniting moment occurred. Because in the Highland Room everyone who could do a bit fronted the mob. And who was in the middle of it all, yours truly. Glasses, tables and chairs, you name it, whizzed past my head till the two mobs clashed. And of course, the soulies drove them back downstairs. This never happened again, as word must have spread what it was like up there in the Highland Room. The number of lads I knew who asked me later on wanting to know how I could stand there and brass out all that mayhem was unreal. I just shrugged it off. Well anyone who has ever been barbed-up to the eyeballs would know!

The Mecca went on to play some fine tunes from Northern Soul, to the later days of jazz funk (My all time favourite Northern track being Yvonne Baker 'Didn't Say a Word'). Yes, there was some incredible music played over the time we went there.

A local club in Darwen hosted DJs Ian Levine and Colin Curtis midweek, where in the early session, they would spin Ian's latest discoveries from the States. We would tape the set, incognito, and play it at home over and over again speculating which new track would break the scene. These were top tunes and there would be loads of them. I too DJ'd at this club years later, it being Tiffanies in Darwen - reputed to have the best sound system in the north-west at the time. I'll never forget hearing Bobby Franklins 'Ladies Choice' – which was banned from Wigan Casino – come blasting out of the speakers. This, I think, was a defining moment for Colin and Ian, and Blackpool in general as the club slanted more towards New York disco type music, which I suppose was good in its own right. Most regulars embraced the sound and fashion of this time even though I look back and wonder how I myself could wear bright green pants and a favourite New York bowling shirt – I must have looked a right sight!

To this day I still request Linda Clifford's 'Runaway Love' on my nights at King George's Hall Blackburn as I hit the floor. A tune I want playing at my funeral, which I hope is a long time off.

I Will Always Carry a Torch

Dave Clarke: *My first recollections of the Torch came about when I was about 16 or 17. I used to hang about with a gang of older lads and we all loved our Tamla Motown and soul music. We started going to a little club under Wigan Casino called the Beachcomber, then we graduated to Wigan Casino most Saturday and Sunday nights. Sundays being the best as it was more for soul followers. (This was when the Casino was only a nightclub before all-nighters began.) Word was also going around about a soul club in Stoke on Trent that was an all-nighter venue and my mate Jimmy asked if I was up for going to the Torch.*

I recall walking with Jimmy to an intersection on the M6 which joined the East Lancs road called Haydock Island. We had the familiar outfits of soul boys in those early days on. I was wearing my made to measure black, Levis style leather jacket, a vest, tan cord baggies with the wide waistband and more importantly, my black Como shoes that I used to polish till you could see your face in the reflection. Como shoes had a leather sole that didn't stick to the floor and you could dance all night in them. I also had my black Adidas sports bag with a change of T-shirt, a towel to wipe the sweat after dancing and some butties along with a soft drink. We soon hitched a lift in a Transit van that dropped us off at the Stoke junction.

But by the end of the night my ears were
singing to the tunes that were to become idolised
at the torch, and later at wigan Casino.
Songs like Roy Hamilton's 'Cracking up over you',
'if you ask me' by Jerry Williams,
'thumb a ride' by the Earl Right Orchestra

and one of the first soul records I ever bought, '
out on the floor' by Dobie Gray.

———————

After walking for a while, with our thumbs out, a Triumph Vitesse – a cool car in those days – stopped and the two guys inside asked us if we were going to the Torch because they'd noticed our 'soul bags' and guessed we were heading in the club's direction. One of the guys hopped out, opened the boot and put our bags in. Once in the car the guy in the passenger seat turned round and asked us if we had any 'gear.' Now like I said I was only about 16 or 17 at the time and still a bit naive so, I innocently told him we did, and it was in the boot of the car in our bags. As I said this my mate Jimmy nudged me in the ribs and asked the guy if he had any? He proceeded to open the glove box and take out a big plastic bag full of all sorts of pills, tablets and capsules that I had never seen before.

Before we arrived at the Torch my mate had done a deal and shoved a couple of pills down his throat. I remember walking to the front door of the club wondering how the night was going to pan out. After refusing the mate's offer to try some pills, I persuaded him to give me the rest of the drugs after I promised I would let him try some more if I was satisfied he was okay later on.

As soon as we went in the Torch, the intense heat and noise hit you like a giant wave. We were soon up on the floor and dancing to soul music I had never heard in my life before. But by the end of the night my ears were singing to the tunes that were to become idolised at the Torch, and later at Wigan Casino. Songs like Roy Hamilton's 'Cracking Up Over You', 'If You Ask Me' *by Jerry Williams,* 'Thumb a Ride' *by the Earl Right Orchestra and one of the first soul records I ever bought,* 'Out on the Floor' *by Dobie Gray.*

As the night wore on I was keeping my eye on Jimmy but I had to keep sitting down every so often because I kept getting stitches in my side. At this time I was playing football every Saturday and Sunday plus training twice a week so at first I couldn't understand why I had to keep sitting down every now and then and my mate was dancing the hind legs off a donkey! He explained he felt as fresh as a daisy. And after assuring me he had no other side effects from the drugs I let him take another one of his pills and away he went for the rest of the night.

Eventually we ended up making our way home on the first train back to God's Country – or Wigan as it's more widely known. The whole experience had blown me away. From just chatting to strangers about soul as though I had known them all my life, to the scary episode with the drugs. Sadly I was only to make one more trip to the Torch before it got closed down. And if I remember rightly, this was because of the growing drugs scene. But I will always fondly remember the Torch as one of the best soul clubs, ever.

The main reason I'd left school a year early in 1971 (it was optional then to stay for fifth year and take exams at Ashton Secondary Modern school) was to get a job to enable me to buy a scooter because my mum and dad wouldn't buy me one. So when I became the proud owner of a Lambretta GP 150cc – chrome mirrors, front-rack, back-rack, front crash bars, back crash bars, backrest, fly-screen, white wall tyres, Colonel Bogey air horn and Florida bars – I thought I was king of the road! Trouble was, when you took a corner in the wet you inevitably came off, and it took two to lift the bugger upright again. Having wheels gave me the opportunity to go to the local discos that played soul and Tamla Motown. Living in Ashton-in-Makerfield, about five miles from Wigan, me and my scooter mates started to frequent a pub every Thursday, the Oak Tree, in nearby Newton-le-Willows that played 'our' kind of music. We also went to Newton Cricket Club, The Carlton Club in Warrington and also Parr Hall in Warrington, where I remember going to see The Real Thing live.

Around the summer of 1973 the word was that there was a venue in Wigan where a DJ was playing good soul music, so we turned up one night. The club in question was Newtown British Legion and the soul being played was spot on, with the DJ being none other than Russ Winstanley – later to be a leading-light at Wigan Casino. At the time Wigan Casino was just an ordinary night club that played various music but still leant towards Motown and soul. The Dog & Partridge in Wigan was our meeting place (nowadays it's a Last Orders chain pub but it still plays soul music) as one or two of us were not yet the legal age for drinking, but the landlord turned a blind eye. A gang of us used to meet every weekend to have a couple of beers before heading to the Casino. We used to stand in the same spot at the back of the dance floor under the balcony; the best place to walk onto the dance floor and also to ogle the girls as they went to the downstairs bar. And every week there was a sort of unspoken *competition to see who was the smartest dressed amongst the lads.*

In the early Seventies soul boys wore shoes like comos, royals and brogues. Sometimes I nailed metal segs to the soles of my shoes so they tapped when I walked. Fred Perry t-shirts and Prince of Wales check parallel pants were the norm. We also used to go to Jacksons the Tailors every Saturday to pay our weekly instalments for made-to-measure box jackets with fancy braiding around the seams.

After having visited the Torch in Stoke, we were all excited to hear that the Casino was having its first all-nighter. As we went to the Casino anyway on Saturdays, me and a mate hatched a plan. The plan was to hide in the toilets at throwing out time of the club and wait till 2am for the nighter to start – which we did. But the bouncers were clued up, they checked the loos, nabbed us and threw us out. Not the best of plans, especially if anybody remembers that urine was over your ankles in the bogs so it wouldn't be very cool dancing with smelly piss squelching out of your shoes on the dance floor.

Although the first time the all-nighter was held it consisted of mainly Wiganers, and it was a great success. The gospel soon spread and people came from all over the world to dance on that springy wooden floor and listen to classics like PP Arnolds 'Everything's Gonna be Alright', 'What Shall I Do', *Frankie and the Classicals,* 'What' *Judie Street and* 'You Don't Want Me Anymore' *by Major Lance, who I had the fortune to see live at the Casino. The all-nighters soon became the number one place to be seen in and 'the' place for Northern Soul. I remember we used to travel on our scooters and park them in my mates' relatives' backyard at the back of the old Wigan Rugby Club; then a short walk was undertaken to the Casino. I also started to take an old cassette recorder and leave it on the stage on record to catch all the brilliant sounds. As soon as I got home on the Sunday morning the first thing I did was play back everything I'd taped the previous night. However usually halfway through a classic song somebody's voice would be heard asking me how I was doing and if I was okay. You had to really shout to be heard over those massive speakers on the stage and I had many recordings ruined because of background noise, but it was the only way to capture the music in those days. What I would give to have those cassettes nowadays.*

After a while Northern Soul and Wigan Casino started to gain worldwide recognition and some songs began to appear on Top of the Pops. It was about this time I began to lose my enthusiasm for the all-nighters. Crap bands like Wigan's Ovation and dance groups like Wigan's Chosen Few dancing to 'Footsie' *made Northern Soul a laughing stock, in my opinion. People who had absolutely no interest at all in soul started to frequent Wigan Casino, acting like the big 'I am' and off their heads on drugs. I remember being introduced to one lad twitching like mad while chewing gum. He promised he could get any drug I desired so I set him a task to test his cred. Needless to say after returning empty handed three or four times with sob stories about how he had just missed out I gave him a wide berth until he got the message. It was funny how I'd spent years spreading the gospel about Northern Soul and when it was at its most popular I began to feel a little resentful, as my love for what had been an underground secret for just a few in the know people was all of a sudden mainstream music masses and in the pop charts.*

Although the closure of Wigan Casino in 1981 was sad, Northern Soul is in revival once more in Wigan and the north-west, with numerous pubs and clubs having soul nights frequented by old and young alike. As I write this story at the beginning of 2010, one of the best places to go is Swinley Labour Club on the first Sunday afternoon of every month. As this finishes about six, you can make your way down Wigan Lane where a couple of pubs continue the soul theme. Another cracking night is at the Monaco in Hindley, which has a large dance floor with a buzzing atmosphere, and King Georges Hall at Blackburn that has regular well attended soul nights. Long may they continue and Keep the Faith.

It's in My Heart It's in My Soul

Jon Huxley: *I started to going to Wigan all-nighters around 1975. Although I was officially too young, the lady on the till was the formidable Mrs Woods, and luckily she was my nan's neighbour, so she knew who I was and turned a blind eye. After a few months me and a mate got a job at the Casino, cleaning up after the rock nights held there. Usually they finished around 11.30pm and our wages were free admission to the all-nighter later.*

It was, and still is (although no longer there) a magical place to have attended and it was part of history of the time. The sights, the sounds, the many friendships I formed with people from all the UK who made the pilgrimage is still part of me. The downstairs bar, which served alcohol during the week, was transformed into a giant record exchange. Obviously due to the British licensing laws back then there was no alcohol on sale.

Some of the money changing hands for 45" singles was mad. For instance I had a copy of an original of 'Wade in the Water' by Ramsey Lewis, and I sold it for £50! And remember this was 1975. Also I had a copy of William Watson's 'Too Late', and the flipside had been pressed with the track – two for the price of one. This sold for £75. God, how I wish I'd have kept hold of them. Mind you, the prices I achieved were a month's wages at least for someone like me in those days.

New lads who turned up to the all-nighters soon cottoned on to the drugs scene at the Casino and realised that, by taking 'uppers', they were able to purchase at the club, they could dance all night without feeling tired and get a buzz too. Most of the drugs that were readily available were the same that the mods threw down their necks in the Sixties, the popular ones being slimming pills. And the most sort-after pills were 'chalkies.' The medical term for these were Tenuate Dozpan, and as the name suggests they were just like little bits of chalk, as well as tasting of it too. They had a quite a high amphetamine content, amphetamine being an appetite suppressant. Depending on who was selling the chalkies on the night you would usually get, for the going rate of a quid, between five and seven tabs. Also on offer were greens, clears, black-bombers, blues and loads of others that were all very similar. It was widely known that to obtain these amount of narcotics, that the dealers would have had to have been involved in chemist shop break-ins or have purchased the pills off whoever had robbed one. And so did the police, with undercover members of the Wigan CID drug squad attending the Casino, mingling in amongst clubbers.

On top of all the attention from the police, who had informed the local press of goings on, Wigan Council threatened the Casino with closure almost on a weekly basis. Only you cannot tar everyone with the same brush, can you? There were many in attendance that didn't touch any narcotics at all. But as with any popular music culture involving people from a wide age spectrum and various backgrounds, there are always going to be some sort of drugs being used; as in ecstasy being connected to the rave scene many years later. In my opinion it's up to the individual whether they take

them or not. No-one at the Casino forced anyone to pop pills. The ones who did drugs, acted on their own accord and knew the lads who would have them for sale. Whilst I do not advocate the sale or the taking of drugs, it was part of the scene. Drugs are out there, and always will be. They are readily available to people as long as they want to experience them, and experiment with them. And like I say, there are folk who are only too willing to provide them, rightly or wrongly.

I've lost many friends to drugs who progressed onto harder substances due to seeking a higher high. Some fairly recently, and some of them many, many moons ago. Of course there are many more who didn't go down that route and to this day, are still involved in the scene in clubs around the north-west, and beyond.

One other thing about the scene that stuck out were the clothes. The lads wore long leather Gestapo type coats – the softer the leather, the more desirable the coat – that flowed down to the ankle. The trousers were as baggy as you could imagine; up to 40-inch wide at the bottom, and the top half topped off with a white vest. And the shoes as flat as possible, usually leather soled, so you had complete movement when you were out on the floor. A splash of Brut *and a handful of* Johnson's Baby powder *on the boards, and away you went.*

Around the same era, the old Burtonwood airbase near Warrington was still operative, and we used to go there for 10 pin bowling. You always wore the oldest shoes you had when going bowling, because once you hired the bowling shoes you never returned them. You then went home in the best shoes for dancing that you could lay your hands on for the Casino, free.

Girls wore similar flat shoes and long, loose fitting skirts that when they danced, and did spins, billowed upwards just like a parachute. And if you were lucky you would get a quick flash!

The thing about the Casino was it was unique. Not only for it being 'the' club of the time but for the lack of any trouble at all. I never witnessed anyone get punched and I never saw any fighting. It was all about the music and togetherness. And obviously romance also blossomed in the Casino.

My best mate, who now lives in Lanzarote, met his wife at the Casino one night. Over thirty years later they're still together and his son is now the youngest Northern Soul DJ on the island. He grew up listening to the music and he also fell in love with it.

I'm now a 50-odd year-old who still loves the music. I have hundreds of great memories regarding the Casino and it was one of the best times of my life. One that will live with me until the day I die.

I'm a Soul-Man

Big Dave: *On leaving school in 1978, I was successful in obtaining an apprenticeship. And with wages in my pocket I was able to spend a little on my indulgences which were most likely the same as any teenager: in no particular order; football, Preston North End, music, clothes, pubs and clubs.*

My mates and I had already started to dip our toes in the music scene on nights out before we'd left school, mainly by the bus into Chorley, or Leyland, and on to the Civic Centre and Fox Lane Cricket Club. It was at the Civic that I had my first experience of Northern Soul – although it would be a few years later when I would finally go to Wigan Casino. A year after I left school the film Quadrophenia *came out which proved to be a real catalyst and reinforced my attitude towards music and fashion twofold. Around the same era the ska scene kicked off again. I remember going to the Preston Guild Hall to see the 2-Tone Tour, and a few months later UB40, then The Jam. During this period we'd also started to venture further afield for nights out in Wigan, Preston and sometimes even Blackburn (God knows why). The Bowling Green at Charnock Richard and the Howard Arms at Whittle-le-Woods were regular haunts too.*

Going to the match also became very important, as in wearing the right gear and looking the part; it was at that time that the casual scene started to take shape, although it was still in its infancy. A good mate of mine was a Chelsea fan and we would often travel to away matches using the two- for-one rail tickets obtained from the Persil scheme, as well as PNE games. In the early 1980s it was becoming apparent that there was a north/south divide, in terms of fashion, with the north getting into the 'casual' look way before the cockneys. Most Chelsea fans of the time were wearing the US style MA-1 pilot jackets, half mast jeans and Doc Martens whilst we were already into casual gear.

Early 1980 was probably the first time I went to Wigan Casino. I remember being out in Chorley with the mates when 'Young Jacko' said he was off to the Casino, and did we fancy it? After a brief deliberation with a couple of lads we decided to go. The next thing you know we were waiting on Chorley bus station for the last bus to Wigan. As I did a block release course at Wigan Tech, I'd heard that a lot of soulies used to get hassle from pissed up Wiganers as they made their way from Wigan bus station to the Casino. Only looking around at the large group of lads from Leyland and Chorley including the likes of Crookie (a terrace legend – RIP), whose company I was in, I thought it would be highly unlikely – and we didn't. Waiting outside the Casino, for the first time in my life, I remember the simmer of excitement as you could hear the thump thump *of the beat escaping from inside when the doors opened letting in set numbers in at a time. There was a buzz in the crowd which comprised people from all corners of the country that had met up with old friends who chattered excitedly about the night ahead. A mixture of cool guys who'd seen it all before and first timers, like myself, who couldn't wait to gain entry into the place to be seen.*

Finally it was our turn to go through the doors and then up the steep stairs. The first thing that struck me was the temperature; it was freezing outside but inside, even though the night had only just begun, the heat was intense, cauldron like, boiling and bubbling away. Jacko said to follow him, and we did, heading upstairs onto a balcony overlooking the dance floor. Below us was a heaving mass of bodies but they all seemed to be in unison swaying from side-to-side in time with the beat and applauding after every track. I could hardly contain myself and get down there and out on the floor. The whole night just blew me away. The friendliness of everybody due to their love of everything soul. I chatted to people I didn't even know before that night, and people who maybe I'd previously just passed courtesies with. Even after leaving the Casino gone 8am, riding the bus back to Chorley and then having a full English in a café once back in town, I was still buzzing. Eventually I got to bed around 10am, only I just couldn't sleep – the whole experience had been so amazing. I was gripped. I was a soul-man.

Many more nights would follow making a near weekly pilgrimage to the Casino in Wigan, until it finally closed its doors in 1981. A very, very sad event. But the show had to go on, so I also made trips to other venues such as The Clifton Hall in Rotherham. It would be many years later before I would go to another 'true' northern night. But listening to Richard Searling's radio shows (firstly on Red Rose Radio *and* Sunset *before he moved to* Smooth*) kept the flame burning.*

Also in the early Eighties I got into modern soul and jazz funk. One club we became regulars at was Casanellis in Standish. When I say club, it was really a motel with a small function room, but the music was great and the atmosphere electric. There would be coaches from far and wide; Edinburgh and Birmingham to name a few. The one thing that really stands out in my memory is during the night's entertainment there would be an interlude when the DJ played an instrumental. He would turn the volume right down and then in a side room hot pot was served, that was fiercely, burning hot in plastic bowls complete with red cabbage. Then the volume would be cranked back up and everyone resumed where they left off. Crazy nights!

At this time I was really getting into the music scene and the lads and I started to visit other clubs to get our fix. Places like Rafters in Manchester, the Ritz all-dayers, again in Manchester, and Angels in Burnley. I also remember all-dayers at Wigan Pier where the DJs sat inside a big frog overlooking the dance floor. Clouds in Preston too, especially the week that Bob Marley passed away when the club's DJ played a half-hour tribute to the father of reggae. And one all-dayer in particular on a wet Sunday in Blackpool when, due to bizarre licensing laws of the Eighties, the bar closed but the music carried on only dancing was not allowed! This lasted for an hour. We left the club along with dozens of other brightly dressed night clubbers to wander the grim streets, bemusing day trippers. Eventually we stopped at the Pancake House for some of Blackpool's famous culinary delights – not.

Back in the early Eighties I also became a member at the newly opened Haçienda, in Manchester; this was well before the rave scene started when it was mostly a showcase for live bands. Although it was never the best live venue for acoustics and sound, I still had some great nights there seeing the likes of A Certain Ratio and The Smiths. Another live venue in Manchester I attended was Band on the Wall. This place was a real dive, but I enjoyed some great live shows whilst the rain trickled in through the roof and your feet stuck to the carpet. Memorable nights there included two great soul / jazz artists, Terry Callier and Carmen Lundy. I've made the odd trip over recent years and had many great night at places such as The Halfway House and The Pines in Clayton-Le-Woods, The Howard at Whittle, The Trafalgar at Samlesbury, Parkers in Manchester and of course, King George's in Blackburn. I'm still into my soul, only nowadays it's mostly putting a rare 45" vinyl on the turntable indoors.

Over the years I've been well into my clothes too; in the late Seventies and early Eighties I did my shopping mainly in Preston. Back then there weren't many places. But I do remember Clobber in the St.George's Shopping Centre and a unisex shop on Avenham Street with a men's department upstairs, but I don't recall the name with a fading memory due to age. I also spent many an hour sifting through the old vinyl in Meldrums record exchange on Friargate.

As the mates and I got older we started taking the train into Manchester, although it was nothing like it is now, being the second best city to shop in Britain. It was still an improvement on Preston, though. We used to shop at the Oasis underground market were all the latest gear could be found, Clobber in the Arndale and Phil Black's in the Royal Exchange, but even back then it was mega expensive. Once we bumped into Frank Worthington in Phil Black's dressed like a cowboy; just goes to show money can't buy you style. Spin Inn Records was another favourite for sought-after tunes. This was the place to pick up the latest soul and funk imports, many a twelve inch and LP bought there. For an example I purchased the album Landscapes *by Cedar Walton, which I only wanted for one track,* 'Latin America', *but what a track! Zico in the Royal Exchange was one of the first shops I recall to start selling the new wave of designer gear, which had started to become more prevalent. Back in the day you'd still to dress-up to get into a nightclub; no jeans, and you'd always have to wear a shirt with a collar, sometimes even a tie.*

Going to the match was a 'casual affair'. Fred Perry tennis shirts and Slazenger V-neck sweaters were these being all the rage in the early days, and I remember a phase when chunky knit cable sweaters where worn tucked into your jeans (thank god that never lasted). The Jazz-funk scene was a riot of colourful clothes. I once turned out in a pair of Chris Soames bright blue canvas pants, quite baggy at the waist but tapering to fit snug around the ankles (similar to MC Hammer's trousers, but nowhere near as bad). They were worn with a white canvas belt with a silver buckle which left the remainder of the belt to dangle in front of your crotch with a silver square tip. And to compliment all that, a blue Hawaiian shirt similar to one of Tom Selleck's in Magnum *(I've gone red while typing and reliving that look, ha). But I drew the line at the fluorescent string vest over the day glow T-shirt and ballet pumps look favoured by some.*

Around 1982 a couple of mates and I travelled to the Hammersmith Odeon to watch Donald Byrd and the 125th Street New York City Band, sporting our wedge haircuts and our usual casual attire. We passed time during the day shopping on the Kings Road, which back then was the bees' knees, grabbed a quick bite to eat, and then headed off to Hammersmith for the gig. In the pubs beforehand all the cockneys seemed to be dressed to the nines, mostly in bright coloured zoot suites and winkle pickers, like a bunch of Kid Creoles, only without the Coconuts.

"We used to shop at the oasis underground
market were all the latest gear could be found,
Clobber in the Arndale and Phil Blacks in the royal exchange,
but even back then it was mega expensive.
Once we bumped into Frank Worthington in Phil Blacks
dressed like a cowboy;

Just goes to show money can't buy you style.
Spin Inn Records was another favourite for sought after tunes.
This was the place to pick up the latest soul and funk imports,
many a 12" and LP were bought there."

Another escapade in 1983 saw a couple of mates and I travelling to Europe on the train. We hadn't booked a holiday unlike the rest of our mates and couldn't decide what to do so at the last minute so we decided to go somewhere hot and plumped for a European jaunt. Anywhere would suffice.

With a brief stop in London before travelling on, one of the lads decided he wanted some Chelsea merchandise which he purchased and then we headed to France on the ferry. After bumming around Paris and the French Riviera, we caught an overnight train to Spain.

Boarding the train, quite away from where it had started its journey, there were no seats available so, we settled down at the end of a carriage in a space adjacent to the toilets and where the carriages joined. Sitting on the floor while drinking bottles of beer we nattered away about our next destination until we crashed-out to get some needed kip.

Then in the early hours the train appeared to slow down, waking us with its jerking, and one of my mates stood up to have a look to see if he could find out where we were. Just at that time a bloke pitched up and babbled something incomprehensible, probably in French. After no reply from us he repeated the same blather to which Andy, a mate, asked if he wanted to get off and proceeded to open the door, even though we were still travelling at quite a lick. The bloke only walked out of the door! "Fucking hell" I said "I think you've killed him", as we all rushed to the window to see if we could see him. But it was pitch black and you couldn't see a thing, plus he was long gone. Contemplating what had just happened we all agreed that it wasn't murder and the most it could be would be aiding and abetting suicide?

As the train approached the Spanish border, Andy decided it was time to have a wash and brush up following the night's weird escapade. Emerging from the toilets after five minutes he declared it was impossible to sort himself out with the train jerking around, and pointed to his half-shaved face with blood trickling down his chin where his razor had cut his skin several times. Is it any wonder later that day as we trawled the bars in a quaint Spanish town we kept getting funny looks. Andy was wandering around in a T-shirt that proclaimed 'You can't ban a Chelsea fan' while looking like he'd been in some kind of knife fight. Priceless.

I've a hundred-and-one tales from bygone days and these are just some of my memories from an eventful youth. I hope that some might strike a chord with others who visited the same clubs dancing to the same music, wearing the same outrageous clothes and having the same, or somewhat similar, hazardous adventures which I'll always remember fondly.

The torch for Northern Soul was kept alive at the Morecambe all-nighters with a gathering of the clans from all over Lancashire and further afield.

Morecambe & Wise

Wayne: *I got into Northern Soul, and wise to the all-nighters at Morecambe Pier, through a good mate Drew (RIP), in the early to mid- Eighties. He'd told me what good nights they were and that plenty of lads attended the Pier from Preston on the last Friday of every month – the only night of the month the event occurred. So when the final Friday came round, I would get my best clobber on and meet up with the lads in town for the usual Friday sesh. After hitting several pubs around Church Street, in the centre of town, we would make our way to the train station, and catch the nine o'clock rattler to the drab seaside resort of Morecambe. Arriving at our destination about an hour later, following a change at Lancaster, it left us time for a few more beers before closing time at 11pm.*

The first time I entered through the Pier's doors I felt a bit let down. As I glanced to the right, there were only a small amount of soulies stood round. I thought 'God. It's tiny and deserted.' Then we walked into the main room, a massive gaff, full of people of all ages, some 50-plus, flying around like they were on drugs to records that I'd never heard before. The dance floor was a huge area, and a bar ran along to the right-hand side of the room.

They'd a licence till 2am and then water was available when the shutters came down. So for a little pick-you-up someone would sort out the Billy (whizz) and a trip to the toilets to neck the gear was undertaken. Now the loos: Well, they made the toilet featured in 'Trainspotting' look five star – the stench was unbelievable.

So, the gear kicked-in and away we go. I'd be on and off the dance floor for the next six hours. There was always a turnout from Preston – The Posses – taking up a large chunk of the wooden boards. Of course there would be many Lancaster and Morecambe lads present who we knew from them coming down to North End for the footy, and their mates too. They were all sound. But a few of them would overdo the drugs and spend most of the night like zombies. I also met a lad from Warrington called Pete, who was a right character. Pete showed us that by spitting beer through a straw into the fruit machines it sent the internal microchips crazy and clock on rakes of credits (the only thing was, the alarm would go off). But with Northern blaring out of the DJs speakers, really loud, it hid the noise of alarm bells ringing. You just played the credits and collected every time you won. (This trick became the norm for the lads whenever they were out in pubs or clubs and could get away with the scam for several years until bandit manufactures sussed how to make the machine shutdown.)

The DJs really took their music very seriously; so when 'Mad Jack', a mate, asked a young, impressionable lad who was with us one night to tap the DJ to play 'Trapped' by Colonel Abrams, which he did, it didn't go well. The DJ's face was a picture. I can also honestly say that in the time we attended Morecambe all-nighters there wasn't any trouble at all. Even though there were lads from Blackpool, Bolton, Manchester and every corner of the north-west, and beyond. Lads would checkout each other's clobber and trainers because there was a large casual contingent amongst the soulies.

The nighters finished at eight in the morning and it was out into the fresh, sea breeze air, still off our boxes, and still chewing the insides of our gobs off.

Normally we would head towards the train station or a café for a brew and then home. Once one of the lads had 'borrowed' a car to get to Morecambe, and he gave us a lift back to Preston the morning after. He drove at a hair-raising speed down the motorway with eyes like Marine Boy, with us lot in the back seats window licking. On arrival back in God's Town, he pulled into a pub car park, the Coconut Grove, next door to where a lad in the motor lived, and said, "Not bad that lads, eh? Seeing I'm wired." He took his foot off the clutch and slammed into the pub – oops!

Another time when I got in the house around 10 in the morning my dad asked if I would pick his brother up from Blackpool Airport as he was busy. I couldn't let him down, or tell him I was off my box, so I jumped in my dad's pride and joy and more or less flew to the airport myself. I picked the uncle up and chewed the poor fucker's ear off all the way back to his home. When he got out of the car and was entering the house, I could see him wiping his face and shaking his head.

During the summer months it wasn't too bad, I would get my head down for a few hours before going out again on Saturday night. But if PNE had a game next day, it was murder because I'd attended the Pier the night before and I was still half asleep. I can remember a match at Wigan once when Preston were causing mayhem on the ground while I'm laid on a barrier coming down big time.

Those Morecambe days were great times and when 'Lady in Red' – not the Chris de Burgh shite – by Ronnie Dyson was put on the decks, all the Preston lads would take to the dance floor – what a 'shout-out'. Going to the nighters for the last Friday until the Pier closed will live me forever – it was a true life changing experience. While I still go to Blackburn all-nighters on a regular basis and other venues occasionally, nothing lives up to Morecambe Pier, just like the older lads told us how they felt about Wigan Casino. Long live Northern Soul.

Today, Blackburn's King George's Hall has become the modern-day hot-spot for Northern Soul aficionados, with events to rival the legendary all-nighters at Wigan Casino in its heyday. Both veteran disciples of the dance floor and new discoverers of northern frequent the Blackburn venue on a regular basis, which hosts soul nights five times a year.

King George's Hall continues the legacy created by Northern Soul clubs across the north of England from a bygone era. Since flipping on a rare groove in 1995, up to 1,500 soul lovers nowadays travel to attend the all-nighters. It's far and away the number one Soul night in Britain. From the humble beginnings of just the main hall, King George's has now a three room set up in place. A mix of old gems and newer music are spun in the main hall, and there's a jazz and funk room and a modern R&B room too.

'Yesterday... Today... Forever... Keep the Faith'

4

THE GLAMOROUS SEVENTIES

With the old grey matter not really being able to recall anything of real substance from the Sixties, my Seventies memories are still recollections I treasure fondly to this day. I suppose most kids of the 'glamorous' Seventies, or any decade really, have cherished reminiscences too from time to time of their childhood. Being the grand old age of four and three-quarters when the New Year and the 1st January 1970 were welcomed in, the Seventies became my grasping of reality and life as I blossomed into a spotty-faced teenager by the time the 10 formative years had lapsed. With wide, blue eyes I absorbed the world all around me while seemingly on my weekly, sometimes daily, missions of boyhood adventures. What a blast. They were absolutely fabulous times for me.

But were the Seventies practically glamorous then? In hindsight, and when the reality of the real social history of the Seventies hits home and becomes tangible, that is once you've researched the facts for the menstruation, it probably wasn't. Maybe it was more an ostentatious, maelstrom of decadence! Manifestly, strikes by postal workers, dustmen and miners led to power cuts and three-day working weeks which weren't truly enchanting; were they? And that's only the preliminary years of the Seventies. The concluding years, 1978 and 1979, saw the 'Winter of Discontent', and 1979 bowing out with the first female Prime Minister in charge of the Britain's affairs – none other than the 'Iron Lady' herself, Margaret Thatcher.

To this day certain tastes and smells can take me right back to when life were so uncomplicated, so carefree. A brief whiff, sip or mere morsel of tucker can trigger harboured thoughts and events that come flooding back from when I was a snotty-nosed kid in short pants and orange wellies, to running down the backstreets – Oi! Oi! Oi! – in half-mast, bleach-splattered jeans and ox-blood DMs.

The tang of rhubarb prompts recollections of rhubarb crumble and custard after a Sunday dinner at the polished, family oak dining table. A swig of lime or cherryade jogs the mind to when the *Corona* pop man would deliver weekly to the home; the mates and I would also lift full bottles of the fizzy stuff from neighbours doorsteps or empty ones for the 2p returns policy. Did you know, *every bubble had passed its FIZZical*?

The scant waft of whiskey, or brandy, can sometimes make me gip. If I'd an upset stomach father always said a nip of whiskey or brandy would either settle my tummy or make me sick. It made me sick EVERY time. The knock on effect of these sickly thoughts then turns the mind to the savour of Milk of Magnesia, and the dryness of the liquid in one's mouth. Also milk drunk from the bottle provokes memories of the milkman, Ernie (Frank really), who would trundle into our cul-de-sac at 5mph in his orange and white Unigate electric milk float. Us Humphreys would be on patrol to see if we could snatch owt when he collected the milk money. You had to, *watch out, watch out there's Humphreys about!*

The cold smack of traditional homemade ice-cream on the palate jogs recollections of the *Cuff's* ice-cream van's hand rung bell. Then there would be a stampede of kids with vice-like grips on copper coins breaking land speed records to make haste towards the ice-cream van. We street urchins would purchase Screwballs, in the main, for the bubble gum at the bottom and would pester the ice-cream bloke. "Mr. Have you any broken wafers?" we'd ask, while old dears tutted as they waited to have three scoops of ice-cream put in their Sunday best dish, with a tea towel covering it to keep the flies off. Or if you were flushed with coinage, double 99s smothered in raspberry sauce, oystershells that had chocolate and coconut flakes on the shell or jam wafers were procured.

The redolence of candle wax reminds me of candles stood in old pie foils throughout our home during power cuts, and me using a pocket torch to find my way to bed. And the torch was also used as a detector to see if the Bogeyman was lurking in the shadows and waiting to get me (where were you when the lights went out?).

A fleeting sniff of brilliantine hair lotion awakens reminiscences of my dad getting ready before heading out to the greyhounds or the local Labour club. The strong odour of polish can make me remember when I would furiously shine my football boots. And later on, in my skinhead days, I'd buff my Airwair until I could see my ugly mug in 'em.

Freshly cut grass takes me back to the summer of 1976 and the sweltering Heatwave and drought. Boy, it was bloody hot. I was going out with a girl four years older than me and got my first feel of bosom after taking an age to undo her bra. This while French kissing and frolicking about in the fields near to where we both lived. I think I got a hard-on too. My nads had descended from my undercarriage with gravity kicking in a few months earlier, and pubes sprouted... that's enough on that subject, though.

As for the fashion stakes in the Seventies: standout time-honoured exemplar pieces included platform shoes (the more elevated the heel, the more highly desirable the shoe.) Pants and jeans went wide. Very wide. Added attributes to synthetic fibre slacks were colossal multiple buttoned waistbands and vast, cavernous knee level side pockets. Figure hugging tops became vogue too – the closer the knit, the tighter the fit. Jumpers with three stars emblazoned across the chest were worn halfway up backs (apart from in aloof Merseyside). Other pullovers were made sleeveless, and were named tank tops. Shirts went loud, extremely loud, garnished in bold, brash patterns together with voluminous winged or round collars.

T-shirts went cap sleeved. Jackets went denim, accessorised with sewn on patches. One type of jacket was pet-named after a tropical bird, this being a Budgie jacket. Hair went lengthy, once more. Lengthy and flyaway. Feathercuts and centre partings became the yardstick.

Music and musicians went glam: archetypal British groups and singers that symbolise the Seventies were, the tartan clad Bay City Rollers; the big haired, big toothed, hairy-chested Bee Gees; and the top-to-toe black hided Alvin Stardust (read on for more personifying Seventies eccentrics).

Wearing make-up was also part of the course. Glam rock, disco and pop was bopped to by some poseurs at trendy, Saturday Night Fever nightclubs while wearing three piece white suits.

The Formative Years

Another Northern Monkey who was also born in the mid-Sixties, and grew up just a few miles from where I did, was Ian. Ian can still call to mind vivid details of his experiences, from innocence, to times when football, music and fighting were his be all and end all. The Seventies made a profound impression upon him.

Ian W: *I've always been in to music from an early age. As a four year old Herman and his Hermits certainly ticked all the necessary boxes, and Rolf Harris with his 'Two Little Boys' was no stranger to my parent's teak Radiogram too. On a more edgy vibe, Johnny Cash 'Live at San Quentin' was another favourite, a taste of the more rebellious path I was to follow musically. My parents had been a little too old for The Beatles; their record collection was more South Pacific movie soundtrack than Lennon and McCartney. And there was always the odd Elvis single knocking about only he was fighting a losing battle with Engelbert Humperdinck. But things were about to change in the Seventies.*

As a seven year old in 1971, I'd never heard of mods and rockers, or hippies, but knew all the words to 'Quando Quando Quando' and 'A Boy Named Sue.' The teenagers of the Sixties had certainly had a good time. When I was born they were all fighting each other on the beaches in some sort of war. And by the time I'd started school, they were all hugging each other and dancing naked in mud while declaring 'peace man!'

My first real decade of true existence was the Seventies: My dad's team – very soon to be mine – had also made it back to the old Division Two. Before this, Saturday afternoons in the late Sixties meant I'd been stuck at home with only my mum and baby sister for company. Oh, and not forgetting Engelbert Humperdinck. Dad would disappear every other Saturday around midday to this Preston North End 'thing' he was so keen on. I don't know if I had been pestering him but one Saturday afternoon in 1971 I made my grand entrance onto Deepdale's terraces. (For the record, we, that is, my football team, PNE, beat Fulham 2-0.) I can't remember much about the game, in fact I don't think I was actually watching it, there were far more interesting things to view as a seven year old. This place I'd entered was mass of entertainment. Behind one of the goals was a huge terrace with a wall near the back, this was the loudest part of the ground. People were singing; what were they singing? My dad kept telling me to watch the game but how could I? To me there was much more going on all in one place than mods and rockers scrapping on a beach, or naked women dancing in mud. Things would never be the same again. Engelbert had released me; I was now a football fan and more importantly, I followed the club my father and his father had supported, our hometown football team, Preston North End.

The early Seventies were also the beginning of my formative years. I had started junior school and even had to catch a bus on my own to get there, the St Marys Junior School bus. It was on that bus twice a day, five days a week, that I perfected my football songs. The bus was an old double-decker and three rows of seats at the back of the top deck were joined together – this was the bus's Kop. And entrance to the Kop wasn't easy. It was almost the end of summer term 1972 before I'd been accepted as a serious, albeit junior, member. Some of the lads must have been almost 11 and knew all the football songs of the time; 'I'm a bow-legged chicken and a knock kneed hen...' and 'Over there, Over there, And if you come, We will not run.' Some of the songs weren't football related but nonetheless catchy little ditties containing lyrics about the IRA blowing the school up!

The school bus went past Wellfield High School, and many of the big lads hanging around outside the school gate had very short hair. I'd seen a few of these on my bi-weekly visits to Deepdale; they had skinheads, and skinhead had finally arrived in Leyland. The high point of any journey to school was sliding the top deck windows open and performing our latest football chants to this willing audience. They must have been impressed as they flicked their fag ends in our general direction, laughing at us in appreciation. One of our lot knew some of the skins and most mornings would take the opportunity to write 'Slade' and 'Skins Rule' on the windows if a build up of condensation allowed, and it usually did. The fag-flickin' skins below seemed to like this, although it must have been back to front. It was the first time I'd heard of Slade and it didn't take me long to find out more. Although still hugely entertained by Captain Pugwash, Mary Mungo and Midge and Hector's House, I began to watch Top of the Pops too, and even try to gain control of the airwaves at home, dismissing my parents' fuddy duddy Radio 2 for the sensational Seventies sound of Radio 1.

Top of the Pops for any kid in the Seventies was amazing; it was even more amazing if you had a colour telly. Sadly we didn't. It was across the road to one of the neighbours for me, the Kays' home. But they were soon to move on to the posh Worden Park estate, where some of the residents had, wait for it... two colour tellies! It was there, Hargreaves Avenue, I was introduced to red and green platform shoes, top hats with shiny silver things stuck to them and musically something they called glam rock. It was only later on when I discovered that Slade used to be a skinhead band, that I figured out why the skinheads in Leyland had now grown their hair and wore checked trousers with big high shoes. Along with Slade came The Sweet. I was nine years-old, and my cowboy rifle had become an electric guitar. It looked about the same size on me as Noddy Holder's real one next to him.

The epic journeys to school continued on the bus but, by now I'd noticed other creatures all around me. These others did not care about Slade, or other glam bands. These other creatures were in love with Donny and Jimmy Osmond, and not forgetting David Cassidy too. These creatures were girls. Girls had their own music and they screamed and swore that one day they would marry Donny or

David. Yes, The Osmonds were for girls whilst Slade were for boys and sounded like a football terrace. And the football terrace behind the goal at Deepdale was becoming more interesting as I reached my tenth year.

I'd been a regular at Deepdale for three seasons now, and we, North End, were still in the old Second Division, but not for long. The Kop during these formative years was a hive of activity. For some reason I wasn't allowed on the local derby games – Blackpool, Bolton and Burnley – but I had witnessed Cardiff City and Sheffield Wednesday swarming all over the terrace from my vantage point on the wall at the front of the Pavilion Paddock.

Preston were relegated at the end of the 1974 season; Bobby Charlton had failed to keep us up after becoming North End manager earlier on that season. His brother though, Jack, had taken over at Middlesbrough, and the 'Boro were in town as Champions of Division Two for the last match of the season. The journey to Deepdale that day had been no different than usual. I was then stuck in the back of a Vauxhall Viva with a bottle of coke and a bag of crisps for an hour staring out of the window at the car park at the back of the Hesketh Arms pub whilst my dad and his mate had their usual pre-match beers, which was the norm too. It was when we got near the ground later that I saw the red and white hordes from the north-east. Middlesbrough were everywhere and these giants were not the usual teenagers I normally saw at the match, they were blokes not much younger than my Dad and his mates. On entering the ground, the Kop to my right, was all 'Boro. If there were any Preston fans on their home end they were making themselves scarce. Preston lost the game 4-2 and on that day in late April 1974 North End returned to Division Three. It was the last time I saw the Kop completely taken, there must have been six or seven thousand 'Boro on there. Once again, I can't remember much about the game but remember the record being played at half-time, 'Sugar Baby Love' by The Rubettes.

Slade had not been heard of for a while; their drummer had almost died in a car crash. The Sweet were still active though, and had just released 'Teenage Rampage'. A call for all teens to 'recognise their age, it's a teenage rampage, NOW!' (The record years later would be put to clips of marauding Man Utd boot boys invading the pitch against Man City, an event that occurred the same day as Preston's relegation. But that day United's Red Army gained worldwide coverage and firmly made themselves public enemy number one throughout the mid-to-late Seventies.) The Rubettes went to number one and to me who liked to ' feel the noize' and have the odd pre-'teenage rampage', they were crap. Even worse was to come, namely Alvin Stardust! Even as a 10 year old I knew this bloke was a phoney, because my mother liked him.

The music was like my football club, going downhill. The summer of 1974 brought more evil to the pop charts. Donny Osmond and co were no longer adorning the bedroom walls of girls. It was in my last year at junior school, it was the time of 'Roller Mania'. The Bay City Rollers had arrived and tartan was everywhere. Also Bobby Charlton decided to make a comeback on the playing field and expectations were high at Deepdale. We beat Plymouth at home in the first match of the season and it was there I first spotted the most beautiful girl in the world.

I was already in position on the Pavilion Paddock wall when just in front of me appeared three teenage girls. The one in the middle had long blonde hair, tight denim flares and a very tight jumper. Her look was completed with a PNE silk scarf tied round her wrist. The pre-match music blared over the tannoy playing Bay City Rollers 'Summer Love Sensation'. I stared at her arse for the entire game, and spent the next few home games doing much of the same. I was 11 and had developed a major crush on this late teen, blonde beauty. Even the visit of locals Blackburn Rovers, and a full away end, could not avert my pre-pubescent lust for the girl next to the dugout. (A few years later, around 1977, she became 'Miss Preston North End', but I would still have been a bit young for her just turning 13?)

Preston were near the top of the table in Division Three as Christmas 1974 approached. I'd also been to my first away game, a defeat at Bury. We stood at the front of the small terrace with most of the Preston fans on the end opposite. But when Bury scored their third, our end was declared a Preston end as Bury fans retreated to the paddock at the side. I'd taken an away end with my dad and his mate without even knowing it, that was before the masses of Preston's boot boys joined us.

In 1974 the UK was on-its-knees with national power cuts and three day working weeks being operated by numerous employers. The music charts offered no respite. As a young lad not yet out of junior school this hardly affected me, but to have Mud being Christmas number one with 'Lonely This Christmas' and a 3-0 away defeat to Blackburn Rovers on Boxing Day, things weren't that good, even for a kid. My first real fisticuffs at a game happened on that very same day 26/12/1974 at Ewood Park and took place in the Nuttall Street Paddock. The Rovers fan was about the same age as me and returned all the punches (sorry, that should be pushes) I gave him and we had to be separated by our parents. Blackburn went on to be crowned Division Three Champions in May 1975; Preston stayed down and in the same league for the next three years. By the time my team made it back to Division Two, I would be 14 years of age.

I started Leyland St Mary's High School mid-September 1975 because all the pupils were given an extra two weeks' summer holidays, this due to someone having taken exception to the ending of their holidays and decided to burn half the school down. High school was a shock to me and most of my friends. The girls at school were women and most of the lads looked like they had just come from taking an away end at the football. It was a far cry from the kiddie tearaways at the back of the school bus. Here different junior schools in the area merged into one Catholic high school, the only one in Leyland. New friends were made as well as new enemies too.

Many of the new arrivals had older brothers or sisters and their elders used to come and check us out and generally take-the-piss out of our brand new uniforms. Uniforms played a big part in school life in the Seventies, and I don't mean the official ones. Most of the fourth and fifth years' lads had long hair with cherry red Doc Martens on their feet and wore the latest Birmingham Bags – massive flares with pockets down the side. Different little gangs would hang round the bike sheds with their hands in the side pockets making them stoop forward looking like hunchbacks. It might not have done much for their posture in later life, but to an 11 year old sporting regulation charcoal school kecks from the catalogue, they looked the business. The girls wore skirts down to just below the knee and huge shirt collars over tight jumpers, with and three-inch high platform shoes making them look more intimidating. Every female seemed to be wearing makeup and smelled like a cross between the Avon Lady and 10 No.6.

The Osmonds and David Cassidy were nowhere to be seen or heard of. The girls at secondary school (well the younger ones) were still into The Bay City Rollers and not far behind, Abba. It was only at break times when fourth and fifth years appeared that I began to notice something called 'Northern Soul' in marker pen daubed across their school bags. It would be a long time before I found out what this Northern Soul was all about; the real stuff anyway. In the meantime, I'd to find my way round this huge school which was slap bang in the middle of Wade Hall, Leyland's largest council estate. The first year at High School passed without any major incidents though.

I was in the school football team and still travelling to Preston to watch the Mighty Whites at weekend. On the music front, Queen had been at number one at Christmas and stayed there for what seemed like months (I hated 'Bohemian Rhapsody', it was far too long). Most of the lads in my class had got into Queen via older brothers; I was more in to Subbuteo and, with a few of my pals, started a league. Music, that's if there was anything decent out there, went way down the pecking order, as either playing, watching or 'flick-to-kick' took over my life.

A mate, Joe, had his felt pitch set up in the garage and used to assemble football stands out of cornflake packets or any old cardboard lying around.

In the homemade stands would be knackered Subbuteo players and Airfix soldiers, as every lad I knew had toy soldiers in the Seventies. Usually just before we'd kick off, crowd trouble would occur in the 'Kelloggs' Stand. The cardboard construction would be set alight and a running commentary would be provided.

"There are terrible scenes here today at the Church Road Ground, the authorities really need to get this under control".

The commentary would be provided by one of us in a John Motson-style, drone. The league only lasted a season due to match fixing, and crowd disorder. Also, the powers-that-be – our parents – had started to take a keen interest in the goings-on in the garage and had cancelled all the following season's fixtures.

We'll keep returning in the book to Ian's adolescence, and his formative years.

Northern Boy

Like I cited, I too had a paralleled infancy to Ian, but I'd not had as comprehensive memories as he has. But what I do remember is I'd had a certain affiliation to a certain green parka.

Every genuine boy is a rebel and an anarch. If he were allowed to develop according to his own instincts, his own inclinations, society would undergo such a radical transformation as to make the adult revolutionary cower and cringe

John Andrew Holmes

From an early age I had my own personal agenda with the clothes that my mother embellished me in and my coiffure, too. During this period there was actually an abundance of poignant, halcyon days though.

Growing-up in the Sixties and Seventies in Preston, your 'run-of-mill' northern town, my family consisted of Mum, Dad, an older brother who'd left home before I'd outgrown my cot, an elder sister and me, of course. Family life while residing in a council house on Brookfield estate on the outskirts of town was quite pleasant, indeed. We had all the up- to-date mod cons; we had a separate toilet and bathroom, a second-hand Hoovermatic De Luxe twin-tub washing machine (including a hand-operated mangle attached) and a Rediffusion rotary selector switch for the three terrestrial channels, plus BBC radio programmes, which was situated on the rear living room windowsill – only the best in our home, I tell you. Outside our home was 'the green'; a 50 foot square grassed area with car parking spaces to the sides. Footy with other lads from the street would be played on the front until our parents called us in. These games would last for hours, with scores reaching 89-90 or until "next goal winner" would be shouted out. Then one day when we'd met on the green after school for another epic game, we clocked there had been a *No Ball Games* sign clamped to the central lamppost by the local council. Some old biddy had complained to PBC (Preston Borough Council) that we'd trampled all over her prized rose bushes and been giving her lip. Guilty as charged, m'lud.

The orange, Wembley Trophy football that I'd received as a Christmas present from Greenlands Working Men's Club, (a local club where my old man was a member) used to get some hammer. If the ball ever got a puncture it was soon repaired by a spoon that had been heated over a gas ring on the stove. Other self-organised entertainment consisted of kick-can, kerby and knock-a-door-run. My dad, apart from going to the Preston greyhound track on Saturday or Thursday nights, when I usually accompanied him, only ever went out for a gill or two of bitter and a game of cash bingo on Sunday dinnertimes, 12 till 2pm, because women weren't allowed in the 'Greenlands' (they should be at home scrubbing the doorstep and cleaning the windows with old newspaper and vinegar according to club regulars). When he arrived home at half two-ish, we would sit round the dining table and have a traditional Sunday roast with all the trimmings and lashings of gravy (northerners love gravy!). Also we would have homemade soup for starters and some kind of freshly-baked dessert for afters. This would be usually rhubarb or apple crumble and custard, or rice pudding. This tradition seems to be a thing of the past, as many families would rather dine out on your two-for-one microwave meals in plastic pubs nowadays.

Anyway, getting back on to the matter in hand, what clothes mother would dress me in: my parents weren't really up-with-the-times, nor neither *a la mode* has you might have already gathered as they were of an entirely diverged epoch. An early distinctive contrast in clothing and hairstyle, compared to other lads my age, became apparent while attending St Maria Goretti Catholic Primary School from the age of five and onwards. My mum use to cut my hair. And because I fidgeted that much while she got to grips with my dome, there were chunks missing out of my mane, everywhere. I also had a very extensive fringe/parting too. Or sometimes, Mother would take me along with her on shopping expeditions to town during schools' half-term or summer holidays and to my Uncle Eric's barber shop to get my hair *styled*. Uncle Eric's was a traditional 'something for the weekend' barber shop with a red and white revolving barber's pole outside and shelves stocked with tubs of Brylcreem, razor blades, black fine toothed combs for grooming while out and about and, little foil envelopes in boxes hidden away in a cupboard; plus he'd a leather foot-pump elevate action barber's chair. I once inquisitively asked what the envelopes contained while Unc' chopped away with his thinning scissors after a bloke before me in the chair had purchased several. Only the question wasn't answered. Through my flick I just clocked a blank expression in the shop's mirror from my Uncle and Mum.

The one thing that kept me I sitting in a stationary position while Mum and Eric chatted about family matters and goings on as he snipped away willy nilly was the promise of a treat later on. This treat would be tuppence worth of periwinkles. These were available from the open fish market, and they would keep me quiet for hours – so Mum was on to a winner on both counts. I would sit crossed-legged on the rug in the front room while gazing at TV watching "Watch with Mother's" *Bill and Ben*, and their neighbour, Little Weed, or sometimes *Andy Pandy*, with a pile of winkles on a old china plate and pin in hand ready to extract my little treat. It became a sort of art form, levering these black and blue fingernail-like shells off the winkle's heads. More than likely I had my tongue stuck out the corner of my mouth, window-licking, as I delved into the wee, sea snail with the pin trying to prise the coiled, brown, worm-like creature from its shell. Boy it didn't half do your box in when the bleeders snapped and the spiralled flesh of the gastropod receded back into its carapace at break neck speed. And no doubt while dislodging the things I would be forever blowing my shock of locks out of my eyes.

Nevertheless, following relentless constant dogging of my parents, plus plenty of conflabbing between themselves, they gave in and finally allowed me to have a fringe. I now fitted in with my schoolyard chums. This apart from my hair being jagged and lopsided, though.

So, with my hair sorted, it was time to pester my mum for an item of clothing I desired greatly. This item being a green canvas parka. These parkas were a must-have for any kid of the Seventies. If proof were necessary as to their popularity you only have to watch YouTube or any TV programme on the day of the FA Cup Third Round. This was when the last round's surviving minnows faced the big-boys and some right old crackers could be pulled out of blue velvet bag. One particular piece of footage features a certain FA Cup game, Hereford versus Newcastle, which epitomises just how ubiquitous parkas were. A fresh-faced John 'Motty' Motson, in his immortal fur lined sheepskin jacket, commentates while celebrating Hereford fans join their part-time Southern League heroes on a quagmire of a playing surface. During the match there were two mass pitch invasions when Hereford scored, and at the final whistle, there was another foray on the pitch by kids clad in parkas. Malcolm 'SuperMac' Macdonald had forecasted he would score 10 in the tie before kick-off, but was left with mud/egg on his face. To add insult to injury, a Bulls' defender, Roger Griffiths, had played 80 minutes with a broken leg while marking 'SuperMac.'

Parkas were a necessity for being 'in' with the 'in' crowd, full-stop. So, the much sought-after fashionable parka had to be had. And surprisingly, after a week of 'I want I want I want', there was one waiting for me after school one Friday, presumably paid for with a Provident cheque. Mother had stitched two small red and white name tags inside the coat too. One on the back of the neck lining, the other half way up the lining of the sleeve. The tags were in every item of clothing I wore to school in fact, including my socks and undies!

The parka consisted of four pockets; two at midriff, and two at breast level with silver shade push button studs for top fasteners. Drawstrings were looped through the base hem, adjacent to the neckline for adjusting the diameter of the hood and around the waist. From under your chin ran a full length zip and more button studs on a flap-over. Inside the coat a red, quilted lining with diagonal stitching kept you toasty. And the hood was trimmed with *real* rabbit fur (I never did get those 'lucky' rabbit foot keyrings, did you?). The parka's core fundamental elements had been lifted from the US Military M-51 and M-65 fishtail parkas that were worn by infantries in combat during bleak weather conditions (anorak facts for you there folks). Such parkas had also been purchased from Army Surplus Stores and worn by mods during combat on windswept beaches in the Sixties. They were ace for riding scooters too, because the 'tail' could be tied through your upper legs so your lower regions were kept warm in temperatures that would freeze the balls of a brass monkey. Seventies' parkas were modified, the fishtail was lobbed off. These resulting parkas bore a resemblance to another US Military jacket, the N-3B Air Force 'Snorkel Parka.' The mid-to-late Seventies saw an adaptation and reproduction of the snorkel in navy blue nylon with orange quilt lining, though the hood was trimmed with fake rabbit fur this time. The brand Lord Anthony became synonymous with the snorkel coat, and Lord Anthony is where I obtained one for school. Such snorkels engulfed (as well as other parts of the UK), Merseyside's tribal youths, who donned them with straight leg jeans and Adidas Samba, this becoming the number one, casual/dresser look.

I can also understand now why my pet rabbit, Fudge, would scurry to the enclosed corner of his homemade hutch in the back garden as I peered through the chicken wire frontaged. I would usually have a lettuce or dock leaf in hand, hunched over while shredding the leaf in-between the wires while wearing my orange wellies, grey flannel shorts and parka hood concealing my face. Fudge must have been going through a trauma wondering if he was gonna end up like one of his cousins as an ornamental frill on a canvas green coat!

Parka pockets could be filled with an array of wondrous small boys' collectables. I hoarded glass marbles containing intense, wavy colourways veining through them or alabaster ones which made my pockets bulge. The marbles varied in size too; oners', twoers' or fourers' were used for pick 'n' nigging with your forefinger into a divot created by the heel of your Clarks on the green out front. Or 'ballies', that could be used, but only if the other player was a willing party. These ball bearings came in handy years later at the match! Sweets from a local sweet shop adjoining a petrol station would be stowed in pockets too; Fruit Salad and Black Jack chews, rice-paper flying saucers, jelly snakes, shrimps, gobstoppers Drumsticks lollies, Bazooka bubblegum that included a foldout cartoon and many, many more delightful delights.

I'd spend an age selecting the 1/2p and 1p sweets for a 5 or 10p mix. The old dear who ran the shop would be done in by the time I'd chosen, with me keep swapping and changing my mind. This while the fag ash off her No.6 ciggy cascaded all over the white chocolate mice. Or I'd request 2oz or a ¼ of bullseyes, or kola-cubes, or sherbet lemons, or cinder toffee, from the jars to her rear, high on the top shelves. This in the hope I could swipe an handful of confectionery from behind the glass screen while she drew-up a stool to reach containers. 'Cheggies' too would be hunted and saved from under leaves on the ground in autumn which had dropped from horse-chestnut trees, or felled off branches by sticks thrown with venom skywards into the trees wilting foliages. Conkers would be soaked in vinegar and baked in the oven with shoelaces at the ready hanging out of your top pocket for a game of cheggies, ready to smash your opponent's cheggie to smithereens (this game is banned at schools nowadays). Even cardboard collectable football cards with a piece of free gum in the greaseproof paper packs were hoarded – the gum also tasted of cardboard. We'd play for hours throwing the cards against the kerbs; nearest wins, tops, or swapping our doubles. I had umpteen scrapes that would ensue after hiding my 'besties' deep in a pocket with boys two or three years older than me. Them pockets didn't half come in handy.

One biting winters day, following being kept behind off a teacher, who dished out a severe lecture over my behaviour in class, I bolted into the cloakroom, grabbed the remaining parka, pulling it on while in motion, and then legged it down the corridor, bursting through the double doors that exited to the playground and at great haste, trapping like a whippet, and headed homeward bound for the game of footy on the green that we'd arranged the night before.

Halfway home, we passed a Methodist Church. On many occasion we had thrown stones through its imposing leaded windows, their value and meaning insignificant to a bunch of feral kids. My fingers on my right hand, which was plunged deep into the parka's lower pocket, felt numb and frozen to the marrow. Taking a dekko at my hand, it was poking through the bottom of the pocket; the stitching had bust, or so I thought. Putting the anchors on, my eyes began to scan the rest of the parka. I soon twigged it wasn't mine. The coat had stains down the front and push studs missing and, on removing the jacket, there were several chunks of rabbit fur absent from the hood. The remainder of the route home was a blur as I hit speeds that the Six Million Dollar Man would have struggled to achieve.

Entering the house through the side door pantry, or a drying or utility or claptrap room, I ground to a halt in the kitchen where Mother was cooking tea (Northerners have tea at teatime, not dinner). Then, like a horse racing commentator on whizz, I gave my mum the lowdown on the parka in my hand. Mother versed me back, the way only mothers do, and said she would be accompanying me to school in the morning to sort the issue out. I'd omitted to tell her the reason why I was the last to vacate school though.

Bright and breezy the next morning, Mother and I set off for school with whoever's coat it was. On arrival at my form classroom, Mum had a brief chat to my teacher, whose name escapes me. Once everyone was sat at their desks, and Miss had their attention, she made an announcement that someone had taken my parka by mistake and left theirs on my hook in the cloakroom instead. And, could everyone check inside their parkas for name tags with my name on. No-one was forthcoming with my parka, nor did it turn-up that day. Unbeknown to me, Mother had also told the teacher that if the jacket didn't appear it might be covered on an insurance policy which was connected to our home insurance; washing line robbery and theft were rife round our way.

During the course of the day Mum had rung the insurance firm, who had in turn contacted the police, who in turn rang my mother informing her that they would send an officer to St Maria Gorettis' the following morning, which they did. The officer addressed all pupils in attendance that day at school in the assembly hall, and asked on the whereabouts of my parka. Embarrassing or what – talk about going beetroot red. The culprit never came forward, or was brought to justice so, the case was closed and a new parka was claimed on the insurance.

When the cheque arrived on the doormat, a spanking new parka was purchased the next day, along with a bright yellow, three-to-four-inch oval long name badge which had red piping and 'Bill' in real writing embroidered across it in red. My mother then stitched the oval patch to the left-hand breast pocket and a dozen name tags inside in different hidden locations. The next day in the school playground I got the shite ripped out of me by each and every one of the mates, plus the girls too, and once more my face went crimson red. From wearing a parka to death like the Asian kid in *East is East*, I now couldn't wait to get the damn thing off. Break times in the coming months were spent running round the playground to keep bloody warm.

That wasn't the only time that the police and parka were implicated. You could also be in the countryside within a matter of minutes from where we lived, and I had plenty of adventures down the woods during the early Seventies. There was an old World War II underground air-raid shelter and a concrete, hexagonal light rifle/machinegun (Type 22) pillbox erected as a observation post in a field no more than 500 yards down the road from ours that we played soldiers in (no girls allowed). These war relics were situated near a couple of ponds full of frogspawn, great crested newts and moorhens during spring and summertime months. The parka's pockets stuffed with bog roll also came in handy for protecting eggs that I'd 'egged' from nests in towering, trees as I climbed back down to planet earth. The trees dominance didn't faze me one iota. I would tackle any tree, no matter its magnitude; majestic oaks or infinite pines, I were 'up 'em' like a squirrel on steds.' Or, was that just the Northern Monkey in me?

Anyway, once, in spring, I'd gone to my sister's barn conversion that her husband-to-be, who was a builder, was working on one weekend. I then wandered off down the multitude of country lanes, egging. Spotting a maggies – magpie's – nest 30 feet up in a hawthorn tree on the roadside, I decided to investigate its contents. Not wanting to snag and ruin my parka on the thorny branches, plus get an ear bashing from Mum if I did, I removed the coat and threw it on the grass verge. When I slipped my hand into the vast, twig nest 10 minutes later I noticed a panda car passing below. It then reversed to be parallel with the tree. 'Oh shit', I thought.

'How do I get out of this one?' A copper then opened the panda cars door, got out, walked over to my parka, which had been left post-box red lining upwards, lifted it from the ground, glanced at it, and then scanned the area for the owner, I presume. I was just gonna shout down "Officer. The jackets mine" when he placed the jacket in the exact same spot, returned to his cop car, and drove off – phew. I haven't a clue what he might have thought to the whereabouts of the owner, or why the parka was there. Maybe he initially thought it were a dead sheep or summat.

"The classic, traditional style parka is still a
withstanding outwear jacket, both functional
and a true king of coats. And long
may they be so."

Who knows? Anyway, I was down the tree in a flash; full of thorns imbedded deep in to my bare flesh, and hundreds of plucks to my jumper. I grabbed the coat, threw it on, and left the lane in haste.

To this day parkas are still celebrated, and contemporary labels such as Engineered Garments, Heritage Research, Garbstore and a magnitude of other brands add their own unique twist to the staple commodity. Rare sought-after heritage brand parkas are also in high demand from American eBay; the likes of Sierra Designs 60/40 – an orange number was seen worn by Robert de Niro in the opening scenes of the flick *Deer Hunter* – Woolrich, REI and several other now dissolved labels fetch big bucks.

The classic, traditional style parka is still a withstanding outwear jacket, both functional and a true *king of coats*. And long may it be so.

Nothing is Original. Steal from anywhere that resonates with inspiration or fuels your imagination

Jim Jarmusch

Shoreham Bootboys

By the mid-Seventies football violence was rife, and scarf bedecked football gangs had began marauding round the country in their thousands in search of mayhem. Ronnie Sharpe was one of these teenagers on the rampage, and in the thick of it.

Ronnie: *By the mid-Seventies the police were finding it increasingly difficult to control hooligans. Thousands of yobs travelled up and down the country and fought in the stadiums, the surrounding streets, in pubs, coach parks, motorway services, railway stations, anywhere really.*

So where did us lot, 'the hooligans', figure in football's grand scheme of things? Were we real supporters? Loyal supporters? Did we love our teams; the Blades, Owls, Rams, Reds, Blues, Millers, Tykes, Spurs, Hammers, Lions, Tigers, Cobblers? Or did we, as the sociologists and anthropologists claim (congratulations for such a fucking mind-blowing observation) just attach ourselves to a particular football club for the violence?

No shit, of course we attached ourselves to a particular football club, and in probably 95% of all cases, our home town football club, that was the whole fuckin' point. Along with the other 91 English tribes we carried on playing the game, a game many of us had played for close on 10 years. Badminton, squash, polo, stick 'em up ya arse; this was the only game, football violence.

There might not have been any secret signs or handshakes, but being part of a mob was like belonging to a Masonic brotherhood. We were grown men who acted like kids, little kids, who called for each other or met up on street corners or in chosen pubs for a full day of fun and frolics. Yes, little kids who went to each other's houses for tea and slept on each other's settees. But we were hooked on something, we lived for Saturdays, we lived for the match day craic and the camaraderie, we were having a fuckin' good time. If we weren't, we wouldn't have done it, would we?

Success on the pitch sometimes meant little to us, or so we'd say!

Now it would have been great to win the league or get to the cup final, semi-final even, but I was a Sheffield United fan, and although I could always dream of achieving some honours, I never really expected that we would; next season, maybe, eh?

The press labelled us 'mindless idiots' and then aided our reputations by printing thug league tables and articles with photos of our exploits too. The daft cunts made us famous, made us newsworthy, and made the hooligan problem 10 times worse. Blame the fuckin' press I say. But fuck the press, they knew fuck all. We loved football just as much as much as we loved our respective teams. Flashes of genius, flowing moves and 30 yard thunderbolts by the opposition always received a polite splattering of applause even from the most partisan crowds.

The focal point of every Saturday obviously came at 3pm when the game kicked-off (could that have been coincidental to the boozers shutting?). But for the lads, Saturdays often started at 6am and ended at midnight, or later. On occasions, Saturdays started on Friday night, and ended Sunday morning. For the really 'unlucky' ones, Saturdays lasted three months which ended with a walk out of the 'Big House' gate. The chance of arrest or injury was always there, but these were risks worth taking.

The fines were still relatively small and could be paid off at a couple of quid or less a week. Magistrates would occasionally dish out a big fine or a short prison sentence to try and convince the establishment they were tackling the problems at football.

A young Hackenthorpe Blade, incidentally, held the honour of copping for the first ever £100 fine dished out for football-related disorder. This happened at Derby in the early Seventies. The lad appeared on the Yorkshire Television news programme, Calendar, after his court case, and the fee he received paid the fine.

Anyone who wore their club colours were fair game, no code of conduct existed back then. 10 lads who turned a wrong corner and bumped in two hundred rivals were written off without a second thought. Even more so than the late Sixties, the early to mid-Seventies was a home and away thing. If the lads got turned over at Stoke, everybody would be ready and waiting for when they came to the Lane. If Birmingham copped it at our place we were certain to get reprisals at St Andrews. Places we'd explored as chabbies in the Sixties were now no-go areas. Only the foolhardy, the brave, or lone drunkards went to Chelsea, West Ham, Tottenham and Millwall. Liverpool, Everton, Leeds, Newcastle, Sunderland, Man City and some of the London First Division teams had huge mobs at home and took thousands away too.

Man Utd (as ever) were untouchable as a mob, and so they should have been. Just like the Grand Old Duke of York they had 10 fuckin' thousand men, and lads. As a young 15 year old in the late Sixties I couldn't help but be impressed by the Man Utd hordes. But in the mid-Seventies I couldn't get my head around what they got out of it. And what must the proper Manchester lads think about the thousands of bandwagon jumping, Bay City Roller clad glory hunters muscling in on their fame? I do wonder.

Anybody could be a Man Utd fan. Following Man U at the time must have been akin to following England in the Nineties and Noughties. Hundreds of lads from every part of the land converging on towns and cities and running riot; what possible buzz could masses of lads get by slapping a few locals? And what about the home games at Old Trafford. Coaches from every part of the country would turn up; how the fuck would you know which ones to brick? Nah, not for me at all that.

There were the so-called easy places (although you could never tell) like Ipswich, Norwich, Coventry, Luton, Carlisle, Fulham, Palace, and QPR. And the inbetweenies like Wolves, Villa, West Brom, Leicester, Forest, Burnley and loads more where it could go either way. At ours: a few of the big boys tried but only Man Utd and Leeds, both with overwhelming numbers, had ever taken the piss at the Lane.

But there was something special and something magic about every mob, even Wednesday. The songs they sung in different regional accents, the way they spoke and the gear they wore. There was a kind of mutual respect for other mobs that nobody but footie lads would understand. Respect, at that time, was a word no footie lad would ever use or even admit to having for others.

The North

So the next incision into the Northern Monkeys fable is by a man that not only overcame ridicule for his Christian name off kiddies giving it large in school, but intense, racist taunts too when growing up in Slade Green, Kent, with his white foster parents. Plus he'd also had to live down the stigma of being born in Yorkshire. He rose head-and-shoulders above all this adversity. Such were the dramatic events during these periods, which read like a script from a movie; he had a film made of his life story in 2008. He is also a best-selling author of eight football fan- related books, five which have been UK top 10 best sellers. Nowadays he is also successful entrepreneur in other ventures; one of these is lending his knowledge as a "hooliologist" to TV and film projects. The man in question, if you haven't already guessed, is none other than Cass Pennant.

I know where I am going, and I know the truth, and I don't have to be what you want me to be. I'm free to be what I want

Cassius Clay

Cass: *I think most of us as teenagers living in Seventies London discovered the north from a football special train. Before that, I had no idea what northern people* *and their towns were like and Coronation Street painted a grimy image (though I thought Ray Langton was a bit of a lad). As for its history, well, the orders went out from London and the armies marched North, didn't they?*

Travelling north for support of your football club was not only an adventure in the 1970s, it was bordering on the suicidal. The West Ham firm were so much younger then, as 12-17-year-olds would bulk up the numbers of the main firm. Most of these lads were typically streetwise, like most cockneys, with heads on their shoulders far older than their actual years – which was useful, frankly, when experiencing the hatred of all things cockney up North.

All this serious loathing for the south just went with the buzz though, and you quickly fell into the mindset. The north really hated cockneys, excelled at brick-throwing and had this great community spirit that consisted of 'our kid', 'our Brian' and all that. I've had several experiences of this community spirit, when locals that had nothing to do with the football would come out of their houses and join in the ruck against the cockneys in the street. Even the police took the attitude that it was all northerners together, and just about every London club fan says they felt the bias when the northern Old Bill fought us on behalf of their own clubs.

The north v south divide did actually unite even those northern clubs with a fierce rivalry, which I have to say was not always the same situation down south. Our first evidence of this would come with a trip to Anfield in the Seventies – which, little did we know, would mean taking on Everton as well as Liverpool. Every cockney has got stories of having it with one northern team, only to get done by another! The Mancs too had a spell of 'all northerners together', until City got into a spat with United as to who was 'proper Manchester'. (It's true though that we never experienced this truce in your north east rivalries between the Geordies, Teessiders, Wearsiders, Mackems and Tynesiders. Ignorance of the day meant that we regarded them all as being Geordies.)

"travelling north for support of your football club
was not only an adventure in the 1970s,
it was bordering on the suicidal."

If any northerner denies this then they were not around in those barmy Seventies/early Eighties, when northern clubs were more likely to grace the FA Cup and League Cup finals and have their day out at Wembley. That's when we saw proof of this 'all northerners together' attitude, after the word went around that this is the way you played it if the cockneys turned up for a row. The London firms too would join together, depending on the level of rivalry; it was unlikely that West Ham would go with any rival London club, yet it did happen on occasions when London firms would hunt around Trafalgar Square for any early arriving northerners on the Friday night, and again en route to Wembley Way next morning. This little war also included midlands clubs, as anything past junction one of the M1 was classed as 'northern'. Geography wasn't our strong point, but the same applied to northerners who classed teams such as Brighton, Watford and Luton as 'cockneys'.

Listening to London away fans just confirmed the whole stereotype of what we thought 'northern' was: 'Tetley's' was not a name I'd ever seen anywhere in London, but up north it was everywhere; nor did I understand the term 'down The Smoke' used in reference to going to London, as our city wasn't full of chimneys and old mills (or mines, come to that). Then there were the donkey jackets that the away fans wore when they showed at Upton Park; everyone of age had a donkey jacket in the Seventies, and the Geordies had them well into the Eighties – but we wouldn't have a name printed on ours, unless it was Wimpey and we worked in the building industry. But all the northerners had names printed on the back of this pit or that road construction firm, I guess it was all part of their 'we're working class and we're men' attitude. I used to be amused though to see the lads around me wearing donkey jackets, when I knew they hadn't done so much as a day's work. I've seen plenty of our own rubbing their DMs into cement and mud to authenticate themselves as 'workers', while I was in no doubt that the other lot came as they were straight from the colliery.

In a world before the package holidays of the Eighties and student rail tickets took us on a European tour, travel meant Lacey's coaches, a Ford transit or a football special train. Going 'up north' was usually a midlands experience for most of us, as that's who packed out the old First Division, while ' far north' was restricted to Burnley, Blackpool and Carlisle. Away games at the bigger northern cities – Manchester, Liverpool, Leeds and Newcastle – were without question payback time from those clubs. Their home ends were never taken by firms like us even though we specialised in it, because big numbers were seriously needed for that. I can still remember the bravado chant that would go up on the North Bank end, "Clap yer hands if yer going to – add such and such – away," and it seemed like half the end joined in. But, come the game, the reality was that no fucker turned up for the morning meet at Euston. The lads that went hid their scarves, and still got sussed and battered.

Considering the police attitude that 'you're on your own if you come up here,' it was unlikely we'd be given any escort, despite the young average age of the firms *back then. The other notable difference was that the grounds always seemed to be miles away from the train stations. I have some great memories (and some not so great) of discovering yer awayday started as soon as you entered town, not when you arrived by the ground. (What a mercy the short walk from Upton Park station down Green Street to West Ham's ground would be, if we had a return match.)*

Northern awaydays to the likes of Carlisle, Burnley and Stoke were adventures, and we took decent numbers too. Carlisle was unbelievable, a Rocky Mountain-style trip. Everyone travelling up would be getting excited, buzzing, faces pressed to the window simply at the sight of sheep – loads of fucking sheep! – on the great big hills we were travelling up and down. The older boys knew where they were, and would simply announce, "We're nearly here, this is Carlisle now." I don't know how they knew, when the train journey was so long that the rest of us couldn't remember how long ago we'd left London. It was the sight of the smog that hit your eyes as you looked out from the train windows – this is what London must have looked like once, and it explained to me why northerners referred to it as 'The Smoke', even though we'd never seen London smog since the Fifties. But with all the mills and factories, the towns were still smothered in smog up north.

All the London clubs – not just West Ham – loved going to Burnley. It's remembered as one of those grounds where the Old Bill would let the fans meet on the terraces, even on the home end and at the sides. They gave you scrapping time, before wading in with a little bit themselves. They were reluctant to nick you too – they'd rather throw you out of the ground so you had to pay your way back in and do it all again. It was incredible, but you knew what you went for and you knew the risks. It was as if they felt sorry for the local inhabitants: "Why not let them let off a bit of steam on the cockneys get it out of their system? Because there is fuck-all else ever going to happen for them up here!"

Yes, it was crazy days on the terraces of Turf Moor, with the skinhead- meets-Bay City Roller-style dress sense of Burnley fans. I recall, in the Seventies, a row going toe-to-toe on the side of the away stand with lads in white bib and braces, bowler hats, sprayed silver DMs, the full Clockwork Orange *attire. It was a real tear-up, but don't blame us – even though it was happening in our section, it was Blackburn and Burnley who were at it.*

When Danny Dyer presented the TV series 'Real Football Factories' in 2006, it featured today's Burnley Suicide Squad. It also showed Burnley today, with the same dust-covered, rundown, shoebox terraced housing on slopping, hilly streets, with corner pubs and flat-capped regulars (now supping what was maybe lager, instead of brown ale). Back in the Seventies, so many asked the question on the trip home: "Do people really live in those streets?" They were taking the piss then, but in 2006 I found it shocking.

If Burnley was somewhere that time forgot, then Anfield was scary in those pre-ICF days. On the walk from Lime Street you would encounter derelict houses, wastelands and bomb craters from the war that ended in '45. But there again, if you weren't from Liverpool then the war was still on. The full experience meant getting run on Scottie Road, those long stick truncheons the 'bizzies' up there carried then, and the terrace song that went, "He's only a poor little cockney, his face is all tattered and torn... I hit him with a brick, and now he don't sing anymore" pre-empting the London supporters' own reply: "In your Liverpool slums ... you look in the dustbins for something to eat, you find a dead rat and you think it's a treat."

I like the way scousers carry themselves, they have a strong pride in the way they are and their accent is very distinct – like a cockney accent, everybody recognises it instantly. They have got an attitude that says, "The world stops at Liverpool, we should be the capital city because we gave the world the Beatles" – blah blah. 'I'm a scouser' oozes independence and bags of confidence in much the same way as 'I'm a Londoner.' Yet the hatred of all scousers from London clubs in the Seventies was on a par with the Liverpool-Manchester rivalry thing of today. The clashes mellowed somewhat in the Eighties, when casual cockneys and scousers found a lot in common with each other whenever they met on designer store shopping trips right the way across Europe.

The stand-alone memories for me of the Seventies period are of how a pal that took a kicking said, "I ain't running from no northern cunt wearing a star jumper!" and of how the northerners influenced the top boys from the South Bank crew into having six-button high-waister trousers, specially made by East End tailors. You couldn't buy such strides anywhere in London, and we started seeing bottle-green three-button baggies first in the midlands, then the waistband appeared to get higher the further north we travelled. They actually caught on down here, which I think was down to those big pockets on the outside thighs – just the perfect fit for the match programme, can of booze, or whatever the weapon of the day happened to be.

The north-south divide was just as evident on the club and music scene, which for me at that time meant soul and funk: Norman Whitfield, Creative Source, Brass Construction, Fatback, Kool, etc. Then we learnt about the all-dayers advertised in **Blues & Soul** *and another magazine called* **Black Music***. It would take us to meet our fellow soul music clubbers from the north, who were doing the same as us in checking out all the good clubs in the south. I got told by friendly northerners who spotted the Motown Gold pendant worn around my neck that, if I was into Tamla, I should check out the Northern Soul scene. They would talk it up like it was something else, not to be missed out on. So, with my close pals I often went clubbing with, we headed north in either Mick's Morris Minor or Bob's Hillman*

Imp. This particular Easter weekend, the targets were the all-nighters and all-dayers of Wigan Casino, Blackpool Mecca and Tiffany's in Coalville, via the ripped-out club-advert pages from Blues & Soul.

I'm not going to bore you with the whole venture or go into detail about the music, because we knew nothing about Northern Soul as we wanted to check out the scene with an open mind. If it was something we were missing out on down south, then we would be going back to let everyone know. Anyway, we had a cracking weekend – even though we fucked up with Wigan Casino, as it was shut or it was the wrong fucking day. It meant driving on to Manchester, the nearest place that could save our night. I knew of the Ritzy but we ended up in a couple of other clubs, watching people doing spins and shit; then the music would change and you had these electro sounds that just didn't sound anything like soul to me. Neither could we get used to this music-being-played-in-different-rooms bollocks, with clubbers congregating in, and blocking, the passageways. The bouncers were putting us on edge too, and people were too fucking strange to talk to us. I guess we'd come from a totally different club scene, nothing like the one we were encountering in Manchester.

So we did the cheap B&B thing and, next day, drove to Blackpool to check out the Mecca. There we found a real Northern Soul set-up; outside, coach after coach pulled up to join the queues forming to get in. (You never got coaches arriving at London clubs.) We went in thinking, "It's going to be kicking off in here in no time," as we noticed the coaches had brought people in from rival areas. We were wrong there, even though the dance floor was like going into a kung fu school, with loads of spins and backflips.

Okay, we weren't ones for dancing as we were there for the sounds and the birds to chat up, who we'd normally start checking out on the dance floor. But the floor was full of lads wearing bowling shirts, whizzing; it was all about their moves; some were tricky, but lacking the rhythm that the guys who could dance down south would show yer. We'd clocked that the birds remained around the edge of the dance floor and the bars, thinking, "Hey, we're in here, chaps!" It was our football awayday experiences that had taught us how northern birds would come up and start showing interest from the moment they heard the London accent, while the local geezers wanted to smash yer. But, because of the way the lads were fighting for space to do their speed dancing, we were getting the freedom to move from one group of birds to another without attracting unwanted attention.

I recall how that first trip to the khazi was another new experience. I was greeted by the sight of a banged-out toilet and all these northern lads making what I can only describe as costume changes. There were holdalls containing fresh clothes all laid out on the polished floor tiles and on the sink tops. Then, in a new dry bowling shirt, back out they went, past all the birds they totally ignored, to the dance floor for more spins and backflips to impress their mates. It was what they appeared to care about above everything.

So you can imagine what we were thinking: the lads that went to the football and the lads that went to the clubs were two different sets of people. It was obviously a pretty serious music scene, but me and the others couldn't get our heads around it, as hard as we tried. They were all getting off on old Tamla Motown B-sides they thought were great, because some DJ said it was rare and they paid big for it. (You dozy Northern Monkeys! It's rare for a reason, and the reason is that it's shit. Not 'shite'.) As for the birds, we thought we'd pulled on the strength of just opening our mouths and where we'd come from. Then we had to think again. When the last orders were called, and those sweat-stained lads in bowling shirts all headed for the gents for one last costume change before getting back on the coaches, the birds we were with, whose drinks we'd paid for all night, just walked off and followed. Worse still, to our surprise they all kissed and hugged as the boyfriends and girlfriends they must have been all along. We stood open-mouthed as to how these girls, now waving us off from the departing coaches, had played second fiddle to their fellah's love of Northern Soul, to the point where we were convinced every bird was single and fancied a cockney.

I don't think anything will ever come close to the north v south divide of the Seventies and all of its basic differences. It was all so simple to define: you northerners preferred the pint jug of ale, we took to the cans and then the bottles of lager, all in a smooth half-glass; you worked the pits, we were on the building sites; you had the factories, we the offices; off the pitch, your crews were 'armies' while ours were 'firms'; on the pitch you had the League titles, the FA Cups and the League Cup – but for all of that we won the World Cup, the one that really matters. So we understand why you hate the cockneys, la-la, la-la, la-la...

*The England team from the 1966 World Cup Final that Cass mentions did include three 'ammers. But out of the starting eleven, only three were southerners – George Cohen, who played for Fulham, and Martin Peters and Bobby Moore (captain), who were both *Irons* (Geoff Hurst is a Lancashire lad). The rest of the squad were born north of Watford. Alright, the West Ham duo, Hurst and Peters, put the ball in the onion bag to win the gleaming, Jules Rimet Trophy, but on balance, the team was mainly a northern one. Only I'm not going to argue with Mr Pennant. Would you?

The Summer of '76

Ian W: *It was now 1976, one of the hottest summers on record, and musically things were 'happening', although it would be another year yet before it 'happened' for me.*

Whilst the Punk Rock Revolution was gaining momentum 200 miles away in London, the only momentum happening in Leyland was a bit of a run up, and then slide across the bonnet of any unsuspecting parked car. Starsky and Hutch the fast moving American cop series, had hit our TV screens. And this duo didn't walk round a car to get in it; they went over the car before doing so accompanied by the latest disco music playing in the background of the mean streets of mid-Seventies America. We had our own UK cop series, The Sweeney. The Sweeney was set in London, and was more violent than Starsky and Hutch, and you even got a flash of the odd pair of breasts. The only problem being Jack Regan and his sidekick George dressed like your father. The American cops wore leather jackets, long thick knit cardigans with a belt around the waist and supported trendy haircuts. Jack Regan of The Sweeney wore a suit, was going grey, and looked like a geography teacher. No contest, really.

The telly and the weather of the time was great. The music, even for a 12 year old, was crap. The charts were ravaged by Abba and The Brotherhood of Man, and all the girls thought they were Dancing Queens and wanted you too 'save all your kisses' for them. Acts like Elton John who had previously stated 'Saturday Night was Alright for Fighting', *pranced round the Top of The Pops studio with some bird singing,* 'Don't Go Breaking My Heart' *It was a confusing time for a soon-to-be teenager. Older lads who had been in the fifth year when I'd started secondary school now had jobs and were going to a Casino at weekends. Some even travelled to their Mecca. Northern Soul was in full swing with Wigan and Blackpool hosting the main events in the north- west. I was too young and hadn't a clue. For me the soundtrack of the summer of 1976 was provided by the still sensational sound of the Seventies, Radio One. Tony Blackburn and David 'Diddy' Hamilton filled the airwaves with watered down disco music and* the *latest hits from artistes such as Demis Roussos, Dolly Parton and not forgetting the summer smash of 1976,* 'I've Got A Brand New Combine Harvester' *by The Wurzels. What did I know; I thought Bowie was boring – although I'd bought Diamond Dogs – and thought Roxy Music were puffy. On the other hand, The Real Thing were a Northern Soul band, I was pretty sure of that.*

The long hot summer finally came to an end with a return of the second year of high school life. It was also a bit of a disappointment just to have the six weeks holiday and unfortunately nobody had tried to burn the school down during the holidays. Arsonists seemed to be in short supply, probably just as well with the reservoirs drying up and a national hosepipe ban being enforced due to the heat wave. The girls in my year seemed to have grown a good few inches taller than the lads during the summer and were getting more interesting as the term progressed as they'd 'sprouted' too.

Preston were still in Division Three, and had their usual good start to the season. And in October they were once again away at Gigg Lane, Bury. This time my father settled for the quieter surroundings of the Paddock of the main stand. On the end to our right-hand side, you could see it was packed to the rafters with Preston fans. And when Preston went two-nil up by half- time, the lads behind the goal were making a right racket. At the other end, trouble had started as 20 or so Preston and Bury fans charged up and down the terrace at each other.

"Bloody hooligans. They're all bloody yobs" my father declared. He wasn't at all happy by the shenanigans at the far end. His mood deteriorated even further as every man and his dog invaded the pitch from the end housing the majority of the Preston following. It was the first pitch invasion I'd seen by Preston. Surely we were now in the same league as Man Utd? The Preston end totally emptied and ran the entire length of the pitch to join the 20 or so lads entertaining the Bury fans at the opposite end. It was an amazing sight as the first invaders reached Bury's stand, as more and more Preston fans were climbing the fences to get out of the away end. My father was not impressed, and having been unable to contain my excitement, I was told to stop acting like the 'bloody yobs' who were currently occupying the Gigg Lane playing surface. A policeman's helmet was being kicked around near the centre circle too, this being a lot better than the half-time entertainment back at Deepdale. All this was played out to the sound of 'Mississippi' by Pussycat, a record my father actually liked and bought, but is remembered by him for all the wrong reasons.

Preston eventually lost the game 3-2. Later that night I was given a talking to about enjoying the spectacle of the idiots ruining our national game, and I wasn't allowed to watch Match of the Day.

Christmas was soon upon us and a chance to dance with the fast developing females at the school Christmas disco, the disco being a record player and tape deck operated by the PE Teacher. And in December 1976 over the festive period, events in London were happening; a new music was shaking up the old guard, feathers were being ruffled in the outdated music industry. It was fast, it was furious, and the fat cat record executives were concerned. Punk Rock had arrived.

Meanwhile on the dance floor. She was a bit taller than me and she'd borrowed some of her mum's Tweed perfume. I'd asked her to dance and she'd accepted. I'm actually moving to the sound of music with a female and her breasts are pressed against me. The High Karate aftershave borrowed from my father mingles with her mother's eau du toilette. It's a perfect moment made more perfect by Showaddywaddy's 'Under the Moon of Love'.

Christmas day 1976 was a good day for the German economy, as Adidas Samba trainers and Beckenbauer football boots were lifted from the famous blue boxes. And a navy blue and white T-shirt completed the three stripe collection. But wait, there was more, as a full Admiral England kit was opened to much joy, this suggesting my father had forgotten his only son's reaction to serious crowd disorder just six weeks previous. And as we entered into the New Year there was a shock in store for me. The blonde one from Starsky and Hutch was at the top of the UK charts with 'Don't Give up on Us Baby' – too late matey, I had. David Soul reached number one with a soppy ballad, betraying his army of bonnet sliding fans in Leyland. I refused to watch the programme ever again.

The charts were still full of the normal shite, and music was once again an afterthought as playing football for the school team and Lostock Hall under 14s filled my weekend. Also Preston North End began their usual slide. And by April, any hopes of promotion to Division Two ended for another season. In London many of the new bands I'd not heard about (yet) had been signed to major record labels. The music industry executives were now falling over themselves trying to catch the wave. Bands and independent record labels were springing up everywhere.

In deepest Lancashire, my mates and I were riding round on pushbikes with cowhorn handle bars and wearing flared jeans that constantly got tangled in the bike's chain. A natty cheesecloth shirt worn with a denim waistcoat completed the look. My tastes in music seemed to be going with the flow and some of the chart soul music even found its way in to my record collection which now consisted of the old Slade stuff, a bit of Bowie and a Soul compilation featuring Harold Melvin, The Detroit Spinners and Rose Royce. The girls seemed to have ditched Abba, some were even ridding themselves of David Soul (the fake) and jumping onto the soul/disco sound of 1977. Donna Summer, Heatwave and Tavares are their records of choice. Girls were high on the agenda as a few of us were now in our first relationships and were discovering the workings of the female, albeit on a small scale. Full on snogging, tongues in-the-mouth and hands up blouses seemed pretty good for a 13 year old round our way. Some of us by then had actually felt flesh inside of a bra!

The country was getting ready to celebrate the Queen's Silver Jubilee; and street parties had been organised all over town. After a ride round on our bikes having a nosey at the events, we retired to Fester's – a good mate of mine – dad's garage. At the time we were getting into a bit of shoplifting, and this was the place we shared the booty which usually consisted of chocolate, aerosol cans (put them on a fire and watch them blow up) and cheap perfumes freely available at Leyland Co-op chemist.

Once a problem occurred with our bowels one day, when vast quantities of diabetic chocolate were consumed within minutes of acquiring it. Four of us developed severe stomach pains resulting in sickness and diarrhoea. We hadn't read the label before stuffing our faces. The girls would be always grateful for the perfume but diabetic chocolate was no longer on our wish list from then on. The music revolution was now reaching fever pitch in London, there was even a band that

was banned from the radio for derogatory lyrics against the Queen. Back in Fest's
garage, we were totally oblivious to the happenings going on in the music world.

Anti-Establishment: 'England's Dreaming'

Punk rock exploded on to the music scene in Britain at same time the brimming pores and pus filled zits erupted on my chubby-chopped face. Poor old pizza-face me... my adolescence kicked-in at an early age. Only I would be fibbing to say I was into punk from the off. After all, I would have been 11-and-three-quarters when the Sex Pistols and their entourage appeared on the *Today* programme on Wednesday the 1st December 1976, hosted by Bill Grundy and shown live at 6.25pm. The infamous Thames Television two minute interview, with the *allegedly* intoxicated Grundy, caused pandemonium and outrage because of the obscenities the group spouted at Grundy, and Grundy asking Siouxsie Sioux if she wanted to meet up after the show. There were thousands of complaints by phone and letter, TVs were booted in by fathers while children were eating their teas, and the headlines in the papers next day read, 'The Filth and the Fury'. Grundy – what a fucking rotter – was suspended from the show and the programme was scrapped a couple of months later. The interview went down in folklore, the Pistols had made centre stage and punk rock had arrived in a frenzied rage, juxtaposed to anarchy in the UK!

Though punk rock's roots stretch back to the United States and Canada, in the earlier Sixties: punk rock was originally used to describe garage musicians and certain bands back in the day, many of these bands using fuzzboxes. Bands like The Sonics, The Stooges and The Kingsmen were playing with no musical or vocal lean and often limited skill. Because they didn't know the rules of music, they were able to break the rules. The Kingsmen had a chart hit with a cover version of Richard Berry's *'Louie Louie'*. Garage rock, garage punk and proto punk was the beginning of the later Seventies punk rock paroxysm. The Velvet Underground, managed by Andy Warhol, then slotted into the misshaped jigsaw puzzle. Next were the New York Dolls, Television and the Ramones; with most of these two-chord wonders having played the country, blue grass and blues club – CBGBs – in New York.

The eccentric Malcolm McLaren had observed bands at CBGBs while in America and flew back to The Smoke in 1975, inspired by the new scene. McLaren had also not long ago renamed an 'anti-fashion' shop he ran with his girlfriend, Vivienne Westwood, to *Sex*, which was situated on Kings Road. The boutique stocked outlandish schummter; bondage and fetish gear too. In less than a year, McLaren had created the Sex Pistols. The rest went down in the annals as pure mania and total disorder.

The Sex Pistols, The Clash and The Damned were recognized as the vanguard of a new musical movement. Rebellious youths expressed their appreciations for punk bands by dancing in a style likened to touching a live electric cable while in the process of having an epileptic fit. At concerts they threw beer – what a waste – over the band members and gozzed phlegm and greenies, containing toenail, into the lead singer's face. Spitting became integral as gratitude and admiration of bands in this major cultural phlegmenon!

Punks rejected everything and they had an anti-establishment, anti-authoritarian, ant-capitalist, anti-social, ant-this, anti-that and anti-anything that there was to be anti about; and they even seemed anti-them-selves–self-harming sometimes – with their, 'couldn't give a toss' ideologies and unreasoning mentality. Punk song lyrics were blunt and to the point, usually containing social and political issues. The groups weren't trend-setters, though; their chief objective was to shock and outrage; a one-or-two fingered salute at society. Punks indicated they wanted to destroy passers-by too. A rather disturbed, but also complex, state of mind? Punk is aesthetically embraced by its legion of followers, but repulsed by bemused onlookers and outsiders.

The classic punk rock ensemble was a ripped T-shirt, motorcycle jacket, and tight, torn dirty jeans. Other clobber could sway from army jackets to flasher macs, military or bondage pants, long sleeve cheesecloth *Destroy* T's or Dennis the Menace black and red stripy jumpers. Charity shops, Army & Navy stores and jumble sales were also raided in a DIY ethos. Safety pins or dangly razorblade earrings through ears, locks and chains or dog collars and inverted crucifixes round the neck, studded wristbands and belts, jam jar lid badges and sewn on group name patches, Swastika armbands and bum flaps accessorised the look. Fluorescent socks with unpolished black DMs, unbrushed beetlecrushers or filthy baseball sneakers for prancing the night away. Hair would be spiked to extensive lengths, elaborately dyed or mohawked. Drugs of choice were speed, to whip oneself into a rabid state or, sniffing glue to hallucinate and let your emotions run wild.

Even the artwork that illustrated albums, EPs and single covers, punk-zines, flyers and gig posters was unique. Glowing, vibrant colours adorned such items with various sized letters; on the surface looking like they'd been cut out of newspapers and tackily glued on. The exemplary example being, the Sex Pistols LP cover, *Never Mind the Bollocks*.

The, *I swear I was (I wasn't) there* gig at the Lesser Free Trade Hall, Manchester, the gig that changed the world *forever*, arguably, occurred when the Sex Pistols performed a set on the 4th June 1976. It was a gig that inspired a Manc generation to form their own bands, or take up a solo career, or become involved in the music industry in some form or capacity. Yes, the gig was a catalyst for the 30-40 idiosyncratic nonconformists in attendance. Though the amount of folk who allegedly state they attended the LFTH gig are twofold: those that have stayed at the Radisson Hotel, in the now converted Grade II Edwardian listed building than have farted under the white linen sheets in its 263 rooms since the hotel opened in 2004. Or twofold, those who say they witnessed Denis Law from the terraces of Old Trafford, score with back-heeler for Man City in a 1-0 win that relegated Man Utd, in the last game of the season 1973/74 to the Second Division. Get a grip, will you.

The legendary concert didn't change the support bands' lives forever, though. Solstice, a Heavy Metal band hailing from a little village, Tockholes, that lies in Lancashire's West Pennine Moors, didn't go on to rock the world. But the LFTH gig was recently voted one of 'the' important concerts of all time, rubbing shoulders with the likes of Woodstock and Live Aid.

The second gig that the Sex Pistols played at the LFTH, on 20th July 1976, saw the Wythenshawe band Slaughter & The Dogs supporting them, along with the Buzzcocks. This may be the gig that everyone *was* at? At the time Manchester's fledgling music scene was concentrated around the Electric Circus club, which gave encouragement to several bands, including Alberto y Lost Trios Paranoias, Buzzcocks, John Cooper Clarke, The Distractions, John Dowie, The Drones, The Durutti Column, The Fall, The Freshies, Joy Division, Magazine, Ed Banger and The Nosebleeds, The Passage, as well as my all time favourite band, Slaughter & The Dogs.

With Manchester having the Electric Circus club for the next budding peer group of rockers, which venues did the rival cities have that were rocking? London had The Roxy, whose doors were bolted shut in April 1978, (it is the flagship store for the swimwear brand Speedo nowadays) and the 100 Club, that still holds gigs and Northern Soul nights. The range of bands for the capital could fill an A-Z phonebook directory from Adam & the Ants to the Zeros. Liverpool had Eric's, closed by the police following a drugs raid in 1980, but recently reopened in September 2011, over 30 years on.

Scousers weren't seemingly that big on forming punk bands; Big In Japan, Elvis Costello and Teardrop Explodes were as near punk rock as you got.

Preston had the Warehouse, and still does; and the group Youthenasia, plus New Suburbia, who turned down a contract with Rabid Records.

King Rocker

Ronnie Sharpe's musical tastes were catered for on the solids of rock 'n' roll. Only when punk rock rocked the world, and Sheffield, did it feed his ravenous hunger pangs for fresh, raw, meat and two veg musical rock that Ronnie needed, as well as his appetite for live bands.

Ronnie: *1977 arrived and booted the music industry straight up the arse. glam rock had run its course and a new underground movement that first surfaced in the late summer of 1976 breathed new life into the disco and Abba dominated charts. I can't remember exactly where I first heard punk, but it was most likely at the Penthouse Club. A rousing little three minute number entitled 'Stranded' by an Australian band, The Saints, became the first single I'd bought for about four years.*

The punk scene in Sheffield didn't really get going until early-to-mid 1977. The Pistols, supported by The Clash – who were playing their first gig outside London – appeared at the Black Swan pub in July 1976. Just four people were in the audience. Over the years I've spoke to at least 20 people who swear to god they were there that night. The truth is though; there was only me and these three punk birds who I was shagging at the time present at the gig… yeah right!

The first punks started gathering in the down-market, yet up-beat Crazy Daisy basement bar on High Street in the city centre. When the Penthouse introduced a 'Punk Night' held every Monday, they made the place their headquarters. With a 10p admission fee, and all drinks at 10p a shot, it should have made the place an alcoholic's paradise, but surprisingly I never saw the place full, or even half-full. A hardcore group of about 30-to-40 punks would hang around the dance floor with few more punters who were there for the cheap drinks, and the regulars who just about lived in the place made up the rest of the audience.

Most of the punks were into the look and the scene, rather than the music. Who could blame them? It was a new teenage revolution, anti- establishment shit, and all young kids, no matter what era they live in, need heads to turn when they walk down the street.

Jonesy, a young Dronny (Dronfield) lad and his bird, Patsy, both aged around 18-19, were part of the punk scene. I use to have a chat with them in the Penthouse, but they always seemed a bit nervous. Jonesy had too much respect to ever blank me, but I could see him keeping one eye on his new buddies, who were maybe thinking, 'what's Jonesy doing talking to that old cunt dressed like someone out of Status Quo.'

There'd always been a scene based around music and fashion in Sheffield, and indeed every other major town and city in the UK. Maybe it wasn't quite a closed-shop, but being on the fringe, I never felt like I really belonged to any of them.

Going back to my mid-teen years of The Esquire and the Mojo clubs, there was a crowd who thought they were a bit better than all the rest. There were a sort of an elite band of middle-class, avant-garde trendsetters who looked down on anybody who wasn't dressed up to the second. Perhaps it went back even further to the days of the teddy boys and the City Hall dances of the 1940s.

Many of the Sheffield punks soon moved on to the next big thing – the mod revival. A couple of years later, the same in-crowd, dressed as 'New Romantics' pretended to dig Spandau Ballet and Duran Duran. It was quite obvious they were following the trend rather than the music.

Tiff (a lass I was living with at the time) and me went to the punk nights every week (it must have been a brief period of harmony we were going through) and we got well in to the music but not really into the scene. At 26, I felt a little bit too old to be a punk. I did, however, have my hair cut short for the first time in over 10 years, dug out my old leather rocker jacket and donned a pair of tight black jeans and baseball boots. So, I was 'kinda' punkish. The Ramones 'Blitzkrieg Bop' and The Clash's 'White Riot' gave me a buzz close to the one I'd experienced when I first heard 'Gloria' back in 1964. Punk had a kind of Sixties feel and that's why I think it appealed to me. The good vibrations had returned, we even got up and pogoed like lunatics once or twice.

Once again rock 'n' roll had reinvented itself. One hundred miles an hour, raw, hard-core rock 'n' roll that grabbed you by the bollocks. But more importantly the three chord, three minute songs of verse, chorus, verse, chorus, verse, end, had made a comeback. The political side of the movement wasn't lost on me, but I really didn't give a fuck how many people were on the dole as long as I wasn't one of them.

The Good The Bad And The Ugly

In an archetypal Northern town like Preston, punk rock made a major impact on some townsfolk when it finally rode into our backwater by pony and trap. Rob (or Trebor, his graffiti tag sprayed on countless gable ends in the concrete jungle where he lived back then), a mate of mine, that punk lyrics encapsulated just how he felt in his teens, also had a desire to watch punk bands live. Once, whilst attending one such gig – Preston's most infamous concert at that – he had observed a catastrophic incident unfold.

Rob: *In 1978, although this was exciting era music wise, I had the misfortune to be at the most notorious punk concert in Preston, ever. Not since the teddy boys of the Fifties, or the mods and rockers of the Sixties, did music have such a conflicting influence over the nation.*

Punk rock had arrived, bursting onto the music scene with its aggressive attitude blowing away all the cobwebs and the popsy insignificant music of the time. Although I never did take to the punk uniform of DIY ethic, Mohican haircuts or safety-pins (safety-pins, were for putting in nappies not holding clothes together). But clothes were, and are still, a large part of my life.

Preston saw its fair share of bands doing the rounds in this era. In 1976 when the Sex Pistols materialised like a thrashing, musical mutation that stuck a finger up to the meaning of conforming, the 'Anarchy Tour' was arranged. This also featured The Dammed and The Clash, and the tour had been booked to play in Charter Theatre, housed in Preston's Guildhall.

An expectant youthful local audience waited with bated breath. However because of what had happened and been broadcast on the Bill Grundy Show, Preston Council pulled the plug. The gig was moved to Lancaster University, which also later declined the pleasure of hosting the bands.

Good: *Being positive or desirable in nature; not bad or poor.*

Having the qualities that are desirable.

PNE had been promoted to the dizzy heights of the old Division Two, on goal difference, under the guidance of the 'King of All Colgate Smiles', Mr Nobby Stiles. The goals from the dynamic duo up front Mike Elwiss and Alex Bruce secured this – 'Super' Bruce finished up the leading goal scorer of Division Three that year too. The only sour note, if you can call it that, saw us missing out on playing the Donkey Lashers again; they went in the opposite direction from Division Two down into Division Three and, "The Blackpool Boys they cried out loud..." If my memory serves me right, they were relegated by just one point, finishing on 37 points and the five or six teams above them finishing on 38 points, putting our derby game on hold, yet again, leaving a very bittersweet taste in the mouths of the Preston Boys. This was also the year I met Lorraine, who was to be, and still is, my wife (having to put up with me and my actions, I sometimes wonder why). Not only is she my best friend, she is also the glue of my life, the bit that holds my world together, even when sometimes it looks like it may fall apart.

Bad: *Misbehaving, disobedient, naughty, unpleasant, disturbing, inferior poor in quality.*

Just over 9,000 spectators turned out at Deepdale to watch North End beat Carlisle United, to keeping them within touching distance of the Third Division leaders. But despite an entertaining match with two penalties, it was the action that took place off the pitch which sparked the highlights of the game, as fans fought running battles on the Town End.

Saturday evening in May 1978, the mates and I went to the Vibrators concert. 'Automatic Lover', their only song to reach the charts Top 40, earned them national recognition and got them onto Top of the Pops. On entering the Polytechnic – now the University of Central Lancashire – the room that was hosting the event was a round venue, a mirrored auditorium (later it would become the gladiators fighting arena) with large carpeted steps circling the dance floor. The room soon filled with a 500 to 600 strong- audience.

The support band, The Depressions, came on stage dressed in black with blond spiky hair. The DPs music was typically three chords stuff – fast and furious. Although not as manic as normal for a punk concert, there was still a great atmosphere and we all surged towards the stage as the chords echoed around the room. Towards the end of their session (the bit where a band likes to talk about "how great it is to be here in this town") me and my mate managed to get our way onto the stage just as the DPs exploded into another track, which turned out to be the last song of the evening. Not knowing the words to the song, or wanting to look stupid for climbing onto the stage without reason, we started to chant PNE songs into the spare adjacent microphone. This was rudely interrupted by us being pushed off the stage by ugly looking roadies, back into the pogoing and spitting crowd below.

Ugly: *Displeasing to the eye, unsightly, repulsive or offensive in any way.*

Within the next few minutes all hell let loose, with fights breaking out all over on the dance floor. People were throwing glasses or whatever they could get their hands on as people screamed and ran in different directions in a chaotic manner. As the main lights came on, attempting to defuse the rioting mob and calm the situation, I started to observe the people around me. In the centre of the floor I saw one lad go down under a barrage of blows from a group surrounding him. As he went down one of the guys in the surrounding group hit him with a chair. He laid motionless with a large pool of blood around his head which looked almost black in colour. The rioting only stopped with the arrival of the police, and simultaneously a voice came over the PA system announcing that the concert had been cancelled and everybody would be required to provide their details to the police prior to leaving.

Once outside, being a local lad, I now felt somewhat safe in the environment. A mate and I started to walk home over hearing different groups telling each other of their actions or what they had just witnessed. It was at this point that we were approached by a group of lads. My mate, who must have had more wits about him at the time than I did, managed to run off. I blame alcohol for the lack of awareness; I was under the influence of drink, but not really drunk though. I was surrounded by a group of five lads who pronounced to be from Blackpool and aggressively enquired where I was from. It's funny how your brain automatically kicks into self-defence mode when things don't look good. I spurted out "Kirkham..." Almost immediately "Whereabouts then?" replied a voice within their group. At this point my knowledge of Kirkham was non-existent, again it must have been the beer, and my brain couldn't react fast enough for an explanation. Being totally surrounded, and the awkward pause before I got kicked in felt like an eternity, although it could have only been a few seconds. Given what I had just seen, my stomach was already turning somersaults and my heart was pounding. Once their first punch was thrown it seemed a signal to the rest of the group to steam into me. When it eventually happened it came as a kind of relief because the waiting was doing my head in – if you've been in a situation like this you know what I mean, and once it starts, you don't worry anymore.

During the one-sided onslaught, of which they were almost knocking each other over in their attempt to tear me apart, I was knocked to the floor and immediately curled into a ball to protect my face from further damage. Almost as quickly as it started they stopped and went looking for their next victim. As I got to my feet, my body was aching and claret was all down my face and clothes. I then dusted myself down and hobbled home.

Over the next few days the concert made major news in the local Lancashire Evening Post and on national TV. 'One man dead and three hospitalised following a punk concert' was the headline with the police making promises to catch the killer.

A Preston man was initially charged with the murder of a 22-year-old, who was also from Preston. But later he was acquitted of the crime. The police then classed the death as football related and turned their attention, towards the Blackpool boys there that night. No-one was ever convicted of the crime. The ensuing adverse national publicity also led to the Depression's guitarist leaving the band, and put an end to the band's career.

Fast forwarding to 2012, some 34 years later and I still enjoy going to punk gigs around the country, with the same mates I still go to football with.

Although these days the only disorder I will be causing is an OCD one. The clothes, like the rest of us have moved on, but being a creature of habit, I still find the articles by CP, amongst others, are classic clothing. Massimo Osti used different innovative materials to create each season's coats, including the Mille Miglia, which have, in conjunction with other British terrace fashion labels, stood the test of time.

Also, the death of a Preston man (RIP) on St George's Day 2009 in Lancaster, after a bar-room brawl involving lads from Preston, Blackpool, Lancaster and other surrounding areas, led the police to believe it was football related... So, you see, things haven't really changed, have they?

The House Ware To Be

I want to take you back to where it all began: my absorption and engrossment of punk came to the fore in 1978, when I'd had enough of coming a cropper and nose-diving off my skateboard. Slinging the thing behind the bin, in the bin-store, with a dislocated thumb and once more a split knee, which bloody hurt, it was time for a change of direction with my feet, ears and dresscode. I'd watched punk mature – if that's the appropriate word – on 'Top of the Pops' and listened to the late night Radio one John Peel Show, on my wireless. I also became a master of tape-recording punk on my birthday present, a Philips cassette recorder. I would sit in my bedroom on Sundays, index finger on the record push button, between 5pm and 7pm, waiting for Simon Bates to countdown the *official* compiled top selling 40 singles of that week, on the Radio one 'Chart Show'. You had to be quick off the mark before Bates jabbered over a punk track near the end of its three minutes airplay. I had stacks of BASF C30s, C60s, and C90s, go! The bleeders were fuckers for snapping, though. Then collecting vinyl became my vice. I had racks of artistic picture sleeves; coloured vinyls and obscure shapes. Some, I have to this day.

By late 1978 I'd began dressing the part too; scruffed up hair, a drawing pin through my ear (done at school, for a laugh), logoed band T-shirts ordered from *'Sounds'* magazine, striped jumpers, Wrangler straight jeans, or 'owt that Frank Clarke stocked, and DMs. F. H. Clarke had an Army & Navy store on the outskirts of the town and many a trip would be made to Frank's on Saturday mornings. Frank always wore a grey warehouse coat, white shirt and tie, his dark hair slicked back with an oil leak disaster of brilliantine, and he always seemed to have a un-tipped Park Drive or a Wills Capstan cig on the go. "Right then lads, I'll see what has arrived this week, shall I?" he'd say as he cut the strings from the brown paper bundles on the counter with a pair of scissors. In his compact shop there was hardly room to let-rip with shelves crammed floor to ceiling with ex-military combat wares, emergence service uniforms and industrial clothing. Standout items were a pair of brown hessian/canvas leg-hugging strides and a beige full-length overcoat, which I adorned with punk lyrics and slogans.

St Maria Gorreti's Catholic Club held an over-18s disco on Wednesday nights, and at the grand old age of 14, I managed to blag a membership and the bar was open. Most of the lads present were under-18 anyway. The DJ played three records on the bounce of each music genre in turn to please the crowd which consisted of mods, rockers (who danced in a long line, fingers through their jeans belt loops and dipping right to left, left to right, each twice, before changing, like a funky chicken to Status Quo) three or four Northern Soul boys, two teddy boys and a gaggle of girls wanting pop and disco – death to disco, I say. Us punks would high kick, pogo and generally go radio rental on the dance floor to our three minute heroes. A couple of pints of sass or snakebite would see us all leathered after raiding our parents drinks stash beforehand. In the backdrop of our schizzing out was a life size Jesus Christ nailed to a crucifix as we loudly sang "I am an anti-Christ ..." Fuelled with booze, the inevitable fight would breakout too due to musical tastes and dislikes. Once we teamed up with the rockers and knocked seven shades out of the soulies and mods outside the club when the disco had finished at 10pm.

The next step on the ladder was to attend the Warehouse. This was either with my mum's blessing, when she advanced me a few pretty greens, (I hadn't dare tell me dad – mums are great, aren't they?) or I'd climb out of my bedroom window when grounded on more than one occasion. Just into the 1980s, I fulfilled my next goal.

The Warehouse – Preston's Haçienda – was a hidden backstreet nightclub at the bottom of St John's Place in Preston town centre, situated to the left hand side of the town's Parish Church, and its bygone hewn gravestones. On Thursday nights the club was a haven for punks, skins, new wavers, waifs and strays, pissheads, oddballs, the curious and one or two norms/squares who'd stumbled across the place in a drunken haze by falling through the doors. The approach to the club was a narrow granite-set street; a bedroom store to the left, a four foot high stonewall that encircled the church to the right. If there was a band on that night, there was usually a 'drunk and disorderly' queue, de-formed, gone nine, waiting for the big black doors to open as the *thud thud* of the base from the DJs speakers would pulsate through the thick, white walls of the building. Or if one the 'biggies' in the punk world had been booked, sometimes on a different week night, tickets had to be purchased weeks in advance. This because the club only held around the hundred mark.

Following visits to the 'normal' punk pub hangouts; the Dog & Partridge, Tom's Tavern and maybe The Britannia, Old Black Bull or The Sun, the lads I went with ventured across town to the Warehouse. If there was no queue, you would *bang* on the door and a minute or so later one of the two doormen would open up. Just inside the doors was the till, and to the rear a secure cloakroom. Entrance fee paid, which varied on whoever was playing, you turned left through a second set of doors under the watchful eye of the doormen. BOOM; the music punched you full in the face, leaving a g-force impression and your ears bleeding. To the left were the lavs, which were covered in bodily fluid stains and graffiti and stunk to the high heaven. The his or hers toilets were only used when the bladder was busting by both sexes in whichever of the two wasn't flooded. Or, the cubical wasn't occupied by some lovers, having a knee-trembler. To the right was a small, 8ft be 8ft dance floor with its own speakers and spotlights and a brick pillar on each corner, situated next to the stairs.

The stairs led to half a dozen dimly-lit alcoves with a central fixed table and benches either side that overlooked the tiny dance area below. The dance floor was routinely frequented by a lonesome pretty vacant, too-drunk-to-fuck punk, giving it his all. Once upstairs an alcove may have a courting couple engaged in activities best known to man – a punkette giving head – or crashed out lads and lasses. There was also a kitchen where you could order chicken and chips, or burger and chips, or chips in a basket.

Back downstairs; the floors under foot were covered in quarry tiles which added to the din as tunes bounced off the surrounding solid surfaces. The walls were painted an off white. To the left were cast iron tables and chairs; to the right was the bar. The hairy-nosed, scruffy old bloke who owned the Warehouse worked behind the bar, as well as a barmaid, serving up dishwater Lion bitter. If the beer wasn't bad enough, it was served in plastic glasses following a fracas with the Morecambe and Lancaster punks one evening down to different opinions of dancing techniques, the night ending in total bedlam and mass carnage.

Coming away from the bar, shaking your head in disgust after taking a sip of the swill in the placcy glass, to your left was the DJ box with its chainmail curtains. Dropping down a couple of steps was the aluminium dance floor, approximately 15 to 20ft square. When beer slops ended up on the aluminium it was treacherous underfoot while attempting to pogo; many an outfit was ruined. And raised up a couple of steps was the stage. The setting behind where the bands strutted their stuff was organic, bare brick walls; profoundly urban chic indeed. All-in-all, a compact gaff. A gaff where bands *should* be watched and where bands *should* be listened to; plain and condensed venues, not venues such as stadiums or open air concerts. *Raw, pure and simple.*

Punk characters that made the weekly jaunt to the Warehouse were christened with some peculiar names: there was a Weasel, a Worzel, a Peacock, a Flid, a Carrots, a Mad Dog, a Boggy, two Kings and many more notable names that have slipped the memory bank. There were the punkettes too. One, who I won't name, was a very accommodating lady.

You know the sort, butter wouldn't melt in her petite mouth, cute smile, girl next-door type but, she liked her backdoors kicked-in. Like I say, this lass would accommodate all comers, and I mean all comers. (And no, I didn't, the truth.) She always wore a black velvet jacket, short skirt and little boots. Lads would disappear with her in the loos or ask for a pass-out for a spot of fresh air. Whether it be a back alley, in a shop doorway or over a gravestone, they'd be back within five minutes – wham, bam, thank you madam.

Even if the river ran red, she'd let them take the dirt road instead. One lad bragged he let both barrels loose all over her face, leaving her mirroring a plasterer's radio. Another lad, came back to where we were standing once with a wide grin and her knickers on his head; his trophy for his conquest. I bet he wasn't so proud of himself the next morning when the scratching began or when a trip to the clap clinic was a necessity.

Outside the Warehouse, come 2am, the beads of sweat that had turned into a flood and saturated your T-shirt during the course of the night, (due to the intense heat created by the sardine can packed venue) now turned to steam and rose skywards in the cold night air as we made our way to the 'Real McCoy' for a flame grilled burger to munch on the three mile walk home. Gone 4am I'd hit the sack; I'd rise three hours later for my paper round, and then school, in a right fit-for-nothing state.

In the first month of a new decade, the Eighties, I went to my first Warehouse gig. On that night were the anarcho-punks Poison Girls, Honey Bane and Crass. I was 14 at the time. And they didn't even ask me my age when I gained entry. I'd recited the 14th of December 1961 in my head all day too, so I wouldn't balls-up if asked my age. I'd asked for a pint of beer in the Bull & Royal pub in town, though. That night walls to the rear of the stage was decked out in daubed, anti-war paraphernalia flags and banners which also promoted animal rights, feminism and direct action. The Crass logo represented an amalgamation of several icons of authority, including the Christian cross, the Swastika, and the Union Jack, combined with a two-headed Ouroboros to symbolise the idea that power will eventually destroy itself. All very confusing to a 14 year old. It still is now! They had a back-projected slideshow and video montages going on before and after each group performed, who were all dressed head-to-toe in black, accompanied with propaganda chanting, speeches and weird music being played too. So what, I don't give a toss.

The next time I crossed the Warehouse's threshold was on the 28th February 1980, when Joy Division played there, and where the live album *Preston 28 February 1980* was recorded (Though, for some unknown reason, it wasn't released until May 1999). Also, the gig was just 12 weeks before Ian Curtis tragically took his own life – RIP. I was lock, stock and barrel hooked on live gigs and the Warehouse by now, and I don't mean Peter Hooked.

Over the coming years groups had me doing an array of weird stuff; the Notsensibles, sick of being normal. Athletico Spizz 80, looking for Captain Kirk. Discharge, fighting the system. Salford Jets, walking round town looking at the squares. The Exploited, fucking the mods. UK Subs, had a stranglehold on me. Theatre of Hate, believing in the west world. Angelic Upstarts, wound me up like a clockwork orange. Black Flag had me rolling round the stage and then the dance floor before getting thrown out of the Warehouse!

The night Black Flag played the Warehouse, I was standing to the right side of the stage next to the speakers and amps. I'd never heard or listened to Black Flag before, so I was observing their stage presence and soaking up the Yankee band's aggressive lyrics and music. Also the distinctive showmanship of the shirtless lead singer and his tattooed, muscular physic – not in a gay way, like. This guy was Henry Rollins. Anyway, while watching them hammer out their fourth or fifth number, the bassist *firmly* nudged in to me. Or so I thought he'd accidentally collided in to me. A few seconds later he did it again. Then once again, harder. He was going to do it once more, so I pushed him, with meaning. He stumbled towards Rollins, regained his composure, while he carried on strumming his bass, and then ran in my direction, sideways. This time he didn't have chance to connect, a fist in the face stopped him dead in his tracks.

Over the following two minutes I had a bass guitar slammed over my head, exchanged blows with Rollins and was then grabbed in a headlock by a doorman and abruptly thrown though the exit doors. In the morning, when I glanced in the mirror, it looked like I'd had a scrap with a cat due to all the scratches and cuts to my head and face. And I'd also found out what slam-dancing was.

Rollins was interviewed some years later on Channel 4's *The Word*, by Terry Christian. Christian asked Rollins if, during Black Flag's rise to fame, he found UK audiences more accepting of the band's aggressive style. In general yes, he replied, adding that there were some very rough places in the UK, though. Like where? Christian asked, a little shocked. "Preston!" stated Rollins.

'I can't remember that I ever had just a minute of stage fright' – Henry Rollins. (Really?)

All good things come to an end, and I began frequenting the Warehouse less and less, with fewer and fewer bands playing there. There was a name change too, to Raiders, but not for long. The club now has three levels with each having its own DJ spinning different themes of music most nights to mainly students and under 30 year olds. Live music is no-more. Though I still make the effort to get over to the Rebellion weekend in Blackpool once a year, where punk bands past and present grace the Winter Garden stages. And I also attend the odd gig in and around the north-west. But those vital days of indulgence in the early-Eighties at the Warehouse are cherished with much joy and glee.

Punk's Not Dead: A New Wave

Although you may be thinking punk has rotted and decayed into the musical crust and mantel of yesteryear – just as dissimilar, off-the-shelf music cults and bands have – punk rock hasn't. Fat punks aren't dead – I know, 'cause I am one. The core punk bands are as strong-minded and resolute as ever. Yes, punk rock is still thrashing to this day; with British bands such as the UK Subs, whose lead singer, Charlie Harper, is at least 70 at the time of typing but, he still has a full-head of green hair and still does two or three gigs a week. The Exploited, a second-wave group, whose *'Barmy Army'* you don't fucking mess with (I know all too well when

I got caught up in the chaos at a gig). And, The Mekons, hailing from Leeds. These are some of the long-standing performers that have never stopped gigging and pogoing from the days they first took to the stage in the Seventies. All three bands' line-ups have changed on more than one occasion, though. They just won't fade away, and keep on rocking to this day.

Outgrowths and by-products of punk rock were/are, New Wave, anarcho–punk, hardcore, Oi!, emo, psychobilly and pop punk (Whatsallthataboutthen?). Looks and un-uniform dress can still be seen worn by glam punks, crusties, skater-punks and goths too, as well as a new generation of punks today.

The newer-style punks putting it out there are the mainstream pop punk band Green Day, who have sold over 70 million records since forming in 1987, and are one of the biggest groups on the world circuit today in any music genre. There's also the wannabe Sid Vicious, Pete Doherty, the alleged poet/artist/singer who thinks he has the attributes of John Cooper Clarke, John Rotten and Billy Idol rolled into one. To me, he's just big baby who takes liberties and is a shambles of a so-and-so, and I can't stand *him* now...

Was punk the greatest rock 'n' roll swindle EVER, and did it leave partisans feeling that they'd been cheated? For me, no, and Ian felt the same.

Ian W: *I'm not sure of the exact date, but it was in our HQ, the garage, after a fruitful afternoon of 'shopping', that a tinny transistor radio perched on an old toolbox was turned up full blast as a Radio one DJ introduced The Sex Pistols and their latest single. A lead guitar started the proceedings followed by a heavy drum beat and then... the speaker on the old wireless almost blew as a huge slab of guitar joined the foray and "THERE'S NO POINT IN ASKING YOU'LL GET NO REPLY" belted out. The lyrics combined with the fast, furious instruments (even on the crappy radio) were like nothing I'd ever heard before. It was like Slade, but louder. It was like Bowie, but faster. And the bloke singing sounded angry, very angry.*

Pretty Vacant was to be my first taste of punk rock. Okay, I'd missed a few other classics in the months leading up to the event, but then again, I was barely a teenager. I'd no older brothers, or sisters to influence me, so this music was all mine.

Over the next few weeks, more and more of this music was discovered by a gang of awkward 13 year olds in a small town in Lancashire. The Pistols had been going for over a year; The Clash's album had been out months, and The Stranglers, The Damned and The Jam had all made singles and albums. We were months behind, but then again, this was Leyland. 'Gary Gilmore's Eyes' by The Adverts was to be the first punk single I actually bought from Brewers Record Shop in Leyland. I'd seen the band on Top Of the Pops and walked home with the singles picture cover on full display for anyone who was interested.

Later on in the year the owner of the record store had the marvellous idea of a punk/New Wave box on the counter. Purchases of vinyl from there would take place on a weekly basis; 'God Save The Queen' by the Pistols (finally), 'Your Generation' *by Generation X,* 'White Riot' *by The Clash,* 'Rockaway Beach' *by The Ramones and* 'Nasty Nasty' *by 999, but to name a few. The singles cost 50 pence each with an album a staggering £2.25.*

And with funds not readily available it wasn't long before our 'shopping' skills were put to good use in liberating the contents of the punk/New Wave box. It was just too easy. As soon as the shopkeeper disappeared in to the stockroom looking for a fictitious release by a fictitious band, it was time for the lucky dip in the box on the counter. At the very worst you could end up with a Boomtown Rats single. At the very best, 'Complete Control' *by The Clash. My record collection grew weekly, and by Christmas 1977, I was trading a few of my ill-gotten gains to kids at school. Musical snobbery was happening at an early age. Loads of acts were cashing in on the punk scene and some of the kids who were just getting in to the music couldn't tell the difference.* 'The Drummer Man' *by a particularly awful group called Tonight, was sold for £1.50, just because of the picture sleeve. My buyers were ignorant and had been probably listening to their older brothers Genesis albums.*

I'd to wait until my birthday for my first album, and I was the last of our little gang to possess it, 'it' being 'Never Mind the Bollocks' *by the Sex Pistols. My Mum actually went to the record shop and bought it. I've no idea how she asked for it without feeling embarrassed. Between our gang we had most of the early punk sounds. Every week more and more groups were found, the more we found, the more we wanted to find. Slaughter & the Dogs* 'Where Have All the Bootboys Gone' *and Surburban Studs* 'I Hate School' *were yet more lucky dips in our local record shop.*

On the football front the usual post-Christmas slump was nowhere to be seen, as Preston were still near the top to the table. Division Three was full of teams with little or no away support but a notable exception occurred in March 1978, with the visit of Bradford City. Running battles took place at the back of the Town End away stand, I was informed. Because two hundred miles away we were having our own running battles at an England Schoolboy International match. It was my first visit to Wembley courtesy of a school trip. The journey down had been like a chimp's tea party with various 12 to 15 year olds giving the teachers a bad time. It was once inside the ground the teachers realised coaches from all over the country had dropped of their contents of unruly teenage boys. Many of the kids on the trip had seen what can happen on the football terrace, and now here was a chance to participate, albeit at entry level. The Spurs fans to our right began taking an interest in Joe's PNE scarf and the first "Where you lot from?" was heard, just before fighting started. Actual punches were thrown as 14 year olds from London and Leyland discovered what the 'buzz' at the match was all about. A passing teacher broke up the junior melee, separating the warring wannabees whilst calling for reinforcements. Further fun was had at half-time when an Arsenal fan spotted my Clash badge. "Give us ya fackin badge."

"Fuck off" I replied as more Arsenal juniors joined him and all of us traded kiddie punches on the stairwell.

The teachers probably thought they'd be in for a jolly day out on a freebie to the National Stadium. Not a chance. There's no such thing as a free lunch but there were was lots of ' free' goodies available at motorway service stations on the way home, much to the teacher's dismay.

By now the good old British jumble sale was becoming our main fashion outlet, numerous jackets were bought for pennies and 'punkified'. Felton's Army Surplus Shop in town was also a must for our DIY punk image. And footwear would consist of black Doc Marten's or 'bumpers' for £1.50. Trips into Preston became the norm mostly when PNE were playing away. For the sum of one pound, we could get a juvenile ticket for the train, a punk single of choice, and still have change for a bag of hot spuds from the Flag Market. There were four or five record shops in town, each having a punk/new wave section, and most of the shops still had listening booths too. The House of Records, up the steps from the outdoor market, was the place I heard 'White Man in Hammersmith Palais' by The Clash for the first time.

The sound coming out of the headphones in the listening booth was like a Reggae record, a bit heavier, and a bit faster, but I loved it – a view not shared by all my mates. Just down from the Flag Market was The Record Exchange and as the name suggests the owner would trade vinyl with any interested parties. I was interested and took my entire Slade collection – four albums and five singles. I came out of the shop with 'Oh Bondage Up Yours' by X Ray Specs, 'Aint Got A Clue' by The Lurkers, and 'I Don't Mind' by The Buzzcocks. Not much for what I went in with, but at the time I was more than happy.

A few weeks later, myself and Joe went into the shop which was full of Saturday morning customers. The owner was serving someone when Joe interrupted him and delivered a line to be remembered forever, "Fuck off please!" The manager just looked at Joe. Again Joe said "Fuck off please!" The shop fell into silence apart from the latest 'pop' sound playing through the speakers. The manager screamed "Get out or I'll throw you out". His face was red and he looked like he meant business. He may have taken my entire Slade collection for the price of three punk singles, but wasn't been told to fuck off twice by a 14 year old junior punk. As he was the manager of a record store selling punk music, why did it not occur that my mate was only asking for the new single by Wayne County and The Electric Chairs, the new single being called 'Fuck Off!'

Located just over the Ring Road, down Friargate, heading out of town, was the record shop that was to bear the most fruit. All above board I must add.

The shop's owner was a Scottish woman in her forties and she specialised in rockabilly plus original sounds from the Fifties and early Sixties. Most of the stuff was second hand too. Dodgy punters would turn up with a bag of singles and she would pay what she thought fit. Some of the records coming in to the shop were our type of stuff and this was an ideal situation. The owner hadn't a clue what they were worth, and the seller just wanted to make a few quid. This would mean hanging around the shop for hours, on most occasions, but it was worth it. Early punk singles were purchased for no more than 50 pence. Eater, Alternative TV, Chelsea, The Rezillos, The Maniacs, The Killjoys, the list was endless and all bought for a fraction of their value. The rockabilly-loving Jock woman liked to do a deal and a bundle of punk singles could be yours for a fiver. Anything not wanted in the bundle would be sold – at a large profit – to kids at school, kids who thought Plastic Bertrand's 'Ça Plane Pour Moi' was as good as it gets!

The Saturday trips to Preston would not be complete without a visit to the Palace Café. This was where all the older Preston punks hung out. Up the stairs and through the door you headed; it was like a different planet and at first quite intimidating for us 14 year olds from the sticks. The aroma of coffee and strange smelling tobacco added to the dingy atmosphere. Punks, bikers and hippies would each have their own tables. It must have been about two months before anyone spoke to us, and when they did, it was usually to take the piss. Most of the older Preston punks had dyed hair and wore biker jackets full of badges. Us upstarts being still at school would have been suspended forthwith at the mere hint of colour on our short spiky barnets. Many of the Palace regulars had seen all the bands appearing round Lancashire and the Pistols too when they'd played just outside Preston as early as 1976. The Rezillos, Adverts, Siouxsie and The Banshees and The Vibrators had all gigged in and around Preston. We'd missed the lot being kids, and some of the older Preston lot filled us in as we were a bit late getting into the scene. What did they expect, we'd just turned 14. What were they doing at 14? Probably listening to The Rubettes. It would be another year before we saw our first live band, but in the meantime it was time to take our music to the youth clubs of Leyland.

The Methodist Youth Club, on Turpin Green, was to become our regular haunt on Fridays. It was run by the church and the epicentre for14 to 16 year olds in Leyland by the late Seventies. The night would usually begin with a concoction of alcohol raided from our parent's drinks cabinet which would consist of anything available, including Blue Bols mixed with Advocaat and brandy. Or for the more discerning palate, Stone's Ginger Wine and whiskey with a hint of Cherry B. It was a case of get pissed, jump up and down to The Clash, and then usually throw *up in the toilets around nine o'clock. The youth club DJ played most of our sounds as long as there was no swearing on the record. And on more than one occasion, his ignorance of the music let him down badly, as 'GLC', by Menace, found its way on to the decks. Everything was fine until the chorus as half a dozen pissed up spiky tops sang "GLC, GLC, YOURRRR, SO FULL OF SHIT, SHIT, SHIT SHIT SHIT SHIT!" The record was banned along with several of us, but only for two weeks (us, that is).*

1978 turned out to be a great time to be a teenager in our part of Lancashire. The punk music continued to come thick and fast, and Preston North End made it back into Division Two. The last home game of the season prompted our little gang's first pitch invasion too. We had come prepared for the moment, unveiling a homemade banner declaring 'Never Mind the Bollocks, Here's PNE.' It was a strange scenario as Preston had not actually been promoted and we had to wait until a week later for Wrexham and Peterborough to draw nil-nil before North End gained promotion. My team were back in the big time – big for us, anyway.

By the time school broke up for Christmas, Blackburn Rovers had been battered 4-1, Burnley had completely filled the Town End, Stoke had almost taken the Kop, and I'd been on the pitch at Sheffield United, all very memorable moments. The Sheffield incident was not by choice, more a case of under estimating the opposition, namely big mushes in leather trenchcoats with the odd skinhead thrown in for good measure. Invading the pitch at Deepdale a few months earlier had been fun, but being chased on to the Bramall Lane pitch by blokes 10 years my senior and four stone heavier – wasn't much fun that day. Preston won the game 1-0. And by the time we were back on home soil, the day had been declared a 'good laugh.' We were ready for more too.

At the end of 1978 the second wave of punk bands was in full flow; Sham 69, Stiff Little Fingers, UK Subs and The Angelic Upstarts had all found their way into my record box. More importantly, my first gig was about to become a reality. The Guild Hall in Preston was to be the setting for what on paper appeared nothing special; Elvis Costello and the Attractions plus a support band. Support was provided by the legendary punk poet John Cooper Clarke and the American inventor of spiky hair, Richard Hell and his Voidoids. At the age of 15 years and three days, I'd witnessed my first live music, and like the forced pitch invasion and shenanigans in Sheffield, I wanted more. In 1979, more of everything was just round the corner.

The 'borrowed' concoctions became a thing of the past as we'd now found an off-license that would serve us. Strongbow cider and Special Brew, became the new pre youth club tipple. It was on a visit to the offy, that one of the lads discovered sherry on draught. All you had to do was bring your own container and the owner would fill it up from a large barrel on the counter for less than a pound. The amount of milk bottles going missing from the area must have been a great concern for the local dairies. A pint of sherry drunk from a milk bottle became many a 14-year-old's party piece.

Rockabilly Rebel

There were other rocking rebels knocking around in the mid-to-late Seventies too, rockabillies; and the amalgamation of rockabilly and punk produced, psychobillies. The rockabilly revival once again emerged from the States, just like original had, with the Stray Cats being at the forefront. Rockabilly is combination of rock 'n' roll, country & western – some cunt from Preston – swing and hillbilly. Lumberjack, bowling or Hawaiian shirts along with dungarees, ill-fitting or skinny jeans and beetlecrusher or brothelcreeper shoes were worn by these rebels. Their hairstyles were slicked-back, upswept pompadours. And the Pole Cats were the UK's number one group. Psychobilly sounds were a mixture of rockabilly and punk. The Meteors from London are credited as the original psychobilly band, though the origins of the name and genre of the style/sound stem from an American group, The Cramps, who first used the portmanteau phraseology, psychobilly, for their approach to music. Their costume was a seemingly thrown together conglomeration of rockabilly, skinhead and punk. The hairstyles were crazy forms of huge, bleached pompadours, cantilevered quiffs and patterned, shaved sides making followers of the cult look like extras in a B-movie horror flick. A well known goggle-wearing, wide grinning, flat-topped 'General of Terror' Chelsea bod, always reminded me of a well turned out psychobilly, for some reason.

Here's a brief insight into the cults from a bloke, Les Fowler, who was well into rockabilly and, who has had a book out there called *Dry Powder* about what else he has got up to during his hectic life.

Les: *It has to be said that the music and fashion of the Seventies was dire to say the least. Glam rock dominated the charts and the style of the day was Birmingham bags, platform shoes, flyaway collars and three star jumpers topped with a feather cut hairstyle! All-in-all, a right bag of bollocks, and none of this was for me. Through contacts in the local Marine Cadets – of which I was a proud member – I found myself a follower of the Fifties cult movement the teddy boys.*

I hasten to add that I didn't wear the ridiculous brightly-coloured suits that rip off bands such as Showaddywaddy favoured, although a skeleton in my cupboard is that I went to see them at the Guild Hall, twice.

Once I left school and found a job, I favoured iconic bespoke Edwardian suits in true Fifties style by an Italian tailor on the edge of the town centre. Gino was the last bespoke tailor in Preston and he closed his door for the final time at Christmas 2009, after 40 years. I also sported a short neat quiff, white short collared shirt, thin black tie and finally a pair of winklepicker boots or a plain pair of black leather beetle crushers that were bought from a shop in Lytham St Anne's.

In 1978 I joined the army and was away from Preston for long periods of time, but on my frequent returns I could usually be found propping up the bar in a town centre boozer called the Gaiety Bar. Despite what modern interpretations of the name might suggest, the occupants of the bar reflected the music and dress scene of the late Seventies and the early Eighties. Punk rockers, skinheads, mods, teddy boys, rockabillies and Rastafarians would rub shoulders, guzzling a variety of strong alcohol laced drinks while being watched over by a couple of West Indian bouncers.

Between 1978 and 1979, I was stationed in Nuneaton with the Junior Leaders Regiment Royal Artillery and was unable to make it to the Guild Hall Preston when Bill Haley played there on a tour of the UK. An ageing Haley provided a poor performance and left the stage early when he started getting abuse from the crowd. A stage invasion followed and all his instruments were smashed up including the original double bass which featured in the cult 1950s movie 'Rock Around the Clock.' The next day the local Lancashire Evening Post had headlines: 'Teddy Boys Run Riot as Bill Haley Stops the Rock.' A mate of mine sent me the newspaper clip and it had pride of place on my bed side locker next to my favourite pin up of the time.

Preston Rock 'n' Roll Appreciation Society was run by ageing throwback teddy boys from the Fifties at the Maudland Club which is just up the road from St Walburg's Church in Preston. The club would open every Sunday evening, and it's fair to say that a good night was usually had with regular bands playing such as Crazy Cavan and Rhythm Rockers. If I wasn't on duty at weekends I would usually travel home on a Friday night and head back to barracks Sunday evening so that I was back in camp bright eyed and bushy tailed for Battery Parade first thing Monday morning.

Apart from attending the Maudland I would spend just about every other available hour in the Gaiety Bar playing pool or just feeding the jukebox. On Sunday night I would be on the piss at the Maudland Club with my Puma holdall containing my freshly washed uniform rammed under a table in the bar area, waiting for me to snatch it up at about 10.20 pm and sprint to the railway station to catch the last train back to camp which left at 10.30pm sharp.

Around 1980 a coach load of lads and lasses headed down to a rock 'n' roll weekender at Caistor Holiday camp and I saw, for the first time, a new style of dress that the London lads were wearing: the Hepcat style of dress and haircut. This usually consisted of shaven heads at the sides, and back, with a flat top or quiff to the front. Bowling shirts and pegged trousers or bleached baggy jeans and moccasins or Ivy League crepe soled shoes were the clothes. The Hepcats favoured rockabilly which was basically rock music with a country & western influenced twist, such as Carl Perkins and Ray Campi.

The head honchos at the Rock 'n' Roll Society hated this new breed of upstarts and did everything in their limited powers to let the Hepcats know they were not welcome. The DJ refused to play rockabilly and the stewards/bouncers on the front door would refuse entry to anyone whose hair was too short or who looked generally Hepcatish! If the hierarchy thought Hepcats were bad, then worse was looming on the horizon with the emergence of rockabilly mixed with punk rock and fans that were called, psychobillies!

Psychobilly bands of the time were the Meteors, King Kurt and The Cramps. The style of dress was usually punk or skinheadish with big ridiculous quiffs on top of shaven heads. Psychobillies usually pogoed or just threw themselves around the dance floor and were most definitely barred from the Rock 'n' Roll society. The psychobilly gigs were usually at the Warehouse which was, and still is, an alternative nightclub down a back street in Preston city centre.

Another favoured venue for rockabillies and psychobillies was Jalgos, a West Indian Social Club that allowed its function room to be rented out for gigs. My most vivid memory of Jalgos were watching young Rastas and old Jamaicans playing dominoes and slamming them down on the table as hard as they possibly could while shouting some kind of insult at the bloke they were playing.

A character who used to be a regular at the Jalgos was a big scouse rockabilly called Frank. He was never backwards at coming forwards when it came to dishing out a bit of fist. And although I never had any problems with him, I knew a good few lads who had their lights punched out for just breathing in the same room as him.

One lad was a skinhead called Carl, who had a run-in with him one night. Frank threw Carl round like a rag doll, but every time we thought it was over Carl would spring back to his feet and launch himself at Frank again. Eventually Frank had Carl by his throat and was choking him till Carl was blue in the face and croaked "Let me go Frank!"

Frank replied "Not a fucking chance. If I let go you'll just come at me again."

Carl managed to squeeze out "I promise I won't Frank. It's over"

So Frank let go of Carl, and Carl flew back at Frank like an Exocet missile!

Frank never bothered Carl again after that.

I knew lads from all three styles of music; teds, rockabillies, pyshcobillies and skinheads too. I socialised with a cross section of them. Also my sense of dress and music influences reflected this, and I began adopting looks from each genre.

In early 1983 The Meteors played a gig at Preston Polytechnic backed by The Riverside Trio, a local band of rockabillies who, to this day, are still doing the circuit. The Poly was packed. I attended the concert with my younger brother who had recently left the Royal Marines and was a raging Hepcat. The audience was made up of psychobillies, rockabillies, skinheads and punk rockers. It was a great night, and at the end me and my brother staggered out and headed off to a chip shop called Umberto's at the bottom of Strand Road near the docks.

As we were staggering past the Fylde Tavern a brick whistled over our heads and we turned to see a group of bikers charging towards us. The Dog and Partridge pub in Preston has always been a bikers' boozer and it was a place that I used to have a quick pint in whilst heading up into town. A few bikers always turned up at rock 'n' roll dos, and were always welcome. So, it was unusual to see such an act of aggression. It turned out that one of the bikers had been at school with my younger brother and still held some kind of grudge. Anyway, we turned and did battle with them which resulted in us rolling around in the gutter of an alleyway next to a gents barbers amongst used condoms and white dog shit – (Why do you never see white dog shit anymore?). We were all too pissed to make any real go of the punch up and it fizzled out. All the strength had drained from my body and as I began coughing up lager which started running out of my nose.

All day dos were a big part of the rockabilly scene and a regular event was Manchester on Boxing Day each year. Big British bands at the time like Matchbox, Stargazers and the Stray Cats would top the bill and would attract crowds from across the north-west. They were usually excellent days out and coaches or mini-buses would be hired to get groups of us across there.

Getting back to my usual haunt of the time; the Gaiety Bar was managed by a scouser called Terry until the mid-Eighties, this until he moved on and took over the Adelphi, another public house in Preston. Terry had been big into the music scene in the Fifites and was involved in signing up some of the big British acts. He was a fountain of knowledge when it came to rock 'n' roll and the styles of the Fifties and he commanded a certain amount of respect from his customers.

When Terry had moved onto fresh pastures a bloke called John took over the boozer. John was OK, but only lasted a year or so. One fateful Friday night I turned up at bang on 7pm ready for a good session only to find the pub was closed. I hung around tutting and checking my watch for 10 minutes or so and with no sign of life I made my way over to the Guild Tavern, which was directly opposite and ordered a pint.

Over the next hour or so I watched through the window as all the regulars turned up and went through a similar ritual as me. We all gathered in the Guild Tavern, scratching our heads. The Gaiety remained closed for about a year. It had been our spiritual home and meeting place. It was the end of an era.

When the Gaiety reopened, it was an Eighties 'fun pub', and we were never really welcome. We adopted the Guild Tavern for a while but it hadn't got the same atmosphere, and lads started slowly drifting away from the scene.

I suppose they call it the natural progression and an ageing process. I also grew bored with the style so I had a number one all over and began listening to, and watching, ska. This was until The Housemartins reared their ugly heads. But I still think back to my rock 'n' roll years as some of the best of my life.

The Mod Revival

When the shock and outrage that punk rock had caused began to be *expected* – which at its beginnings would leave not only old dears with blue and pink rinses in their tight permed hair dead in their tracks gawping open cakeholed at the speed generations glued-up, mohican hairstyles and schummter but, by society in general – two new, well second comings really, appeared on the music and cultural front. Mod revivalist and 2-Tone rude boys and, ska and skinhead. The suited and black & white booted/shoed group, The Jam, had led the manor since hitting the charts in 1977 on the mod revival foray. Only The Jam, from Woking, couldn't be 'niched' mod. They'd slipped into the slipstream of the vacuum initially created by the purest, punk hardcore bands, only they were approved and held in high esteem by punks, New Wavers and, the then, new breed of mods alike. The Jam wore sharp suits, not ripped or tatty attire, but their music was fast and their lyrics expressed events in everyday life and the modern world.

On the back of the pre-eminent success of The Jam were Secret Affair, who had a following called Glory Boys. The East London Glory Boys decked themselves in basket-weave shoes, camel-hair suits and madras checked shirts. But, Secret Affair weren't the first second coming mod revival band of the Seventies to rear their pristine head. A former punk band, the Killermeters, from Huddersfield, were! More mod bands soon appeared on the scene: The Chords, The Merton Parkas, The Lambrettas, Purple Hearts and also plenty of others but, within 12 months, the mod revivalists took side stage to a newer commixture, 2-Tone and rude boys.

2-Tone: the movement, and record label, originated in the West Midlands, to be precise, Coventry. The brainchild behind the checkered 2-Tone music, label and rude boy movement was Jerry Dammers, with the succour of his chum and fellow band member of the Specials, Horace Panter. Dammers smelted ska, rocksteady, reggae and up-beat punk/new wave collectively and forged the music and term known as 2-Tone. Bands that strummed harmonized 2-Tone were The Specials, The Selecter, The Beat – the odd ones out due to their London location, Madness. Contrasts of black and white toned togs were *sine qua non* to the camp. Black, snug- fitting suits or Sta-Prest strides were partnered with white, button-down collared shirts; narrow black ties, pork-pie hats and tasseled-topped loafers was the preferred choice of outfit by their following. The only splash of colour was red; top-pocket hankies, socks or half-inch wide braces. Hair was cropped to a number-three or four crewcut or, a box-top/ flat-top with the sides tapering up from a number-one. Wraparound or Ray Ban Wayfarers shades consummated, to some extent, the businesslike, crisscrossed, cloned look.

An Adventure Into Two-Tone And One Step Beyond

An exception to the ebony and ivory twosome and the *piece de resistance* was two-tone material. On the whole it's a polyester and nylon fabric mix which shimmered two hues under intense light and came in tones of purplish claret/navy blue and copper brown/olive green. This eye-catching textile was utilised into suits and pants. And who is sartorially placed to inform us of such man-made, commodities of clothing? None other than the man of a million-and-one phraseologies and cogent theories, the ska'd for life Ian Hough.

Ian: *Manchester has a secret history, one that remains out of reach of latter-day scribes and social commentators. This history centres on an underground youth movement closely related to several others but always lying just outside them. It is the proto-form of what became casual, and it only properly surfaced in the absence of competitors. Taking over a decade to be fully assembled, the soul boy in a Fred Perry polo became the Bowie boy in a leather blazer, who finally made it onto Manchester's football terraces in chunky-knit jumper and Hush Puppies. This creature didn't spring from nowhere; he just seemed to. Throughout the Seventies glam rock, punk and disco were mainstream radio fodder, but these kids were into something slightly off-centre. When the plastic mod revival hit Manchester in mid-1979, it was temporarily folded in with this other youth trend, as others had been before it. It was inevitable; this thing seemed to share aspects of itself with* *virtually every cool thing that ever came along, but it had bags of reserve enough to never quite commit itself to any of them. As such, it had survived in one form or other since before most anything else. There are even those who claim it was a direct descendant of the notorious "Scuttlers": street gangs from Manchester and Salford known for bloodthirsty battles and a curious lop-sided hairstyle that obscured one eye. It metamorphosed over time but its fundamentals never changed.*

In the late-Fifties, British youth was finally allowed to express itself, albeit through American vehicles like Elvis, Buddy Holly and Jerry Lee Lewis. This stark cold English crew were there, waiting. They had rock 'n' roll in their blood before they'd ever heard it. They were the Real McCoy, the ragged-trousered ones with the sharp cheekbones, the healthy glow and the sinister accents. Like a molecular memory passed through the evolution of species, or a latent virus waiting for the ideal conditions, it was always ready to hit the light of day in some new guise. From teddy boy to mod to Northern Soul to Bowie to perry to casual to Madchester, this Nameless Thing had raced ahead of the herd, a locomotive energy fuelled by initiative and style. It's been well documented today but in 1979 it still represented something dark, unknown and uncontrollable. Like the blue bear and the giant squid, it kept to the shadows and crannies where the average punter feared to tread. Its violent proponents closely resembled mods and this soon caused problems for the plastic Johnny-come-latelys of the time.

By the time Secret Affair, The Lambrettas, Madness and the reissued/redone Quadrophenia *was 'in', Manchester's bad lads were pretty much sold on this almost-mod look, but plenty flirted with two-tone and inch-wide ties for at least a month or three. Stolen From Ivor in central Manchester was one of those shops that catered to the trendy crowd and they were all over mod in mid-1979. There are people today who laugh at Stolen From Ivor's and say it's a crap shop, but back then it wasn't; it was a crap world and Ivor's catered to a minority. They sold two-tone suits, ties, Hush Puppies, Fred Perry polo shirts, the lot. There were two big windows on one side, facing the steps that went down to the underground market in front of Oasis. Mannequins stood in each window. In the left-hand window was a green and orange two-tone suit and in the right-hand window was a purple and blue two-tone suit. The crêpe backing paper was appropriately-coloured. Both windows were illuminated by coloured spotlights that complemented the suits. A variety of accessories, such as trilbies, chunky-knit jumpers and button-down shirts were pinned to the backing paper or draped tantalisingly for all to see. These objects were the fetish items of a violent sub-culture. The Fred Perry laurel wreath in particular represented a fist in the face, not from the mods, but from those other kids, the ones who seemed to defy classification. They had always worn the Perry polo.*

They weren't skinheads and they weren't mods. They were known as Perry Boys. Most curiously, they sported a girl's haircut; a fringe that came down over one eye and whose length was continued in a layered bowl across the top of the ear to a point at the nape. They'd adopted the David Bowie look a couple of years previously. They were also very fond of soul music. Some even liked disco, and the trendy shops around town played a weird mish-mash of these and other sounds as background music.

In the dark weeks prior to my discovering Stolen From Ivor, I'd never seen two-tone material before. A lad at school called John Clucas (who sadly is no longer with us) first told me about it. "I'm gonna get a pair of two-tone pants after school tonight," he said one day in the yard. I could tell it was a thing of importance. Mod was sweeping through my neck of the woods and Clucas was a trendsetter. He had different coloured eyes like Bowie and a space-face decorated in strange cosmic freckles. He was one of the Perries and wore expensive clothes, but like others he also had an appetite for mod gear. I asked him what two-tone was and he explained. I could see it in my mind before I ever set eyes on it. But once I saw him in his green and orange two-tone trousers, Fred Perry and Hush Puppies, I became obsessed. It lived up to my expectations for a change. A friend of my mother's described the material as 'iridescent' after listening to me mithering my Mum for a pair of two-tones and somehow this word was even better than 'two-tone.' From what my mum's mate said, it was obvious that this fabric wasn't some closely guarded secret from a secret American military base full of aliens — it was a well-known fashion device from decades past. It seemed the choices in two-tone were limited to those two featured in Stolen From Ivor's window; green and orange or purple and blue. I admired Clucas for his good taste. The purple and blue were a little too iridescent, and made the material appear almost plastic.

Then one day my parents surprised me. They'd been out on their shopping travels and had found me a pair of two-tone pants at a market in Bolton or somewhere. Back then Bolton may as well have been Bangkok, it seemed so far away. I was horrified to discover that these were blue and orange! They fit me okay, but were perhaps a little too wide all the way down, unlike Clucas's, which followed the shape of his thigh and calf. The inseam was a kind of nylon that chafed between my thighs at the top, and after walking in them for any length of time I would be raw. I was ashamed and proud of them in equal measure; they weren't the de rigueur kind sported by all the 'professional' mods, but at least they were two-tone. I would caress the material and wonder at it. How the fuck had anyone come up with such a notion, much less assembled it in real life? Finally I encountered Clucas whilst wearing my secret pants, and I braced myself for the mockery. But a strange thing happened. Clucas, the main face, looked interested rather than disgusted. He bent down, felt the cloth, walked around me with eagle eyes, scrutinising every contour and seam. Then he offered to buy them off me! Well, this was a turn up. I had to refuse, naturally, if only because my parents had bought them for me. But every time he saw me from then on he offered me money for the pants. For the life of me I couldn't work out why. I even went so far as to tell him how they chafed and how awkward the metal clasp at the top of the zipper was. The zipper was nylon, as opposed to the metal zippers of the popular kind, which featured a button, not a clasp.

This only served to make Clucas even more interested. The fact they had a slit pocket at the back – just the one, not two as the others had – with a button holding it closed, drove him to new levels of distraction. The popular type had a simple slit on either side, which I thought looked brilliant. My back pocket was a slit, with a nylon zip under a thin, horizontal flap about a quarter-inch wide, plus a button which fastened to a loop of two-tone material fashioned the same as the rest of the pants. Hesitantly, I asked would he be interested in swapping trousers. This might be something I could get away with. He instantly said yes, and I became even more confused. Now I am older and wiser, I realise it is because nobody else had a pair like that. They were a hybrid of the two popular colour-combos and as such a thing of value.

But that was 1979, when Wrangler sweatshirts with massive eagles emblazoned on the front or Fruit of the Loom bib and braces were considered cool. It was an age when jeans were subconsciously noted as fashion items, when Brutus had been replaced by Jesus. Brand marketing had inserted the thin end of the wedge into British culture, with Adidas training shoes at the forefront. They were a black and white basic version of what came after, but they were the perfect bait to dangle in a pool of hungry disciples. What the then very naïve brand marketers didn't realise was that the kids were about to take that rudimentary offering and forcibly invoke a catalysis that was to colour and enhance our world for generations to come.

Rainwear in 1979 was limited to two choices; an Adidas cagoule or a fishtail parka. The Perries became mods for a while. Many bought fishtail parkas, of which there were several degrees of authenticity and snideness (as there was with the Adidas cagoule). The best kind was a peculiar-looking all-green type that had webbing on the inside, and enshrouded its wearer like a sea devil from Doctor Who. These were the ones the perries favoured. Inferior versions tended to include a red lining. The second-best featured red lining down to waist level where it was intercepted by green. The worst type had a full red lining, and they were considered major 'divvy'. 'Divvy' was a word used to describe an article of clothing that was a counterfeit of another, much hipper product, or more accurately, those who chose to wear it.

The difference between then and now is that everything was still innocent; brand marketing had barely begun its assault on our existence. As such, products like Fred Perry, Adidas and Puma were manufactured by skilled men in Germany, not starving nine-year olds in East Asia. Those brands were relative unknowns back then, and the media was utterly ignorant to them. Today we see middle-aged 'collectors' hunting down vintage Adidas trainers and Lacoste cagoules online, half-demented with the hope they'll find something different and original. Adidas reissued trainers today weigh less than half what the originals weighed. Whether this is down to the removal of since-banned chemicals in their manufacture or simple cost-cutting I don't know. 1979 was a crap world because of the media's ignorance. But Stolen From Ivor were one of the few shops that actually catered to Manchester's perries, and occasionally they stocked things that were top notch. One of these was obviously the Fred Perry polo shirt. Fred Perry polo shirts cost seven quid in 1979, enough to make my old man choke on his bread and dripping. As summer turned to autumn, the short-sleeved Perry was usurped by the long-sleeved Peter Werth. This was an important development.

Throughout 1979 I'd been going to a weekly disco every Thursday night. It was in the centre of Prestwich, in a place called The Longfield Suite. The DJ, Les Barry, was something of a local legend. Hundreds of kids, male and female, would be drawn there every week. Les Barry sent them sillier than Little Willy with his masterful tune combinations. Punk and new wave were played between long bouts of soul, Northern Soul and disco.

John Clucas got up one night to R. Dean Taylor's 'There's a Ghost in My House' in a massive pair of exaggerated flares and a fetchingly mad shirt. He shifted his body gymnastically about a sizeable gap made by hundreds of dancers, who stopped their shenanigans to watch his fluid moves. It was the first time that I realised there was at least some musical heritage to this queer hooligan path I was embarking upon. Les Barry's Longfield disco was the perfect barometer to gauge what was hot and what was not.

Some of Manchester's coolest kids went there, and most of them lived right in my neighbourhood. The Longfield was where Clucas debuted his two-tone pants. He and his mates would hang out near the bar, an assortment of vicious brawlers; thieving waifs, vandals, gang-bullies, semi-mods and other ne'er do wells. They weren't necessarily match goers, but football was certainly high on most of their agendas; it was Manchester after all. Some of them were City fans and some were United. The hair ran from basic crew-cuts, to modish short back and slapnecks, to soul boy (read: Perry Boy) style. The soul wedge was like a goal they all seemed to be racing toward; skinheads, growing into side-parting, growing into flicks, heading straight for wedge status. Burgundy was the colour, of the hair as well as the chunky jumpers. They wore Fred Perrys in all possible colours or baggy long-sleeved burgundy Peter Werths. Baggier small-collared shirts made from expensive thick material, billowed out where they were tucked into their tight-fitting Levi straight-legs. Adidas Kick or Mamba trainers and Hush Puppies were *the chief footwear. Clucas also favoured Clarks Polyveldt. I owned a pair of Polyveldt too, having been impressed by Clucas's. I also owned a pair of shitty Gola Jet trainers, because I couldn't afford the Adidas Kick. But I was getting older and learning to translate a lifelong shoplifting addiction from sweets and books to clothes.*

For Christmas 1979 I received an all-black Fred Perry, a cotton green and orange two-tone button down collar shirt and a French Connection No.2 herringbone two-tone brown and purple shirt. The thick cotton shirts matched with new brands of jeans like Lois, Lee and Inega obviously represented a new breed of street fashion – one that was dovetailed to designer sportswear and crowned with a wedge hairstyle. From New Year 1980 to New Year 1983, everything that could possibly be called 'Casual' came and went. Most of it already existed and was simply discovered and consumed by the hungry tendrils that combed the shops looking for quality and originality. The hooligan element at the football was treated to a new coat of paint, one that could be appreciated by Alpine skiers and German tennis pros, as opposed to their previous suppliers – market traders who sold snide versions of silly Seventies attire.

It literally evolved; there is no other word for it. Adidas was the apex species that set the pace; Stan Smith then Nastase then Grand Prix then Wimbledon then Grand Slam was a very definite sequence of improvements in tennis shoes that spanned the years between 1979 and 1981. Puma, Le Coq Sportif and pretty much fuck all else tried to challenge Adidas, trainer-wise, but it was never gonna be any other than the brand with the stripes. Le Coq Sportif Arthur Ashe and Puma Argentina were reasonable facsimiles of Stan Smith and Trimm Trabb, but it was too little, too late. There were other shoes that ran concurrent to the Adidas story, such as Pods, Clarks, Kios and Kickers, but again they were flashes in the pan compared to the mainstay. The tales of lads going onto the continent are worn out, but suffice to say the 1980-81 forecourt at OT became a jungle of familiar and unfamiliar sportswear from Germany, Italy and France. Most of them slept rough and were on the move the entire time, and their brand new shoes often looked months old by the time they'd made it home. A pair of 30 quid trainers bearing that jaded soiled look was a badge of rank and one in the eye for the lads from other teams on match day. The crews were huge, always several hundred strong, and the scousers definitely came to Manchester looking for it back then, whatever some of the more biased United and City fans will tell you.

Personally, from a home game perspective (and I went mostly to home games as much for financial reasons as anything), I don't remember anyone but the 'Mickies' coming in proper firms to Manchester between 1980 and '82. Leeds brought some lads in late '81, but they were little more than a hundred strong and got mullered at White City. They never made it to the ground, but they tried.

Liverpool and Everton were a different proposition altogether. They'd been running in proper casual firms before anyone and the average age was probably late-teens. These mobs of skinny scallies would turn up at Oxford Road on a 10 o' clock train and take the piss in town until United's main team tracked them down and it went off royal.

I remember one morning in 1980 going with a mate to Oxford Road station, ready for a 10 o' clock train coming in from Liverpool. United never played on Merseyside in 1980, by some strange quirk of the fixture list. This is the reason they think we never became casuals until 1981. Consequently, their view of how many boys we had was limited to Old Trafford meetings. United were away at Forest that day and some of the older lot told us to meet them there; Liverpool were at Maine Road and well up for it. My mate Kenny and I were walking towards the station when an oddball crew of about 20 poorly-dressed dossers surrounded us. We knew they couldn't be scousers and it was hard to believe they were Mancs.

"Where you from?" a lad in a shite leather with an elasticated waistband and a green and white gypsy kerchief round his neck asked us. We were puzzled by their appearance.

"Errr, Manchester," we told him.

"Whereabouts?"

Kenny pulled the corners of his mouth down and lazily flipped his finger in the general direction of Salford. "Over there…"

One of them smacked me. We tried to run but they trapped me against the wall of the Refuge Building and gave me a harmless few punches and kicks. We trotted down toward the station, hoping to see our mates waiting for the scousers and turn the tables on this weirdly-dressed little team. The train was just pulling in and there were literally hundreds of scousers on it. They were waving to us across a cinder carpark; our cords and colourful ski tops probably made them think we were from Liverpool. Our mates were nowhere and this huge mob poured off the train and was walking up Oxford Road towards the library. We were walking parallel to them up a wasteland street at the backs of the warehouses. Every few seconds we'd pass the opening of a connecting alleyway and this mob looked like a police escort it was so big. At first one or two heads turned. At the next opening it was eight or ten, and by the time we reached the third connecting street the word had gone up and 50 lads were already halfway down it towards us. I have no recollection of what happened next, but I imagine it involved running like fuck in the vague direction of anywhere. Later that day we saw them (or it could have been a different firm of scousers) right in Piccadilly bouncing along, laughing their balls off. Hundreds of boys. I'm not sure where City were. Probably smoking weed in Oasis café and playing Space Invaders. As for the mystery crew of wilburs it recently occurred to me they could have been some smaller team from outside Manchester or Liverpool who happened to be nosing about on their way to a match.

Through this era United would have hundreds, sometimes thousands, of lads out in force on match day both home and away. You'd be on a train and it would be totally packed, everyone sporting the wedges, an array of spot-on designer gear that changed week to week. The odd trendsetters would stand out in the crowd, usually in something very subtle, like a heavy knit brown cotton sweater with suede trim, or a mental dark green hiking coat bristling with dangly bits and alien labels. At the destination it would be chest out and arms swinging, hair flicking, accents loud and clear. Hundreds of boys pounding down some main road and as soon as we saw them it went off. The new style gave a confidence, and there was always that same body language; the sideways bounce towards the opposition, the almost chest-beating, and the pogoing right in front of them before someone steamed in. It was irresistible and looked brilliant, guaranteed to set nearly everyone confronted by it on their toes. Some never budged though and there were many near-mythic accounts of full-on kickoffs like Man United's mass brawls against Leeds cavemen or confident cockney firms. And the Stanley knives of the scousers loomed like a spectre over our every meeting, as well as their out-on-its-own style that only a fool would deny they started exclusively at the football.

1979's button-down/small-collared shirts and polos had become silk French Le Coq Sportif football tops that became bike tops that became jockey jackets that topped out in the form of expensive multicolour smooth cashmere ski jumpers with ribbed padding, silk underarms and snug knitted waistbands. What had been in 1979 an alternative form of jeans, the Inega and Lee, multiplied in spring 1980 to include Ritzy, Razzy, FUs and eventually – at the end of 1982 – Levis. Levis had been big in late 1979 due to the mod revival and now they bounced back with a new ice-wash blue faded selection. An earth-tone knitted jumper, Levi ice-wash jeans and a pair of brown Adidas Korsika was for me the final composite in the evolution. The Milk Cup Final against Liverpool at Wembley and the FA Cup quarter against Everton at Old Trafford were the highlight, football- wise of 1983. For me, at least. Something else was about to take control; drugs. Sometime in mid-1983, after years of skullduggery, thoughts turned to music, to the Sixties, to drug trips and inner discovery.

The Wilton Lounge pub in the centre of Prestwich was the local den of iniquity. The Wilton is half-built into the precinct and a curved section of it looks down upon the main bus-stop to town. This was the era when pubs were utterly hammered on the weekends. One memorable stoned night in the Wilton, Clucas approached the Wilton jukebox and played Chris Montez's 'Let's Dance', followed by Dion's 'The Wanderer'. The entire place began doing a Fifties-style hand-jive, everyone crippled by hysterical, psychedelic laughter. After several years of sober, tepid loitering outside train stations, we were ready to fuckin' dance, believe me. The rest, as they say, is history.

The rest of the country was totally clobbered up in designer gear by the time Mancs started to explore drug music and dancing and to leave the shiny tracksuits behind. A lot of people point the finger at hip-hop and Chicago house, etc, as the root of Manchester's (and Europe's) rave culture, but I think there were influences coming from other directions, too. It wasn't all about dancing but we did like to do a line or two in Band on the Wall and bop about. It might be electric bluegrass from some American band with a mad triangle player. Another favourite was Victor Brox, who was from the Manchester area and simply magical to watch, as he blew a trumpet, played piano and sang amazing blues all at the same time. The bands, the roadies, and the regular punters were all one, just a mob of Saturday night pleasure hunters. It was easy to meet new people and the possibilities seemed endless. Other times it could be some wannabe shower of shite like the idiots who broke my nose with a pint pot who came to cheer on some crap band and ended up kicking off. You always had to watch your back, which wasn't easy if you didn't give a fuck and spent most of your time out of your brains like we did.

This was after everyone had started taking the piss out of the dole in London by signing on at various offices around the capital. They were now on the move, well and truly, jetting off to distant places in a continual cycle. Dropping back in Manchester after a stint of cement mixing in Tel Aviv, or yacht-waxing in Miami which would always entail a crazed few weeks of sampling all the new clubs in town and exploring how much the psychedelic scene was growing. The older lads who'd schooled me in acid, speed, pot and worse, were bang into their sounds. They loved all these obscure bands from the States, Europe and Australia like The Rain Parade, Plasticland, The Nomads and The Lipstick Killers. The influences were pure LSD and 1960s trippy heads like Roky Erikson, Sky Saxon and Syd Barrett. There was a whole scene around the Salford-Prestwich border, always a fertile place for trends in fashion and music. Lads who'd started off listening to The Fall, V2, Bowie and Buzzcocks turned onto John Martyn, Gil Scott-Heron and Talking Heads and finally the haunting sounds of The 13th Floor Elevators, The Seeds and The Soft Boys. The music trip was just as evolutionary as the training shoes years earlier. Most of it featured the same blend of a lunatic singer with a youthful, fucked up voice, backed by a squad of gurning goons who'd done their homework in the acid rock department. I'm not denying that hip-hop and house were the direct influences of rave, but I think there's a lot more to it at the street level in Manchester, especially where the hooligan-hipster-stoner element is concerned.

Quite a few of the old casuals went into dealing and bouncing, and when the rave thing made clubs massively popular they were in charge of it at all ends. A fair number just disappeared, went and married women in Sweden or New Zealand or Thailand. The Eighties ended in the midst of a mass drug trip, and Hillsborough. It was a paradisiacal sea with a drop of hell in there for good measure. The Taylor Report led to what we have now; plastic seats and plastic fans and plastic players who are in it for the money and nothing else. It makes you wonder where it's all going to end. But all things do end, that's for sure.

Skinhead Resurgence

The second coming of mod, or ska/rude boy – apart from The Specials' meaningful lyrics and accelerated beat – weren't for me but, skinhead and Oi! music were, for a time. My prevailing tastes in Oi!, its working-class roots, and its sound of the streets led me to do my oral English Literature dissertation on the movement. This dissertation went towards my O-Level in the final year of secondary school – much to the disgust and horror of my English teacher, because I informed the class that the expressive lyrics used in Oi! band's songs contained expletives and four-letter profanities to get their points across.

The second generation of skinhead had re-emerged alongside punk in London; the focal groups they followed from The Smoke were Sham 69, Cock Sparrer and Menace. On the attire front, things weren't dissimilar to the original 1969 skinhead look: Baracuta G9 Harringtons, either in red or black with Fraser tartan or a rip-off version of the jacket. Same with the Crombies that were worn too – copies would do. Sage green nylon MA-1 bomber jackets, lined in Indian orange fibre, were at the spearhead of second coming of skinhead. The Ben Sherman Oxford shirt in gingham or check with button down collar came back with a roar. Screen printed band pictures, or full frontal Union Jack stencilled flagged T-shirts hugged slender torsos. And shitstopper Levi jeans with a ½" turn-up or Sta-Prest pants, were at half-mast. The only slight differential between rude boy and skinheads were their choice of footwear; Rude Boys wore loafers, skins 12-hole ox-blood DMs, but it ain't necessarily so, though.

Garry Bushell, while writing for *Sounds* music mag tagged certain second-wave punk groups with the term, Oi!. Bands that fell in to this bracket were the Cockney Rejects, The 4-Skins, Combat 84 and many other southern based bands. From the North were the Angelic Upstarts, Slaughter & the Dogs and Skrewdriver, briefly, plus others too. Skrewdriver went on to be the most prominent white power rock band

and help set up Blood & Honour music promotions. I saw many a Oi! band at the Warehouse club and within the old Lancashire boundaries.

I remember once when a half-a-dozen of us skinheads were walking through St George's Shopping Centre in town heading to the Black Cat café – a skinhead haunt –near the train station after we'd listen to that weeks latest releases in the sound booths in Laskeys and old dear stopped us. "Well..." she pronounces "I don't care what they say about the likes of you lot; you're always well turned out smart, and you've neat haircuts" and then she carried on her merry way.

Though there were downsides that blighted the second coming of Skinhead, the association that some held that 'all' skinheads were right-wing racists, neo-Nazis and members of either the far-right NF (National Front) or the BM (British Movement), this seed planted chiefly by the gutter press. And I was on the receiving end of a couple of severe beatings proving this accusation. These beatings were due to my sense of dress, the length of my hair, not being able to put forth a case or explanation as to why I chose to crop my locks down to a number two, my political beliefs, and why I had a *Rock Against Racism* badge pinned to my red Harrington. The perpetrators dishing out the pummelling mustn't have clocked the badge and their minuscule mind psychology had tarred 'all' skinheads with the same brush already. Tell me why, tell me why, tell me why why why!

A badge seller in Preston town on Saturdays wouldn't stock Union Jack or St George's cross badges, such was the stigma back then for doing so. That's not to say that there weren't skinheads who held fascist and racist tendencies and voiced these views in more ways than one. Such acts as monkey chanting, racial abuse, sieg-heiling salutes and banana throwing went on inside football grounds routinely in the late Seventies/early-Eighties. An incident at Upton Park once epitomised such goings on: West Bromwich Albion players Brendan Batson and Cyrille Regis had run out of the tunnel to warm up before a game against West Ham, to a barrage of bananas being thrown on to the pitch, in their direction. Only Batson picked one of the bananas up, peeled it and feigned to eat the fruit. And, he also launched one over to Regis, who only shoved it down his plum-crushing, skin-tight shorts. They then both volleyed several back into the hostile crowd. Put that in your pipe and smoke it.

Once when I visited Stamford Bridge to watch North End versus Chelsea in early 1980, I observed outside The Shed, the handing out of NF and BM leaflets and the sale of copies of the magazine *Bulldog*. The *Bulldog* magazine encouraged its match-going buyers to make their grounds the most racist in Britain and top the NF's most vocal league table printed in the publication. Some seven months or so later, on a dark winter's Thursday night, I'd decided to stay in to watch *Top of the Pops* on the box featuring one or two miming Oi! bands. The next programme was either *World in Action* or *Panorama*, and it threw an in-depth spotlight on the British Movement and their followers, showing a large portion of skinheads on marches in MA-1's. Nexus, *Minder*. This episode of *Minder* was titled *All About Scoring, Innit?* The episode showed Arthur looking for Terry at Stamford Bridge when Chelsea had entertained the mighty Lilywhites; a game ending in a 1-1 draw and featured my own good self on the North Stand away end for a nanosecond. It's a funny old world, innit?

Manchester Calling To The Faraway Towns

Ian W: *By 1980 I was now travelling further afield for the latest additions to my collection, and Manchester was just 45 minutes away by train (its record shops were light years away from anything in the Preston area). As the train pulled in at Victoria Station you could see and smell Boddingtons Brewery. The next few hours would be spent trawling the many record stores and bringing home sounds only available to those in the know, or more so, those who thought they were in the know.*

Virgin Megastore would be the first port of call. This place was huge and although most towns had a Virgin record shop, this one had an entire punk/new wave section, the size of a normal record store. Just down the road was the underground market and a stall with thousands of picture sleeves on the walls of records that would soon become rarities (little did I know back then) which were all readily available. All the main independent labels were represented; Small Wonder, Rough Trade, Step Forward, Fast etc, along with more obscure labels. Before the entrance to the underground market was a shop selling punk clothing; T-shirts, mohair jumpers, bondage pants and much more. The shop was called Oasis. Along with a couple of other stalls, the market became the new choice of punk outfitter for us, replacing jumble sales and Army & Navy surplus stores.

Travels to the Far East – East Lancashire – for both music and football were also occurring on a regular basis too. Preston were now in the same division as Burnley and Blackburn Rovers, the latter being the home of King George's Hall. After a steady gig-going start at the Guild Hall in Preston, King George's Hall in Blackburn town centre then became 'the' place to be in 1979. Within a space of 12 to 18 months the venue played host to most of the punk/new wave big hitters. The Damned, The Clash, Buzzcocks, Stiff Little Fingers, The Ruts, Slaughter & the Dogs, The Skids, The Jam, Adam and the Ants, the list was endless, with most having a good support bands like Joy Division who supported the Buzzcocks. Waiting for the doors to open was an adventure in itself as various chancers went up and down the queue with their carefully scripted "have you got 10 pence mate" routine. It seemed to work for a couple of gigs until the younger punks who were getting older and wiser decided enough was enough and the local in question was left in a heap outside the Jubilee Pub with a nasty gash to the head. His little gang of 'ten pence poncers' disappeared in the direction of the shopping centre, never to be seen again.

Football rivalries were never far away at punk gigs in Blackburn in the late Seventies, and on more than one occasion it seemed the entire audience was at war. A four way mini riot involving Blackburn, Burnley, Preston and Blackpool added to the atmosphere as Stiff Little Fingers – it might have been The Damned – provided the background music for Lancashire at war. It wasn't exactly a walk in the park for the bouncers who also had the added bonus of making sure no-one clambered on to the stage while the war raged on. At the time most of the bands encouraged the odd stage invasion; an invite wasn't always necessary. Being prone to the odd pitch invasion, invading the stage seemed a natural progression for myself and other mutual friends. Pete Shelley, lead singer of the Buzzcocks, was not entirely impressed though, whereas Captain Sensible from The Damned seemed to take it all in his stride. And the stage antics would guarantee a few bumps and bruises once the bouncers had regained control, because the stage at Blackburn was a good six foot above the crowd and safe landings were not always possible.

The best gig I saw at Blackburn was The Damned supported by The Ruts and it was one of the rare occasions when the support band blew the headliners off the stage. Malcolm Owen, lead singer of The Ruts, was like a man possessed. He threw himself round the stage throughout their set and was the best frontman I ever saw. It was only natural to join him for a few seconds and help him with the vocals to 'In a Rut.'

More cuts and bruises were collected from East Lancashire at the Burnley v Preston game. My mate Tommy, and his dad, although they came from Leyland, were Clarets fans, and myself and Joe cadged a lift to the game with them. Tommy's dad parked his car up in the town centre. It wasn't long before we left our Clarets friends and joined up with the huge Preston mob who'd come by train. A few pockets of Burnley fans made themselves known en route to the ground but were despatched by the older lads with relative ease. It felt good to be part of such a big mob even though we were tucked away in the middle, well surrounded by lads a lot older, and gamer.

The match ended in a 1-1 draw with Alex 'Super' Bruce netting for the North End. As we made our way out along the alleyway next to the cricket pitch, once *again we felt invincible as hundreds of Preston youths got ready for the real action in the town centre. Mounted police were waiting at the end of the alley and began pushing the Preston mob to the right in the opposite direction of the town centre. A few Preston fans in cars went through the horses and turned left. We followed them but noticed they were getting fewer and fewer by the time we reached the crossroads at the corner of the cricket ground. The whole road was swarming with Claret and Blue heading in the direction of town and Joe and me stood out like sore thumbs. The Claret hordes were all in denim jackets and flares, most of them with some sort of Claret and Blue attachment. For two 15 year olds in black drainpipes and various punk badges, the situation was far from ideal. As we reached a roundabout we saw a few older Preston lads and one of them was on the floor with blood pouring from a nasty head wound. The police surrounded the rest of the North End, stopping the Burnley fans from finishing the job off. We kept our heads down and walked just behind the coppers in the direction of town. Two of the boys in blue must have noticed two very quiet punks behind them and offered to walk with us in the general direction of our lift. Twenty yards later the coppers got a call over their walkie-talkie and were off down a side street where sirens were blaring. It doesn't take long before a small mob of Burnley sussed us out. "Where you lads from?"*

"Erm... Rishton." "Where's that then?"

Joe takes the first blow to the head followed up by a smack in the mouth for yours truly. It's all over in seconds as a lone copper arrives on the scene and backs off the four laughing Burnley fans.

We eventually reach Tommy's dads car and after a quick "Enjoy the game lads?", it was back to Leyland with more tales to tell.

By the time school came around on Monday morning, a few bits were added and at 15 years old, we had become part of the Preston mob that had humiliated Burnley before the game. After was a different story! School was put on the backburner as the only things grabbing my attention were music and adventures at the football. The music scene now had another youth culture about to explode, the ska and a mod/skinhead revival. I didn't mind The Specials and Madness, and The Jam were about to become the biggest band in Britain with their 'All Mod Cons'. Many of the kids at school adopted the look but for me there were plenty more bands to discover who didn't appear on Top of the Pops.

Whilst UK Subs, Angelic Upstarts, Stiff Little Fingers and the likes were still thrashing around fast and loud, more experimental post punk groups were appearing on the scene. The Gang Of Four and the Pop Group were mixing punk with funk. And Killing Joke had just released their 'Turn to Red' EP. In Liverpool, Echo and the Bunnymen and Teardrop Explodes had also released singles. Over in Sheffield, the synthesiser and drum machine became the sound of Human League and Clock DVA. The raw sound of guitar based punk was still a must, but now there were sounds for all occasions. I was still a massive Clash fan and their first album, 'The Clash', and 'Give Em Enough Rope', still took pride of place in my vinyl collection. The collection had by now grown into a couple of hundred singles and around 50 LPs. From Crass to Throbbing Gristle, I had music for every mood. John Peel was now the only radio show I listened to. The two hours between 10pm and midnight were a must. I sometimes waited for a 10 minute of a dub reggae song to end, to hear two minutes of vinyl heaven by an unknown band.

The Clash had changed their sound more than most, and on a trip to Manchester in December 1979 I found myself in a two hundred strong queue outside Virgin Megastore. 'London Calling', The Clash's third album, was about to go on sale and I wanted it the minute it did. The album took a bit of getting used to, but over 30 years on is still my favourite album of all time.

By now most of my mates were not just listening to music, we were actually playing it. I managed to get £40 together and bought a knackered second hand drumkit. Tommy, the Burnley fan, picked up the guitar and was soon a natural guitar hero. Fester, whose garage had first introduced us to the Sex Pistols, got himself a bass. And Joe, as yet undecided, soon changed his mind and joined in the fun. Soon we became the X-Cells.

After a stint on drums, I moved to the more prominent position of lead singer. Joe became the drummer. The line up was now complete. We practised in the school hall and anyone's garage who would let us. The sound was a bit raw but getting better all the time. Early songs included a version of Punctures 'Mucky Pup' and Jonathan Richman's 'Roadrunner.' The X-Cells were just about to start gigging when we all fell out. I could say it was due to musical differences but I honestly can't remember. I left and was replaced by a lad nicknamed Tag. In the meantime my best mate at the time Wolfie, had just purchased a top of the range drumkit and with two other mates, Woz and Alan H, we became Dielektric. We only gigged half-a-dozen times, but one of the most memorable was at Jalgos Club in Preston. Jalgos was a Caribbean club that hosted a punk night every Wednesday. We were paid four pints of lager each for which we did eight songs and a punk disco followed our best gig ever. I had a hangover from hell the day after at school. Whilst the X-Cells went on to make a single on Burnley's Snotty Snail Records, Dielektric went down in history as the greatest punk outfit in the Preston area never to appear on vinyl – honest.

Margaret Thatcher was now prime minister, and things were getting much worse on the job front. It wasn't an ideal time to be coming to the end of your school days, either. As the Seventies ended and the Eighties began, I had just turned 16 *and was more interested in music, alcohol, Preston North End, terrace warfare and girls. I hadn't given a second thought to future employment and I had a casual approach to school work and exams. I was also working part-time in a supermarket which meant I'd enough money for my vices. What more did I want for after leaving school?*

Punk nights at Jalgos ended in 1980 though, after a police raid, with most of the underage drinkers present cautioned and other things confiscated. The local youth club had become a little boring; we were ready for a new adventures and Thatcher's Britain was in full-flow.

One of the new adventures came in the shape of The Warehouse just round the corner from Jalgos. Thursday nights at The Warehouse became the stuff of legend as Preston now had its own punk venue. The night would usually begin with a bottle of cider on the Fishwicks 111 bus service to Preston, and then we hit the few pubs we could get in, albeit at the other end of town where the students drank. Tom's Tavern, The New Britannia and the Sun Hotel became the meeting places for Warehouse goers. A hop, skip and a jump across town would then be undertaken to the Old Dog, and then into The Warehouse around 9.30pm. One of the first gigs I witnessed at The Warehouse was Discharge. These boys were part of the more hardcore punk scene and played two-minute songs that were pure distorted noise. The Warehouse was a tiny venue and you were almost on the stage with the band. The dance floor at the front of the stage was metal and not entirely safe and if 20 people were on it, it was full. And most weeks you could expect chaos. It was one of Discharge's first gigs outside their native Stoke on Trent and they went down a storm in central Lancashire. Other notable bands that played in 1980 included Joy Division, Crass, The Wall, UK Subs, The Exploited, Fad Gadget and a host of local bands; The Fits (Blackpool) The Stiffs (Blackburn) Notsensibles (Burnley) and Prestons very own X-Cells and Blank Students.

Like King George's Hall in 1979, The Warehouse was the place to be in 1980. As the word spread, punks from all over Lancashire and beyond would flock to this tiny venue every Thursday night. Later on in the year, Discharge were booked for a triumphant return gig. By this time they were the number one band in the more hardcore punk movement. Their first three singles had all been at the top of the indie charts and they had built up quite a following.

On entering The Warehouse that night, something did not feel quite right. There were faces that I didn't recognise and these faces didn't appear too friendly. No-one was dancing and you knew it was about to kick-off, and someone, or something, was about to light the fuse. Then word spread round that the group were not turning up. It didn't take a genius to realise this, as the stage was empty and no speakers or instruments were likely to appear at 9.30pm. The DJ carried on playing but people had turned up to watch Discharge, and Discharge were nowhere to be seen. Then all of a sudden The Warehouse ignited in a flash as locals and out-of-towners went to war. I don't know how it started but it was sheer bedlam as bottles flew through the air crashing against walls. Tables were tipped over as cover and studded belts became lethal weapons. Toe-to-toe fighting ensued and covered most of the club. Run in, have a dig, then get back undercover to hide from flying objects. Heads would be split open as another bottle made a direct hit. This went on for about 15 minutes until it was time to head for the doors as the sound of police sirens can be heard outside. I just got through the doors as more cops arrived with truncheons at the ready. The mates and I hid in the graveyard opposite as we saw people being carried out on stretchers, one bloke holding his hand, blood gushing out with half a finger missing. The Morecambe and Lancaster punks seemed to have come off worse but casualties were high on both sides. No-one was the winner and The Warehouse eased off for a while – Thursdays nights were put on hold for a time.

December 1980 and John Lennon was fatally shot outside his apartment in New York. And on the way home from a mates house, I felt like I'd just been shot too. This after a vicious beating from three heroes who didn't like punks. Two black eyes and a split lip suggested my injuries weren't fatal, and my girlfriend looked after me in a special way once she'd cleaned me up at her house.

And so a new year dawned: I woke up on New Years Day at my mate Keith's house. Keith's mum was a bit of an old hippy – candles were lit all around the living room as a gang of punks rose from the carpet to the sound of John Lennon's 'Imagine', on the first day of 1981.

Later that year things didn't look too good for Preston North End. It had been an eventful season on and off the pitch, but a return to Division Three was on the cards. Swansea had brought thousands as they completed their romp through the lower leagues and into Division One. It was the biggest away following I'd seen, as massive Welsh lumps made their way up Deepdale Road the worse for wear. The game ended 3-1 to the visitors who were now swarming all over the pitch. Outside, Moor Park was like a warzone as different mobs of Preston tried their chances against superior numbers. Swansea had been promoted and four days later, Preston were relegated.

There was more to life than football anyway. Music became my number one priority with decent bands returning to The Warehouse; UK Decay, Theatre of Hate, The Dark, UK Subs, Exploited, Chelsea, Angelic Upstarts and more. Talk about being spoiled. And across town, Preston Polytechnic had got its act together again with the Killing Joke and TV Smiths Explorers playing within a few weeks of each other. The John Peel Road Show even came to town; who said Preston never had a music scene!

And so to the summer of 1981: The country was in turmoil, riots were happening in every major city and unemployment was at a record high. But the music was still coming by the bucket load. I also started working for a mate on his market stall, selling punk and indie T-shirts with the odd few badges as well. It was just on a casual basis, which supplemented my casual lifestyle. I'd just turned 17 and an even more casual way of life was to follow very soon, as casual clobber took me, the Eighties, and the north-west like a raging storm.

| The author's dad's boxing medical card and boxing billings from 1939/40

The author with his mum and dad on holiday at Butlins, early Seventies.

The author's brother, centre, looking slick.

The author's brother, central, having ditched the denim.

Dave Hewitson's dad, Glynn, on the left, with his mate and fellow Cunard Yank, Brian, in a dockside bar, Savona, Italy, early Sixties. Glynn is wearing Levis obtained in Baltimore, USA, and moccasins from the West Indies. Dave's dad also brought back, amongst other items, KDs – khaki denims – from Curacao in the Caribbean Islands.

Dave Hewitson and the missus in the Big Apple.

Derek, in the white polo shirt, still out on the floor at the Twisted Wheel in the late Noughties.

The author (top left) with his Cubs football team in the mid-Seventies. *Note the green parkas.

Ian W, PNE fanatic.

| The group Left, Right & Centre 1966; Phil Eaves on the left.

| Scooter Boys: Yob, ready to roll.

Ian W, the moody punk rocker.

Cass Pennant wearing white 'Lionel Blairs'.

'ammers donning terrace attire of the Seventies.

The author stood on the base remains of the WWII Type 22
hexagonal pillbox in a CP Company parka. This is the spot where
he played army with his mates in the early Seventies.

The author flicking his wedge haircut out of his eyes on Bonfire Night in the early Seventies while wearing orange wellies.

The author skinned and shackled in his local rival's manor in the late Seventies.

The author slightly intoxicated in the Casually Acceptable Eighties.

Rob K, viewing hateful graffiti.

The Beatles: The biggest band in the world ever. Tamla Motown: Yesterday... Today... Forever in Northern Souls. The Spirit of Skinhead and the Trojan Explosion went hand-in-hand in '69. 2-Tone: Complete Madness, and one step beyond that a cockney band had to leave The Smoke for a record deal – Tell me why, tell me why, Tell me...

The author trying to smile after Santa had left an Everton kit under the tree on Christmas Day, instead of a North End one.

Nobby and the gang on an away day, early-to-mid Seventies, with the skinhead look long gone.

The Warehouse, and The Exploited 'Barmy Army'.

| Ronnie Sharpe, setting standards on the terraces.

| Ronnie Sharpe and his merry men.

An assortment of Preston punks.

The Warehouse.

5

SCOOTER BOYS

Owners and riders of scooters are part of a phenomena that has been much misunderstood and under acknowledged since the Sixties. And while many involved in the scene can trace a radix back to the mods, many scooter boys have strong ties to casual/dresser as well.

Scooters, or more so motorised machines, have been tearing up the highway before Queen Victoria not-so suddenly vacated her throne. And as mentioned earlier in the book, the main two scooters (that are also still seen on the roads to this day) were manufactured by Italian companies Piaggo, Vespa, and Innocenti, Lambretta. Both these two scooters have dominated the British scooter scene since rolling off the production line in the 1940s. Any other scooters assembled in Europe or by their Italian brothers, Ducati and Capri, have been frowned upon by scooter purists – they just haven't got the eye-candy appeal. The other reasons for scooters being so popular were affordability (a couple of farthings filled the tank with juice) they gave you independence, and most of all, they were a bloody good hoot to ride – figo!

Since the mods of the Sixties had embraced the scooter, the future changing cults did so too. Each faction passed the baton on and kept the 10″ wheel in motion; mods to skinheads, skinheads to Northern Soul boys, Northern Soul boys to the second coming of mod – this in the form of the rude boys of the late Seventies, and beyond. This new breed of the late Seventies/early Eighties mod, would rummage through dusty sheds and rickety garages in their pursuit to unearth an old scoot after watching the classic 1979 film *Quadrophenia*. The movie featured re-enactments of mods and rockers fighting on Brighton beach and a multitude of scooters. There had been exceptions in the scene, though, during the Seventies. Manchester and some parts of Scotland had scooter clubs that were throw backs to the original mods, and Merseyside was seemingly home to mod, and later casual/dresser scooter enthusiasts. The south *also* held onto some old mod beliefs. And scooter riders, of any persuasion, in the London area, were virtually extinct, according to some clued-up authorities. The north and south weren't totally at different ends of the spectrum, but you might have thought so.

Only during these transition periods of modulation there was a clear north/south divide, and scooterists from different segments of the British Isles very rarely crossed lanes en masse, northerners converged on seaside resorts such as Morecambe, Skegness and Scarborough. Southerners rallied at old mod haunts along the south coast on Bank Holidays just like their predecessors. If they did rally together, Northerners were scowled at by their southern counterparts for wearing sheepskins, MA-1 pilot jackets and parkas with club and rally patches and beer towels sown on. These jackets were usually accompanied by ex-issue army pants and lengthy, ox-blood DMs. In the main, southerners who attended meets were mod revivalists and glory boys.

But in 1982, lads from all around the country began to somewhat distance themselves from the mod revivalist element off the late Seventies and started to ride under the banner 'scooter boys', and made their own codes of rule. More practical attire was to be worn for riding like waterproofs, specialised motorbike clothing and even leather bikers jackets. Adding to these changes a mixture of musical tastes that lads listened to had begun to be played at rallies. DJs would perform sets in marquees or night clubs with the odd all-nighter at some venues. This sparked various bands to be booked by organisers and perform on special stages set up for certain events. Also highbred, customised and cut-down scooters were not as widely dispelled anymore – modifying was now accepted by most. Scooter lovers were once again *united*.

I've never been too stable on two wheels. My dad gave up teaching me to ride my bike without stabilisers when I was seven or eight, this while pushing me round the green, red-faced and out of breath, at the front of our home. The law of gravity just kept making me fall over. Years later I taught myself to ride a bicycle, somewhat perilously. I jumped on a mate's push-iron one Sunday afternoon on the local Gamull Lane Bridge, a bridge that spanned a railway track, but a bridge that was a main road for traffic too. I nearly went head on into a trilby-wearing, elderly chap's prized battleship grey, Morris 'Moggy' Minor while out on his Sunday trundle. He'd had to swerve out of my way as I struggled veering from lane to lane out of control on the bike doing close on 30mph. I had to slam the breaks on when I reached a T-junction, slid off the seat, and squashed me nuts on the handlebar's swan-neck. Now that did hurt.

So, like I've mentioned, I'm not overly confident on anything with two wheels, let alone a scooter. The missus owned a rev-and-go, briefly, that I used a couple of times to nip to the shops on. And, I had to hand back a similar rev-and-go in Thailand once after an hour or so, 'cause I wasn't risking life and limb on the thoroughfares there due to the conditions of the roads and the maniac Tuk Tuk drivers. Thais, though, would fit full families on rev-and-go's, this including grandparents and their pet dog! There are other reasons behind never owning a scooter or motorbike. Two lads I knew were killed at the tender age of 17/18 in accidents; one in road accident while on his small-framed 50cc Vespa, the other on a blind spot down a country lane on his mate's Yamaha 'Fizzy' FS1-E – RIP. Also, a lad who I'd gone to school with, and a fellow apprentice bricklayer, Tomo, got knocked off his 50cc Vespa and was left severely paralysed down one side of his body. Sadly, he passed away some years later from a sudden illness. These untimely deaths and a brush with the law concerning a blue and white Honda Super 50cc Cub, made me think I'd better steer clear of motor powered wheels.

The Honda 'placcy' escapade happened when I was 14. A lad I knew had liberated the placcy from a shed near to where I'd attended infant and junior school, and as he was pushing it towards the close by football pitches (where I scored many a goal and won many a trophy) the five us who were out and about bumped in to him. For the next couple of hours we ragged the shite out of the thing on the fields after hotwiring it. We also caused alarming damage to the pitch's playing surface. This until it ran out of petrol. We then hid it in some bushes for the next night's scrambling, when we'd chance to get some juice from the petrol station. Only another lad had stumbled on our evening's entertainment, but we wouldn't let him have a bash and he got a major monk-on. He only went and grassed on us to the police, who'd turned up the following morning at the bloke's house (who our mate had *borrowed* the placcy off) after the owner had found it missing, and hadn't been able to get to his daily graft. The lad lived across the road from the bloke. One-by-one we were rounded up and taken to the cop shop with our parents. The coppers informed our parents that if they paid two-ton between them, we wouldn't be charged; this 'cause we weren't *midnights*. The placcy wasn't worth two-ton, more like 50 quid, but we weren't in any position to barter. I got a good ear-bashing and a long list of chores for the coming months that came my way when we arrived home, this to pay off my £33.33p. Ironically, the lad who bubbled us to the Old Bill went on to be caretaker of the very same school, chasing kids off the same playing fields that we'd razzed round on the Honda placcy while doing comparable, mischievous monkey business.

Preston's scooter club since the mid-Seventies are the Wildcats, who are still going strong to this day. And there is many a tattooed limb and torso depicting a black panthers head with 'Wildcats' underneath it on display during the summer months on various advancing ages of torso. On Fridays in the early Eighties I would meet up with some of the Wildcat Club members in the White Hart pub, come opening time at 6pm. These lads wore differing togs: from MA-1 Flight jackets, combat kegs and DMs right down to market stall bought shirts, Jekyll & Hyde jeans and Tommy Ball shoes. Who gave a fuck, we were all mates. Friday nights weren't nights for riding scooters – maybe fighting, though. Gone 7.30pm, several drinks later, and a rousing departing sing-along to The Jam's *'Going Underground'* or *'Down in the 'Tube Station at Midnight'*, it was, 'hey ho, let's go', and we'd board a bus to Meadow Street on the periphery of town which had over 10 pubs within staggering distance, and got totally wankered. And then, somehow, we'd catch the last bus home at 11pm or head to a nightclub. The subsequent morning I'd wake up wondering how I made it home in one piece or hadn't been nicked.

I also went on a couple of rallies in the Red Rose county with the same lads. We went to Morecambe, putting in an appearance by train. Row after row of scooters would be lined up along the seafront, a very statuesque sight if the truth be known. Supercool. Venturing further afield wasn't for me, but many of the Wildcats did travel far and wide. Scarborough, Weymouth and the Isle of Wight spring to mind. Not that they rode their scooters to those destinations, they'd hire a tranny van, and shove their scooters in the back for the long haul. They would then offload the scooters on outskirts of wherever, and then ride in to town, park up, and receive pats on their backs for the achievement of a 200 mile-plus, bone-rattling jaunt. Also, there was one lad, Shieldsie, who had a permed mohican and wore a parka covered in rally patches. He who would walk round the resort all weekend with his arm through a full faced-helmet, even though he hadn't come on a scooter, or even owned one at the time! Great lad, all the same.

Preston is also home to the acclaimed Frank Sanderson's Scooter

Innovations Ltd. The main man, Frank, supercharges up scooters to the supererogatory of 350cc and upwards superiority, namely the Scomadi. Superfluous, some scooter purists say. Other scooter boys feel Frank's scooters are superlative super symmetries. In his laboratory he supercharges scooters by inserting Italjet Dragest, Gilera Runner or superbike engines between customised side panels. He was also involved in the late Eighties with the Rosser Project which transplanted Yamaha YPVS 350cc engines into Lambrettas. Also, the superpowered scooters that the superordinate has worked on were raced regularly at Three Sisters Race Circuit in Ashton-in-Makerfield.

Anyway, the stature of owning a scooter and being part of the cult/ movement is second-to-none for some, and the experience of the endorphin rush while on a mass ride-out straddled over a vintage Lammey, or Wasp, with a warm breeze in their faces, is sheer utopianism.

The Bad Old Days

While the Northern scooter lads were keeping the faith (like Paddy & S.M.S.S.C., whose knowledge of scootering down the years and differential in dress follows the next tale) down south, things were a little different, to say the least. Here's an account of southerly goings-on by Robin Williams, probably known to most scooterists as Yob, and also the originator of the Moderaphenias Scooter Club.

Robin: *This is a personal account starting long before the formation of Modrapheniacs Scooter Club, and before the name for the club was even thought of. It is not intended to be a fully documented, comprehensive history of the club, though. I make no apologies for going back has far as I do, as many letters and articles in the scooter press refer longingly to the early National Runs as 'The Good Old Days', but very little seems to have been written about the previous years and, 'The Bad Old Days'.*

I was born and grew up in Poole, Dorset, and my first sighting of scooters en masse occurred during the mid-Sixties when, as a youngster I was taken by my parents on seaside outings to the local resorts of Bournemouth, Swanage and Weymouth. These outings were often interrupted by pitch battles between mods and rockers on the seafronts from which I was hurried away from by my worried parents. I was only about eight or nine years-old, but the sight of scooters tearing round corners with sparks flying from their exhausts, registered a vivid impression that was never to be removed.

This impression stayed with me till my teenage years, and developed into an obsession that actually took a hold in the early Seventies. By this time mods were virtually extinct, and Lambrettas were rapidly disappearing from the local streets.

At this time I was thirteen years old and I purchased my very first scooter; a Lambretta Li150 series one. It still had its original paintwork and was purchased for the vast sum of £5. This was to be the going rate for several years as Series Threes and GPs were the only scooters desirable to the few that still rode them. Everything else was considered old fashioned junk.

Not collectable, just junk. Hopefully this excuses my next action; I then proceeded to remove the leg shields with an axe! Thus modified, I fitted it with knobbly tyres too. So it became a scooter scrambler. There was about half a dozen of us with various models of Lambrettas – including a TV 1! These scramblers we steadily destroyed by scrambling on the local heathland, much to the amusement of the local motorcycling fraternity. This continued through my early teenage years, when we were guilty of destroying countless Series 1&2 Lambrettas on Canford Heath.

Poole was a real biker town so, during the summer of 1971 I started to hang around the amusement arcade at Rockley Sands holiday camp. The Rock- Ola would be booming out tunes like Dave and Ansel Collins 'Monkey Spanner', Slade's 'Coz I Luv You' and Family's 'In My Own Time' all in the new fangled stereophonic sound. I had the 'Royal' loafers, red H&J 'Indestructible' socks, bottle green Levi Sta-Prest, pale green gingham check Ben Sherman, ½" red braces and a blue/green tonic single vent jacket complete with sloped and flapped fob pockets. My hair was not too short, but smooth, just right. I could have been cool, I could have pulled, but I lacked one vital ingredient.

The girls would be wearing tonic suits with short skirts, white thick lacy tights paired with crêpe-soled loafers or Levi's 'red tag' shrink-to-fit jeans and boys loafers (girls never wore Dr Marten boots; these were boy's wear for football matches). They had long feather haircuts, and they were beautiful! But they hung around the guys outside, who as well as being a couple of years older than me, had the one vital missing ingredient: a Lambretta.

My fanatical obsession with scooters lost me many friends and potential girlfriends during this time; but I would watch these local smoothies and skinheads posing around the holiday camp on their Lambrettas and I couldn't wait for the day when I was old enough to join them. Around this time the scooters consisted of left over mod-type Lambrettas; still well turned out with mirrors, bars, racks aerials etc. Also starting to make an appearance was the earliest form of cut downs. These merely had the legshields cut or removed and the sidepanels removed which were favoured by the skinheads. The Innoccenti Lambretta GP was still available, but was only ridden by the lucky few that could afford a brand new machine. These tended to be left in standard trim with an Ancillotti seat and possibly a large Amal carb poking through the sidepanel. My total and utter fascination with these machines, and the accompanying cultures, continued through my school years until I left at the age of 16 and purchased my first road-going Lambretta; a second-hand late model SX150 with clip on panels. I had also been going into Arnatts in Bournemouth, the local scooter shop, and paying £5 a week until it became mine.

Boy was I the odd one out. I was about two years too late. The whole town was now full of 16-year-olds on Yamaha FS1E and Fantic 50s. Accompanied by a similarly obsessed and fashion displaced friend, Alan Prax, I rode my scooter illegally through my 16th year. (This was also the last year that you could legally ride without a crash helmet.) To our knowledge, we were the only two 'scooter boys' in the whole of the Poole and Bournemouth area. We would spend blissful, happy sunny days fantasising about the days when scooters ruled the roads. Only we were to come under frequent attack from local greasers, who were determined to stamp out what they saw as the last of the mods. Little did they know this was just our beginning.

As I rode into my 17th year (1974) we would meet the occasional skin/suede who was getting rid of his Lambretta and was more into a Ford Cortina or Anglia. We would pester them to sell us the accessories from their scooters before they sold them. This was because the numerous local scooter shops were rapidly disappearing and even the most basic spares and accessories became unavailable. We would even knock on the doors of houses where we could see a disused Lambretta in the garden. The skinhead/suede cults were now in massive decline – glam rock was displacing reggae and Motown in the charts, and scooters were going out of fashion with a vengeance. The Innoccenti GP range had gone out of production and the only new Lambretta to be seen in the remaining shop, Moordown Scooters, was the appallingly finished Jet 200. This was available in the single colour choice of yellow, ochre panel work, teamed with bizarre under panel colours like purple, orange or yellow. All of which seemed to have been applied with no undercoat or primer. These truly were grim times.

Just when I thought it couldn't get worse, my mate Alan went and got a steady girlfriend. I was left with my newly purchased 1966 SX200, my dreams, and precious little else. However, I persisted with my love of Lambrettas and the scooter cult image that was firmly implanted in my mind, much to the amusement of all those around me. Just in case you were wondering about my sexuality, I also acquired a steady girl about this time who I quickly brain washed into Lambretta submission for the next five years. (I often wonder if she's ever recovered and has ever forgiven me.)

My persistence eventually paid off, and by 1975 I had persuaded a couple of friends to purchase Lambrettas. Initially, this was just a cheap form of transport for them, but it didn't take long for the bug to bite and not long later four or five of us would cruise the streets together. We were nearly a gang.

During the spring of 1976, I heard rumours about a mysterious group of Northern Soul fans in Swanage that allegedly rode scooters. So, one Sunday afternoon I headed off on the 15-mile ride to Swanage in search of this lost tribe. I rode my accessory laden SX around the town for a couple of hours and I was just about to give up when a couple of soul boys flagged me down. They were astonished to see someone from out of town on a scooter but, they were friendly and soon introduced me to some of these strange people that rode scooters too. They had long feather cut hair, wore sports shirts and high waister 24" 'Spencer Soul Bag trousers. They explained that although they had seen other scooters on their pilgrimages to the far away land of Wigan, they believed themselves to be the only members of the tribe in the south of England. In order to prove them wrong, I arranged a meeting in Swanage for the following Sunday.

Three of us duly arrived to be confronted by 10 immaculately turned out, gleaming, chromed up Lambrettas. The excitement and atmosphere of this meeting was unbelievable, and a bond had been formed from that day on. These Sunday Swanage runs continued for many months. And on one such day, we had the unbelievable figure of 23 scooters. So feeling pretty confident we set off on a 20-mile trip to Weymouth. We had only gone a few miles when we confronted by a red GP200 hurtling towards us, weighed down by two outrageously large rectangular spotlights and a ton of mirrors. A grinning lunatic called John Loving, from Dorchester, piloted this machine. He had ridden to Swanage after hearing about the gatherings of scooters taking place. Due to a firefight with local greasers the trip was abandoned but, we agreed to meet John in Weymouth the following Sunday.

The day arrived: and scooters gathered from Poole, Swanage, Weymouth and Dorchester. There were at least 30 of us; we were now officially a gang! It was probably the largest gathering of chromed up Lambrettas seen on the south coast since the Sixties. These meetings continued, ad hoc, until we decided to form a scooter club. In late 1976 the Dorset Scooter Club, known then as the 'Lowriders', came into existence. For me as Secretary and John Loving as President, this was a mutual dream come true. At this time we believed ourselves to be the only road-going scooter club in existence. To put this in perspective you have to remember that there were no scooter magazines in print and the motorcycle magazines had deleted the word scooter from their titles and copy, full stop. Internet, email and mobiles had yet to be invented. We were in a communication wilderness. However, we were shortly to discover a photocopied magazine called 'Scooter and

Scooterist'. This was only available by post and was compiled by a guy called Norrie Kerr. This was about to end our isolation.

In 1977 we read about a scooter rally organised by the Vespa Club of Britain to take place at Havering near London. So 15 of us duly set off on the 110-mile trip, the longest we had ever undertaken on scooters. It's hard to believe but we were so unprepared, that the trip took nearly 24 hours. We only had the vaguest idea where the rally site was too. When we eventually arrived, we were greeted with looks of disbelief from about 200 Vespa riders, who were mainly from the north. I should point out that no-one from Dorset had ever seen a customised Vespa, or even a flipover backrest. The south coast was 100% Lambretta at this time. Yes there was a Vespa shop in Bournemouth, Harveys of Westbourne, only no-one cool rode them. Our occasional recces of this shop had led us to the conclusion that these machines were for incontinent old men and people who'd had style lobotomies. This illusion was disappearing before our eyes.

Many of the people at the rally were under the impression that no scooters, let alone Lambrettas, existed south of Watford. Once these mutual myths were shattered, we set about making beer-flavoured friendships that were to last many years. In particular, one with the crowd from Burnley and Pendle (Terry Burns, Terry Pratt, Earl and many more characters). They made us more than welcome by letting us share their hotel bedrooms (not in the biblical sense, I hasten to add). Some of the older Vespa riders (who did fit our earlier impressions) were slightly less than pleased to see us and declined to make us eligible for any of the awards at the rally. This owing to the fact that we rode Lambrettas. Overall, though, the welcome was warm and we got to hear about unofficial 'runs' that took place in the north, and in particular Scarborough, where hundreds of scooters were rumoured to gather.

Three of us were so hyped from the Havering experience that we set about preparing for a trip to Scarborough on the August Bank Holiday. Myself, Steve 'Stick' Evans and Ricky Kashir made this epic trip to the other end of the country with some trepidation, as we had nothing to go on other than a few encouraging phone calls from the Burnley lot. What we found at the end of a 14-hour trip was beyond our wildest dreams. We were met by clubs from all over the north of England who treated us like gods from another planet. We couldn't believe the sight of so many customised Vespas and Lambrettas. There were probably three or four hundred machines spread amongst the cranes at Scarborough fishing docks – the atmosphere was supercharged. We found to our amazement that we could leave our possessions, helmets etc on our scooters, disappear for a drinking session and when we returned everything would be intact.

On the way home from this momentous weekend, the three of us were still absorbing everything that we had seen, and we knew that things had to change in *order to become part of this scene. We decided to drop the 'Lowrider' tag, rename the club Modrapheniacs, and dedicate the club to travelling the country on scooters to meet new people who shared our vision and to spread the faith too.*

The name: 'Modrapheniacs' was a name that I had dreamt up some years earlier whilst listening to the original Quadrophenia *album and avidly studying the black and white picture book that came with the record. It had been put in the frame when we were originally naming the club but had come up against one of John Loving's titles, 'Dorchminster Mountain Coal and Oil Scooter Club'. In order to end the interminable discussion about these two names, we opted for the Lowrider option. But now I knew the club had found its rightful name, and if anyone didn't like 'Modrapheniacs', they could leave the club. I should emphasise that, at this time, there was no stigma attached to the word 'mod'. Many scooterists considered themselves to be mods although they wore wide jeans, DMs, greatcoats or parkas. There was no animosity between the north and south, it was just a feeling of belonging to a tremendous brotherhood. You had to be united because; you knew when you went home you would once again be outnumbered by the local greasers or NEBs (Non-Educated Bastards), as they were known in Burnley. There was also no nicey 'we all ride two wheels' camaraderie back then. They hated us, and we hated them. It seemed that scooters had never really gone out of fashion in Lancashire and Yorkshire. So, we were going to ensure that the south now came out of the wilderness too.*

On our return to Dorset we told the club about our visit to the scooter Mecca and the next trip to Scarborough became the hottest talking point. At this time, I sent the famous 'Greasers in the Sewers' letter to Scooter and Scooterist, and people from all over the country responded positively to the letter.

Also whilst we'd been in Scarborough, we'd been plagued with requests for club patches; you couldn't buy these treasured items for any amount of money (this was pre-Paddy Smith), they could only be swapped for other club patches. We returned to Scarborough the following Easter, 15-strong and armed with club patches plus wooden shields mounted on our rear racks. We had also adopted the phenomenon of road sweeper mudflaps (from York SC) which had left many Dorset lorries mudflapless!

Now a strong healthy scooter club, we attended the LCGB Southend Rallies of 1978 and 1979, which were to see the first outbreaks of large-scale scootering violence since the Sixties – the local teds and Hells Angels being the enemy. These scenes were quite unbelievable, with scooterists from all over the country being bound together by an unspoken bond of loyalty and actually taking the upper hand. In 1979 the rally ended with a torched police car and the SPG waiting at the gate. There were to be no more Southend rallies. Because of this, Modrapheniacs became the last club ever to win the Southend Rally Cup.

If this cup was to be the clubs first claim to fame, it certainly wasn't going to be the last. We, amongst other clubs, had been approached at the Southend Rally to play an active part in the filming of a new film, this film being 'Quadrophenia'. We thought the whole thing was a wind up until one of the directors turned up at the New Inn in Poole waving a chequebook.

Before the filming began there was a Northern organised run to Brighton. The Daily Mirror reported 'On the 19th August 1977, mods will celebrate an anniversary of anarchy. This weekend, 10 years after bloody battles with the rockers, the mods are planning a reunion in Brighton.' I don't know about a reunion, I shouldn't think there was one person from the Sixties there, but it was certainly the first time that northern and southern scooterists had united on the south coast. Sixties' mods had only really ever travelled within their local region, the new generation, being less numerous, were travelling hundreds of miles in order to achieve reasonable numbers. This was to set the scene right up to the noughties.

After the filming of Quadrophenia, *and during the 18 months before its release, there was so much hype that the Modrapheniacs membership went into three figures and we saw the first Vespas joining the club, one of which was ridden by Phil (Gormont) Birch who was later to become 'Number One.' The Modrapheniacs were to be an inspiration to a horde of new south coast scooter clubs, and we paid frequent visits to towns such as Torquay, Plymouth and Seaton, often becoming allies against the overwhelming numbers of south coast greasers.*

On a local level, the club existed on a diet of weekly Sunday runs starting from our meeting place at the Sandford Hotel, Wareham. A cross section of people including skins, punks, mods, soul boys, even a couple of really camp lads (that's a story of its own), were all bound together by a love of scootering. However, whilst we were popular with scooterists, the same was not true of the many local bike gangs. This resulted in many skirmishes in which we were always outnumbered. One such incident led to me sacrificing four teeth whilst biting a hammer that a biker was waving. Indeed this scrap was so big, involving about a dozen of us, and nearly a hundred bikers, that as well as sustaining injuries and providing local and national press with column inches, we lost our meeting place. It was subsequently decided to hold meetings on alternate weeks at the New Inn, Poole, and Goldies Bar, Dorchester.

"Of the ... new mod type clubs that sprung up around london. these were afflicted with the typical London delusion that they were the first

and the best at everything but in reality had
no idea of what had been occurring in the
true underground scene for the
previous eight years."

Also during the late Seventies some of us were to venture into scooter racing, but this didn't sit easy following our often public hostility towards non-road scooters. This led to the mainly Weymouth section breaking away to form Wessex SC, a racing club led by Colin Taylor.

Upon the release of **Quadrophenia***, scooter clubs became deluged with new members and the numbers on national runs went from several hundred, to thousands, culminating in the 1980 Scarborough rally where the town nearly collapsed under the sheer weight of numbers which made the front page of many nationals.*

A spate of local clubs sprang up due to alleged views of the Modrapheniacs, their members disillusioned with what they saw as the Modrapheniacs lack of interest in the 'new' mod scene. This couldn't have been further from the truth, but these were the early cracks beginning to appear between two new sub-tribes, the mods and scooter boys. The club also tried to distance itself from the north-south divide that occurred during the early Eighties. I believe that this was mainly caused by some – not all – of the more arrogant, new mod type clubs that sprung up around London. These were afflicted with the typical London delusion that they were the first and the best at everything, but in reality they had no idea of what had been occurring in the true underground scene for the previous eight years.

Towards the end of 1982, John Loving and myself tended to take a back seat and let some of the young whippersnappers run things. I am very pleased to see that the club has survived and thrived. I know that John has been there all along, and I continued to be a (honorary) member whilst spending far too much time pursuing my scooter interest through Hi Style Products and DJ work at scooter and soul gigs. Then, latterly, due to a mortgage, kids and an ex, plus a career in the car industry, I took a backseat. I still have my Lambrettas, and a fierce burning pride in having helped to start what has become one of the institutions of British scootering, the scooter boys.

I would like to thank everyone else who helped, rode, drank, fought, laughed and bonded but, having the memory of a goldfish with alcoholic amnesia, I'll just have to assume you know who you are.

The Lean Years

Another old scooter boy, Paddy, who did, and still does, ride out of the Stockport Mod Squad Scooter Club since the Seventies, will now shine the beam of his old Lambretta front headlamp on to briefly explaining the 'lean years' of the social history of scootering, plus, a hilarious tale of a Seventies trip.

Paddy: *There wasn't so much a north/south divide on the scooter scene; it's just that after the mods of the Sixties had all but vanished, scooters were seeming abandoned 'down south' along with the mod look. But we kept bang at it 'up north'. Scootering was a way of life for some of us.*

When southerners got back into the reincarnation of mod in the late Seventies, they mainly rode Lambrettas, while most from northern clubs only rode old, fat Vespas with huge road sweeper mudflaps acquired from Arctic wagons. Seemingly, York Scooter Club was the leader in this trend. Southerners were more mod orientated in dress, once again. Before the resurgence of 2-tone we tended to be more up-to-date with fashions, wearing high top pants and French flares with leather bomber jackets and parkas for riding. I personally wore a Harrington under my parka. Everyone wore open face helmets with chin-cups, and some of our lads put silver tape all over them to make them shine. Most of our club had the same helmets, so when we went to Southend-on-Sea once we stood out from the pack. And even though we were called the Stockport Mod Squad, we really only had three proper 'mirrored-up' mods in our club – most had no chrome at all on their side-panels, just nice paint jobs with an Anselotti or Sneterton seat. Also, we had our own membership numbers sown on our parkas, which is a story in its own right!

There was only one kind of rally patch back then and it was done by a bloke called Paddy Smith, not my own good-self, I hasten to add. Paddy made them for each rally and you could only get a patch if you went to the event; he destroyed any he had left over so it was proof that you had attended and arrived on a scooter. A badge of honour amongst those in the know. He also made an end of season patch which you could only get if you had the full set for that year. We had our own club patches as well, one we would sell to other clubs plus a members-only patch. Another thing the northern lads did was to stitch northern breweries' bar towels on their parkas, or even make them into scarves. I still collect towels to this day.

Anyway, in 1978, 18 of us set off from our Stockport Mod Squad Scooter Club base at 10pm for our yearly ride to the National Scooter Rally in Scarborough. As we drove through Buxton we decided to grab a late night drink and pulled up at what looked like a quaint, old traditional pub. A few minutes later drinks were ordered. Then the pubs regulars arrived, about 25 Hells Angels who weren't a happy bunch. We were sat in their pub, and not wanting to upset them anymore, most of us drank up quickly. But every scooter club has its nutter, and ours was Mike Lee. He decided that it wasn't time to leave; it was time to order another drink – the Hells Angels surrounded him. So to save his life we shoved our way through them and dragged him outside for a quick getaway, with him shouting he was going to take them all on single handed. We convinced him it wasn't a good idea, and rode off swiftly into the night.

Lucky we hadn't had any breakdowns en route by then. When we were halfway to Scarborough, one of our club members, Chris Gardener, (also known as Skitz, who had finally caught up with us after leaving home about an hour later than us) began to have problems. He was riding full out on a Jet 200 Lambretta with a tuned barrel borrowed from a mate of his. I was riding at the back the pack on a Lammy and I heard him coming up behind me. I was doing about 50mph, so I knew he'd been fair bobbin' on as he flew past me with his girlfriend fast asleep on the back of the scooter, held onto his flip flop back rest with bungee straps.

The next thing, about a mile further on, it looked like he was riding backwards. He flew past me going sideways, speedway style, back down the road with the scooters rear wheel locked solid and his girlfriend still fast asleep. Shit!

He disappeared out of view so we all turned round and went back to find them both in the pitch black, hopefully without any serious injuries. We found him pushing the scooter out of a field in a somewhat damaged condition, the scooter that is. The pair of them were just shaken up, luckily. He decided that fixing the scooter was too big of a job for the side of the road, so he asked for someone to tow him. Everyone went quiet as most had new scooters that were piled up with camping gear, and they also didn't fancy burning out a clutch. So as I had an old £40 Lambretta Li 150 I said it was OK and I'll do it with girlfriend and gear passed on to the others.

Another drop of luck we stumbled on was an old, closed petrol station (in the Seventies most didn't open all night). And, following a bit of rooting around some old bits of rope were found and we managed to make a tow rope about 20 feet long. We set off again, now at a slower pace, because I was learning how to tow someone without burning out my clutch, and was getting the hang of towing too.

Several miles later I thought we were getting the hang of the towing lark while doing about 40mph, and I turned to check that Chris was OK. On glancing back he seemed like he was waving me to speed up, so I did. I did this a few more times and he did the same each time. Eventually we were doing about 60mph down a long hill, and as we went round a sweeping left hand bend I looked back. This time

I thought I heard Chris shouting me to speed up even more. But what he had been doing was frantically screaming, while waving one hand, for me to stop! Only with the speed we were going, and coming into a left-hand bend, his scooter had swung to the right, out-of-control like speed boats do with water skiers. I now realised what was happening. Looking straight ahead there were two bollards in the middle of the road; I went to the left and Chris went to the right with the rope getting caught on one bollard uprooting it. Not before the rope wrapped round the bollard nearly pulled both of us off at the same time. Chris had been slung shot and over took me. Once again we'd had another slice of luck with no damage done.

After that we kept the speed down but we still had a final near miss. This was when an old bloke in a Mini overtook Chris, and then tried to pull in between the two scooters, totally ignoring the bits of rag tied to the rope. Chris would have killed him if he could have caught up with him after the night's events.

When a few of us noticed that we were on reserve – Lammies didn't have petrol gauges – a decision was made that around 10 miles further we'd pull over and wait for daylight to find a petrol station rather than run out juice. So we pulled over to the kerb in the middle of nowhere, shone our six volt Lambretta lights on the grass verge while setting up our tents and got some well-deserved sleep.

At 7am the next morning we were rudely awoken by a loud voice shouting for us get up, and shaking our tents as well. When I opened the zip I was surprised to see a load of angry coppers standing there. Eventually when everyone had surfaced the coppers demanded to know exactly why we had pitched out tents there. We tried to explain why, but this big sergeant wasn't having any of it. He then demanded we had to get off Scarborough Golf Course, double sharpish.

So we had the police standing over us shouting that we were in deep trouble unless we packed up double quick and got ready to move within minutes. We hurriedly did so. All, that is, except Chris who refused to hurry and said his scooter had broken down and he couldn't move it. The big sergeant came over and shouted at him to move it right now, or else! Chris, who was kneeling down at the scooter casually said "Why don't you put it in your big mouth and move it for me then."

The sergeant went ballistic and grabbed Chris and, with the help of another copper dragged him off to the Black Maria van. The two coppers then got in the back with him and, we're led to believe they explained to Chris why he should move his scooter right away with the help of Mr Truncheon.

Eventually we moved off, with me towing Chris again, and arrived at Scarborough where we found the camp site. Chris stripped the scooter down to find both the piston rings had gone because of over tuning, he said. But we knew it had not been run in properly and it was thrashed. One of the lads phoned a mate who was coming over to Scarborough later and got him to bring a spare engine in his sidecar.

Finally, with things sorted, we carried on to have a blinding weekend. Remember it was the Seventies; we had around £15 in our pockets for food and beer, and with petrol at 39 p a gallon we'd no need to worry.

We were young; we were The Stockport Mod Squad Scooter Club.

Power To The Scooter Boys

With the second coming of mod, so came a seconding coming of scooter riders. But not all second coming scooterists jumped on a motorcycle with 10″ wheels and an enclosed engine because of mod, or the time-honoured flick *Quadrophenia*. One of these lads was Ste.

<u>Ste:</u> *If you ask anyone on a scooter rally nowadays how they got in to scooters, probably 99% will say* Quadrophenia, The Jam, Northern Soul, *mod revival. They'd seen older lads riding them and fancied getting one because they looked cool, and other similar answers. I was a bit different. I loved watching Citizen Smith as a kid and he rode a scooter – yes really! One episode the local gangster came in pub and said "Whose is the Lambretta outside?"*

Inquisitively I asked my dad what a Lambretta was, and he got some old photos out. Himself, and my uncle, had had them in Sixties; proper mod affairs, loads of extra lights and mirrors, the full shebang. At first I thought scooters were just the same as the mopeds the old fellas who lived on our estate rode around on, but with all the accessories it became something completely different. At that time I still didn't know about mods, and over the next few years I completely forgot all about scooters (but I still carried on watching Citizen Smith).

Then punk happened. To be honest I thought it was a right racket and they were all a 'clip' (clip meaning, a right state and badly dressed.) So when one day in the school playground aged nine, some older kid came over and said "Are you a mod, or a punk?" I just said mod straight away not knowing what a mod was; I just knew I wasn't a punk. Good thing I did. The kid next to me said punk, and got put on his arse. The strange thing was, me and the other kid were dressed the same; polo shirt, V neck jumper and Adidas Kick – but he'd said the wrong thing. That night I asked the old fella if he knew what a mod was. Once again he got them same photos out from few years before. He then told me all about the fighting at

Brighton, the bands and the clothes, but missed out the 'speed' that was necked for some reason.

Well, it was just before my tenth birthday.

A few weeks later I stayed up late one Sunday night, and The South Bank Show came on. Featured on the show was Quadrophenia, *and it started with the clip where they all ride into Brighton. I was hooked. The problem was, the look and the clothes were 15 years old, and how did you get hold of them?*

Gradually the shops wised up, but at first it was just our idea of mod, which looking back was more perry influenced than mod anyway. I'd been shoplifting mod gear, and records, for quite a while and how my mother didn't realise when she gave me a quid pocket money and I came back home with bags of gear every Saturday, is beyond me. Maybe she just buried her head in the sand. Then one Saturday I went into W H Smith and the book 'Mods' by Richard Barnes was in there. Straight away it was under the parka and on its way home with me. After reading the book, something wasn't right. It kept saying how the original mods, the main faces, were always getting new gear and stopped wearing certain attire when others caught on. The revival mods were wearing things at least 15 years old in design or two-tone suits.

Then when I started going to Old Trafford and watching Man U, I noticed slightly older lads at match wearing different clobber; this style was what became known as casual. They seemed more mod than mod, as it were. So the parka went. My preference in clothes changed, but I still loved the Sixties music, especially soul, and the scooters – my love of scooters never died.

It would be another six or seven years though before I owned a scooter, and when I did get one, I wore clothes that lent more to the Paninaro, the Italian look (Chipie, Chevignon and late Eighties' labels) nothing at all like mod.

If you read some of the books on mods and scootering you would think it had all but died off by 1966/67, then it suddenly reappeared again in 1979. It didn't die off, it just moved north, out of the London media spotlight. A strange world still existed in the north of soul all-nighters and lads in flares riding scooters to Scarborough on Bank Holiday weekends. The southern revivalists didn't really have a clue about these, so when a rally at Scarborough was attended by both parties for the first time, they didn't really see eye-to-eye. It was the same when the 'new' mods in cheap Sta-Prest suits shuffled onto the dance floor in Wigan Casino; they were mocked. Something had to give, and it did.

At first it was a north/south divide, of sorts. Then many of the lads who were sick of the mod elitist attitudes, and their clothes snobbery, wanted to distance themselves from the mod revivalist. A new name was born; The 'scooter boys'. Violence to mods started too.

Over the coming years various contrasting tastes in clothes, music and diverse, customised scooters were seen at rallies, with the odd bit of fisticuffs still. But every one of those individuals had a love and a common bond for one most important item, the scooter.

To this day I attend rallies on regular bases, DJing at most events. The biggest rally of the calendar, and in the world, is an annual event on the Isle of Wight during the August Bank Holiday period. The island is awash with scooters from around the globe, and nowadays the local community welcomes us with open arms – not like back in the day. The scooter boy culture has never gone away, it has simply moved more underground, once again.

6

CASUALLY ACCEPTABLE IN THE EIGHTIES

Britain's 1980s embarked with the first female leader of the western world in power; from behind the solid, oak black glossed door of number 10 Downing Street, and in parliament, *she* also introduced widespread economic reforms including the privatisation of nationalised industries and the de-regulation of stock markets; and on the second day of the new 10 year period in the 20th-century, British steel workers downed tools and went on strike. And so began the Eighties decadence.

Strikes in the core industries were instigated at the drop of a hardhat from then on in the Eighties, thus setting a precedence for rail, ferry and transport staff – even Channel Tunnel workers stopped boring – to decide enough was enough too; they joined their brothers on workers' rights marches and also formed their own picket lines. The yearlong 1984-85 'Coal Not Dole' miners' strike was a defining moment in British industrial relations, because the miners were defeated. The strike defeat significantly shattered the backbone of the National Union of Mineworkers and the British Trades Unions; this being a major political and ideological victory for Margaret Thatcher, the queen of mind-games and the holder of British citizen's destinies and livelihoods.

The miners' strike became a symbolic struggle, and was seen as political rather than about jobs by some, which exposed deep divisions in British society and caused considerable bitterness, especially in the north. Southern Old Bill and Met coppers had waved their overtime slips and banknotes at the ravaged and pot-less miners from behind barriers during the strike, just like their southern counterparts and cockneys did to scousers and northerners at the match. In return the southern fairies received tenners and twenties raised aloft to the tune of 'thank you very much for paying my Giro, thank you very much... !' Distressingly, though, 10 deaths resulted from events around the strike: six pickets died during pitched battles with the police, three teenagers perished searching for coal, and a taxi driver was killed while taking a non-striking miner to work.

Also, mass unemployment hit the UK hard and a recession hammered the manufacturing industry. Figures for folk on the scrapheap/dole rose to 3,500,000 at the midway point of the decade and no-one in authority was listening to their voices.

Riots also became commonplace on the streets of the Britain, unconnected to the troubles that were happening across the Irish Sea in Northern Ireland at the time. The Brixton uprising/riots were a confrontation between the Met Police and protesters between the 10th and 12th April 1981; these conflicts resulted in large scale injuries on both sides with hundreds of vehicles and buildings being vandalised and torched. Riots spread like wildfires, and the fireball effect and petrol bombs then engulfed Toxteth, Liverpool, with disorder occurring in July 1981. These disturbances arose, in part, from long-standing tensions between the local police and the black community with CS gas used for the first time (legally?) in the country. Then Moss Side, Manchester, went up in flames. So did Chapeltown, Leeds, and Handsworth, Birmingham, as well as many other towns and cities too. Preston town centre would have, but it was raining. Further riots manifested throughout the Eighties in Broadwater Farm, London and Dewsbury, Yorkshire; and once again in Brixton, Handsworth and Chapeltown, plus the overcrowded prisons regularly saw major disturbances.

Then there was the overnight Argentinian invasion of the Islas Malvinas that ignited the Falklands War in April 1982 (British forces recovered the Falkland Islands and emerged victorious four months later). Wars aren't the answers to anything – but whom I to question these actions?

There were major tragedies at football matches too. At Valley Parade, on the 11th May 1985, the home ground of Bradford City, the main stand caught fire during a game between Bradford and Lincoln City; this on the day when Bradford City were supposed to have celebrated their winning of the Football League Third Division trophy. A total of 56 people died and more than 265 others were injured. On the same day as the Bradford fire, an innocent teenager was killed when a wall collapsed on him at

Birmingham's St Andrews stadium after a game against Leeds. And only 18 days later fans were crushed against and under a wall in the Heysel Stadium in Brussels, Belgium, before the start of the European Cup

Final between Liverpool and Juventus. 39 Italian fans died and 600 were injured. The disaster resulted in all English clubs being placed under an indefinite ban by UEFA from all European competitions until 1990–91, with Liverpool being excluded for an additional year. On the 15th April 1989, at Hillsborough, Sheffield Wednesday's ground, 96 people lost their lives and 766 were injured; all of them were Liverpool fans. The official inquiry into this disaster, the Taylor Report, concluded that the main reason for the deaths of the fans was the failure of police control.

Hooliganism also reached a violent peak when a riot at Luton Town's Kenilworth Road at an FA Cup sixth-round match between Luton and Millwall saw the ground and surrounding areas totally wrecked. This led to a ban on away supporters by Luton Town and Luton's expulsion from the Football League Cup in the 1986–87 season. The club also began to enforce a membership card scheme, which Thatcher wanted to have adopted at *all* grounds across England. 14 arrests, numerous stabbings and other injuries occurred in a lawlessness incident aboard a Sealink boat, the Koningen Beatrix, bound for Amsterdam. Followers of Manchester United and West Ham fought a savage battle on the cross-Channel ferry which forced the boat to return to Harwich, England, following the setting off a distress signal and the captain fearing for the lives of 2,000 passengers aboard. FIFA added an additional year exclusion ban for English clubs in Europe because of this incident. There was trouble nearly every week at grounds up and down country back then.

But the nemesis, Maggie T, had it sorted! Didn't she? Big Brother had begun watching and the thought police were in control.

Music genres ebbed and flowed through the Eighties, from home-grown sounds and cults, to once more the Yank influx of influence on UK kids; post punk, new wave, new romantic, goth, hip hop, indie, synth pop, house music and, God created 'Madchester.'

Fashions were loud, and were tasteless. The most exceptional foreign items being Miami Vice rolled up sleeves, shoulder-padded suits. Magnum Hawaiian shirts, and Cowboy boots and legwarmers. Say no more.

By New Years Eve 1990, Thatcher was two-and-a-half years in to her third term has Prime Minister. And another recession was on the horizon. Yes a pattern – and I don't mean a diamond Pringle pattern jumper that southerners adored – had formed in the Eighties, one that seems not too dissimilar and all too familiar of today's environment in the UK.

But right through all the aforementioned, there was a culture making waves, tidal waves, bigger than the pioneers, or anyone who had noticed the movement's progression, could have perceived. This cult being, casual/dresser. The groundswell and upsurge of casual/dresser took the UK by storm and had gathered its velocity by 1983; a cult that had made quantum leaps from its humble beginnings and its under the radar crescendo in the north-west. The cult was unaffiliated to any one music category too, having no specific alliance. Lads would spend fortunes on, or 'acquire', labels and looks that came and went like night and day. There were more labels and looks than towns and cities in the song 'It's Grim Up North' by The Justified Ancients of Mu Mu (The JAMMs). And yet for all the consumerist elements, as a cult it still seemed avant-garde and set benchmarks.

1980 was a transmogrification for myself and the threads hanging in my wardrobe alone by the ass-end of the year that consisted of the remnants of an assortment of punk attire, a fostered London look of an MA-1 flight jacket from a shop in Preston called Easywear, and two Lonsdale of London sweatshirts (a grey one with black velvet writing and a mustard short sleeved one with black logo both purchased from the men's outfitters Burtons, because you got bags more buzz from the gaff). I wanted/needed the grey one after watching the flick *McVicar* at the ABC picture house in town one Friday night. I had a red and a black Harrington jacket with mandatory tartan lining, a chunky burgundy knit jumper and a blue & white/silvery flecked, oversized fisherman jumper – these had been bought in Stolen From Ivor, formerly Clobber. Clobber had stocked funky gear such as bowling shirts, baggy topped strides – that you tucked your jumper in and polished tin-tipped, dangly white belts. A fine, woollen long sleeved grey two-button polo, with horizontal quarter inch yellow and burgundy adjacent looping stripes. Two Ben Sherman shirts; a gingham and a Prince of Wales check, plus varied colourways of Fred Perry from an indoor market stall. Fruit of the Loom white T-shirts. Straight leg Levi's and Wrangler cords and jeans out of Lord Antony, Millets and a large Army & Navy store. In the Army & Navy I use to browse the circular rails and sneakily hang two pairs over one hanger, hold them up, at a distance, and ask the female assistant if I could try *the* pair on. Less than five minutes later I left the shop after replacing the hanger on the rail, with now only one pair hung-over, the other pair under a pair I'd 'obtained' previously that I was wearing. A yellow Le Coq Sportif cycling top with navy piping and wording with a ribbed zipped collar. A white and navy blue three stripe trefoil Adidas T-shirt, a golden panthered, brown Slazenger jumper and an ST2 adi black cagoule – because they had no navy blue left – with obligatory red quilted lining. All these were from Merigolds Sports Shop situated in St John's Centre, near the bus station in Preston. And a Crombie that my Mum had treated me to, and which hangs in my wardrobe to this day.

Under my bed were a pair of ox blood Doc's, adi Kicks, navy and white slip on yachting shoes, burgundy loafers and a pair of beige, soft-soled mesh shoes (who I'd borrowed these off in an intoxicated state is anyone's guess). I had an 18" Spanish gold belcher chain and sleeper earring. And I had the developments of a wedge with a burgundy stripe above my right ear from a semi-permanent sachet of hair dye, or a crewcut. (The initial influence of the casual/dresser came from the soul boys round our way who'd made pilgrimages to their Mecca, Wigan Casino, and other Northern Soul all-nighters following conceptualises.)

There was also an influence from New Romantics who wore elaborate showy clothes, a somewhat backlash to punk's 'whatever' scruffiness. Both male and female supported motley, miscellaneous costumes. Only the males ventured towards their feminine side in dress, and the wearing of make-up came hand-in-hand with the diversity! Image-conscious, mirror-hogging, Prince Charming trendsetters trimmed themselves in a mixer of over-the-top flamboyance. A manifestation that couldn't be pigeonholed. 'Futuristic', poseurs' schmutter ranged from theatrical pirate rigouts – add facial war paint and eye patch – right through to tailor made, wide lapelled pizzazz silk suits. They crowned this semblance with a dyed or bleached bouffant barnet or a heavily lopsided wedgehead. Yes, it was a right potpourri. All very strange to outsiders of the cult.

Now then, round my neck of the woods at the time there were plenty of sorts who adorned the flap-over shirt and baggy topped trousers with burgundy flick but, only a few went the full hog. One lad that had gone to a secondary school near to where I resided, and his buddy, took to slipping on red, 6" high stilettos and an abundance of jewellery. Boy, did I giggle when they caught the same bus to town on Friday night and alighted at Preston Bus Station – a Brutalist iconic building. I wasn't really laughing at what they were wearing, but for the way they struggled to toddle across the bus apron with their dignity, grandeur and panache intact as they twiddled with their beads. I asked someone once who knew the chaps if they were homosexual or summat? "No. They're definitely not. It's their sense of self-expression, and 'cause they like Boy George!"

In 1981, intense stimulating sportswear came to my attention (I could hark on perpetually) and by the autumn of the year, I began an apprenticeship in the building trade so had a bit of brass in my pocket. The materialistic world was my oyster, or so I thought...

Saying that, this opened the door to wearing pastel shades and poofy pink in the early casual days. And I'm as culpable has anyone on that one. Apart from nearly every Pringle and Lyle & Scott I owned being camp as you like, I once wore a combination of pink Fila T-shirt, yellow Sergio Tacchini trackie bottoms and Nike Wimbledons. Get me!

Yes, the Eighties were a weighty part in my social history, and a learning curve. Spatial continuums when you'd to be simultaneously instantaneous with your head, fists and feet too!

Take It To The Limit

Situated near the confluence of five rivers, with its primeval foundations laid on the site of seven hills long before the Iron Age in South Yorkshire, lays the now fifth largest city in England and one of the eight English core cities group. This city being Sheffield, where folk are hard, where the music is forte, get around town. Sheffield's history is forged in the hardness of the steel industry. It is also home to the streets in the sky, harsh and eerie estate, that is, the Brutalist Park Hill Flats – a bohemian urban enclave when constructed. The city can boast, though, that it has the oldest football club founded way back in 1857, Sheffield FC. But, there is an intense, bitter divide and shattered harmony among 'Steel City' dwellers, with hostilities rife. Because most town folk either follow one of the other two football clubs based in the city; Sheffield United, the Blades, or Sheffield Wednesday, the Owls. These rivalries and revulsion for each other's teams are well documented in such books has Blades *Business Crew, 1&2, Flying with the Owls Crime Squad, Steel City Derby* and Ronnie Sharpe's *Sharpe as a Blade, 1&2* – segments of which you may have read earlier in the book. There isn't much brotherly primate love betwixt these two sets of Yorkshire Northern Monkeys.

Sheffield is also a city where 'men are men' and drink at least 15 pints of bitter on Friday nights in spit and sawdust gadger only pubs. They spill more ale down their waistcoats than their southern counterparts could ever sup. They consider moustaches cool as hell and trendy too. And, in the late Seventies/early Eighties the city was the heartbeat of the New Romantic movement which drew their musical inspirations and sounds from glam rock, David Bowie and Roxy Music while also blending early punk with new wave. Most were also hugely influenced by a synthesiser using German band, Kraftwerk. Then adding newly developed technological, musical artefacts and computers they produced an electronic beat. New tunes throbbed. Amongst the audiences at gigs were followers from the south, the Blitz Kids, who travelled up north to watch these new bands and they also attended the Blitz nightclub in London, were they'd got their nickname from. New Romanticism thrived in Sheffield's inner city pubs and clubs with local groups that formed at the forefront of the scene setting standards second to none. London was where it began, but Sheffield was where it was at for bands. A man who witnessed the development of New Romanticism, and was involved in the chain of events, but didn't don any lipstick, powder or paint – he just dished out plenty of slap though – was Steve Cowens, author of *Blades Business Crew 1&2*, and co-author of *Steel City Derby* amongst other books.

Steve: *There are not many football lads who will admit to being heavily involved in the New Romantic scene! After all, it was very effeminate for a start and the name New Romantic hardly makes you feel, and sound, like a hard-case, does it? Well, I for one was well into it. In fact, I loved the cult at the time and Sheffield was one of the major flag bearers for the scene. By 1980 we had several bands carrying the New Romantic banner:*

Human League, ABC, Heaven 17, and Cabaret Voltaire were some of the first big bands to emerge in a new electronic synthesised sound from in and around Sheffield. Other bands from round the country included Japan, Soft Cell, Duran Duran and Spandau Ballet. The latter two went on to become massive names when they later commercialised and went mainstream.

The New Romantic scene actually emerged in London at the back end of 1978. Steve Strange had began hosting a few evenings titled 'Bowie Night' at a club called Billy's, in Soho, then the Blitz Club. Boy George actually worked for Strange as a cloakroom attendant at the Blitz, but he was allegedly sacked after being caught helping himself from women's purses that had been left behind the counter.

Bands replaced guitars with synthesisers and traditional drum kits made way for electric drum pads and beat machines which pulsed out pulsating beats. Sheffield was very much the music capital of England at the time; such clubs like the Limit on West Street gave little known bands of the time an arena to play in. Ultravox, U2, UB40, Madness, B52's, Pink Floyd, UK Subs, Cockney Rejects, Siouxsie and the Banshees, Joy Division, The Damned and New Order all cut their teeth in the Limit, often playing gigs to small crowds.

The Limit was brilliant, its low ceilings created a moody atmosphere, almost spiritual. Its name spread so much so that people came from far and wide to sample, and inhale, the smell of stale piss, the cannabis smog and fusty old rotting carpets. If you stayed in the same place too long your Gazelles stuck to the carpeted floor – you had to keep moving. By '82 the Limit was probably the best known club in Yorkshire: think Haçienda circa the Manchester indie scene 1988. Well, the Limit was our Haçienda, a place where New Romantics, punks, skins, mods, rockers and casuals all mixed peacefully. This until the casuals of United and Wednesday stopped mixing with each other as war broke out in '83. Before that, both sets of lads would often drink side-by-side, although there was always an atmosphere and edge to these situations.

The New Romantic birds used to look like sexy toned down punk girls: spiky frizzed up hair complimented with long, dangly earrings and other piercings; heavy standout make up and mohair jumpers completed the look. Apart from the outlandish clothes that the lads wore, some of them went a bit OTT by adding make up to their faces for the look, which was never my bag, I hasten to add. I was a bit more conservative, preferring the tailored look of Bowie rather than the frilly shirt camp look.

In late 1980 I celebrated my 16th birthday and moved away from the scene in dress terms and swapped Bowie trousers for Lois cords, side buttoning shirts for Slazenger or Pringle jumpers, and daft pointy shoes for Adidas Barringtons or Gazelles; the casual movement had taken off in Sheffield.

In 1981 a trend war broke out, and for two or three months, skinheads and trendies (casuals) went into battle most Saturday afternoons. This was a throwback to the mods and rockers battles for supremacy in the city in the Sixties. The aptly named 'Peace Gardens' in Sheffield was usually the starting point of the hostilities. But week-by-week, the casuals' numbers grew-and-grew, and the skins soon realised they had bitten off more than they could chew. Not so long later, the skinheads stood side-by-side with the casuals; be it in town or on the terraces at Bramall Lane.

Other big nightclubs later emerged in Sheffield, most notably The Leadmill, The Music Factory on London Road, and Occasions in town (or Coke-asions as we called it). The Music Factory and Leadmill were Blades strongholds whilst the Limit was mainly Wednesday with Occasions a mix of the two.

The Police were happy with the fact that on Friday and Saturday nights the two rival firms were a few miles apart as they went to their clubs after 11pm which left them to put their feet up and dunk a gingernut into their strong, sugary tea. On a personal level, I could go in most clubs without getting a tug off my Wednesday enemies. The Wednesday lads knew I was a fair enough lad and I carried a code with me, and many a time I stepped up to the mark to stop one of their lads taking a severe beating.

In 1983, a new war broke out, and United and Wednesday would never be seen together again. A visit from Leeds to Hillsborough saw 80 Blades turn out with Wednesday meeting in the Blue Bell pub on High Street in town. Wednesday turned a good mob out that day and had around 120 lads in their midst. Inside the Blue Bell it was strained to say the least. It was weird, really. The furthest apart from each other in the pub were the lads who hated their rivals and wanted to rip into each other. The middle ground was taken up by the lads who could tolerate each other; I was stood in that bracket. And, the lads who knew each other, and were friends, stood chatting – this no doubt helped stop an inevitable battle. Then, a shout went up that Leeds had arrived, and Wednesday filed out. United stayed put.

Whilst we were out for Leeds that day there was no way we would fight by Wednesday's side. After five minutes or so news got to us that Leeds had gone through the Wednesday firm and were walking through the hole in the road subway which brought you out around 30 yards from the 'Bell. We piled out of the back door and filed up a narrow alleyway that led to High Street. Leeds fans came up the escalators and it kicked-off. United's lads had armed themselves with stiletto shoes stolen from the display outside a shoe shop and battle commenced in the narrow alleyway. After some initial to-ing and fro-ing, the Leeds firm backed off. Later that night, United and Wednesday clashed on West Street, and never again would there be peace between the rivals.

By the time I was 19, I'd become totally embroiled in violence at football. I'd also started to get a name for myself, and I knew I'd arrived because the older lads that I looked up to began taking me to games with them. Also, I never suffered the taxing that other young lads had to cope with, which was totally wrong. Some lads were relieved of clothes, money, and gold, by a couple of United's main actors. I hated the fact that this was happening and once confronted a tax collector after he relieved a pal of his Kappa coat. This only led to my reputation growing for sticking up for our younger element.

By '84, the numbers of United's casual youth were seemingly growing by the week and I knew it was time to challenge Wednesday's undoubted supremacy in the city. This we did. And one small scale scuffle outside the Penny Black pub in town, between 30 of our pups and around the same numbers of Wednesday's main actors saw a change in the way we looked at Wednesday. I'd ran into them as they belittled us by spitting and slapping us. This led to all our pups steaming in. And although Wednesday didn't run, we had backed them off a few yards before the police came and saved us. As the audacity of our attack sunk in, they had a go back. We were buzzing and I knew in my heart-of-hearts that the fear we had carried for their firm for years had been lifted. It was now a time for a power shift in Sheffield.

Anyway, getting back to the music and clubs: The Music Factory was a brilliant club, which was frequented by United's lads, but things took a turn for the worse in the late Eighties. A few of United's lads were making a small fortune selling 'disco biscuits' in the club when the rave scene took off, because the bouncers were local and powerless to stop this trade taking place under their noses. Only this fact came to the attention of The Music Factory's management. Then, one weekend, all the door-staff were replaced by a hired troop of bouncers from Nottingham. With this, almost overnight, the BBC were barred from what they saw as their club. Trouble erupted almost weekly from then on as United's lads clashed with the doormen whose numbers grew to cope with the attacks. The power struggle saw a firearm discharged in the club one night. Also, the club was CS gassed; distress flares fired at the doors and a van that the bouncers came up in was set on fire. For my part, I never really got involved, I wasn't going to risk my liberty so a couple of United's firm could line their pockets selling 'E's.' I'd back my team and firm up to the hilt against other mobs and such, but not so they could get rich selling drugs. After 18 months of trouble, which led to several lads being jailed, the trouble died down and the Nottingham firm of bouncers were replaced by well-respected Sheffield door staff.

North Of Watford

I tended to emphasise the secular, the casual, the colloquial, the vernacular against the sacred

David Antin

It is well documented by the northern sector of knowledgeable writers who were there when 'things happened', on the emergence of the casual/dresser look. And if you haven't read about these events in Phil Thornton's *Casuals*, Dave Hewitson's *The Liverpool Boys are in Town* and Ian Hough's *Perry Boys*, I can't stress enough you go out and purchase copies, *now*.

So, let's allow the southerners have their say on matter-of-facts and rectify the allegory that the majority of southerners weren't dressed like hackney carriage driving Del Boys, Sticksmen style, or skinheads, when the cockcrow of casual kicked-in, and in its onset dotage.

Here's an investigation into the north-south divide on the dawning days in casual, from a southern source. A southern source who has attended football matches at grounds worldwide – 340 plus at last count – including every English and Scottish league club since the Seventies. So, if ever there were a source that has clocked the origin and the fountainhead of the casual/dresser, Iain could be the man?

Iain: *I go up pub and drink 10 pints and I get really plastered, then I go home and beat the wife, dirty Northern bastards!*

Sound familiar? Well, file it alongside norvern monkeys, northern bastards, pie eaters, southern shandy boys, southern softies, cockney cunts and assorted other insults. There you have a few of the names both sides of Watford Gap Services have called each other down the years. It is not a new phenomenon. The abuse and distrust of one another has been going on for centuries, not just decades. The industrial revolution may have propelled the north versus south debate just that one step further but the seeds were sown a very long time ago.

I won't bore you with a fully illustrated history of the social classes and differences as you can find that in detail elsewhere written by people with far greater knowledge than me. Indeed, some folks can't even agree on whether the dividing line is in Watford, the midlands or somewhere else. It matters not. What is important is to examine the regional variations in a football context, and in particular the terrace fashions of both the northern and southern regions of England. And I'll pay particular attention to the north-west and London areas during the late Seventies and early Eighties.

I would like to set the record straight though on a few myths which have come out of the northern sector, especially in Liverpool and Manchester. Some like to portray cockneys as all being skinheads, punks or flare wearing Boot Boys up until around 1981/82. The reality is somewhat different and as much as certain people may like to believe that, it simply is not true. I personally knew nobody who wore flares after 1977 which was the last great flared jeans/trouser year regardless of their overall dress sense or affiliation to various youth cults of the time. By 1978, more and more numbers of both sexes had begun to sport narrower bottoms. Straights, drainpipes and pegs became more the order of the day. You also need to remember that like, London, Liverpool and Manchester also had skins and punks as well as donkey jacket scruffy type hooligans.

Unlike in modern times, the late Seventies saw a vast number of youth cult movements across the UK. The majority were music related such as punk, skinhead, rockers, teddy boys, soul boys, mods and rude boys. They were not area specific and you could find most of these types in any town or village up and down the country. Despite punk often being cited as a capital culture, a healthy proportion of the better bands came from the north of England and specifically Manchester; The Drones, Buzzcocks, Slaughter and the Dogs, Ed Banger and the Nosebleeds, John Cooper Clarke and Subway Sect were all prime movers in the early years of punk rock between 1976 and 1978.

It is the influence of some of the soul boys which first appeared to inspire a sharper and smarter look in the south, and more specifically the London area. Scousers often claim that cockneys simply copied their look but as we shall see many of the clothes they wore were never sported down south. The scally look of Campri blizzard coats, Razzy jeans, Peter Storm cagoules and the majority of Adidas training shoes cut no ice at all with lads outside of the north-west. In London for instance, both Diadora and Nike training shoes would often be preferred to Adidas. Pringle, Ballantyne, and Coxmoor were more popular than the Lyle & Scott, Munsingwear and Braemar brands typically seen further north of Watford.

Whilst the Manchester Perry boy and Liverpool scally look were associated with football, the southern soul boy culture had its roots in music. Some of these lads went to the football on a Saturday but by and large, most didn't. The better dressed lads on the terraces in London were very much in a minority in the late Seventies. It is certainly true that at this point there were still large numbers of skins about and other assorted youth movements on the terraces. A typical mob from this period could often be made up of scruffs, smoothies, punks, skins, soul boys and other assorted types. Most of the people I knew around this time didn't belong to the nationwide youth cults but were soul boys or straights/smoothies. I'd been into punk since 1977, but my mates were starting to have an influence and introduced me to soul, jazz-funk and reggae music and bands like The Trammps, Bob Marley and the Wailers and Steel Pulse.

Many of the soul boys I came across didn't wear anything special clothes wise in terms of big designer brands. One however stood out. He was a lad who had been in my class at secondary school. He was sporting Farah slacks and Christian Dior shirts with Grenson leather shoes from around 1977/78. He wasn't unique; there were others like him too. Although more soul boys just wore the fashions of the time like peg trousers with dangling belts, slashio shoes, plastic sandals, bowling shirts, trench coats and mohair jumpers, the better dressed ones were one step ahead. They preferred bits of Burberry and Aquascutum with Fiorucci and Lois jeans, ski jumpers, Croc and expensive leather shoes, Farah slacks, cashmere jumpers, leather jackets and Lacoste. This was the look which appeared alongside the roll neck, v-neck jumper style sometimes referred to as the London cab driver look on the terraces across the capital. Mingled in with these lads would be straights and smoothies wearing threads like Lonsdale of London sweat tops with straight Levi jeans and trainers along with the standard fashions of the day.

Evidence of this type of style can be found in several books including Paul Wombell's 1978 outing Tottenham Boys We Are Here, *featuring a photograph near the back of three soul boys wearing straights, trainers, complete with smart haircuts and one sporting a Burberry house check scarf. Elsewhere in the book there is a photo of Millwall v Tottenham from 1977 showing a couple of lads sporting drainpipes and trainers.*

The Aston Villa 'Villains' volume shows an encounter on the pitch at Highbury in May 1981 with lads from both sides dressed in this early style. In fact it was Villa's C-Crew which was one of the first dressed firms from outside of the London or north-west areas which I came across in 1980.

Their boys were displaying ski jumpers, burgundy cords or drainpipes, leather jackets and black Adidas trainers like Samba. At Ashton Gate in Bristol during the same year I noted one lad in particular had a neat wedge style haircut, drainpipes, crew neck sweater and Adidas footwear. Although a smarter style was gradually being adopted during the years 1978 and 1979. It was around the 1980/81 season when larger groups started to appear and with it more organised firms. During this same period there was also a sharp decline in all the youth cults as only the rockers survived in any great numbers with mods, second wave punks, rude boys and skins all taking heavy casualties as times changed.

It is of course all too easy for people in both northern and southern camps to stereotype and base opinions on only one or two experiences of each other. I travelled the UK from one end of the country to the other during the Seventies and Eighties and had visited all 92 league grounds by 1989. I got a good feel for things and it was easy to see that all towns and cities had both well-dressed and badly-dressed folks. By the early Eighties, most football clubs had a mob, firm or crew attached to them made up of mostly young lads in their teens and early twenties clad in expensive designer sportswear who liked nothing better than a good tear up at the match.

So how did we go from this early smoother dressing style to ending up looking like tennis stars? Personally I believe this probably was influenced by Liverpool and the sportswear labels robbed from European away days. It is hard to say for sure as we are talking about 30 years ago since the expensive Italian sportswear labels first started to appear in London and being worn by match going lads. This would have been around 1981. Before then it was really stuff like Farah, Gabicci, Pringle, Lois, Fiorucci and Levi jeans, leather jackets and that type of outfit.

Nobody was writing books about it then or keeping detailed notes. Photographs are scarce due to the ridiculous size of the cameras during this period. They would often typically be five or six times the size of one of today's all-singing all dancing compact digital age models which can simply be popped into your jeans front pocket. In those days cameras were big and heavy, too bulky even for most coat pockets, so had to be worn around the body or neck via the strap. Photographs then were often only reserved for weddings, holidays and trips abroad and it was very rare to see somebody with a camera down the game as they didn't want to have to carry it about all day.

The wedge haircut was the normal style for both the scally and perry boy cultures, but was more commonly associated with soul boys in the south than football lads. Even later on when Tacchini, Fila, etc, were widely worn, there were plenty of lads that didn't have the wedge. Boxer cuts and other short smart styles usually with a side parting could often be seen amongst the ranks. It was really only between 1981 and 1982 that we started to see a similar style develop between both northern and southern based lads which consisted of expensive track tops worn with tennis polo shirts, v-neck knitwear, drainpipe jeans or cords and training shoes. The branded clothing was much the same and revolved around labels such as Tacchini, Lacoste, Fila, Ellesse, Pringle, Lyle & Scott, Adidas and Diadora. This was the look which became the uniformed nationwide Casual style.

Certain items of clothing were more synonymous with particular areas as previously mentioned. Although Adidas models like Trimm Trab, Forest Hills and Grand Slam were popular across the country, many more of the range was not as well thought of down south. Diadora Borg Elite in both silver and gold stripe versions (often the stripe was referred to as a 'flash' around this time) were the preferred choice for many. The gold flash version simply known as Diadora golds was undoubtedly seen by many as the must have training shoe of the early Eighties. Diadora Borg Ace, Top Spin, Master, Player, Tie Break and assorted Borg signature models from the 234 series were all sought after shoes. Adidas Tobacco and many of the City series shoes like Dublin, Stockholm, Bern and so on were rarely seen on London lads and remained largely a northern choice. Nike were another brand that had proved popular especially down south with the Ace '82, Legend, Wimbledon and Wimbledon Supreme all being in favour at one time or another. Neither Diadora or Nike still to this day have ever enjoyed as much popularity in the north-west as both scousers and Mancunians have largely stayed loyal to the Adidas stable. Kappa was another label that was always more popular up north. Cockneys largely frowned upon the brand and dismissed it.

There is some debate as to where the term 'casual' first came from. Some Northern lads think that it is a London expression first used by the media.

But my research suggests otherwise. Nobody I have ever spoken to, be it in London, Manchester, Birmingham or Stoke, ever used this phrase back in the early Eighties. It was always lads, boys, firm, dressers or trendies when talking about the well dressed football hooligans of other clubs. The first time I personally came across usage of 'casual' in a football hooligan context was in the 1983 **Face** *magazine article written by Kevin Sampson and Dave Rimmer. Analysing the London scene, Dave used the now famous quote "they haven't got a name, though some call themselves Casuals". An Aberdeen lad I know has newspaper cuttings from several Scottish papers that used the term 'casual' in 1981/82 to describe young football hooligans of the time in Scotland which certainly pre-dates the Face article. This was backed up by several other Scottish lads from various teams who also confirmed that was the case. The term started to be used more down south and was picked up on in music journals such as Sounds in 1984. And later became front page headline news when used to describe 'The General', the Leader of the Cambridge casuals, who received a long prison sentence for his part in an attack on Chelsea fans.*

It should be stated that there is no definitive story to casual culture. Different people will have experienced things others didn't, and vice versa. How much money you had, where you lived, how clued up you were, what access to good shops you had, who your friends were and what items you could beg, borrow or steal would all have played a part in how each individual saw things and dressed. Everyone has a different story to tell. The bigger cities generally had the better shops, which made things a tad easier when hunting down that elusive purchase. Labels came and went very quickly and could be deemed old hat in a matter of weeks or months. Some led the way, whilst others followed. If you didn't get the look right you risked being called a div and ridiculed in front of your mates. There is no exact timeline to follow and it would simply be impossible to accurately list every brand along with where and when it was worn.

The trackie top era burnt itself out pretty quickly though as the better-dressed amongst the football fraternity simply moved on. Lads up north took to what was later dubbed the 'scruff' or 'dressed down' mode with scousers and Mancs togged up in suede and leather jackets, crew neck sweaters and wider bottomed jeans. London had seen the introduction of both Burberry and Aquascutum to the table as early as 1982. Particularly prized were the golfer jackets which had the famous house check underneath the collar. The look was starting to move away from the track top/v-neck jumper style and throughout 1983 new items and labels appeared.

Giorgio Armani jeans became the big thing followed by the knitwear range. Polo Ralph Lauren was another early addition. By 1984 a less sporty more casual style had emerged down south. Expensive Italian and French leather jackets were all the rage from brands like Zilli, Ricardo Bini, Sikons and Daniel Hechter. The early Paninaro style was about to descend on us only nobody knew it yet. Shoes by Bally and multi-coloured jogging trainers replaced the white tennis models. Drainpipes were out and a looser Italian fit was in.

Late arrivals at the party: school kids and the cast of Grange Hill got there too late as it was finished by the time they had paid over the odds for their first Fila Bj tracksuit. The sportswear slowly started to disappear between 1983 and 1984. By the start of the 1984/85 season you needed a whole new wardrobe and complete change of direction. But that as they say, is another story.

Playing Up

From the deep, deep south of England, there is another chap that could perhaps give an unvarnished account of the rise of the casual/dresser?

The British Isles were formed many moons ago following the 'Big Bang' and the glacial period. These pleasant green isles have a barrier of seawater that surrounds their shores which sets them apart from the rest of Europe, and the world too. They stand alone. And situated within the British Isles, on the south coast of England, in the ceremonial county of Hampshire, is the only United Kingdom city island. This being Portsea Island, where the age-old city of Portsmouth originated. Today, the historical naval city port is more densely populated than London when statistics were calculated from the last census. Included in the city's boundaries are the Portsmouth Urban Areas: Fareham, Portchester, Gosport, Havant, Lee-on-the-Solent, Stubbington and Waterlooville, this trebling the conurbation's inhabitants to a near half-a-million.

From Pompey's port over the centuries, many an armada, flotilla and lone watercraft have dispatched, setting sail where the Solent joins the English Channel. These sailing vessels rollicked boisterously around the worlds' five oceans and 110 seas – and quite possibly the three landlocked seas as well – with bountiful swashbucklers and explorers aboard in the quest of prolific adventures and to discover new-found lands or, to return with forbidden fruits and acquired treasures aplenty. They also voyaged to do battle at sea or on a crusade through Europe.

Portsmouth is nowadays connected to the English mainland by three road bridges, a pedestrian/cycle bridge and a rail bridge. On leaving Portsea Island nine times out of ten you shall begin heading north. And from Portsmouth and Southsea train station in the late Seventies and right through the Eighties at 6:57am, on Saturdays, left a train.

Onboard this first service to London's Waterloo Station were the aptly named group of football following Pompey lads, the 6:57 Crew. These characterful, multicoloured clad lads in the Eighties weren't half a sight for sore eyes when they rolled in to town playing-up – and Mr Pompey, though for other reasons, that is. And I can bear witness to this on several occasions, tales that I've chronicled before. Preston North End never had the opportunity of entertaining the likes of Liverpool, Man Utd or

Tottenham from the fashion conscious metropolises during the Eighties, just their seemingly dowdy neighbours Trammere, Rochdale and Crystal Palace. The acclaimed pace-setting scousers, Mancs and cockneys in their casual clobber weren't to be seen on Deepdale's Town End wooden terracing, seated in the stands or on the nearby cobbled streets. But the vista of the 6:57 Crew masquerading around Preston in pastel shades is still very vivid to this day – they didn't half leave a vibrant imprint in my mind's eye, an extremely virulent one too. No-one could ever call them monoculturalists, that's for sure. They once even baffled the Heddlu De Cymru with their well turned-out spruced-up dress sense and cunning pre-plans. Read on...

Over the years the 6:57 have been lambasted by columnists, news media and inspectors of police forces in every county of the UK. They've also taken to task nearly every football 'firm' nationwide – the majority of takers, coming out second best. But what the lads of the 6:57 had a real ardent affection for, beside the odd scuffle at the match, was their ensemble.

One Pompey chap, Eddie C, wants to enlighten us about the psychological state of mind and the close, bonded working class community spirit that Pompey lads upheld. And, their like-mindedness wasn't just a geographical one contained to the boundaries of Portsea Island. They were much more than just a small island race. They closed tight ranks, and set forth to put a place on the map. The 6:57 were free spirits, unconstrained by location, and travelled 'op noff' in abundance, on a many a *'Teenage Rampage.'* I also think that Portsea Island has analogies to the north-west, in a way. We are both somewhat detached from the rest of Britain.

Eddie: *Portsmouth Football Club play (up) on Portsea Island: an island roughly four miles in width by four miles in length. And back in the halcyon days of the late Seventies/early Eighties – before mobile phones, computers and the internet – if you were a youth entering your teens, or in your teens, it was seen as your duty to support, and protect, the city's football club from invaders on our island. Very few people on our fair island supported any other team. Even our ex-manager Harry Redknapp noted as much when he commented something along the lines that 'when you go past the parks and commons ALL the kids are wearing Pompey kits. It's as if no other team exists. (Yeah Redknapp, one heart, one club, know what I mean?). And another thing, Pompey followers have always upheld, a dapper sense of dress.*

The first game I attended at Fratton Park was the FA Cup 3rd round on January

3rd 1970. Portsmouth versus Tranmere Rovers. And, of course, we lost, 2-1. I went that day with my dad and uncle (my mums' brother) who had lost a leg at 16 in World War II, and who had a prosthetic plastic one for getting around on (they weren't called heroes back then, they were just a 'statistic'). All I really remember about the day was sitting at the front of the North Stand, and playing with the red gravel on the running track.

Following this glorious start, I somehow caught the Pompey bug. Occasionally I would go with the old man or I would walk the two miles from home to the ground with a mate (or even sometimes on my own) and hang round waiting for the gates to open for the last 20 minutes.

I had to wait till the 1975/76 season to travel to my first away game. After pestering my mum and dad for weeks, I was allowed to go with two school pals and their dad to Ashton Gate, Bristol City's ground on the 8th February. So, clad in my green parka, and armed with my cheese and pickle sandwiches, we set off.

After entering the ground on the side where the players ran out, the terrace seemed mainly full of Bristol fans. At about 2.50pm, a loud roar went up. To our right a big gap opened up in the crowd, and in the middle of the parting there was around 40 fellas stood in that time honoured stance; legs and arms akimbo, barrel chests and bellowing "Come on then", in Pompey accents. The Bristol lads needed no second invitation and steamed in. As it went off, the Pompey on the end behind the goal to our left decided to join the fray. Hordes of youths decked out in flares, three star jumpers and white silk scarves flapping in the wind clambered on to the pitch as the players emerged from the tunnel. What a sight of bedlam greeted the teams: to an impressionable 13 year-old, the scene of a mass riot was unfolding in front of my eyes. Following an inglorious 3-1 defeat, outside the ground there was fighting occurring everywhere as we made our way to the car at the side of a park.

When we arrived home, I was full of it. My old man sternly informed me that it would be my one and only game because a young lad had been knifed to death at a match in the north, at Blackpool v Bolton. Only I did manage to get to Craven Cottage with a mate and his dad by car to watch us play Fulham. (Fulham were to play in the FA Cup Final in a few weeks). It was events off the field that captivated me, as it kicked off once again. It always seemed to back then. But I'd well and truly caught the footy bug.

From 1974, 'til I left school in 1978, I went to as many games within reason: Swindon, Palace, Oxford, Charlton and so on. Although, I was told in no uncertain terms, I wasn't to travel to SCUM in 1975. (SCUM standing for, Southampton Company Union Men, who scabbed during a Portsmouth Dockers strike many moons ago). But SCUM has a meaning a whole lot deeper to Pompey fans. I wasn't going to miss a match against our bitterest rivals, was I?

So, I made up a story that I would be going round to mate's house for the day. I left home wearing my reliable green parka, only when I reached the top of the road I took it off and hid it in some bushes putting on another mate's crombie that I'd borrowed – which was two sizes too big. Off I trotted. Pompey lost 4-0, again. It kicked off everywhere, again. And it pissed down, with rain again.

Heading home I returned to the bushes, only there' was no parka. Shit! I nervously knocked on the front door at home and my mum swiftly opened it saying, "Had a nice day love? Where's your parka? You seem all wet!" Before I could come out with a white lie I notice, hanging up in the hallway, my parka... CLUMP! I was in deep, deep trouble. It took several weeks of washing-up and other chores to smooth things over, I tell you.

By the time I left school in 1978 Portsmouth were in the old Fourth Division: I was determined to go to every game or, at least as many as I could afford. A little mob of us from round our way were of the same persuasion; fresh out of school, mostly working as apprentices in various jobs, into football (Pompey) and finding music, fashion and girls of great interest too. What more do you need in life? And what could possibly go wrong?

Our tight, game firm, made a decision to call ourselves 'The Harry Gang' after watching the infamous Panorama documentary on Millwall's F-Troop, and their main man 'arry the Dog. We began travelling to away games, mainly by minibus, with an older geezer (who was a bank manager by day) driving the bus. We attended matches at the likes of Brentford, Cardiff and Newport, as well as far flung northern outposts such as Bradford, Darlington and Hartlepool plus many other grounds around the country. We would more often than not arrive back indoors in time for a full English Sunday breakfast. Great times to be young and not have a care in the world.

Like I mentioned, we were also getting in to our clobber and music. We began ditching traditionally worn donkey jackets, scruffy jeans and Doc Marten boots at the match for smarter Harrington jackets, Levi 501s, Fred Perry polos and Doc Marten shoes. This quickly evolved to button down shirts, pegs and Jam shoes or, for the soul boys in the crew, granddad shirts, bib 'n' braces and bowling shoes. Bowling shoes could be 'borrowed' from a bowling alley in town on Arundel Street. I had a lovely dark and light blue pair that I 'borrowed' myself.

By the late Seventies and early Eighties, most who followed Pompey were into the soul boy and skinhead look. But, I remember once going to Blackpool in 1980 and among us was a lad nicknamed 'Frank Spencer'. He donned a green Peter Storm cagoule, pale Lois jeans and white, Adidas Stan Smith trainers. The look was completed with a mushroom-topped head of hair. Richard 'Frank' Spencer was, in my humble opinion the first real dresser in Pompey. He had picked up the lead from scousers, as he would occasionally slope off on his own to watch other games. Even down the road to Plymouth he would go, to spot what was 'in' on the terraces.

The 1980/81 season, saw further changes in the lads' dress sense. I also remember when we played at Home Park, Plymouth Argyle's ground in the League Cup, August 1980. It went off quite badly inside the ground with a proper old Pompey face Fish (RIP) leading the charge into Plymouth's lads after grabbing the corner flag as we steamed in. But what really stuck in my mind that day – apart from having a truncheon over the head – was that Plymouth's mob had a skinhead girl right at the front dishing it out. Also, because the game was a draw, in the replay at ours the same geezerbird came in the Fratton End with only one other bloke giving it large. This before being moved out by the Old Bill to a standing ovation from Pompey's mob.

During the same season, we played Millwall at The Den on Boxing Day, and one of the lads, Fooksie, ran a special train to London. A lot of chaps had their new Christmas clobber on and we'd a bit of a mixed look on that trip. There were still plenty of skin/suedeheads aboard the train mingled in with lads growing their hair decked in diamond jumpers and Lonsdale sweatshirts. Lonsdale sweatshirts weren't available in Portsmouth so a trip to London's Lonsdale shop on Beak Street had to be undertaken. Some of the chaps present were influenced by the London look too – West Ham and Chelsea were wearing the likes of MA-1 flight jackets, Fred Perry polo shirts and Doc Martens. And some wore crewneck jumpers with straight jeans and Adidas Samba trainers or Adidas Nizza Baseball sneakers.

Over the next season or two, things worn at the match began to move at a rapid pace, weekly in some cases. You would clock something new and vow to have the said item by next week for the catwalk only for it to be out. *That was the football terrace fashion for you. Pac-a-macs or tracksuit tops, Pringle or Gabicci, Farah or Fiorucci, Nike or Diadora, and even Deerstalker hats came and went. But amongst it all we still had the Pompey punks, Fareham rockabillies and of course, the reliable Pompey beer monsters.*

In season 1982/83 we were in the Third Division and just before Christmas we played Chesterfield at Saltergate. A mate that came that day was well pleased with this, new-to-us, white and grey jumper he was wearing, an Armani jumper, that is. Despite it being freezing he decided not to wear a jacket over his newly acquired threads so it was on full display for all the natives to see. On the ground we were stood on the side as the Chesterfield hordes, separated by a flimsy fence.

The hero of the day, our mate, sauntered right to the fence giving it "Look at this" while pointing with both hands to his jumper "you scruffy norvan mankeys. It would cost you lot a month's wages. It's Armani. In case you've never heard of it..." and so on.

With that, a Chesterfield punk on the other side of the fence launched a bottle of blue ink in to the air which landed all over our mate, and his new jumper. As he stood there with ink dripping off his face, fans from both sides were roaring with laughter. Then one of our lot shouts "I didn't know Armani did tie-dye." Safe to say the mate sulked all the way home and his early Crimbo present never did look the same again.

The other highlight of the same season was the last game away at Plymouth which saw the 'Mighty Portsmouth' crowned champions. On the way there we passed some strange sights: Stonehenge had PFC sprayed on its stones and some sheep by the roadside were painted blue and white!

The Face magazine was a popular read at the time, and a few firms from the country were writing in with anecdotes. So one of our lads called Ze wrote in, replying to a letter from a Millwall chap to inform him they weren't the only firm dressing for football, and going in the seats at games. This was in July 1983, and he signed it; The 6:57 Crew.

Pompey had started to get it organised by now and all the different fractions like The Harry Gang, Porkys, Air Balloon, Cosham Commandos, Wicor, Leigh Park, Emsworth and Fug, to name a few, began travelling by the train en masse under the banner 6:57, the 6:57 train being the first out of Portsmouth on a Saturday morning. Sometimes, the old favourite, the furniture van, was used. One such excursion was to Cardiff in September 1983 – although not with such a good outcome for yours truly. The game was a blur but after it had finished we were driving round Cardiff looking for a row when the three in the front banged on the dividing between us and shouting "There's 30 lads ahead on our left, get ready." As the van slowed down, up goes the shutter, and out we piled. The Taffs were caught unawares and took off as we gave chase for a hundred yards or so when the Old Bill showed. It was back in the van, shutter down, waiting for the engine to kick-in.

But no. 'Bang bang bang', "Open up this shutter!" barked someone, presumably the OB.

"There's no-one in here" came the reply. We chuckled.

'Bang bang bang', again. "There's no-one home" a lad blurted, as we guffawed loudly in the dark.

Then the shutter rattled open. A copper stood there cradling a German Shepherd in his arms a couple of inches away. And with no further ado, he launched the snarling beast into the van. The hound then decides he fancied me for tea, only my new mustard Pringle was in the way. As the mutt and me were rolling around the vans floor the 20 mates exited the back in a world record time. After a minute or so of wrestling the rabid savage, the copper called it off. I'm left sat there in a ripped jumper, ragged Fiorucci jeans and a gaping hole in my forearm pumping blood at an alarming rate. The Old Bill then kindly helped me from the van and made us all sit in a line on the pavement while giving us a rollicking on our behaviour. Well, up went the chant "Oops Upside Your Head", the title of one of the Gap Band song. We then did the rowing boat dance that was all the rage in the late Seventies and early Eighties, rocking side-to-side sat on the damp, flagstones. The police didn't see the funny side and showed us in no uncertain terms, too.

"Right... you lot. Get out of Cardiff and Wales double quick. And if we see this van again, you're all nicked."

"What about me arm..." I mumbled.

"Tough. Now do one."

The lads felt sorry for me, letting me sit up front 'til we reached Pompey, where I was then dropped at the hospital, receiving 18 stitches to my wounded arm. I had no such luck with my beyond-repair jumper and jeans though.

Like I mentioned, we had started going in the seated areas at grounds, usually where the home fans went: a notable one being Millwall on a Sunday morning supposedly arranged at that time to quell crowd trouble. (Millwall were an unhappy set that day). And Cardiff again – a different season from the aforementioned incident – when they had a right go at us. Also Preston, and Swansea on the day of the Harrods bomb. We had a long trek by train to Newcastle too. We came straight out of the station and had the waiting Geordies – who I don't think were expecting us to travel by train en masse – on their toes while laughing at the complete lack of fashion sense. I mean, grown fellas in kilts, what's all that about? Unless they were the first New Romantics? On the whole we found them to be a right scruffy bunch.

Bournemouth away, 1983: this saw the first, and I think only time, that our mob did a mass steam-rolling of shops, relieving them of their wares. Sports shops and gentlemen's outfitters were looted of large amounts of stock. And a Benetton store received special attention. Well, they did have one before us so what did they expect, eh?

Leeds away 1983: this was a funny as we'd got wind that the Old Bill would have a waiting committee (how, I've no idea in the days before mobile phones). Anyway, a decision was made to pull the emergency cord on the train in Wakefield to avoid them. The train ground to a halt on a bridge near the centre of town and we all bailed out clambering down an embankment much to the bemusement of Saturday morning shoppers. One old lady asked one of the lads what we were in town for. "For an NF march love!" came the reply. She scurried off double-quick.

By now the colours of clobber worn were getting louder: Kappa, Fila and Tacchini, to name but a few, were seen in a multitude of shocking and pastel shades. One week a certain pair of trainers were in, the next suede desert boots, then another make of trainers again. And the 6:57 had grew into a massive firm; we travelled to every corner of Britain in numbers. The saying on Friday nights went, 'The only excuse not to go is... if you're banged-up!'

During the 1984/85 season it was the norm to all head for the seats on our travels, notably a night game at Birmingham. Another notable excursion was when we took our pushbikes on the train to Cambridge for a laugh, which caused a bit of a stir. When we were on Liverpool Street station in London waiting for the train, a certain Taffy Aldridge (ICF in-fame, RIP) came over and said "This'll never catch on, Pompey." There was also the lengthy jaunt to Middlesbrough in deepest winter, when we were refused entry into the seats at their end of their old ground, Ayresome Park. So, a cry went up "We'll go home then!" There was a bit of a stand-off for a few minutes until the dibble relented and we were allowed to sit in the seats behind one of the goals. The snow that day blew right in to our faces from the start of the second half 'til the final whistle. It always seemed cold up north, not like the sunny south.

Proving a point, we got badly caught out by the weather in a preseason trip to Dundee once. We left Pompey late afternoon on a Friday in T-shirts, shorts and flip-flops, and by the time we arrived in Dundee that Saturday morning there must have been a near 20 degree temperature change. Never mind, I went straight on a little shopping spree. Well, I did need a new sweatshirt, jeans and trainers!

During the season clothes had transformed to Ellesse ski jackets, Aquascutum shirts, Munsingwear, Burberry and for the well off, (or light fingered) Armani.

October 6th 1984, Cardiff away again, and a 'first' too. About 20 of us came up with a plan to travel separately from the firm by train and the order of the day was to turn out in Aquascutum blazers, shirts and ties, Farahs and loafers or brogues, which we did. We also had invites printed for a warm welcoming in the valleys for a family wedding.

The plan ticked like clockwork when we disembarked the train at Cardiff station: the bulk of the firm went one way attracting the attention of the local constabulary, our 20 the other way, quick march. But, like most well-thought-out ideas we'd counted our chickens before they'd hatched. As we trotted off from the station, rubbing our hands with wide smiles on our faces, a police van began to follow us. After about 200 yards it pulled to a halt in alongside of us. "Rightyo, lads. Where you off to?" a copper asked, as two of them got out of the van.

"Cardiff away again, and a 'first' too.
About 20 of us came up with a plan to travel
separately from the firm by train and the
order of the day was to turn out in, aquascutum blazers,
shirts and ties, farahs and loafers or brogues,
which we did. we also had invites printed
for a warm welcoming in the valleys
for a family wedding."

"We're going for a drink before heading to a mates wedding" I answered.

"Oh yeah. Who's getting married?"

"Steve and Sharon."

" Well... I asked your mate and he just told me it was Dave and Kerry who were getting hitched."

"I don't really know them that well, I thought their names were Steve and Sharon."

"C'mon you lot. Get in the van and we'll take you up to the ground, shall we?"

"Nah, I told you. We're here for the wedding."

"Bollocks! Mr – I know exactly what you're up to, 'cause I've been watching your every move for weeks – such 'n' such informed us that..."

He then began to reel off all our names and past events. It dawned on us like a lead weight that Pompey Old Bill had unleashed a new weapon, spotters. Either within our ranks, or they'd been observing us from a distance. Take a bow the two Pompey spotters. And there ended our cunning plan. We were in the ground by 12 o'clock. The rest of the firm had had a right tear-up in the city centre.

Togs changed and changed as the Eighties rolled on with the firm peaking around 1987 too. But, with a heavy police presence wherever we went, and a definite stretch of bird if nicked, the lads sought new pleasures away from football. More of the boys were dabbling in new exotic substances and travelling to far flung places to dance till dawn. This led to many of the lads being unfit for duty on the 6:57 or, they packed in going altogether. Plus the rave stuff they were dressing in just wasn't right – in my eyes anyway.

I personally never got into the rave scene, I was more into my soul and Indie music and I carried on going to football and concerts. Oh well, all good things come to an end and we'd had our heydays – 1982 to 1987.

And, if you weren't there in those days, boy you missed a blast!

Although our away following was getting smaller, we still had some cracking laughs. We played Newcastle up at St James' Park in 1989 just when the pubs had started opening all day (remember 11-3 and 6-11.) After the game about 20 of us were in a boozer and I'd liberated a Sky TV baseball cap (remember only having four channels). The lads had begun larking around when this Geordie Thalidomide walked over and offered me outside. I looked at it him with his malformed arms and said, "You're joking, aren't you mate?" But he wouldn't take no for an answer.

He replied "You think you're all that in your Sky baseball hat..."

My mates were crying with laughter. In the end, I managed to swerve the offer, patted him on the head and said, "Well done mate, nice effort." And bid my goodbyes, quickly.

Back in the early Eighties it was a strange time with fashion evolving so quickly, and obviously being from the south we thought we were the bee's bollocks. But to be honest with you, I think areas of the north, especially Liverpool and Manchester, should take a bow because they were at the forefront of what was happening. London in 1981/82 still seemed to be into the skinhead/mod revival theme; we used to go and watch the The Jam and likes and all the cockneys wore clothes influenced by Mr Weller & Co.

In the same era we were in the Fourth Division and although we travelled to some right dumps you could still see some interesting sights while on the move. Places like Birmingham New Street or Crewe station is where you would clock other firms of lads. Maybe Man U on their way to Spurs, us to Oldham. Or Everton going to Villa, while we would be heading to Wrexham. Looks would be exchanged and up-to-date fashion notes taken.

I'm not saying all the clubs caught on at once because at some grounds locals were stuck in a time-warp with flares still in evidence. But most chaps in the know would suss out what was going on and dress accordingly. Both northern and southern clubs would have fellas who dressed for the terrace catwalk come weekend, and others who were more into their music tastes for looks or others who hadn't a clue. Only any mob that based itself just on clobber alone would soon come unstuck, even taxed. Also, regularly travelling with England over the years most of the lads I've encountered have taken a certain pride in their appearance, be they from the North, the midlands or the south.

Thirty-five years on and a dependable few are still going. We've even had our time in the Premiership, a period that nearly ruined us with crippling wages demands paid to foreign players who didn't give a damn about Pompey, our club. We've had FA Cup success, and Europe too. Time is catching up on us, but we still like to dress the part: Barbour, CP Company, One True Saxon, Ralph Lauren, YMC, Heritage Research and many other labels are worn with more discreet logos than in bygone times. Going round the country nowadays means meeting similar-aged lads from other clubs and reminiscing about past events. They've even changed the time of the first train out of Portsmouth to lose the stigma. Although there's still a piece of us that longs for the good old days. Play up Pompey!

Have A Butchers

With PNE spiralling down the leagues in the early Eighties, and no European trips on the horizon – apart from the odd game at the Racecourse Ground, in Wales – I'd make do with shops in the north-west to obtain my sportswear or trainers. Or sometimes I'd have the occasional venture to London. Only Preston did have one or two shops worth popping in to; one such shop, Gibsons Sports, is where a very good mate of mine, Cuey, worked.

Cuey: *Many moons ago, in between being sent on errands for long stands, tartan paint and glass hammers, I worked (allegedly) at Gibsons Sports. This was the early-to-mid-Eighties at the height of the casual boom so it was a great place to be for a label-chasing youngster.*

The shop itself was quite a scruffy looking place; it had been a butchers before becoming a sports shop and still had two tree trunks in either corner that the butcher had installed – for effect presumably. In hindsight the quirky appearance probably added to the shop's appeal, and anyway, the important thing was what was on its shelves. Gibsons had a few other shops dotted around Lancashire and Greater Manchester, and they'd been stocking what went on to become football casual staples long before they became de rigueur on the terraces. The labels trip off the tongue: Pringle, Lyle & Scott, Sergio Tacchini, Lacoste, Pierre Cardin, Cerruti 1881, Robe di Kappa and so on.

There were also lesser known labels such as Australian, OP and Lhuta as well as the brands more associated with footwear such as Adidas, Nike, Puma, Diadora and fledgling Reebok when their entire range consisted of about a dozen running shoes and not much else. In addition to new and current stock regular buying trips to Germany were undertaken. The owner would hire a box van for the jaunt with the warehouse manager accompanying him on the ferry across the North Sea, this in the search of bargain booty to fill the van to the hilt with and bring it back to the north-west. This meant the shops became a magnet for people looking for something a bit different, or unusual. After one such trip to Germany looking for old Adidas stock for the January sale, Gibbo returned with piles of Forest Hills, Tobaccos, Samoas, Handball Spezials, Fresno Bleus, Trimm Trabbs and Triest amongst others, all put up for sale for under £20. Then after the sales, I binned umpteen pairs! Of course, this was before the advent of the retro trainer revival and eBay.

There were a few obvious perks of the job though, like getting first dibs when anything new came in and the staff discount, although there was a massive downside, especially as being a football fan and having to work Saturdays.

I could still get an occasional mid week fix of football for fisticuffs and the odd Saturday booked as holiday though. And, now and again, the mountain would come to Mohammed.

Because of the shops close proximity to the railway station, and the football 'casuals' obsession with sportswear, it wasn't unusual to get a visit from football fans on the rob plus you had a ringside seat whilst the Preston lot slugged it out with whoever was visiting Preston that particular week. Blackpool were particularly active in the 1980s, and for obvious reasons had to change trains at Preston regularly. They're not a very bright bunch, though, because invariably they would announce their arrival with a 'Sea-Sea-Seasiders' chant as they came up Fishergate. So on hearing the racket we had time to lock the door and man the barricades. On one occasion, after trying to force the door, they turned their attention to the big plate glass window and took turns at trying to boot it through. Poor mites just kept bouncing off and landing on their arses, ha. They did have a bit more luck at Glacier Sports, the ski shop round the corner on Lune Street judging by the number of them sporting brand-new quilted ski jackets when they all legged it past five minutes later.

A few months after the Blackpool fiasco, it was the turn of the Wiganers, although this time Wigan were actually playing Preston and a reception committee was waiting. We'd already bolted the door after hearing the customary chanting and thought 'here we go again.' But this time as the motley looking crew of Wiganers got near the shop the singing stopped, and a few of them started to turn on their heels whilst others seemed unsure what to do. I pushed my cheek up against the door to try to look up Fishergate towards the town centre to see what was going on and was met with the sight of dozens of Preston's finest running the Wigan lot back down Fishergate.

There is photo evidence of the battle as it unfolded that was taken off a Wigan lad. To us at Gibsons, it was just another Saturday at the office.

The Friendly Crocodile

I'd been well and truly bitten by the dressing lark and spending (wasting) my coin on clothing and trainers most weekends. The following tales detail such:

When the little green reptile kicked in with us Preston casuals/dressers, I made a short bus journey to a shop called Fulwood Sports, which was in the close proximity of Preston's main tennis club. I presumed they held the lines of sportswear that were 'in' at that moment in time; so I pushed the door open and ventured into the cramped, well stocked store as the bell above my head rang out. This alerted an elderly lady to my presence as I entered with bated breath to what treasures awaited and that I might uncover on my sub-cultural, designer label apparel mission. I supposedly thought she would make her way over to greet me and also help me on my mission. How wrong I was. She hovered over my right shoulder with a stern look on her face as I browsed through the rails, intensively scanning each and every item of clothing's trademark brand.

After five minutes of rummaging, and with not even as much as a 'good morning' out of the old dear, I hadn't found a piece of substance requiring me to part with any of my hard earned coin. I also began to wonder why I hadn't clocked any tennis wear that was worth purchasing.

"Are you looking for anything in particular sir?" the shop assistant eventually asked. Replying, I rhymed off the chosen attire I'd made my early morning trek for, only to be informed that they now didn't stock any of the clothing. They used to, though. But prior to my visit – over the previous weeks – they'd had endless Liverpudlians turn up at their doorstep on a shopping spree, only these cheeky-chappie-scallies hadn't spent a penny in the store. These loveable scousers had either relieved the rails of whatever they wanted and forgot to pay or, cut off (probably with their Uncle Stanley) all the labels.

So, like she'd mentioned, they wouldn't be stocking the more expensive end of the market anymore. "But... we've two items of Lacoste left in the back storeroom that might just fit you, out of harm's way. I will go and get them."

She returned with a medium sized Lacoste V-neck squash shirt and a pair of 30" waist white tennis shorts. Trying them on in a minute changing room, they both fitted snugly (how times change, I wouldn't get my leg through the waistband nowadays). I purchased the V-necked squash top for £9 and the shorts for £15. Yes the pair of them for a grand total of £24, bargain or what?

On the subject of Lacoste, there was a clothing shop in St George's Shopping Centre, called Pele & Polo that sold Lacoste and its American brother brand Izod. Izod's crocodiles weren't just your regulation green, they came in several colours more befitting of a chameleon, I suppose. Anyway, when you entered the boutique the assistants were all over you like a rash, pulling jumpers and shirts off shelves and rails at an alarming rate. They'd flash merchandise before your eyes while reminding you that if you spent over a certain amount you'd also receive into the bargain a 'free' pair of box-cords or slacks. If they persuaded you to try any of the articles of clothing on, and you came out of the fitting room for a gander at yourself in the full length mirror in the shop, I could guarantee whoever was chasing their commission that day would come out with one of the following statements; "That suits you sir. And that's the way they're wearing that style this season, fitted" – seam splitting, skin-tight. Or, "That suits you sir, and that's the way they're wearing that style this season, loose" – baggy as fuck. And this could happen within a week or two, or in some cases, the very same day!

On one of my early Eighties shopping excursions to Manchester, I visited Hurley's, the legendary northern haunt near Piccadilly train station.

When you entered this Aladdin's cave you saw clobber dripping from the ceiling like stalactites for your wide eyes to behold. Shop assistants would stand round holding long poles with hooks on the ends, waiting to reach for the sky and lift your choice of breathtaking wares down so you could literally swoon over the item after seeing the price tag. Anyway, I'd all but spent up by the time I'd stepped over the threshold one day, only there was a cap that had grabbed my line of vision. The gem in question was a white Lacoste tennis cap with green and red piping, a large oval badge on the front boasting the croc and writing above and below it, and a green, transparent plastic, sun visor peak. Cool or what? So, not having enough pretty green on my person I'd to give purchasing the cap that day a miss. But I made a promise to myself that day; I would return shortly to acquire the said cap.

We'd drawn Rochdale away in the Sherpa Van Cup, or whatever it was called back in 1982 or 1983, and I made a strategic, down-to-a-tee, plan for the hat to become mine. However there might be a few problems to harmonise and achieve before I did.

Seeing as these cup games took place on weekday nights, I had to get my priorities on both fronts sorted. Also my casual clothing obsessive-compulsive disorder was developing – along with my other compulsions – at an alarming, unstable rate. So when the game was announced, I decided to kill two birds with one stone, only there was a stumbling block. This being on the day Preston were due to play Rochdale I had to attend college on day release from work. I had another problem as well; this one, a cash flow problem, but I had plenty of assets to trade in for needy funds. These valuables were my precious vinyl collection of punk records.

On a Tuesday morning in September, I set off for college, Adidas holdall over shoulder, listing to one side because of the weight of the anthology of my generation. The full catalogue of UK Subs singles and LPs in different coloured vinyls were in the bag (boy do I regret the decision to sell them). Stage one of my assignment was in place.

At the end of the opening period at college, the 15 or so from the class of clay artists set off to Elsie's Pantry for our usual meat and tatty breakfast pie (butter pies on Fridays, an old Preston tradition). While walking to the confectioners, I disclosed to a lad who was severing his time at the same company as me my plans for the rest of day. That was that I would be heading over to Action Records to trade in the records in my bag, jumping on a train to Manchester and then purchasing a diamond of a hat from Hurley's. Come back to Preston, meet up with the footy lads and then trek over to Rochdale for that night's match. And maybe have a bit of 'fun.'

"I'm up for a bit of that", the lad declared. So we slipped off from the rest of the boys and sauntered down to the second-hand and new musical haven, Action Records. Gordon, the owner and proprietor of the store, I'd known for years after obtaining many a rare slice of vinyl from him. Before he'd set up his Preston-based shop, he would advertise in the *Sounds* music magazine. And if you desired any of that month's goodies, you'd to go round to his home in a dodgy estate on the outskirts of Preston.

Once, when I was round at his gaff, flicking trough his vast back stock of records, one of his children came running in the house shouting "Daddy, daddy. Someone has done something to your car."

"Right son. I'll have a look in a minute", Gordon replied. I bid my farewells with a rare single tucked inside the lining of my leather biker's jacket, and Gordon went to access the damage to his motor. A full tin of white gloss had been poured over the car! Nice place back then, that Farrington Park was.

Anyway, I placed my holdall on to the shop's counter, unzipped it and took out my prized UK Subs collection. Gordon skimmed through them with no facial expressions at all, he just slid the odd single out of its sleeve, spun it round while inspecting for scratches and noted its colour. "Nine pounds for the lot of 'em", he announced in his Northern Irish accent, without making eye contact.

"You're having a laugh. Aren't you?" I blurted out, followed by a sarcastic laugh. "Come on Gordon pal, you know the score." And we began a bartering of mind over matter.

Not much later the mate and I left the premises, leaving my holdall with Gordon for safe keeping. And I'd another miserly 11 green pound notes off Gordon added to the clobber stash stuffed into my pale blue, Levis jeans front pocket. Happy? No! I'd traded one of my favourite bands' entire works for a pittance. I bet they were worth 30 to 50 quid, easily.

The two of us then walked down to Preston station, invested in 2p platform tickets, boarded the next train to Manchester (avoiding Hector the collector en route), and alighted onto Victoria station's platform, beating a path to Hurley's.

On entering Hurley's, the music from the scene in *Life of Brian* when the Three Wise Men humbly enter the barn bearing gifts of gold, frankincense and myrrh came into my head. Only I brought sweaty pound notes and silver coins. I then spotted the Holy Grail behind the counter and asked an assistant to try the cap. He lifted the hat, which had distinguishing characteristics, and passed it to me whilst he placed himself between me and the door. I adjusted the Velcro strap at the back and slid it on my wedge-head, hairstyle noodle and struck a pose in the shop's mirror. Sheer unadulterated, out-and-out perfection. And without any hesitation I declared, "I'll take it", to the shop assistant.

We exchanged pleasantries as I counted out the £16, the cap's price-tag, onto the top of the cash register, stacking the fifty pences into pounds, and rounding off the full amount with unravelled, creased sterling notes. Where upon I was presented with a small carrier bag containing the sought-after 'crown'.

Hastily I left Hurley's, pulled the Lacoste hat out of the bag, placed it on my head and threw the carrier bag in a litter-bin. If the cap fits, wear it! Job done. We then moved at pace back to Victoria station, caught the next train to Blackpool that stopped at Preston, and if I remember rightly, we got collared by the ticket collector and had to purchase a ticket. (To pay is to fail. This time we failed, I think.) By the time we ascended the ramp on Preston's station concourse, it was nearly four o'clock. So, we had just over an hour and a half to kill before hooking up with the rest of the lads outside the Bull & Royal public house, in the centre of town. A decision was made to go for a coffee in the Black Cat café next to the station on Butler Street (this was way, way before pubs opened all day). The Black Cat had been a haunt of diverse fashions and music cliques since the swinging Sixties. Through the years mods, skinheads, scooter boys, punks, and then once again skinheads had frequented the greasy spoon. Apart from the café's fine cuisine, the extensive range of tunes on the jukebox and pinball machines, were major attractions. The café was also a handy location for the football lads to launch a surprise attack on the unsuspecting away fans arriving on football special trains from around the country. And like I say, the main reason for being a client in the caff: the tucker was bob on (pie, peas and gravy, that is) and the brews were cheap too.

After downing our coffees we ambled up to the Bull & Royal just gone five. A couple of the mates were already there loitering. And come half past the hour, there were 40 plus lads intermingling while chatting about last weekend's activities, clothes and football. And, asking 'would Rochdale show?' I also received quite a few complimentary comments as they admired my newly-purchased Lacoste cap and how natty it looked. All of a sudden two white Transit vans ground to a halt, one driven by Eli, our regular van-man, outside the Red Lion opposite the Bull & Royal. The lads bounded over the road, opened the back doors of the vans and filed into the back of both of them in a flash. We were all agile and nimble back then, and in less than a minute rubber was a-burning. It wasn't the preferred mode of transport, 20 odd of you crammed like sardines in the back of a Transit van, but it had to be done.

Lads were either sat down with their knees drawn tight to their chests or doubled over, swaying with every slight turn and touching of the brakes, some lads ending up on top of each other. Jaunts in the back of a van would be even worse when the cramps set in on the long hauls. The good news tonight though, the journey was a relatively short one and was achieved in less than an hour.

Nearing the ground, Spotland, a shout went up in the front of the van from Eli, "They're 'ere", as he anchored on. The back doors burst open and we were out in a jiffy, trainer-clad feet hitting the street. Running at the already moving mob of 30 odd or so of Rochdale fans, they turned left at a junction. (Thinking back, if they didn't want to know, why bother chasing them, only it was the done thing, wasn't it?) WHOOSH...! A gust of wind lifted the peak of my new acquisition, my prized Lacoste cap, off my head. I managed to catch it mid-air and shoved it back on as our firm turned left on Rochdale's case. And as we banked left, more Preston lads joined us, who'd run along the road we were now on from the right. Both groups were jogging side-by-side and I was holding the cap down with my right hand. "Orite Bill", rang a familiar voice. It was a lad I'd been to school with, Big Bob. He hurriedly informed me they also travelled in a van and had been pursuing the same lads as us for the previous five minutes.

The chase didn't last long; we realised it was a lost cause, they'd trapped like greyhounds, disappearing down the warrens of side streets. I breathed a sigh of relief because I could now take my hand off my head and walk at a normal pace to the ground. Well, with a slight swagger! We had just run the mighty Rochdale, hadn't we?

Entrance fee paid at Spotland, we stood on the open terracing mulling over whether Rochdale's lads would stand their ground after the game. The lads I'd made the journey with were very finical. Then, when play on the field began, half-a-dozen of us made our way down to the front of the terracing to lean on the hoardings, to the right-hand side of the goals, for a better view. Also, we wanted to cast an eye over any potential sports wearing Rochdale lads and clock their labels. Preston North End in this period of their history were, abysmal, to put it politely. And halfway through the first half North End finally had their first chance on goal. A wayward ball fell to one of the 'Mighty Whites' strikers, unexpectedly, on the edge of Rochdale's box, at our end of the stadium. He lashed out his right boot, slicing the ball and sending it wide of the goalmouth. Our side of the goal, so I was directly in the line of where the ball was advancing at a rapid rate. Instinctively I positioned my forehead so that the ball would hit it bang on the button. I would head the scud missile back onto the field of play, take a bow, and accept a rapturous, round of applause. SLAM! Wrong. The rocket-propelled weapon hit me exquisitely in the centre of my bonce, but... I'd forgotten I was wearing my brand new, pristine, snow white, Lacoste cap. The cap flew off my head landing on the grimy, filthy terracing. My misfortune was met with roars of laughter from the lads, and from others stood in the nearby proximity. Timidly I made my way to where the hat came to rest, picking it up like lightning, to more cheers and guffaws. I then commenced inspecting the now mucky soiled specimen. The green, transparent plastic sun visor peak was bent and twisted. There was also an imprint of where the mud-splattered ball had hit the hat, just to the left of the once grinning croc, (It looked pissed off, and sullen jawed now, just like myself). I tried brushing most of the grit, grime and soil off, but to no avail, so I gave it up as a bad job. I shoved the dishevelled, twisted cap in to my velour, Terrinda Fila trackie top pocket, acting like I wasn't bothered, all poker-faced. I was really fucking gutted, I was. I'd sought out my Grail, only to see it ruined forever in one fell swoop. The cap was total ravaged and devastated. A tear-jerker for any casual purist.

The rest of the game was spent in a self-induced trance, avoiding any niceties with anyone. The gates were opened five minutes before the end of play and we were out wanting 'action' – especially me. Only there was none to be had. No willing parties were found following nearly a half an hour search. We then clambered, not as agile, into the back of the van and set off home. I sat to the front of the vans divider in the corner, silently sulking.

Getting dropped off at the end of the road where I lived, I gave a half-hearted thumbs up and a muffled "See you Saturday lads", to whoever was still left in the van. I entered my home going on midnight, trotted upstairs, flung the cap in the airing cupboard which housed my work clothes, and slammed the door shut.

The hat was never the same again, no matter how many times I returned to the cupboard to try to repair the peak's crease and restore it to its former glory. Within a year it became a work hat; another costly lesson learned: Duck when a football's heading towards you when wearing your Grail.

Where's The Beach?

Labels and looks came and went nearly as rapidly as working-class bread-winners lost their jobs and found themselves having to join the lengthy queue to sign on and collect their UB40 in the early Eighties. And one such sportswear label from those bleak, sombre days was Ellesse.

Ellesse's famous half-ball logo was created by the combination of a pair of ski tips and a cross section of a tennis ball that symbolised Ellesse's heritage in these sports. The label was a firm favourite with casuals in the early Eighties too. The Ellesse badge is often cited as one of the first ever logos to feature on the outside of a garment, a move copied by other companies worldwide ever since. The Italian Leonardo Servadid and his team of designers banged heads and came up with the eye-catching symbol. They also produced both stylish and innovative ski and tennis wear and went on to create the 'it' coat, the quilted ski jacket.

Once, when I'd ducked work (or it might have been after one of my many court appearances) I was walking past PSD, a sportswear/outdoor wear shop in Preston with the other-half and thought I would bob in to see if any new lines of tennis wear had arrived. Preston Sports Department was a small, compact split-level shop that stocked Fila, Ellesse and other such brands. This made footy lads yearn for the destination. They never had a large selection of stock, so when it was gone, it was gone. The aforementioned company's togs can be purchased at retail park megastores for less than a tenner these days, but back in the Eighties tennis shirts cost £25 plus, a tracksuit top or bottoms ran out at £40 or more and a jacket, well you were talking big money, easily a week or two's wages.

Getting back on track; I tried to gain entry to the store only I noticed a sign taped on the glass panel in the door. 'Sorry we are closed for stocktaking'. I then noticed three blokes rummaging through brown, cardboard boxes as I pressed my face against the glass frontage pane of glass. On seeing them, busy busy, I nipped up the narrow, cobbled side street to the right-hand side after remembering they had Ellesse Aspen skiing jackets on display in the side windowpane. They still had. These quilted marvels, if the memory serves me right, were around the £150 to £200 mark. So, I quickly hatched a plan with the love of my life for her to obtain the said 'it' jacket, which went along the lines of; tap tap, on the door. Tap tap again. And she then gave the three gents a cute, friendly smile through the glass. One of them came over to the door, opening the lock and instantly began to explain, "Sorry love the shop's shut..." Before he could explain anymore about what was happening inside the shop, or that it had changed hands, the sweet little thing stood in front of him informed him that she'd come to town especially to acquire a present for her love of her life, me (I'd wandered off). She then went on to disclose to the bloke she'd set her heart on buying her darling a dark blue coat that was on display on the dummy in the window. The funny thing is he hadn't a clue how much the said jacket retailed for, there wasn't a price tag inside it, and by his and the other twos dress sense, they weren't in the know on the casual scene, so my little scam might work.

Not long later my diamond of a manipulator left the shop with a navy blue Ellesse Aspen skiing jacket with detachable zip-off sleeves and concealed hood in the collar, unsophisticatedly shoved in a black bin liner. Deal done. The jacket had cost the un-pricely sum of 60 spondulies! She'd told them, all puppy eyed, that she only had three twenties in her purse, in near tears, and they'd taken the bait. What a touch, ha. They'd split the twenties between themselves – their palms had been greased – and stuck a note each in their undesigner jean's back pockets. Naughty, corrupt, boys, I know. But I wasn't complaining, was I? No! What a result. 'It' looked the business with a matching Ellesse ski hat in winter which I wore both to death at the match. This until a Burnley versus Wigan game when it got slashed, but I won't go there.

I also once remember a game at Springfield Park over the festive period in 1984. It was lashing down with rain and we'd paid into their crumbling, small seating section, dripping wet, following a non-eventful wander round Pieland. At half-time about 20 of us had gone looking for a refreshment bar to obtain a Bovril or anything that would warm the cockles. Anyway, we only ended up in a boardroom, or a similar room of the sorts where a few well dressed chaps were sitting round a grand, old oak table discussing some in-depth goings on or other matters at the club. We'd marched in wearing an array of various vibrant ski coats and ski-hats on our nuts.

These gents were suited and booted and announced, "Can we help you boys", while looking a bit confused as to why we were in their gaff. Well, one of the lads blurted out "Where's the beach?" And with that we all burst out laughing, about turned, and left, leaving bewildered kippers on humble pie eating faces. What a classic.

Never Ever Run... For The Bus

Down the M61 from Preston, happenings were happening and had happened. It's sometimes easy to rely on the faces at the centre of a scene to make things happen, but the footsoldiers who follow have their stories too. Jeremy Bramwell is one such mucker.

Jeremy: *I'm from a non-football family; we never had football on our telly in the house (apart from the FA Cup Final), it was never talked about, I never played for the school team, and I never ever even got close to going to or wanting to go to a match during my childhood.*

I was brought up in a neat Sixties detached brick house about 11 miles south of Manchester in a large village called Marple, just in the foothills of the Peak District. We had a front and back garden and middle-class aspirations from lower middle-class parents. I was a late developer and spent most of my youth and early teens going down the woods with my mates, lighting fires, making dens out of any old stuff that flowed down the River Goyt, going out trying to shoot rabbits with our air-rifles, making go- karts, and then, in my teens, getting into skateboarding.

This was until the start of my alternative take on life, eschewing organised 'team' activities to pursue, with my small group of mates, off-beat and anti-establishment shenanigans. We first started a little craze we called hedge-hopping, basically sneaking through people's back gardens. We would do this at dusk on pre-planned time-trial routes, jumping over or through fences, hedges and walls, wading through fish ponds, narrowly avoiding various yapping or growling dogs and their petulant owners. I'll never forget the sheer physical thrill of crawling on all fours across a wide expanse of lawn no more than 15ft from the back of the house in question whilst observing a family going about their evening meal. The funniest and most thrilling times were when the mother was washing-up right in front of the window, staring aimlessly out at exactly where we were crawling. She would then cup her hands around her eyes and put them against the glass to get a better view, at this point we knew we were spotted and would sprint like a herd of wildebeest crashing and scrambling into sheds, greenhouses and fences until we had made it to the next garden.

Also at this time there were various 'gangs' knocking about the estate, groups of lads who wandered around looking for trouble or making mischief; they would often affiliate themselves with football teams usually United or City, occasionally Stockport County.

My little gang of hedge-hoppers knew the streets, back gardens and woods around the estate better than anyone else. We knew this and always fancied a bit of sport and thrill-seeking. So our little game was to find and track a gang from a distance and wait until we had identified which team they supported. This wasn't through football colours as they weren't worn unless you were going to a match, so we had to get close enough to hear what they were talking about, then retreat to a safeish distance before we started chanting the name of the team we knew they didn't support, we had no allegiances to. Of course the gang would be sparked up and come running after us, we'd run a bit, stop, turn round and taunt them then, wait until they were close and split-up and skedaddle usually over a wall or hedge, through a few gardens and back to a pre-arranged meeting point.

We were the masters, we never got caught, or beaten up, and also were never identified by the other gangs as we always wore handkerchiefs over our nose and mouths a la the bad guys robbing banks in cowboy films. The only other accoutrement associated with us was we all wore Dunlop Green Flash pumps; our mums bought everything else we wore.

When I was about 15, Harry (not a hooray, it was his nickname), a mate from school, asked if I'd like to go to watch a football match with him. He usually sat with his dad only as he was now 15 he didn't want to, and would I fancy coming along – why not? I said yes for no good reason.

The team in question we were going to watch was Bolton Wanderers. I'd barely heard of them and had no idea where Bolton was but I was getting a lift so I was 'in for a penny...' and all that. So off we went the next Saturday in Harry's dad's Jag. I think it was around 1980.

You know the feeling at your first football match, the sights, the sounds, the smells; it was all there for me in spades, but on top of that I was encountering the massed ranks of the northern working class for the first time ever. Bolton were in the 2nd Division at the time so it definitely wasn't a glamour match, but to me the whole experience was oozing with glamour.

Being Bolton, a northern football outpost, there were plenty of scraggy feather cuts, sheepskin-lined lumberjackets, loon pants, clumpy footwear and scarves and more scarves, round necks and wrists. We mooched along to the corner of the Manchester Road stand which apparently was the place to be as it was next to the segregated away fans. Then about 10 minutes into the game three or four lads with thick Lancashire accents bustled passed and stood in front of us. I was transfixed. I had never seen or heard the like of them before. They all had these enormous wedge haircuts, huge side-parted fringes, 'tashes, skin-tight pale jeans, suede loafers and although it was the bleak mid-winter, brightly coloured sweaters and sort of silk scarves (Paisley I think). They started laughing and chatting away to each other and anyone who'd listen. They said they were actually West Ham fans, which absolutely staggered me, and they were just at the match because West Ham's game at Barnsley, or wherever, had been called off. Then they started flitting between their Bolton accents and fake mockney.

"Aren't you cold?" I wimpishly enquired.

"Bloody freezing" they replied. "That's the point in wearing these clothes though; people think you're 'ard."

And with that experience burnished on my mind forever, I went home.

I continued to go to the occasional Bolton home match and even a couple of away ones, but always with Harry and his dad. I remember observing the away fans more and more beginning to recognise 'brands' such Lyle & Scott and Slazenger for the first time in my life and thinking 'wow my dad is actually quite trendy.'

The big turning point came when I was about 18 and started to go to pubs for the first time (I told you I was a late developer) and my sister started going out with a lad called Geoff. He was an avid Man City fan and had a nice line in Adidas trainers, bright pink and yellow Slazenger jumpers and super tight Lois jeans. Geoff talked and acted like a true Manc with tales of drinking, partying and football exploits of what he called 'The Perries'. He was also good mates with the Top Boy in Marple (well Compstall actually), Phil Jennings. Now Phil was an exotic character to say the least, uber cool at all times with a mischievous glint in his eye, a ready smile, almost white blonde hair with an enormous flick and wedge, mousy 'tash and the most outstanding dress sense I'd ever seen. He was always immaculately turned-out and seemed to have a different outfit every time I saw him. He worked, which nobody else did, so he would always spend his wages each week on pints of Stella, but also clothes, and mainly really strange names that I'd *never heard of like Tacchini, Fila, Puma, Lacoste and Kappa. I'd still barely graduated from Marks & Spencer apart from in the trainer department. "Where do you your gear from" I'd asked.*

"In Manchester. Either from Kendals or Hurley's" he replied, "or places in Europe when I'm there with work."

He was an apprentice surveyor or something like that so would go on trips abroad, now and again, coming back with all sorts of weird and wonderful sounding brands.

There were a few more lads in this crew making about four or five. I of course jumped at the chance to join up and take my first steps into this new and unreal nether world of football supporters. Very quickly, I realised there were rules, some said, some unsaid, that had to be adhered to at all times to remain part of the group.

The Rules:

- *Never wear football colours; the only concession was a tiny Man City pin badge that was always worn, day and night.*

- *Never use organised transport to go to the match, always make your own way there.*

- *Always be on top of football fashions and change regularly to catch the away fans Perries on the back foot.*

- *Never ever run anywhere, ever. Not even for the bus; walk coolly, and if you missed it, pretend you never wanted to catch it in the first place.*

- *Always remember the police are the biggest enemy, more so than any away fans, they absolutely hated football fans and would brutalise them at any opportunity.*

So off we went; rules, haircuts, trainers and jumpers perfectly in order on various adventures seeking out new brands from the most obscure places and often inventing a new fashion for a week – just for the hell of it. The great thing about the Kippax Stand back then was that with only metal railings separating the away fans at the back of the stand you could get a good view of each other. I remember well the time we wore yellow leg warmers with burgundy keks which we very bravely wore against Cardiff that elicited a raucous reaction from the deerstalker wearing masses in front of us! Of course we responded with the song 'Where did you get that hat?' I even remember the time we decided to dress in the style of a

German U-Boat captain; four days growth of bristle, cream cable knit polo sweater, and black boots with chunky hiking socks. It was of course a bit hit and miss as you can imagine.

We started adding city centre wine bars to our pre-match routine, usually Henry's for home matches and then we would all jump in a taxi to the ground, get out and find the away fans and then do a sort of fashion 'stare-off' that had to involve taking the piss whatever they were wearing. But secretly taking notes at the same time of the few we thought looked the part.

For all our bravura we were not fighters or even runners, just daft fashion dandies, living the life and trying to keep our good looks intact. We would hang around the periphery of City's firm, 'The Guv'nors', but never got too close. They were really hardcore and some of the tales they relayed scared the living shit out of us.

The early morning trains to away games were often the best days out, avoiding all policing and giving us plenty of time to have a few beers and a mooch round the town before the game. It was all about the craic and the clothes, never the aggro, (the closest scrape I got into was getting 'lightly' beaten-up in Boots in Brighton in 1983). I'll never forget the explosion of hairspray, shampoo and conditioner bottles flying around as the trainer-footed kicks rained down on me. Sort of appropriate when you think about it really.

Memories Of A Non-Leaguer

Football is in my soul: I could regale for an age about certain football grounds and matches of yesteryear that I've attended over the years, each club's unique one-off stands and elements of the ground that struck a chord on my visits and, how unwelcoming the locals were too. Whereas I'm nonplussed with the stagnant, nondescript bowl stadia of today and the clapstick clapping, face-painted replica kit-wearing *fair-weather* fans that fill the plastic seating in the cloned, identikit sterile sections and, how welcoming the locals are nowadays too. And how, in today's football environment, the preponderance of *true* fans of professional league teams feel somewhat disconnected from the game. Yes, fans are somewhat detached, somewhat disunited, somewhat pissed-off fans with the game they *love*. Fans just don't seem to feel a real bond towards their clubs and teams anymore. And more so, with the players. The list about my gripes on modern day football bores into infinite, and I could waffle and rant on and on, forever. Plus there's no Bovril and Wagon Wheels at the majority of grounds nowadays. I *hate* modern football with a passion.

Some passionate fans and ardent, enthusiastic investors have formed new clubs like phoenixes from the flames. Following over 100 years of history, and the relocation of Wimbledon FC, which caused outrage amongst fans, AFC Wimbledon were established by a crazy gang in 2002. And within less than 10 years of their formation they gained promotion to League Two. Also, disgruntled Man U followers hacked-off with a variety of events at the club founded FC United in 2005, a team who are on the march to league status in the not too distant future.

The game I once loved is well and truly riddled with a terminal illness. Yes, football isn't the game it once was, or ever will be again. But, there is, and always has been, grassroots football; this being non-league football, which is sometimes closer to home than your boyhood heroes. And one such watcher and person who has always had a preference for such football is Julian Thomas (not all lads who looked the part followed the big clubs he'll have you know). Non-league football has always had its fair share of obsessives. Julian also had a thing for the clothes and the look of the era. He still does.

Julian: *Just how cool were those guys? It must have been 1982 and I was still a little 12 year old in east Manchester. The lads: Adi, Rick and Paul all dressed in their full Sergio Tacchini and Fila tracksuits wearing Adidas Rom, Adidas Jeans and Diadora Borg Elites. Their clothes seemed to dazzle and then I looked at myself. I was wearing a pair of drainpipe jeans, Slazenger sweater and black Gola pumps.*

Shopping for me was Mossley Sports or Ron Hill in Stalybridge. Clothes were a birthday or a Christmas treat. Fun trips to the swimming baths in Oldham would involve a diversion to Romida Sports to gaze along with the multitudes at the Fila, Ellesse and Lacoste gear all locked in glass cabinets like jewellery (I later learned this was to deter gangs of 'steamers'). Legends arose of infamous lightning raids by Moss Side and Hulme gangs on Hurley's Sports in Piccadilly.

At school, kids would turn up in the regular uniform with the additions of Pringle sweaters, Farah trousers, Kickers or Pods. School trips became mini fashion shows. I remember being about 14 and turning up for a trip to an old coal mine in Longton dressed in a Cerruti sweater, Lois jumbo cords and a pair of lovely tan Adidas slip-on golf shoes.

Even though I looked the business, I wasn't going to league football regularly. My mum was scared because of the bad reputation of the game and I was always interested in the football rather than the bother. I preferred going to the non-league; it was cheaper, a lot of my friends – and my dad – went and I could always have a cheeky beer in the clubhouse without anyone being too bothered. My team was, and still is, Mossley AFC, my hometown club.

Whilst the early Eighties saw trouble at league grounds, non-league had the reputation as a 'bit of a one man and his dog' pastime. And to an extent, that was and still is true. The only exceptions were cup matches, local derbies and games in dodgy towns. An FA Trophy quarter final at Bangor City in 1981 attended by some 2,500 saw running battles in the North Wales town, before and after the game. Also as the train pulled away from the station after the game bricks came flying through the windows.

An Easter derby against local rivals Hyde United resulted in large scale fisticuffs once too. The other place where trouble was always guaranteed was South Liverpool FC, based in Garston, a tough old dockers' area of Merseyside. Little wonder the club went out of business after vandals burnt down the clubhouse and trashed the rest of the place.

The high – or low – point was the Northern Premier League Cup Final in 1989. The game was played at Maine Road, just days after the Hillsborough disaster and attracted a good non-league crowd of just over 2,000. The plan was to split the main stand between Mossley and Fleetwood Town fans and a couple of friendly Bobbies to oversee events. Those two officers were quickly on their radios calling for back up as gangs of opposing fans faced off against each other and began rushing backwards and forwards throughout the game. Back up was called for from a United versus City reserve game. Those fans ejected continued the battles in the Moss Side streets. The result and goings on were front page news in the Manchester Evening News the next day, and Manchester City were banned from holding non-league Finals at Maine Road. A ban which has continued over to Eastlands, where the new stadium will never see a repeat of Mossley's 2-1 triumph that day.

My choice of clothes had changed by then. Favourite shops in Manchester were DeGuy and Voi in and around the Royal Exchange. Brands were C17, Radio, Ciao and Sonnetti. I also loved the Manchester music scene with the band t-shirts, Go Vicinity flares and multi-coloured Kickers.

A return to my home town some three years ago after an absence has seen me renew my interest in football and in Mossley AFC. I've gone from a few games when I first returned, to most games home and away – my interest has been rekindled in my home town team. Ironically, there are a few lads my age who for various reasons don't go to City or United anymore; so you spot a few labels around Seel Park. The sight of Lacoste jackets, Fjallraven coats, and a vast number of Adidas Eighties'-style trainers is not uncommon amongst other brands. And a few nods are exchanged at the match when you see lads in similar garb from visiting teams.

The clothes are now back to the early Eighties look of Fila trackies, Lyle & Scott polos, Levi's 501s and Adidas Stan Smith trainers for the younger element too.

A look at the non-league scene today still sees a very homely, some would say nerdy, view of football. Again this is not an unfair view, there are quite of few rather square chaps at games. That's not to say there isn't trouble. Chalfont St Peter versus Glossop North End in the 2009 FA Vase semi-final witnessed trouble. Though this was certainly due to drunken excesses, as opposed to any organised activities. Our old friends at Fleetwood Town have a reputation when travelling away and reading on the many non-league forums their reputation goes before them. FC United of Manchester, the breakaway club from the Glazer-owned Manchester United, have attracted many hangers-on and I've witnessed personally local Mossley youths face off with their so-called support after a league game in 2008. For a regular game, there are no distractions from the football; although an away game at FC Halifax Town or an FA Cup game at Curzon Ashton can have you looking over your shoulder.

The truth being, there is not enough people to develop a scene as such. Not that I'd want a return to bygone days. Average crowds at Mossley are around the 200 mark and we are one of the better supported teams in our division, the Northern Premier League Division One North. Only I would rather watch non-league than any other form of football nowadays.

Saturday best: Braemar jumper, Sergio Tacchini Orion Star trackie top, Lois jeans, Tacchini Young Line polo shirt and Adidas Trimm Trab.

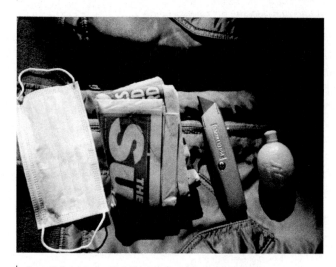

Essential match day kit in the late Seventies/early Eighties.

Fila track top, Lois drainpipe jeans and Adidas Trimm Trab.

Fila velour tracksuit top, Pringle jumper and Adidas Koln trainers that were part of the popular City series.

Diadora: To share gifts and honour. Original Diadora issues from left to right, top to bottom: Borg '79, Borg Ace, Borg '77 from the 234 series and Borg Elite '81 alongside an original 'free' Bjorn Borg shoe bag.

Ellesse: serving up 'it' gear.

Part of the author's Punk vinyl collection.

The author's bedroom back in the day splattered with posters.

Ian Hough, Blackpool seafront, 1981.

The Portsmouth 6:57, flat caps and woolly scarves – usually a
Northern look! Burberry and its 'checkered' past. Ian Hough
contemplating the 'Nameless Thing' in 1980. The author in his
first, of many, Pringle jumper 1980.

The 6:57, suited & booted.

The 6:57 wedding party.

Adi dazzlers.

A young Steve Cowens proud to be a 'Blade.' 'tashes were all the
rage in Yorkshire in the early Eighties, and still are today.

A scene repeated in most towns and cities in the UK during the late Seventies and Eighties. Preston and Wigan clash outside Gibsons Sports. Gibsons Sports was a Casual haunt for one-off trainers in the early Eighties.

The author looking 'scruffy' with a long flowing mullet too. The author contemplating his waning love for the once beautiful game outside Preston North End's ground Deepdale, just before the bulldozing of the last stand from a bygone era to complete the modernistic, benumb stadia several years ago.

Steve Cowens: Burberry tweed jacket and scarf, Armani cords and Adidas Samba – smoking.

Big Dave, a casual soul boy. Preston Wildcats Scooter Club.

Wigan rugby lads out on the prowl.

Wigan and Leeds rugby lads exchanging 'views'.

Old skool trackie tops; Lacoste and a Dallas Sergio Tacchini.

7

SOCIAL ENTREPRENEURSHIP

'I have far more respect for the person with a single idea who gets there than for the person with a thousand ideas who does nothing...'

Thomas Alva Edison

Actions speak louder than words, so there is no need to go great detail briefing you on the next three bloke's actions. Because the next three stories speak volumes about their entrepreneurial actions!

Adi Love Handles

A Yorkshireman by birth, Robert Wade-Smith is an honorary Scouser. His influence on the burgeoning years of casual is one that has long been acknowledged by Liverpudlians who understandably regard him as one of their own. On Merseyside, his retail outlet enjoyed mythical status. Tapping into an insatiable thirst for rare, unreleased 'trainees', Robert made his name selling Adidas sports footwear to young scousers.

Sporting activities weren't on their minds though. During the first wave of what is now neatly pigeonholed as 'casual', the only thing they wanted to exercise was their sartorial superiority over their peers. That one-upmanship is what fuelled the fast growth of Robert's business.

Scousers sought to out-do each other. Indeed long before Robert opened his eponymous retail outlet in the city, the young men of Liverpool were hotfooting around Europe in search of adventure and tennis shoes.

The story of the Robert Wade-Smith shop has been covered in detail in Dave Hewitson's *The Liverpool Boys are in Town*, but how did Robert find himself perched on the axis of one of the biggest youth movements in the 20th century? What follows next are those details, in Robert's own words.

(Interview by Michael Taylor.)

Robert: *I went to private school and didn't do very well. But my dad told me I had to get some experience so, he persuaded me to take a job at a manufacturing company where I could get some sort of an apprenticeship. He then made a phone call to one of the big suppliers and said: "Look, my lad thinks the world owes him a living and, you know, thinks money grows on trees."*

I joined Peter Black in the September of 1977 at the age of just 17, and I stayed with him for five years. What was interesting was that they had a multi-faceted business; they had this huge manufacturing business, one of the most successful in Yorkshire, and were the biggest supplier to Marks & Spencer. They were the main manufacturers for the bags and luggage for M&S, and also their slippers and ladies' sandals. They had over 2,000 people working in that factory in Keighley too.

From day one I was thrown in at the deep end. The factory had 13 manufacturing rooms with sewing machines and I was put in the big Adidas sports bag room, with 40 sewing machine girls. I was given a job of cording the handles of the Adidas sports bags, which in those days was the biggest selling sports bag of the Seventies. It had a loop handle on it and that handle is a piece of material that was folded in half, sewed and therefore hollow inside and in order to give it the grip, it had to be plugged by a plastic tube, and that tube came in rolls by the thousands of yards in length. So the raw material was then cut into one foot sections and my job then was to thread that tube into the handle.

Now if you imagine they were producing 50,000 bags a week at that point, that's 100,000 bag handles being made!

So my first four months was spent purely threading the handles. They would be heated up to make them soft, and then you'd then thread the tube in with what can only be described as a Phillips screwdriver with its end sewn off; a blunt screwdriver piece of kit. You'd to push the tube in so that it left at each end of the handle just short of three inches. The ends of those handles could then be looped into the hoops and then put onto a riveting machine and attached to the bags. You can imagine there were probably a hundred little processes to making an Adidas bag done by hand back then.

That first year in that factory they wanted to if I had the resolve to work my balls off. Coming from a pretty good background, public school and in amongst all these women, it was a proper test. It was all about whether you could understand the work ethic and the sheer dedication going on the production line to create business, product and trade. And it was just a very interesting lesson. By about month three I'd caught up with the girls opposite me and they were threading three or four thousand handles a day each. So you were working at a hell of a pace.

From that point onwards they moved me round the factory to various other jobs like turning bags inside out after they'd gone through the oven. I had three months just sweeping the floor in the M&S luggage room and other similar jobs. When you're producing, like I say, 50,000 Adidas bags, plus probably 50,000 Marks and Spencer suitcases, it's poetry in motion to see it. But you certainly get a sense of the work ethic that goes into how you make a successful business.

I worked my arse off, so they moved me to the Adidas distribution warehouse for a year. That was another eye-opener as well. The Adidas bag had been so successful that they gave our company the licence for distributing their trainers and sportswear, much to the annoyance of Umbro, who had up until then the distribution order for sports shops. Peter Black had persuaded Adidas to give them the distribution to department stores and the mail-order business, as well as some of the up and coming trendy menswear stores such has Topman; (Ralph Halpern had launched Topman after Topshop in the mid-Seventies). Topman became the fastest growing menswear business in Britain and Adidas had 20 shop-in-shop concessions – small areas within Topman stores. These were just a few wall shelves areas of trainers.

I had the ambiguous title of assistant, or personal assistant, to the warehouse manager. Of course the lads who worked in the warehouse, about 15-20 of them, felt that I'd got special treatment. I was actually earning less than they were. Naïve as I was, i soon turned it into the concept that I was the assistant manager, not the assistant to the manager. But I learned the hard way, and I was certainly brought down a peg or two and had to work my bloody arse twice as hard as everybody else, stacking boxes. I bet they had 200,000 trainers in that place; it was 50,000sq ft of warehouse.

At the time it was a £10 million pound business, which would be equivalent to £80 million today. It was quite an operation. And then the day came when they gave me the big break I'd been looking for, which was to go into the concession business. One day I was stacking boxes and working my arse off in a horrible warehouse, the next day I was suddenly on an airplane to Aberdeen to open an

Adidas concession, not the first, but a new Adidas concession in the new Topman Aberdeen store. The trainers' boom was just about to begin. And there I was, with my new job and new job title travelling around the UK visiting two concessions a day.

They gave me a company car and I would visit each member of staff in the concession stores. I was working out of a very nice office in Ilkley, the Adidas headquarters for the UK, and learning the shop-in-shop day-to-day business.

I was working for a bloke called Steve Dawson, who was running the concession side of the business. And what was fascinating, is that he said to me before the call came in from the Liverpool concession, "You watch this, watch Liverpool's figures." Because all the figures that were coming in were around the £500, £600 and £700 mark. "You watch this in Liverpool" he kept saying "it will be two grand at least!" And sure enough, it was over two grand. Steve said Liverpool's figures had been ahead by a mile, every week, since setting up there six months ago.

Anyway, when I got my feet under the table I started to realise, after going over to Liverpool, what was going on. The scally phenomenon of the trainer. It was the Adi Stan Smith in that first few months leading up to Christmas of 1979; I think we sold a 1,000 pairs in November, 2,000 pairs in December, and then, sales went up to 3,000 a month.

At that point in a little concession in Liverpool, it was pretty clear that something was going on. Also, the ST2 padded jacket, the navy one, with the three white stripes down the arms became the cult jacket of the time. We were selling 50 jackets a week in Topman. The next two years were just absolutely mind-blowing with what happened. The average prices of trainers being purchased in Liverpool next Christmas jumped from £19.99 a pair to £29.99. The average selling price in the UK at that point was £16-£17. And in Glasgow it was about £14. What had happened in Liverpool was there was suddenly a step change from just wanting ordinary sneakers to wanting pukka top tennis shoes. The Stan Smith was the first, then it went oneupmanship. So for the next two years, Liverpool was selling thousands of pairs of the most expensive tennis shoes.

Manchester happened a year later; but it didn't really kick in until 1980-81, with Liverpool being 1979-80. It was just mind-blowing. The sales figures went to 5,000 pairs a week. Imagine: sales figures are coming in from 20 odd concession; Liverpool's are at 5,000, the Manchester's at 1,500, and Ediburgh's shop at 900. Then all the other shops are in the hundreds.

The total business was running at about 12,000, maybe 15,000 pairs a week. I was involved in this concession business for 150 weeks/three years nearly. Not only was Liverpool number one for all 150 weeks, it was three times bigger than the number two. The total business for Adidas was three quarters of a million, with Liverpool doing quarter of a million on its own.

I was just turning 20 at the time and I thought, I've got to open my own shop. And that was 'the' moment, if you like. I'd seen an opening and opportunity at a young age and a burning ambition to open my own shop. but I could never pluck up the courage.

Anyway, we always had a drink on a Friday night after work – the Adidas reps were all a bit older than me, they were all in their early 20s – and I'd be in the pub and saying I was going to open my own shop one day soon. And after about three months, one or two of them had heard this half a dozen times, at least. One of the reps, on the old piss take, sort of, after about six pints at 11 o'clock one night, had this eureka moment for me. He said: "The problem with you, Robert, it's just entrepreneur bullshit talk and no action." I was a bit pissed, but I thought 'yes' I was giving too much talk and not enough action. I talked a good shop, but I was just one of those people who have got a great idea and never follow it through. (I told the same guy at a dinner three years later that it was him who gave me the impetus to set up on my own.)

This was just about the end of 1981, going into 1982. So one Monday morning I rang Tom Black, the chairman I worked for, and asked his PA if I could come and see him the following morning, and he said yes; Mr. Thomas will see you at 6.55am for a few minutes.

The next morning I entered Tom Black's office at 6.55am; and he was surprisingly nice at that time of the morning. I told him what I wanted to do and if he would agree to supply me with the Adidas trainers for a shop I wanted to open in Liverpool. He said, "I've got to say, my friend, I started in this business just like you, sweeping the bloody floor, at the same age, and had to work my way up the ladder to run this business for the old man. I'm an entrepreneur myself too. I would have loved, at your age, to do what you're on about what you want to do. I admire you a lot, and I wish you every success. And yes, we will supply you." And at 7.03am I was out of the office.

As my dad said to me, "You didn't go to university; you went through the school of adversity." This was quite true, really. Though it was harsh at the beginning, and I couldn't get any money from the old man. He gave me an absolute slating for giving up a good job and read me the riot act – I had a phone melting experience with him. He absolutely launched into it saying, there's 2,000 bloody shoe shops going bust in England right now, and who of sane mind would put money into that? I said there's a trainer boom. He replied "I don't give a bugger about the trainer boom; and I'll tell you something else, Robert. The concept of opening a shoe shop in fucking Liverpool has disaster written all over it." And he really was ferocious – too ferocious, in my mind. And his final answer was, NO. I was absolutely fuming. I said to Angie, my young girlfriend at the time, she was 19, "That is fucking it. That is fucking it. I'll never speak to that guy again. He's a twat!" And I didn't actually speak to him for seven or eight months. As far as I was concerned, he was over. But one thing did jolt me, I knew I was completely on my own at that point.

I had already resigned; and time and money was running out. I then had to have a complete rethink. So instead of opening in Bold Street, Liverpool, which would cost me £12,000 a year in rent, I then went to Slater Street, which is 'the' back street. Yes 'the' famous back street where the shop was £30 a week rent. I worked out that if I just sold five or six pairs of trainers a week I could survive. So I sent a little plan up at £25,000 turn-over, which is £500 a week; and also worked out with this turnover I could even make a small profit, but I wouldn't pay myself in the first year.

Fortunately, Neil Cowan, the finance controller at Adidas, who loved the idea, was an accountant who lived in the same village as me. We were mates, though he was a bit older than me aged 25, but he really put me in the right direction of how I would go about getting some financial help. We both went to see the Natwest in Ilkley, and there was a lovely guy called Ron Reekes.

I had about a £1,000 in my house in equity and I had £500 quid in my bank account. Neil had got a bit more equity in his house. Ron said, "Look, Rob. I'd love to get involved and if you're giving up your job and moving to Liverpool I would help you get the overdraft to fund the venture." So we got a small overdraft agreement secured on my house, and Neil's house, plus my money, £500. Ron gave us a facility with Natwest of £10,000 to start the business.

We budgeted on £2,000 to fit out and stock the shop, and by hook and by crook, and by borrowing stuff, we did it. Adidas did actually give us some shop fittings too. We gave the shop a lick of paint, and we were ready for business. All we needed now was stock.

Nike would supply me. Puma wouldn't supply me. Le Coq Sportif supplied me. New Balance wouldn't supply me, though Reebok would. So, we made our £2,000 spread. But, the most important part of the story is, that we got broken into on Sunday/the early hours of Monday. Angie and I had merchandised the shop on the Saturday, and when we arrived on the Monday morning, the shop had been ransacked.

I mean, they'd gone in through a side window which had been boarded up, and there was about a hundred little burnt out matches on the floor. So obviously kids had broken in using the matches for light. They'd basically nicked about a hundred pairs of shoes, half my stock, my only stock. So it was one of those moments, talk about adversity. It was one of those disastrous situations when what do you do next; and at the age of 22, it knocked me sideways. But this was the school of hard knocks and you've to pick yourself up. I phoned Neil, and he said, "Look mate, you need a bit of advice and encouragement. Mate, you've just got to brick up the windows, for fuck's sake, and learn from it. Things will pick up, for sure."

He was right, fortunately. I'd been into the Norwich Union on the Friday, and got myself an all-shops policy for £142.50. An all-embracing shop starter, starter pack. I rang the insurance company and incredibly, the lady that sorted the policy answered the phone and I explained that she wasn't going to believe it; we'd been burgled in the first weekend. I was in tears about the whole thing. I reckon she could hear and sense that I was absolutely shattered.

She sent the loss adjuster to the shop within half an hour and he could see for himself; he was a good man. He told me he could see what had happened and the insurance company wouldn't let the shop fold and go bust before it had begun trading. He was going to do everything to push the claim through as quickly as he could. And by Friday, a £2,000 cheque landed in my bank account.

The phenomena of what happened next: in the first week, I sold a pair a day. At the end of the first week I'd done £141 in sales. Though what was interesting was, I'd had a number of scallies in the shop, and they were all wearing these different coloured Adidas Trimm Trab trainers which had the big thick polyurethane sole, with new buck suede uppers. But these were the rare ones from Germany, Austria and Switzerland. Some were in red and white stripes, some were in royal blue with red stripes and some were the rarest of all, green with navy stripes. I couldn't get them from anywhere. So I said to them "where are you getting Trabs from?"

Apparently they'd been launched in the mid-Seventies under a name called Jaguar Super and released in the UK, but they'd been a disaster – too Germanic. Of course, that was too early for trainer explosion, like a lot of things. So, they'd been renamed by Adidas to Trimm Trab. In Germany they were one of the biggest sellers. And because Liverpool FC were in Europe, and 2,000 regular scallies went on tour, they were 'acquiring' Trabs from shops across the continent. Actually, a lot of these scallies were robbing Lacoste and Fila tracksuits and Ellesse ski jackets from department stores and sports shops. Again, you couldn't get any of those labels in the UK.

"It was really those lads who followed
Liverpool who were bringing the stuff back to Britain.
It was well known they'd go into the luggage
department of a department store, nick a head

> bag, and then fill it to the brim. That's how the
> head bag trend was started – you couldn't get
> those in the uk either. They would arrive
> back home in Liverpool and sell £600
> worth of gear to pay for their trip
> they'd been on plus an earner."

It was really those lads who followed Liverpool who were bringing the stuff back to Britain. It was well known that they'd go into the luggage department of a department store, nick a Head bag, and then fill it to the brim. That's how the Head bag trend was started – you couldn't get those in the UK either. They would arrive back home in Liverpool and sell £600 worth of gear to pay for their trip they'd been on plus an earner.

That was quite a common thing that was going on back then, and what became known as the casual boom of the designer sportswear. This then led to the designer and jeans boom in the mid-Eighties. That whole oneupmanship of expensive sportswear worn as casual wear was created by the Liverpudlians. Which explains why Liverpool was so way ahead in the charts. It was Liverpudlians going round Europe; and they, the scousers, always wanted something different, they always wanted something that nobody else could get.

Yes, there was a little bit of dressing up going on at Tottenham, and you're dressing up going on at Arsenal, and also dressing up going on at Man U. You know, you read some of those stories about that, and the sociological thing were going on, a movement, but obviously from the scousers' point of view, they didn't like second best, so they turned out with the best gear. There was that joke about going at the time too; Leeds United were still wearing the long leather coats when the scallies had visited Elland Road in 1982.

By the time I was properly trading in 1982, it was pretty obvious I just hadn't got enough of these rare trainers in stock. I constantly got asked, have you got this, have you got that, you've got a great range but you haven't got these, have you? Well, I had 70-80 per cent of the Adidas range and other trainers but, I didn't have all these top end tennis shoes and top end running shoes. I'd outdone Topman straight away in sales as they only had Adidas and I had about twenty styles of Nike plus, other brands.

The shop was the first shop in the world that actually pointed the concept at a casual fashion side as opposed to a pure running shoe shop, Footlocker in America had already been three or four years into the running shoe boom in California. Cobra, the running shoe shop in London, had opened around the same time as me.

But I was the first fashion trainers' store. And then the biggest breakthrough of all came; when in the second week of trading I went with my empty suitcases to Brussels, by train.

Like I said, I'd turned over £141 in the first week, then £180 the following week, roughly a pair a day. So, I shut the shop; I put a sign up on the window, "Gone to Brussels for more stock". When I'd been asking the scallies where they were getting their trainers from in the main they'd say, "Brussels, la." And that, unbeknownst to me, was the standard answer, because they certainly weren't going to tell anybody where they were really from. It just so happened that my cousin, who had become a director and an investor in my company, was doing his Price Waterhouse apprenticeship at the Brussels office. I stayed with him overnight in Brussels, and scoured the city for rare trainers, only to find absolutely fuck all of any worth.

Nothing. In the shops they didn't even have as good a range as the UK. That was an absolutely downer. But, what they did have was some rare Puma; and as Puma wouldn't supply me, I bought a load of Pele Rios, which was a suede Trimm Trab lookalike. I bought 20 pairs of Puma; 15 pairs of Pele Rio and a few pairs of Adidas shoes, which were quite cool. I also got a 15 per cent discount; and the currency exchange rates were in our favour in those days. So I was able to get them at roughly £17.

On that particular trip I came under the radar. But what was absolutely brilliant about that trip was, when I got to Ostend, on the way back, feeling a bit compromised, I went into the café at the ferry terminal and on the bloody deck were five scallywags, proper scousers with the wedge haircuts, and they were wearing the most expensive Ellesse ski jackets, all of them.

And, they all had these amazing trainers on; Grand Slam, Zelda, two pairs of rare Trimm Trabs and a pair of Munchen all brand new. They were sat there as casual as you like, classic scouse, sitting on their Head bags; and I thought they're loaded up, they've been on tour. So I went and got a beer and went up to them: "Lads, you from Liverpool?"

"Yeah, la." Came the reply.

"I'll tell you what. If you've got any rare trainers in those bags, I'll buy every pair you've got." I responded.

"Fuck off, la. Wheres yous from anyway?" one said.

"I've just opened a shop in Liverpool selling Adidas trainers, and I'm looking for rare trainers. If you've got any stock, I'll buy it." I stated.

"Fucking hell, la. Yous fucking having a laugh, like?" another chirps up. They were casing me up thinking am I some sort of bizzie, CID, or whatever.

"Fuck off, la. We've got fuck all. We're on our holidays."

"Fine. Okay." I said, and got on the ferry and I began to feel a bit nervous. Especially as they might turn me over.

Then one of the lads came up to me on the ferry and asked, "Hey la, where's this fucking shop, la?"

"Slater Street" acknowledging him.

"Fucking never heard of it. None of us have never heard of it."

"I know you might not of heard of it, I only opened it two weeks ago" I enlightened him.

"We've been on the Transalpino for two weeks" he then informed me.

I had a little chat with him. He didn't really say anything about the trainers, though. But I got very nervous then and thought I'm going to have to shake these guys off, so I went to a different end of the ferry and tried to shake him off.

When the ferry docked, I got on the train as quickly as possible to Victoria. Anyway, they were on the same train and were getting progressively more pissed. I thought they were definitely going to have a go at me.

Then, at Victoria, I was running out of time, at half-seven, to catch the tube to Euston. So, I ran and got down the tube station, jumped on the tube, and couldn't see the scallies; I'd lost them. Got the tube to Euston, ran up the escalator and it was 7.55pm, with the train leaving at 8pm. I ran straight through barrier onto the platform after hastily paying for a first class ticket. Fucking hell, I'd paid for first class, which was totally alien to my idea of not spending a bean and not paying myself for the first year. I boarded the train in first class as it was just about to pull off; thank fuck for that, I thought. And then, down the platform the rogues came. They were proper laid back, they were being monkeys; they knew the train was going to wait. I thought, shit.

The train had just got past Watford, and who turns up in the next seat, one of the fucking scallies. "Hey, la. We've been having a chat down the carriage. Why don't you come down and have a look what we've got, la?"

Nervously, I put my suitcases under the seat and headed down the carriage where they opened their bags. They had 20 odd pairs of, fucking gold dust. They'd got all these different colours of Trim Trabb, even burgundy ones.

They'd Munchen, blue and red. Grand Slam, too. And, they'd a pair of navy Zelda. They'd all sorts.

I offered a tenner a pair.

"Fuck off, la. We'll be getting 18 quid a pair all day long when we get back" one snapped.

"I'll pay you £14-£15." I responded.

"Half and half, la" they bounced back, quick as.

They're ripping me, in typical scouse humour, and taking the piss a bit. So, I sat down and had a beer with them. "We'll think about. We might do a deal 16 and a half, maybe 16." They debated between themselves out loud, but for my attention.

"You're getting nearer. Make it 16 the deal's done." I threw into the mix.

"Right, la. We'll come to your shop tomorrow morning and we'll bring them." One of the lads said looking directly at me.

So I went back down the train, got back home to my bedsit and to Angie. It was a Friday night. I rapidly informed Angie, "You're never going to believe this but, I've got a load of stuff coming to the shop tomorrow, so I need to get some money out of the bank to pay for it, alright?" She was fine with it.

Amazingly, when I got to the shop, the sign on the window had got me a little queue of six or seven people waiting. I then saw one of the lads from the train with two bags; I thought he was going to try to trade them to my queue, so I got him through the doors double quick. I also said to the queue, "Would you wait for another 10 minutes guys, please?"

I did the deal with the lad that we'd agreed and bought 25 pairs of trainers off him, he buggered off happy as Larry. He'd also given me a receipt on the back of an envelope that he'd bought them from some department store in Hamburg, and then sold them on to Robert Wade-Smith. So I was happy,

I'd got an invoice off him too, ha.

Soon as he'd fucked off, we opened. Angie and me sold six pairs of trainers within 10 minutes to the queue of six; in 10 minutes we put £200 in the till, more than the first week's takings. Those six kids left the shop with the trainers and the word went out. And during the next four hours, until 2 o'clock, we sold a pair every 10-15 minutes. We sold every pair bar three.

We put £800 in the till, talk about the day of magic. That one day on its own was the whole thread, the start of the thread of the whole Wade-Smith story.

Everything after that was a phenomenon, really. Never mind magic, it was a fairytale come true.

I then rang Neil, at 3 o'clock, and I told him how much we'd done and he said, "Jesus, for Christ's sake, Rob. Hire a van, I'm coming over – we're going to drive to Germany." We drove to Germany on the Sunday.

On putting the phone down on me, Neil then rang Ron Reekes at home, the bank manager – he had got his number out of a telephone book. Neil asked him could he get hold of our overdraft, the other seven thousand quid, in deutschmarks for us. He said he could fix it. If we drove to Lombard Street, in London, for nine o'clock in the morning, it would be sorted. So we drove to Lombard Street, to NatWest's main branch, and we took out the whole of overdraft from our account – £7,000 in 30,000 German marks.

It was bloody funny really; because having been burgled two weeks earlier, I was so nervous, but I was cooking on gas now, it was just amazing and, I was so fucking shit nervous about us losing the 30,000 marks. Neil had got this leather wallet, a big leather wallet, and it was stuffed full of the money. When we set off to Dover, I asked Neil if the wallet was in his pocket. When we stopped at the petrol station and Neil gets back in the van after filling up, I ask him if he has still got the wallet in his pocket. Again on the ferry; getting off the ferry. "Stop worrying. I've got the wallet" Neil kept saying "Nobody's going to get it off me."

Driving along once in France, I began asking over the wallet again. "Rob. Shut up about the wallet, will you?" Neil would reply. "Okay, okay, okay" I kept saying, but I still asked every three or four hours, it was a long journey. We'd been travelling for 12 hours at this point and I dozed off. On waking up, you might have guessed, I asked Neil if the wallet were safe? "Fucking hell, Robert. I haven't even stopped the fucking van. I've got the wallet. Will you fucking shut up?" But it's just one of those incredible things and that's how much was at stake. You see, it was not just our lives, it was our houses, it was our business, it was everything. And when we finally got to Germany, the shops were full of all these fucking trainers.

I don't think anybody from Britain went to Germany to buy trainers in bulk, only people that trade. So, we to went to Aachen first, and we met these guys there who put us on to the chief man in Germany. In those days they had territorial agreements so the shoe industry was split into the six territories of Germany and this one guy had the territory of Cologne and Aachen, the north-west side of Germany. He had three or four shops in Aachen and he had eight shops in Cologne. When we contacted him we said we'd like to buy maybe 2-300 pairs of Trimm Trab, Munchen, and other trainers that he stocked. Yes we have them, but not in Aachen, you have to come to Cologne. So we drove to Cologne, with my heart pounding away.

When we get to his office, it was the first computerised business I'd ever seen in November 1982. The building was a mega shoe stores too; a massive three or four floors of shoes in thousands of different styles. They were mainly Adidas and Puma. But he had 157 pairs of Trimm Trab in about six of his shops and he would get them all together. "Yes. I have Munchen too" he said. "We also have this... and this... and this..." he rhymed off what we'd come for. We could have the eight styles that we wanted, and it all came to 30,000 deutschmarks. We knew we could get to 400 pairs.

"Yes, everything's okay for you." He said in broken English. "But you come in the morning and with a banker's draft, we couldn't take a cheque. So if you bring, speak to your bank, bring a banker's draft tomorrow, we'll have it ready. I'm sorry but I only just met you but you must have a bank."

"No. We'd like to pay you now!" I replied, and Neil got the wallet out.

He says, "You are paying in cash?" So we got the cash out.

"In 30 years I have never once done one transaction for 400 pairs with one customer, and I've never done it in cash like this before!" He then turned to his partner and announced, "This is incredible. Get the wine, get the wine out."

He brought the wine in and I paid him in cash, he was absolutely mind blown. He loved it. I think we had paid him about £17 a pair or something, so he was happy. He'd given us a 10 per cent discount and, we saved 15 per cent tax because they were retailing at £22 in the German shops and we'd got them down to about £16 or £17 which we knew we could get £34.99 a pair for them in Liverpool. He had them all at the office within a few hours.

I mean you cannot believe what happened, we sold the lot. So, we went back before Christmas to get more. And can you believe it, in the middle of a Cologne high street, a scally I met in the shop comes up to me, "Hey, fucking hell, Wayne (because he thought I was called Wayne Smith) what's going on here, la?" It was quite obvious really, because we were loading these Adidas trainers in to a van.

But the fairytale carried on: we did £110,000 that first year, and did £250,000 in the second year; you could never have predicted that in your wildest dreams? We'd made something like a £40,000 profit in our first year. Neil was very good at building the stock levels up, so I reckoned we made near on £70-80,000 profit in the second year. When you consider I had been earning £4,000 a year at Adidas; though I'd had two magic years there. And it taught you everything you needed to know about trading.

I probably had more 'moxie.' I called it moxie, the ability to trade, the hustling ability to trade, more than any entrepreneur.

We went through the Eighties opening a number of shops only to find nothing had changed much, that Liverpool was still a one off. Unlike JD, we didn't find a scaleable model. JD were sitting a couple of levels below us in their average price and they were also into clothing a lot earlier than we were.

So the fashion sports shop that they created had a more commercial appeal when they began to open. They started in Bury, so they modelled it more at a sensible price. We were in Liverpool, and were enjoying this all at the top of the range. We took our very expensive trainers to Manchester, to Birkenhead, St. Helens and Wigan. We eventually got as far as Birmingham, Leicester and Sheffield.

We got up to nine shops at one stage, but it wasn't a bed of roses at all. Firstly when we got to Birmingham, JD were already there. Allsports were there, so were JJB and Olympus, as was Footlocker. So when we arrived in Birmingham, we were already late. The rare imports had run out of steam because Adidas had seemingly ran out of options. Reebok, of course, had a big boom, and Nike too, which took over in 1986/87. And as the Brummies liked their Nikes more than they did their Adidas, we were off the mark, and we were too expensive as well.

I actually then went into stocking Timberland – the rugged boot business – which, again, started in Liverpool, typically two or three years ahead of everyone else. After the scruff look, the move from trainers to a more rugged shoe fell in line with the change from designer sportswear, which had run out of steam, to the Italian and French sweatshirt and jeanswear labels; and therefore in 1985-86, there was a bubbling over in Liverpool. This was from Fiorucci, to then Chevignon, then Chipie and one or two other brands coming along.

And therefore there was a big step in change between 1985-88. I watched that unfold thinking, here I am, in the sports business, and I'm opening these chain shops, and they're not working. I also had a huge frustration that all my profits were going into opening these shops and they weren't delivering. Three or four of them were marginally profitable, but Manchester never made any money. I was in the wrong site there. I thought I could go into another backstreet site, like I had in Liverpool, and take a fortune over the counter. My golden goose in Liverpool was laying me golden eggs but, in Manchester, it was just like a… dead duck.

But Hurley's were doing well, they had a massive footfall from Piccadilly, so they were doing things right. JD were already in the Arndale making a lot of money, and we just couldn't compete. We were selling to the likes of the Gallagher brothers and people like that. They were all buying Gazelles, which was the big thing back then in different colours; there was a slightly different trend going on in Manchester than Liverpool. And there was a little rare import market thing down in the Oasis market where they were selling really old school trainers. Then there was that whole Haçienda movement; that whole period was slightly different to Liverpool.

I did branch into designer wear, and I was quite hated by a few of the local boutiques and ruffled a few feathers. I opened a shop on the famous Mathew Street. Within a year we'd got Armani, then Ralph Lauren and Calvin Klein and it just snowballed; Donna Karen, Diesel, Chipie came in and went, and we had runaway successes with Timberland. Suddenly we were selling 50 pairs of Timberland a week at £120 a pair. So the sales in Mathew Street did a million in the first year on its own. We were selling more Timberland than any other shop in the world. More Armani jeans than any other shop in the world. More Lacoste product than any other shop in the world. We had all these world records. Bernard Lacoste came to see us; he couldn't believe how we were outselling the whole of Paris. Sidney Swartz, the founder of Timberland, even came over from America and gave me a bloody gold watch with Timberland on the back of our sales.

But those early days in the Eighties, selling trainers to scousers, it was just mad, really mad, what happened in Liverpool.

The High Street Boom

With north-west lads having an unquenchable thirst for sportswear in the early-to-mid-Eighties, it wasn't long before retailers of such coveted components cottoned onto these yearnings. Only sportswear shops, and more so tennis and ski stores at this stage of standing, were usually one-offs owned by ex-professional sportsmen or sportswomen. But also young, enthusiastic entrepreneurs twigged on to these up-to-the-minute events, with a chain reaction proceeding on the sportswear and trainer outlet front. And one such northern outlet in its infancy during the early Eighties was JD Sports. From their unpretentious beginnings in Mossley and Bury, JD Sports now have emporiums in every major town and city in the UK. Someone who was involved with JD not long after its conception and right through its proliferation was Barry Bown, currently the chief executive of JD Sports, now a £1bn business.

(Interview by Michael Taylor)

Barry: *The fundamental thing about JD as it is now, and certainly the ingredients of the business, is first and foremost, that we are always turned on by great products. And that all comes from wanting to wear these items back in the day, when you had to save up your paper or milk round money before you could buy a* *round-neck Adidas T-shirt; so when you managed to get something like that, you treated it with real care and attention. We've always, always been product driven; and that's been the ethos of the business really.*

I started at Olympus sportswear when they opened a chain called 301, which were the big flagships. They had one on Oxford Street in London and a second one in Market Street in Manchester. I joined Olympus at the end of 1982 and left 18 months later. At that time they were the absolute kingpins of the sports fashion industry. They had the most stores, they had all the brands, they had the best retail presence. They were the ones that were really, really setting the scene. But equally at the same time there were all of these smaller retailers which were probably a lot sexier in their own right, but in terms of mass there was nothing in it, because they were very independent. There was one in Manchester called MC Sports, which was in the Arndale, where they used to hang all the Australia, Cerrutti, Fila, Ellesse and Head clothing from the ceiling, which at that time were about £40; a lot of money in 1982 for a polo shirt.

Whilst Olympus was the big corporate vehicle and the one which had the big turnover behind them, what they didn't have was the sexiness of all these Italian brands mentioned and Scottish brands like Lyle & Scott and Pringle that were coming through too. You could only get these from Gansgear and Wade Smith in Liverpool or MC Sports and Hurley's in Manchester. Only at the time there was this small retailer called JD, which, again, was trying to get in on that labels.

John Wardle and David Makin were the owners of JD, and they had moved into Manchester city centre around at the back end of 1982. They founded it all in 1981, and they had a store in Mossley. Prior to that, they had a store in Bury. That's where I got to know David Makin; he was a real obnoxious 16-year-old lad that I used to see in their tiny JD store where I would buy T-shirts and shorts. He was this kind of 'abrupt bordering on arrogant' young lad and he was busy telling me that the shop was half his.

After a while I got to know David and John a bit more. At that time I was the manager of an old menswear company called Greenwoods, and David used to come and borrow Barclaycard vouchers off me, the ones you used to have to put them through that machine by hand.

I didn't see them both for quite a while when I left Greenwoods, this until they came into the Olympus store and it was probably in around about November/December 1983. When they walked into the store it was literally, "What the fuck are you doing here?"

I just said, "Nice to see you as well!"

I informed them I had been here for a while and they asked would I be interested in coming over for a chat at their shop? So I did; and the next thing I knew I started at JD on the grand sum of £6,500 a year and that was when they had stores in Bury, Manchester and Sheffield.

Because I was at Olympus I was in a suit at work, which was what was expected of you because you're at the front of the business, so you had to portray yourself as a professional individual. Immediately after joining John and Dave, it was Adidas polo and a pair of pants. It was fantastic because you could wear the gear to work that you wanted to wear.

I'm also a football fan – lifelong Man City – only I was not in the slightest bit athletic, but I used to love trainers; I still do to this day and obviously clothing as well. There's something about a pair of trainers which is difficult to explain. They can be absolutely magical and it can't be really put into words but, I think once it's got you it's got you.

Back then manufacturers were still selling training shoes for sport, but the lads were buying these great pieces of footwear to wear on a football terrace. It was those lads that turned sportswear into being a real fashion thing, not the brands. And some of these brands, without a shadow of a doubt, were bigger in Europe than what they were in the UK. So lads literally hopped on a train and went to Europe and 'picked up' a dozen pairs from a retailer and brought them back to sell on.

There were times when we certainly drove to the suppliers to pick up stock ourselves because we were selling it quicker than we could keep it in store. At that time it was all beginning to become a kind of movement; we were fortunate, we were one of the placements, so it was a natural fit for us to work with those brands.

When I first joined JD, and I walked into the store, there was a wall full of tennis racquets and badminton racquets; we decided quickly they had to go and we are going to offer the latest and greatest in sports fashion products.

Some of the brands, way back in the day, are no longer around now. Patrick is a brand which has been almost rubbished in retail nowadays. They used to do a shoe called Patrick Colarismo which was unbelievable. People just wouldn't understand that today. It was very like the Adidas Munchen. All brands were new and exciting to us, really. So, as I've mentioned before, Australian, Fila, Cerruti and Head were absolutely cool as they come; and on top of that, you've got Adidas plus Lyle & Scott and Pringle. Nike came along a little bit later. Peter Storm cagoules were absolutely massive too.

The store was always going to be rooted in sports by reference to the brand, but it was going to be worn by the guys that went to watch football as opposed to want to play football, or tennis. So we wanted to supply the guy that went to the sports events as opposed to participating. We were also very instrumental in driving that element of retail. Outside of Olympus there wasn't really that many other sports retailers which emerged; First Sport and then Allsport. But I like to think that JD was one of the pioneers of really developing that product.

I think at this time you've got to give credit where it was due to the people that were involved in the business and the products. David Makin was, and is, an absolute visionary. Although we don't talk anymore, you've got to be fair and give praise where it is due. He was very, very quick to spot the newest trend which was coming, and if he believed in it, he went for it. He had the conviction which enabled you to either get it wrong or you got it right, and in fairness to David, he got it right a lot more times than he got wrong.

As a business, we were a lot smaller then, clearly a lot closer to the consumer because of the size of the business; we used to work every hour God sent us. You'd have done your Monday to Friday, but we were a retail business, so Saturdays were important and even if we didn't have a shop, at the time, in somewhere like Newcastle or Glasgow, we'd go and walk the streets of Newcastle and Glasgow and look at what people were wearing and observe and learn. Our life then, and probably to a degree now, was consumed by having the right product proposition for the consumer, we were infatuated with it.

I tell a story, and I only tell them to the people that have been with us for a while because they're the only ones that actually get it. When I was at Manchester we didn't have a head office facility or anything like that, though we had an office in Blackfriars in Salford, where David and John would operate from, and a temporary warehouse just outside of Prestwich. All the deliveries would come into Manchester and I'd literally just open the backdoors of the store and put boxes in the car after sorting through them. This could be seven o'clock at night, and I would drive over to the Sheffield store to take the stock. I'd have to get hold of the manager beforehand and say "Whatever you do, don't go, I'm coming over tonight." When you get there at 8.30, 8.45, I would, with the manager, actually unpack the delivery and put it on the shop floor. We actually merchandised it as well.

In those days there was no such thing as staying in a hotel. A luxury to us would be after you'd done the delivery, you'd lie on the cardboard on the floor in the shop and that's what you'd sleep on. That was how you had to do it. We just didn't have the money to stay in hotels and things like that.

I think one of the things we do take credit for, even though nobody will probably give us credit for it, but we were the first retailer that presented it in a way which was sexy at the time for the consumer, that in turn made the consumer want to buy it because of the way that it was displayed and presented in the stores. And those would be some of the components about what's really made us, to a degree, evolve as a retailer and stand the test of time.

We were always eager to learn: One, we were always keen to make sure we were doing the right thing. Two, if we had any aspirations of becoming a bigger retailer and going into other markets then our proposition was going to be right for it. Three, to see if the culture was the same in the different areas. Fairly quickly after Manchester and Sheffield, we opened a store in Birmingham. After Birmingham we set up in Liverpool, then Bradford and Leeds; we saturated the north and then slowly started going further and further afield.

The key heartlands have always been, and probably always will be, very sports-fashion friendly and brands that resonate extremely well in those locations. It's not that different on footwear and sportswear nowadays, because you still have the same kind of variations in different locations. The south is still driven by clean-looking footwear, white-white, or black-black as footwear offerings which will always be the key staple diet. Whereas in the north they tend to like court shoes but colour. Apparel does too, but that's by brands as opposed to looks really. Adidas and Nike as a brand do carry nationwide, but within that there will be certain things which are more relevant.

I actually don't know whether we ever, at that particular time, got Adidas to wake up and latch onto this, but there were a myriad of products coming through which were developing into more things. We weren't saying, "Oh, now you've done this, can you do that?" we weren't like that then. It was only when we had probably 20 stores that we actually started to say, well actually, that's great, but we need it to be done a little bit different. That could be done in a different colour way or have a different sole. We then started to develop our point of difference because other retailers were becoming evident in the marketplace so we had to make sure we had something different to make the consumer buy from us. That took us to another level again.

In fairness to David Makin, whether it was an apparel item or footwear trend, he was able to take what the brands were presenting to us and then adapt it for our consumer and be sufficiently different to attract them. Paul Fox has been instrumental in going through the Nineties into the early Noughties on footwear for us, he has been quite pivotal.

Take Size? for instance. Size? started life as a business called JDFC, which was JD Footwear Concepts, with shops in Kensington High Street, Kings Road and Carnaby Street in London. At that time we recognised that if JD as a business wanted its position as being a place to house new and innovative product, we almost had to have something sat above JD which enabled a fascia to operate at a *different level of footwear, which would ultimately evolve into mainstream footwear for JD. JDFC wasn't right and we needed something a little more sexy, so Size? was born. Size? has built our reputation at that level on footwear. We had a good reputation anyway, certainly at a JD level, but to we needed add newness into the market, to get the early adopters, all those trainer aficionados visiting Size? for the 25th edition of Adidas Superstar. Lads sleep outside the store all night, and queue round the block now. Even recent re-launches for Adidas London, Manchester, Birmingham and Glasgow virtually every pair was sold out within a day or so of release. People still have an appetite for that.*

When Size? started out, we quite frankly weren't overly bothered that it didn't necessarily contribute to the financial dynamics of the business, it was offering the business something completely different. It was offering JD a food supply for tomorrow. It was really important to do that. We then recognised that Size? had to have something sat above it, so we bought Foot Patrol. Foot Patrol works with a distribution which Size? can't access; Consortium from Adidas, and Tier Zero from Nike; both higher level of products which ultimately will drip into Size?, which will ultimately drip into JD. The food chain of the pyramid keeps going. It's nothing other than product-driven.

As we've grown as a business what we've tried to do is attract the widest consumer base that we can possibly get into the JD sports fashion group. JD caters for a certain consumer that wants the latest and greatest in sports fashion wear and comes for the latest round of PTs or Max 95s from Nike. But there was also a new emergence of brands which JD wasn't working with. Brands like Henleys, Superdry, Gio Gio, Jack Jones and Game which JD didn't have access to but clearly there was a big consumer out there.

At the time we had the Scotts fascia which was dealing with the likes of Lacoste, Paul & Shark, Hackett, Penguin and Henri Lloyd the more classic, mainstream labels. But there was all these new era brands going on which we weren't really part of. This was the perfect chain to stock these new brands though.

Then again, we felt that if we want to become a bigger player and operate with a wider brand portfolio, we had to be strategic in our thinking. So Bank was acquired when it had 50-odd stores. It's now grown to 70-odd, and we believe it could go to upwards of 150. We've still got some fine-tuning to do but we've still got that as a goal.

We've had to buy brands as well: The best way to describe is it is immunising ourselves a little bit. Some retail operators out there deal in a more "value-driven" manner which perhaps doesn't uphold the integrity of a brand. I often tell the brands we care more about your brand than they do, because of the way they end up selling it into the market in certain places.

So we also felt that a reasonably safe course of action was to acquire brands ourselves, develop them as brands, but we never, ever tell people that they're an own-brand. We market them as brands. McKenzie is an example. To the consumers out there, it's a brand in its own right.

We supplied all the Sergio Tacchini for the remake of the film **The Firm** – we had to have runs made especially for it. It was a fairly costly exercise for us but an important one for brand recognition and we're now beginning to explore development of the brand. And we have a deal with Fila too.

I do think that the trainer culture and football thing have always been hand-in-hand. But while the football fan has been a strong adjacency for us, so has music. You only have to look at the bands on stage to see the clothes they're wearing and they'll also be decked out with a pair of trainers, whether it's one of the Adidas City Range or Converse pumps or Nike hi-top.

Because I'm still a big kid at heart, I still go to a lot of gigs and love music, I always have done. And we've staged and sponsored music festivals, whether it's been by being the main sponsor of the Carling Academies, or whether it's actually working with a band and paid for them to go into the studio to record an album. We've tried to do a lot of that; communicate extensively through the music media. The NME is a prime example; we take a page in there once every three weeks, usually in the front inside or back inside cover, where, there'll be a product shot, no editorial, but the best of the best available at JD.

As long as I'm around then JD will always stand for what JD stands for and it will always behave in the way that JD behaves. This is to offer compelling product in a really nice retail environment and displayed in a very highly presentable manner with great differentiation, and exclusivity. These are just some of the things which I think a lot of people take for granted but we actually work hard at achieving.

One other thing that we've always had over the years and continue to have is, a very strong relationship with our suppliers and we'll continue to do that. We challenge them, we work with them, our relationships are partnerships and that's not a flippant word, really. They are guys we've known and worked with for years that understand what we're about and vice versa, especially Adidas. Adidas originals are back in vogue again, but it's not a particularly new look.

While you have to embrace the internet and work with it and make it a fundamental part of your business, it's also been responsible for killing things as well, such as the music industry. The fact that people have disappeared off the high street as the internet's become more of a powerful force. It's one of those things. Love it or loathe it but you've/we've got to go with it too. The internet has become a big part of our business and we're even putting kiosks in stores so folk can *literally surf the net and we can either deliver their purchase to their home or they can pick it up in the store the next day. It's the way the world is going.*

Personally, I'd never, ever, buy anything off the internet, unless it's a collectable pair off eBay that I've not been able to get anywhere and I don't care what size it is. I've been able to fill in some of the collection what I never got round to getting at the time. If I've been on eBay and wanted a pair of Odyssey from Nike from 1989, and there's a box fresh pair with tags and things like that, you will have to pay top dollar, but you will get them. But if your mindset is that way that you want to collect, then you collect. It's like the Haçiendas. Adidas released an Adidas Haçienda where there was about 130 pairs worldwide and fortunately I managed to get a pair and it's got part of the Haçienda floor in the bottom of the box. And the last time I looked on eBay they were going for £2,600 a pair.

Impossible Is Nothing

In the late Seventies, and more so in the early Eighties, slipping on a pair of training shoes became fundamental nature and a sine qua non for the UK soccer tribes who attended the match. Only down south, Diadora Borg Elites (made of kangaroo skin tanned white with a gold or silver Y flash , embossed on the side along with Borg's endorsement signature) or white, leather Nike Wimbledon (with a pale blue tick/swoosh) were worn by the bulk.

But up north, Adidas, and their infinity of designations, formulations and variegations, were seen on the crumbling, concrete terraces in cornucopia – as you've already read.

And one lad who fell in love for the plenteous range of Adidas was Gary Aspden, born in Darwen, educated in Blackburn and Preston and at the University of Central Lancashire. As he says here, he's had an incredible life, mixing with the stars of sport and music through his work for Adidas and setting up partnerships and endorsements. But it's his upbringing that has been vitally important to everything he's done.

(Partly recorded at a Creative Lancashire event, 2011, and in conversation with Michael Taylor).

Gary: *My first contact with fashion was at the age of 11. There was a local disco called Bogarts and my friend Paul Ryder said we should attend. I turned up on his doorstep on the Thursday night, and knocked on the door all excited. He took one look at me in my flared jeans and said: "You cannot come out looking like that."*

I went back home and I asked my mum to take the flares in. She wouldn't. So I ended up sitting in that night watching Top of the Pops *with my dad and didn't go to Bogarts because Paul wouldn't go with me wearing those flared jeans. That was my first contact with fashion and I've probably been emotionally scarred ever since.*

I guess that was where my interest in clothes started, while my older brother got me into music. When I first got into clothes around 1980 it was primarily about a look more than brands. It was skin-tight jeans, white socks, Adidas trainers, anything burgundy, preferably with a Slazenger sign on it, a Fred Perry T-shirt and an anorak. I always wanted one of those kind of Human League haircuts too, but I used to struggle with that as I have wavy hair.

Labels started to play a bigger role as time went on. We got into Pringle and Lyle and Scott lambswool sweaters first, and then onto brands like Lacoste and Ellesse. It was the look of the working-class kid in the early Eighties.

My first music I discovered for myself was electro: I remember seeing a bunch of older lads wearing Fila and Sergio Tacchini tracksuits rolling about on a piece of cardboard with a ghetto blaster blaring out Street Sounds albums and I was fascinated. Soon enough I got into that whole breakdance thing and became obsessively interested in it – I was going to 'all dayers' all over the country when I was still at school. Me and my mates saw what American kids were doing on TV, only the stuff that the Americans were wearing wasn't available in this country at that time, it was a different environment then, things weren't globalised as they are now. Kids here appropriated that look and wore Tacchini, Fila and Adidas, which kind of crossed over with what football lads were wearing.

The gang of kids I hung around with were racially mixed, three of my closest mates were three brothers who moved to Darwen from Hulme whose dad had gone back to Nigeria and left them with their mum who was unable to cope. They were adopted by a local family in Darwen so we used to go into Manchester regularly to visit their mum. Another couple of my good pals were Asian.

This is important to mention, because the north-west during the early-to-mid-Eighties, particularly in Blackburn, there were real problems with racism; and because we were a mixed gang of kids, we used to regularly travel to Manchester, Bury, and Bolton where it didn't seem as prevalent. That exposed us to a lot of cultural scenes that I wouldn't come across in Darwen.

In the early-to-mid-Eighties' fashion was always changing, it was street fashion in the truest sense of the word, because there was no internet, we weren't reading magazines, there were three TV channels – you wouldn't even have come across a McDonald's unless you went to a big city.

As the whole breakdance thing died out around 1985/86, I started to go to football matches – at that point it was all about Armani, Boss and Valentino and European casual wear brands like Ciao, Ball and Pop 84. I was always brought up with football as my dad was a season ticket holder at Blackburn Rovers but I was never into the violence (or racism) like a lot of the lads who followed Blackburn were. That was one of the great things about Acid House in 88 – it finished all that nonsense almost overnight.

I'm not big enough to be going round starting fights. I was more concerned with keeping my clothes nice. If you get 300 geordies running up Bolton Road and screaming at you, your outfit pales into insignificance. Most of the psychopaths I came across on the football terraces were not overly concerned with clothes. In the early Eighties a full Tacchini tracksuit was £75, which was a lot of money back then. I would be very cautious in what I wore on a shopping trip to the Manchester Arndale on a Saturday afternoon. It was a risky business. People would want to tax you or chase you to the station for your clothes.

Looking back I guess a lot of it was just about fitting in with your mates – feeling a part of it. The early 80s were pretty boring so music and clothes were everything to me growing up. It was exciting to seek out trainers and clothes in the kinds of shops that sold tennis rackets and golf gear. It wasn't pre-packaged for you.

I remember, in probably 1984, going on holiday with my mum and dad to Spain for two weeks and we are all mad about Lacoste at the time. My dad got this tracksuit for me with a huge crocodile on it. I couldn't wait to get back home to show all of my friends my new tracksuit; I thought they were going to be really impressed with it. When we'd got on that plane across to the Costa del Sol, all my mates were wearing tracksuits.

We got back two weeks later and I'm sat in the park waiting for everybody to arrive. Three of the older lads came walking to the park and they're all in Burberry jackets, with flared cords, one of them even had a walking stick. They were kind of dressing like English country gents – I'm sat there in this tracksuit – and they were like "Nice one. But now you need to get one of these" pointing at their jackets. That was how quickly it would change.

My mum was desperate to get me off the dole so I did an art course and then applied to what was at the time one of the worst fashion courses in the country at Manchester Polytechnic (I'd put that down as my first choice). At that time, me and my mates had got into getting InterRail tickets and going off around Europe. When I got the interview at Manchester, I bought myself a new rig out and I went down there and told them how I had spent time in Paris and Milan – I also borrowed a few pieces of work off the walls from the previous years to beef up my portfolio (I was rarely in college back then).

They swallowed my 'presentation' and gave me a place on the course. By chance, by fluke rather than by design, I got a job in a clothes shop and worked with a girl called Fiona Allen, who is now a comedian. She was on the TV show Smack the Pony and she also worked on the door of the Haçienda. I lasted about four Saturdays before they fired me. I was also spending more time in the Haçienda than I was in college. Coincidentally, at that time Blackburn was beginning to put on the very early Acid House parties. Within a couple of years, I watched these parties go from 30 to 40 of us in our house, to 10,000 people on a Saturday night with loads of riot police waiting outside a warehouse.

For me, 1988 and 1989 was – the Haçienda on Wednesday night, the Haçienda on Friday night, Sett End in Blackburn on Saturday night before going on to an all night party and coming home at 11am. Sundays were spent trying to recover, and so were Monday/Tuesday and then it was back out on Wednesday. That was pretty much the way it went for a good 18 months and I ended up dropping out of my fashion degree. I got a first year pass and went off partying on every night for a couple of years. I absolutely don't regret that to be honest, but in the early Nineties it was like the big come-down from this huge party that we all had been having.

Culturally, it was certainly the most exciting thing that happened in Blackburn in my lifetime, and people want to make all this into films and books nowadays. At the time it was happening it was berated by the local media and the local pillars of the establishment did anything but support it.

The early Nineties was probably the worst time of my life. I was broke, and I was very unhappy, and I knew I needed to do something with myself and make some changes, so I moved away. I stopped partying and drinking, and said to myself that it was time to grow up so I went and applied to Preston College. I explained what I'd been up to, and they put me on probation for my first semester (they didn't know if I would adapt to being back in education) so I got stuck in.

I then treated college like an apprenticeship. I was seeing a girl who was in her fourth year of a Fashion Design degree. After she graduated her mum and dad were ringing the lecturers up demanding they put her in touch with someone who can give her a job; and I watched her coming out of the Job Centre crying her eyes out. This really woke me up actually to the fact that in three years' time, I was going to be in that exact same position if I didn't use that time wisely. I quickly realised I needed to make some contacts and connections.

When I was at Manchester Poly, I never had any of the work ready on time and when we used to critique each others work I was always waiting for everybody to verbally lay in to me. Whereas at Preston, I used to sit there smug knowing that I worked really hard on what I had done. One of the lecturers introduced me to this bloke called Kenneth Mackenzie who had just started a label called 6876. He *introduced me to the head of marketing at Diesel Jeans and I went to work in their press office as an intern.*

I did that on my student loan basically – I was working for them for free. It was tough getting by; my mum and dad didn't have money and I was eating food from the Iceland bargain freezer and sleeping in a bedsit.

I also used to do a lot of stuff in my own time that could be seen in some ways as a little bit altruistic, and through that I was introduced to head of press at Armani. She invited me to come and be like her 'pet northerner', which was quite an experience. I remember one day I picked up the phone in the Armani press office in Knightsbridge and said "Good morning, Armani press office, how can I help?" And it was Mr Armani's right hand man from Italy, an American guy and I put it through to my boss. Five minutes later she finished the call and said, "I don't quite know how to say this, but only answer the phone if it is a dire emergency, like if there is no-one else in the office." I took the hint.

Yet from the Armani thing I met the people from DKNY. I did work experience there for a while and then I went to work for DKNY before going to work with Kenneth at 6876. I then went back to Preston to finish my degree.

I graduated in 1998, and moved back to London, only I was unemployed for about six months. I worked temporarily at Diesel and then registered again at the dole office. It was quite an uncertain time, I wasn't able to pay my bills and didn't know what was going to happen next.

When I was in my final year of college I met up with one of the kids I used to breakdance against (he used to dance with Street Machine) in Manchester. When we were all going partying in the late 80s he'd got into kickboxing and so had kept himself really fit. And in the early Nineties, he started breakdancing again, and had become number one in Europe. I began helping him get links to clothing companies and through that got to know the people at Adidas who handled that stuff.

In 1997 during my internship Armani gave me a little project relating to all that Britpop scene that was going on. There was a lot about Britpop I disliked – it felt like a lot of middle class people celebrating working class values. People getting drunk, wearing trainers and waving Union Jacks about. So, the Armani press office asked me to put together a portfolio of 'hip bands' that we could invite to the Armani fashion shows, because they didn't have a clue. I started contacting these bands' managements and setting up meetings between them and Armani so I had a bit of a contact base in music. Out of the blue, an opening at Adidas came in February 1999. I was originally employed by Adidas UK to work on entertainment marketing; basically, building relationships between the Adidas brand and the entertainment industry. At that time, Adidas was a very pure sports brand, but on the back of Britpop, they were getting all these requests for product from different bands and TV shows.

The idea of this job was basically to have somebody who could be the arbiter of what was right for Adidas to get involved in and what wasn't. I basically cleared the decks of a lot of people they were already dealing with. I felt that Adidas was a very credible, iconic brand that had lots of natural synergies with music culture. It is not something that has to be forced. If you look back on Adidas it has a rich history with music: Jim Morrison wore Adidas, and so did the Rolling Stones on the Exile on Main Street tour. Lennon wore Adidas, I've got pictures of David Bowie wearing Adidas in 1976 and Paul Cook of the Sex Pistols wearing Nizza Hi's. Bob Marley wore Adidas; the reggae culture in the Seventies was completely besotted by Adidas because the majority of the artists were huge football fans too. Then the Eighties hip-hop scene came along in the US which coincided with the whole casual thing that was evolving in the UK.

In the UK you had an Adidas trainer culture that was very specific and didn't travel well at all, particularly the trainers worn in the north-west of England. If you look at most of the youth cultures, there is a definitive look to them. Casual, or whatever you want call it, is still a look that will be forever evolving and forever changing.

"In the UK you had got an Adidas trainer culture that was very specific and this didn't travel well at all, particularly the trainer worn in the north-west of England. If you look at most of the youth cultures, there is a definitive look to them. Casual, or whatever you want call it, is still a look that will be forever evolving and forever changing."

When I finally got 'the' job at Adidas, I was looking for bands where there was a natural synergy with the brand i.e. they were already fans of it. My first year was about building those relationships with bands. These bands included people who I'd seen as a kid; Public Enemy and LL Cool J – as a 16 year old they were my heroes. I'd seen Run DMC and the Beastie Boys at Manchester Apollo, after crashing through the fire doors. So, for me to actually meeting these people, was an incredible experience.

The year I joined Adidas was the year that the Happy Mondays reformed, and they would go on to play in Japan at the Fuji Rock Festival as the headliners. I said to Shaun Ryder, "If you wear Adidas on stage on the night, I can probably justify getting a flight out to Japan" and I would get to see Tokyo too. So he said, "Consider it done." Shaun looked out for me from day one, so I'll always be grateful to him for that. Japan became very influential in the projects I worked on further down the line.

My partying days were finished a long time ago, so I was not waking up in the morning scratching my head wondering who I had given my business cards to. It has been great to experience all these moments stone cold sober because I can remember every second of it. As a fan of music and a fan of popular culture, to be able to actually meet these people and interact with them both on business and leisure time has been really exciting.

When I joined the PR strategy of Adidas was pure to sport, and if we received a request for products that wasn't a sports-related request, then we weren't meant to send anything out. Adidas reissued the Micropacer, which was a shoe from 1984. At the time I knew a stylist who worked for The Face magazine, which was incredibly influential around then. I said to her, under the radar, "If I give you a pair of these shoes, will you stick them in the magazine?" I wanted to try and educate people internally in Adidas about the opportunities that we were really missing out on – make them see the value of promoting the lifestyle properties of the products. She featured them and gave them a full page feature for this specially numbered range. I was then asked to put together a list of musicians that we were working with who might be into them to send them shoes. Working inside the corporations you face two battles; one is an external battle, trying to make a difference in consumers' lives but you also have internal battles.

When I started doing the entertainment marketing for Adidas, most people who worked there were very straight. On my first day at Adidas I met all these very straight laced, very sporty, macho blokes with their chinos pulled up to their necks who spoke like Alan Hansen, and had little in common with someone like me. My job was to try to get the high profile people that wear the Adidas brand to keep wearing the brand and to feel like they are part of Adidas – a connection to Adidas. I started to work with some of the independent labels up in Manchester like Twisted Nerve and Fat City Records with Andy Votel. It was around this time that Adidas brought in trend marketing which was about looking for ways to communicate the brand to a more, what they would call, opinion-leading, media savvy, design- conscious audience who our traditional advertising and PR were not reaching.

When I was growing up, there was a range of Adidas shoes based on cities; there was an Adidas Dublin, Adidas Stockholm, Adidas Paris, Adidas Barcelona and so on. Plus these naming of trainers went right through to running shoes like,

Adidas New York and Adidas Boston. I felt that the north-west of England was such an Adidas heartland, Liverpool and Manchester particularly were so loyal to the Adidas brand, so we did an Adidas Manchester to tie in with the Commonwealth Games of 2002 that were being held in Manchester. We went for a kind of a red stripe on a blue body because we didn't want to alienate Manchester United or Manchester City fans. We also went for a handball silhouette, which was a very classic terrace style. They were snapped up very quickly and became quite a collectible item so they were reissued a few years later by Size?. Once again, there were queues around the block for the second reissue. They also did a trackie top, which was nothing to do with me.

In 2001 Adidas had decided to split the brand into different divisions – I guess this was an acknowledgement that the consumer had been ahead of the company. Consumers had adopted sportswear for a lifestyle for years and the brand itself needed to catch up with that so they set up a three division structure – they made Adidas Originals its own division within the company. The first Adidas Originals collections were quite small and we were tasked with doing the global launch in London. We partnered with The Face *magazine and took over a warehouse space in Shoreditch, building this giant Adidas shoe box as a stage. We also created animations of the first Adidas Originals collection and projected them onto a giant cube in the middle of the space. We did a run of posters too, plastered all over the venue, and Ian Brown performed at the party. It was great, to be honest. It was like you've been given a load of corporate money to put a rave on, which was totally different to the rawness of the raves we'd been involved in Blackburn a decade earlier.*

I was then invited by the sports marketing team to meet David Beckham, because he was becoming as well-known for what he was doing off the field as for what he was doing on it. It was right on the cusp of 'Beckham Mania', and they wanted somebody to meet with him and look after his requests for products for his day-to-day wear. All his boots and his sports equipment for training kit was taken care of by sports marketing, but when it came to the stuff off the field, they wanted somebody with some understanding of style and what he might want to wear.

I went up to Bury where he was doing this ad shoot. I was sitting in this trailer waiting for David Beckham to arrive and the people from sports marketing informed me, "He's got this hairdresser who does his hair and he is a right oddball, a weird character but this is the guy who cuts and styles his hair, and David insists he does it." The door opens and his hairdresser walks in, and he was only an old mate of mine called Tyler who I used to go to the Acid House raves in Blackburn. He said, "Gary?!? What are you doing here?" It was the first time I had seen him for years and consequently it saved me a lot of aggravation later, because he told David Beckham that I was an old mate of his which saved me hours of trying to build a relationship with somebody like that. Consequently Beckham gave me his personal mobile number and would call me direct from then on.

I then get this call from Beckham out of the blue saying, "You can't tell anybody this, but I've been asked to open the Commonwealth Games" – which was in two weeks' time – "and I want a special outfit for it! Can you help?" He had put me on the spot and I was sort of puzzled what to come up with, plus I was sworn to secrecy. Luckily, I had these basketball tracksuits. Back then, before the Adidas Originals division became as big as it is now, I would trade products with all the different licensee countries that produced Adidas products. So, what I would do is send an autographed Oasis poster to

Adidas Argentina and in return they'd send me a box of product that was not available in England – that was my best currency because we weren't paying these people. I had just been sent a load of basketball products from the US and there was this white basketball tracksuit, and I thought "who in a million years would wear an oversized white velour basketball tracksuit?" when this light bulb went on! So I called Beckham back and said, "I've got this idea. I've got this white tracksuit and I think you might be able to carry it off."

I then sent him pictures of the tracksuit, and he liked it. He then asked how we could make it more 'blingtastic'. Off I went to a bunch of ladies who worked for a tailoring shop in Soho in London, and got them to sew sequins onto the tracksuit and across the chest and down the three stripes too. As it was something that represented the UK, he also wanted a sequinned Union Jack on the back of it. These women who were sewing the sequins on the tracksuit were asking, "Who is this for? Liberace?"

We got my intern to hand carry the top from London up to Manchester because we couldn't take the risk of it disappearing. I was out in Japan at the time and I rang my mum up and said to make sure she watches the opening ceremony of the Commonwealth Games. I couldn't even tell her why, only that if it comes off that it would be like the Great Train Robbery of PR.

And, it did; making the front page of pretty much every newspaper globally. There was a PR manager at the time in Germany and he was quite annoyed as he didn't know anything about what I'd planned. He got me on the phone and he said "Why didn't you let me know about what you had arranged? Only if I'd have let us know about it, we could have done something around it too."

My reply was: "A billion people watched it live and it made the front page of every newspaper globally. What else would have you planned to do exactly?"

Japan has always been important in the work I do with Adidas. I would go to the

Fuji Rock Festival every year, and in 2002, Ian Brown was performing there. He had a friend called Kazuki Kuraishi who worked for a Japanese street wear brand called 'A Bathing Ape'. He introduced us, and we stayed in touch. Kazuki is a big football fan so I used to send Adidas products to the Bape football team and he used to send products over to me. The team at Bathing Ape were huge fans of pop culture and brands, they would take existing products they love and would do their own twist, their own interpretation of brands. They would take a Ralph Lauren piece, but instead of having a polo player on the horse, it would have a guy from 'Planet of the Apes' on the horse instead – they would just twist things a little bit to pay homage for their love of certain products. I initiated a collaboration with them, which was another milestone project for Adidas. We really went to town with this and took it on to a whole different level. The Japanese are incredibly into product and the detail and will take something like British popular culture and take it to a whole new level. There were limited edition shoes, three different colour ways in two styles, and a ' friends' giveaway version. The first release was a Superstar, then there was a second release called the Superskate. A week before the shoes would be going on sale, a frame containing the raw components would appear in store windows – and I had never seen in my Adidas career, until that point, that kind of frenzy for trainers. They were limited to one pair per person; people were in sleeping bags outside the shop. The prices were going crazy as people started putting them on eBay. This went on to inspire the Superstars 35th anniversary trainer too; the Superstar is one of the biggest selling shoes for Adidas. Obviously, the shoe has got strong association with different areas of popular culture particularly hip-hop, which is a truly global culture. They wanted to basically resurrect and inject new life into what were becoming quite a tired shoe for Adidas. I had this idea about a range within it called Consortium. I was basically trying to think of ways in which you could create the excitement that there used to be when I was a kid before things were globalised, when you would have certain licensees, because in the Eighties, the whole Adidas culture saw people going into Europe to buy Adidas shoes. In the different countries, you would have different product ranges and I thought of a way to contemporise that. There were a group of stores, Foot Patrol in London, Union in New York, Undefeated in Los Angeles – essentially a group of six boutique stores whose endorsement appealed to a particular type of customer who would cultishly queue for their products. We did this release of shoes where each store would get an allocated number of the shoes. What this did was to create more value for the shoes in different territories.

We worked with Tomato on their shoe; we did a shoe with Missy Elliot, we also worked with P Diddy on a Bad Boy Records shoe and with Jay-Z on Roc- AFella shoe. We worked with the Red Hot Chilli Peppers and did one with Ian Brown, I guess to represent the shoe's connection with British guitar music. We also did a Run-DMC shoe because they are important in Adidas' history.

I worked with Ben Kelly and Peter Saville to create a shoe for the anniversary of the Haçienda too. Peter said he wanted it to represent 'the look and the life' of the club – he said he and Ben were all about 'the look', and I as an ex punter was all about 'the life'. He said he never used to go in the Haçienda because it was too sweaty and scally for him. I was sitting there and I had to pinch myself that I was actually exchanging ideas with these people who I was such a fan of.

They really put Adidas to the test; first they decided they wanted a shoebox that was in the shape of the Haçienda dance floor. They wanted the design language of the club to translate into a shoe. In the late eighties there was a very clear differentiation between the people who were going out with shiny shirts and slip on shoes and us lot that were going to the Haçienda in painters jeans with hooded tops and Adidas trainers. We wanted to celebrate the fact that that club was the first to embrace casual wear and sportswear. There was a maple base put into the box which was the same material used for the Haçienda dance floor. There was also tissue wrap paper around the trainers, where we used Kevin Cummins photographs that he originally took in the club in 1988 – it also included some of the blueprints of the architecture of the club from Ben.

There was the Adidas Darwen, which I guess was a vanity project. Kazuki came to me after we did an ad shoot with Noel Gallagher and Ian Brown; he is a huge, huge fan of British music and particularly Manchester music and culture, and he's been on tour in the UK with Ian Brown a couple of times and hung out with us over here. He's very aware of the north-west, with the Darwen Casuals and the Blackburn Youth and that type of stuff, and so he wanted to work with me on a shoe that would work well in Tokyo and acknowledge his experiences here. The shoes were originally supposed to have been called the Adidas Aspden, but somebody put the blockers on it in Germany because they thought I might be getting carried away with myself. We then decided to call them Adidas Darwen after my home town. It was basically a hybrid of one of my favourite Adidas trainers and was a sort of a nod to the leisure shoes that were around in the Eighties that they used to sell in the Oasis underground market in Manchester. I never had a pair as a kid but I always remember them, so I wanted to acknowledge them. The shoes are based on the Adidas Winter Hi, which have a running shoe sole but are more like a winter boot. We changed the materials, and the colours, and put a little logo on the side. Kazuki then did his magic on the tongue, and hey presto, we had the Adidas Darwen. A lot of people from Blackburn on the Lancashire Telegraph website were not happy about them though – there's always been that rivalry.

By this time I ended up running the entertainment division globally. I used to manage a team in Los Angeles and people in London, plus some folk in Tokyo, as well as some people in Germany, but I'd hit the buffers really because I couldn't go any further doing what I was doing based out of the UK. The real power of Adidas, as a German company, is in Germany. They didn't want me to move out of London, which was kind of a good thing for me as I didn't really want to live in Germany. We worked out a compromise and I now freelance as a consultant to the company.

Nowadays I am free to work with other people on a consultancy basis as long as Adidas give their prior blessing, but I cannot work with any other competitive brands.

Since going freelance in 2009 I've worked with Barry Bown, the CEO of JD Sports, and with Paul Fox, who both knew me from my career in the sportswear industry. They were just setting up the Size? stores and basically they nicked an old idea of mine to use Polaroids of the customers when they walked in the shop – there is no hard feelings though. They are both fabulous to work with, and are both based in the north-west, plus they are product-mad like I am.

I also helped Kevin Sampson on the 'Awaydays' film about Tranmere fans in the Eighties. I remember reading the book and knew the film had a very limited budget so I helped out with the wardrobe; in particular with the footwear. They dressed very much the way I dressed when I wanted to go to that disco when I was younger so it was a certainly nostalgia trip for me being involved. We did a viral campaign for Adidas using the outtakes from the film.

I supported The End book too, based on a fanzine which came out of Liverpool in the Eighties by a bunch of football fans documenting what was happening on Liverpool's street fashion at that time, particularly football scallies. We were approached by them to support the compilation and there was nobody better suited than Adidas. I contacted a local designer up in Darwen called Gary Watson, who used to do a fanzine in the Eighties called Dead Good, and who is very au fait with the whole Adidas culture in the north-west in the Eighties. I asked him if he could basically do some bespoke Adidas adverts that would speak to people from that culture.

His interpretation of the Eighties included all the travel essentials: a passport, an InterRail ticket, sunglasses, a shopping list and, of course, Adidas trainers.

8

SCRUFFY NORTHERNERS

In your northern slums,

You look in the dustbin for something to eat,

You find a dead rat and you think it's a treat,

In your northern slums

*This chant has been chanted to an array of teams' fans north of Birmingham since the dawning days of football.

Getting back to the prerequisite roots and growth of the splendid barked, intensely grained, northern casual/dresser tree; the trees solid trunk establishes stronger, elongated branches every season, which in turn sprouts new awesome foliage – unless they're an evergreen – after the wilt and abscission of the last fall, and the tubers strengthen too. Each year deep inside the bole another ring flourishes that is a reminder, and an ingraining, of past personal idiosyncrasies. These prepossessing new buds spore leaves that are a representation of the Photoperiodism of northern culture. And us Northern Monkeys weren't hanging around and still swinging in these trees while resting on our laurels in the Eighties. Only according to most southerners and cock-er-nees, we were!

Civilisation, of sorts, did/does exist outside the metropolis, you know.

Vibes and underlying currents do spread and do occur north of Watford – so be aware. And unthinkable, unpredictable events and happenings were occurring again in the 1983/84. The north created another new cult and scene all of their own. Yes, a scruff/dress down look came to the fore. Most northerners thought (and some still do) that cockneys were cockalorums full of cock-and-bull and cocksure cockeyed cock-of-the-walk cocks in their taxi driver habiliment. And north-west lads knew that southerners had latched on to casual/dresser movement and *the* look.

However, as a backlash to every dog and his best friend cottoning onto the casual look, scousers and Mancs moved the goalposts on the raiment mien, leaving onlookers at sixes and sevens and not knowing if they were coming or going. They'd took a step backwards, to move forwards, from the herd.

Because northerners strive to achieve, rather than follow, they seek out and find, rather than let the mountain come to Mo'. They get out there in the world, no matter what the conditions, in appropriate, essential ensemble, in extreme circumstances sometimes, while on missions to find new idealism – they go all the way. I would state that northerners endeavour to be somewhat proud connoisseurs on issues and events that have moulded exactly who they are. They learn about their roots, about their ancestors, about their fellow brethren and just how their forefathers mapped out how they live their lives to this day; and then, pursue new all-singing, all-dancing groundbreaking advances. There is nothing casual about their approach and what northerners choose to accomplish. Really, to Northern Monkeys, it's what makes them tick. It's their culture. It's their way of life. They don't see life through rose tinted lenses, though.

They take themselves further, deeper and higher. Northerners have Northern Soul. The north is a state of mind. The northerners mind-set is second to *none*.

The Scouse Retro-Scally

The scouse 'retro scally' was a semi-flared trousered philanthropist of all things scousekind; brotherly Liverpudlian love and peace, man: During the early-to-mid part of the Eighties, if you ever ventured to Liverpool, Manchester or even London on a shopping trip, there was every chance similar dressed, sovereign-clad lads would want to serve a benevolence on your sportswear purchases. Only this changed in and around '84. Not the taxing of clobber, but the appearance of the perpetrators of these actions; in Liverpool, especially. The etymology hunter-gatherer society hanging round Lime Street train station and St John's Shopping Centre now looked rough and bedraggled, vagrant-like. The flocks of scallies wore woollen fabric jackets (and they called others woollybacks?) with semi-flared jeans or cords and suedies. Their flicks and mushrooms were also morphing into primordial mullet hairdos. Up until then I'd never clapped eyes in the flesh on anyone bar an old bearded geography teacher from school, who also decked his plates in Clarks Polyveldt, that wore tweed, never mind deep-set, scary eyed youths of my own age. I'd observed Harris tweed on TV coverage of gentry on a pheasant shoot and toffs coordinating an annual village fox hunt, though. Only tweed was chic, in Merseyside too. All eminently, and all ultra twee.

You'd always have to be cagey in Liverpool if you'd frittered away your hard-earned meagre apprenticeship pay packet on fabric, or wheels. Once outside the shop, following an acquisition, I would remove any purchased goodies from the logoed plazie bags and boxes and ditch the evidence. I would then try and conceal the products upon my person or under my trackie top before being asked, "What time izit, la?" If the answer wasn't in a localized articulation a Kirby Kiss could be forthcoming or Uncle Stanley's Sheffield's forged steel might get an airing – not that I ever had such a pleasurable occurrence, but plenty did.

But now, these street urchins were fuelled with a narcotic of their preference as well as a sweeping change of demeanour and clothing choice. Somewhat natural features of a detached region were becoming evident, once again. An appraisal of these neo-hippy hipsters/earth-studying types, from outsiders, couldn't or wouldn't be understood until years later. Scousers had moved on, stepped back, and rebelled against slavish conformity, baffling onlookers. Never the ones to expect apish peer pressure, Liverpool's youth didn't hang round debating about an identity crisis; they crafted their own idiosyncratic look and milieu.

They didn't need no thought control.

Greenwoods, Dunn & Co, 'suit you sir' stigmatised gents' outfitters and tailors were paid visits by skeletal teenagers, to the worry and bamboozlement of owners, management and senior old-schooled, tape-measure-hanging-round-the-neck staff. Both cord and tweed jackets were necessities; olive green or fawn cord strides, no more than 18" wide, were a must. Marks & Sparks crewneck lambswool jumpers and cable pattern knitted cardies with suede or leather elbow patches became a second layer over country check buttoned-down collared shirts and no doubt the odd waistcoat would have been worn. Also, a smart pair of brogues were requirements. Alternatives were traditional Barbour

Beadle, Beaufort and Border wax jackets – Sloane Ranger, Ra Ra Rupert's they weren't.

Well worn faded flared jeans, Levi's chambray denim or cord shirts were an alternative. And Clarks Desert boots or Adi Stan Smith tennis shoes, once again. Or even elderly relatives' closets were rummaged through and the contents adopted, if they fitted,or not.

Just like 'casual' wasn't used to describe other fellow dressers between each other back then, nor was 'retro-scallywag' used as a characterisation by themselves in Liverpool or interlopers at the time on the scouse dressing-down. Only it wasn't *just* a look. Drugs, music and politics – militant tendencies – played a big part in their way of life too. I won't go there on the politics front, though.

Mainstream dress sense, hairstyles and music had somewhat diversified in the early Eighties, for the worse in the scouse discerning orb. The spectrum of talentless, mutant pop stars and pretentious groups in the charts, wrapped in outrageous multifarious clothing, just didn't do it for your 'lad type' so, what tunes were worth listening to then? A back-catalogue began to be rediscovered. Along with this relaxed sense of dress and sounds, a relaxant drug would be needed, and in abundance. And what better drug, on the cheap, was knocking about? T'weed!

Yes weed, began to be tooted and drawn deeply from Stanley blades used as hot-knives into lungs intensely by scallies wearing smoking jackets in bedrooms, pubs and clubs, to chill. Mass unemployment had hit Britain hard with Liverpool at the epicentre, and long queues formed at both the dole office and the city's Job Centres. If teenage Liverpudlians were lucky enough to have a job, these would be basic paid, low income ones or YTS's – Youth Training Schemes. Bread was scarce, no-one was Brewstered, pot was economically priced. The only building work going on was that of elongated joints brimming with herbs; this leading to a shortage of king-size Rizla papers. Prescribed downers, LSD and hallucinogenic seasonal magic mushrooms also worked a treat for getting 'spaced' while trying to forget such misfortunes as no foreseeable future. Smack would also soon grip the city, and the nation, claiming many a youthful soul.

Golden Brown had become readily available and plentiful at bargain basement rates due to dope being sparse – the dragon was chased. And so, Merseyside became lost in a haze of purple fumes, euphonic and mellifluous music. Welcome to the dark side!

Musical accompaniments and tweed are also part of history, in the form of Tweed Fender amplifiers. Vintage, battered amps would have been used by bands in the Eighties starting out on the rocky road to stardom. Also, established progressive rock groups from back in the day used tweed amps. In the Clash's video for their classic song *'Bankrobber'*, which was shot in a studio, you can clearly see in the background that the walls are lined in tweed. Secondhand 12-inch vinyl LPs from bands and artists such as Cat Stevens, Led Zeppelin, Frank Zappa, Gong, Captain Beefheart, Jimi Hendrix, Genesis, Bob Marley, Yes, Bob Dylan, Santana, Supertramp, Pink Floyd and so on were in *high* demand. The back catalogue went on and on of every maverick hipsters who'd recorded from far and wide and were listened to at 33 and a 1/3 rpm on hifi's constantly, again and again, by lads monged out in the sanctuary of their habitation of four walls. Revolution rock gurus would constantly hound DJs at clubs and pubs in and around town too, to slow down the music and change the tempo from fellow Merseyside groups that were being spun. Groups like Echo and the Bunnymen, Wah!, Orchestral Manoeuvres in the Dark, The Teardrop Explodes, A Flock of Seagulls, Lotus Eaters, Big in Japan, Dead or Alive, The Icicleworks, Elvis Costello, controversial chart toppers Frankie Goes to Hollywood and loony tunes *Ullo John! Gotta New Motor?* Alexei Sayle, to mention a few.

Liverpool lads had gone all organic: and they wanted to watch local bands at local venues, choosing homegrown talents Groundpig to follow round town, who in the main, did cover versions of the bands that stoner-scal's were digging. Groundpig had had a resident midweek spot at the Philharmonic for three years before becoming hero-worshipped and absorbed by scallies en masse. They then went on to play packed-out gigs come weekends at the Bier Keller, Apple, Checkmate, and Scotty clubs.

The nucleus of the folk / country / pop group were John O'Connell and the charismatic, be-'tashed banjo / violin / acoustic guitar playing character, Graham Evans – RIP. Another band who were making their mark on the local circuit were the The Farm, whose lead vocalist Peter Hooton, a youth worker and editor of the football fanzine *'The End'*, arranged a tour of Liverpool's secondary schools with the help of council funding for Groundpig plus a bunch of Evertonian lads in a band named Drama. This so they could spread the word on the evils of mind-altering stimulants as part of a anti-drugs campaign. The tour had to be abandoned, because unemployed lads had got wind of the tour and arrived in droves at schools, off-their-boxes, with faces pressed against windowpanes dribbling – what window-lickers. Hooton also gave Groundpig the chief supporting act at several of The Farm's gigs; the pinnacle being a gig on the Royal Iris boat as it cruised up and down the River Mersey one night. This was a night when John Peel DJ'ed while dumbstruck and flabbergasted by the sight of the outlandish, tweed arrayed long haired lovered crowd in attendance. They were a phenomenal Eighties subculture generation, on the surface, isolated to his hometown.

Whereas Groundpig never went on to national success and stardom, the 'Soul of Socialism', – The Farm – did, some five or so years later. Although, another band, The La's, who crystallised in 1984 playing acoustic, rootsy melodies, had a fair to middling ascendance in Merseyside, the north-west and nationally, never reached their full potential before splitting in the early Nineties. Eventually, boredom, drugs and ever changing line-ups are alleged for their disbandment. The La's had gone back to basic ethics, strumming skiffle and Mersey Beat but, they were still cited, by many, as forerunners of a new evolving music scene that had taken the country by storm as the euphoriant Eighties bowed out. A scene that wasn't dictatorial domineered to, by the tyrannise south!

Northern Monkeys undertaking this exploration of the new musical prodigy, and accessories, set off enwrapped all warm and toasty in Berghaus, Sprayway and a myriad of branded puffa/ski jackets. Boots were hiking, jumpers thick knit. Sweatshirts had mansized logos printed across. Titfers were beanie/bucket or ski, some two teamed. Leg wear was either dungarees or baggy topped, tapered bottomed, stonewashed jeans. And so began this enigmatic, embracing expedition. The Italian Paninaro look was wedged in between the crazy dancing and Madchester scene that beckoned lads to 'la dolce vita'.

Sound Made Of Sound

But before embarking on this *trip* to sweaty, environmentally friendly climes, Phil Thornton, author of *Casuals*, and co-editor of *Swine Magazine*, has let me swipe an article from the archives of the mag, on the sounds retro-scallies were listening to. Phil Eaves enriched and enlightened us earlier in his account of 'Supergroups' and their music, but Phil gives a pastoral insight on why they were popular, again – well in Merseyside, at least.

Phil: *It was in the pool room of the Cherry Tree pub in Runcorn that I first noticed it; one of the scousers from up the road, a lad well known as a bit of a 'Stanley' merchant in his youth, was sat down wearing a tweed jacket with what appeared to be a Genesis t-shirt underneath. Genesis! If any band at that time – this was 84ish – symbolised the bloated, pompous excesses of the past, it was this bunch of pretentious public schoolboy plums. As a former punk who'd discovered* *soul and funk and was now listening to nothing but black American music at the time, the nearest I got to this kind of stuff was Funkadelic, who remain my favourite band ever. There was a crossover of sorts there. Post-punk, most of my mates had got into the weed scene whereas I got into the speed scene and it was this choice of narcotic that decided which music you favoured; music to dance to, or music to mong to. They got into Marley, Santana, Gong, Hawkwind, Captain Beefheart and even, cough, Pink ' fucking' Floyd! This being the very essence of everything we'd Stalinised from our musical past in 1976's Year Zero. Hippy music! Mushy music! Indeed it was their ingestion of fungal and herbal substances that resulted in what I considered to be a very backward looking and self-defeating cultural cul-de-sac. But as many of them were on the dole it was entirely reasonable to fill the day watching Apocalpyse Now, Cheech and Chong, Easy Rider and Pink Floyd Live at Pompeii, or listen to Tubular Bells, or Trout Mask Replica whilst scoobied up to fuck, I suppose. The hippy ethos had been applied to the unemployed working class; they'd turned on, tuned in and dropped off. Once skag got mixed into the scene, I decided to swerve some of 'em to be honest. And over 25 years later, some are still bang at it!*

"Only in Liverpool could bands such as groundpig
play to packed houses. Only in Liverpool could the la's
act as a catalyst for the type of unashamedly retrogressive
generation of so-called 'cosmic scally' bands such as the Coral,
Zutons and maybes? Only in Liverpool could the pale
fountains / strands / shack be worshipped as the last true
Carriers of the flame. there is a light that
never goes out indeed."

But this lad in the Genesis t-shirt wasn't one of our lot, he was one of the scousers who used to dance to the likes of Gino Soccio, Rick James, Tom Browne, Chic, etc, at the Cherry's disco annexe. What had turned him from a funkateer to a stoner scal? Fashion! Turn to the right: Liverpool at that time was almost a separate country, a city that prided itself on its isolationist stance to the rest of 'woolsville.' Liverpool turned its back on the world, in a climate of self-preservation against all odds, what became known as 'retro-scal' first developed from the chong ashes of a disenfranchised young population. The clothes obviously first symbolised this strangely perverse scene; a sloppy scally-hippy hybrid of loose change and broken biscuit conversations. It wasn't for me but I remained fascinated by it nevertheless. This manifestation of cultural contrariness seemed to symbolise all that was unique about Liverpool, about how it didn't like being dictated to by self-appointed taste makers and opinion formers. What did they know? Who voted for YOU?

Only in Liverpool could bands such as Groundpig play to packed houses. Only in Liverpool could The La's act as a catalyst for the type of unashamedly retrogressive generation of so-called 'cosmic scally' bands such as The Coral, Zutons and Maybes? Only in Liverpool could The Pale Fountains/Strands/Shack be worshipped as the last true Carriers Of The Flame. There is a light that never goes out indeed. When the likes of The Bandits, Tramp Attack, Hokum Clones and Cracatilla started gigging in the early Noughties, it was clear that far from being musically purist the bands were in fact the opposite and open to anything and everything. They absorbed all kinds of music, regardless of whether it was deemed hip or not, they worshipped Hank Williams as much as Arthur Lee, and Leadbelly as much as Neil Young. Okay, they didn't listen to music that pre-dated 1970, but at least they had taste and it was refreshing to meet young lads in their late teens and early twenties who had a genuine and sincere love of music for its own sake; not as a way of getting sucked off or getting rich.

And now, all these years later, at last I'm beginning to understand the appeal of these bands I'd dismissed so arrogantly years before. If you view music holistically, if you want to look through pop's kaleidoscope and watch the patterns flow into each other and stare as the colours mutate and morph then there are no boundaries, no meaningless genres, no marketing pigeonholes with which to compartmentalise and package music as just another consumer item. So, I now dig out ancient LPs by the likes of Roger McGuinn or Steve Hillage or Pentangle or Caravan and at least give them a listen. And it's not just me. The self-appointed 'crate digging' aristocracy with deep pockets and lots of free time have been excavating this seam of progressive-psyched, acid-folk, space-rock to put on their fancy Sohocentric compilations and mixes. But they're over 25 years too late. Now, like me, they've finally cottoned on to what that lad in the Genesis t-shirt and the tweed jacket knew all those years ago. What goes around comes around.

Sound made of sound.

Back To Ours – The Stoner Scal Tapes

Adding to the story of the regeneration of these pastiche groups is Dave Richards, also a contributor to *Swine*. Dave informs us of his favourite recordings that were chonged to in bedrooms, from bongs, while impassioned, magnetic tunes pulsated from tape recorders. Turn on, tune in and drop out, man...

· · ·

Dave: *It's nearly 25 years ago since Pink Floyd played their infamous show at Maine Road. Floyd 'were' the essential band back then, no doubt about that. There was a time when you couldn't move for lads with scraggy jeans and suedies who were sporting a Hammers or Dark Side T-shirt, or even changing their name by deed poll to Seamus Atomheart-Mother and painting their house like the cover of Obscured By Clouds, but all the Floyd albums used to get heavy rotation. I know loads of lads who owned Roger Waters's unlistenable side project album with Ron Geesin called Music From The Body, along with all the solo Syd Barrett stuff and the hard to get compilation of early rarities Works. Early Floyd from Piper and Ummagumma, was far superior to anything on The Wall if you ask me.*

Genesis's The Lamb Lies Down On Broadway, was another must-own album in Liverpool in the mid-Eighties. For some reason Fly On A Windshield was a favourite drunken sing-a-long tune on the Friday night post alehouse walk home, usually followed by The Jam's Down In The Tubestation At Midnight. On the cover Rael Imperial, our hero, is clearly seen sporting Adidas trainees and a pair of semi flares, which to this listener were almost certainly a pair of Flemings Supa-Tuff. Genesis (aka Genno) were a weird one though – quite a few disagreements would breakout over the merits of the post-Gabriel (or even post-Hackett) incarnations of the band – "What's this shite – Three Sides Live? They were cack after Gabriel left you tit". The later stuff like Duke, Abacab and Genesis (with Mama and Home By The Sea on it) were huge as well, but as a staunch Gabrielist I'm not letting none of that shite on. The Genno cult reached its logical conclusion at Glastonbury 1991 when, as yet another festival was taken over by hordes of scousers and Mancs. One well known Everton head set up a giant tent – Southfork – installed his own decks, and treated the crowd to classics from The State interspersed with snippets from Foxtrot, and the gurning masses all chanted "Mum Diddilly Washing, Dad Diddilly Office, You're All Full Of Ball". True story.

Zappa and the Muffin Men: There's no explanation as to the huge popularity of Zappa in Liverpool. Zappa-heads have always been with us. There was a famous cartoon in The End of a cockney 'casual' and a scouser stood next to each other. The cockney is sporting some complicated Italian jumper and his speech bubble says "Nitto you sigh", no idea what it means, while the chonging scouser is saying "Sound this draw" and is wearing a Zappa Ship Arriving Too Late To Save A Drowning Witch T-shirt. God only knows how that 'difficult' album became an underground classic round here, although Valley Girls is on it so it could be that. Years later I worked in London for HMV and I got talking to some cockney sales rep who used to supply vinyl to all the big cities HMV megastores. Turned out he was into Frank and he told me that other than the Oxford Street Megastore, the Liverpool one was the only shop that stocked the entire Zappa back catalogue. He never knew why either! So big was Frank on Merseyside that it's only right that the greatest exponents of Zappa's music ('tribute' band doesn't do them justice) should come from here as well. The Muffin Men are still going strong and are just about the best live band you will ever see, so get on them.

Stephen Stills/Neil Young: All their stuff was big back then; Neil Young in particular had a huge following amongst the lads, although personally his whiney voice used to get on my nerves. I preferred Stephen Stills, and one of the lads copped for a Crosby Stills Nash and Young video that featured Stills doing Treetop Flier (it's on YouTube), a boss little fingerstyle guitar number about the Nam Vet chopper pilots who could only get work as crop sprayers when they came home. I think it may well have been inspired by Stills's own legendary coke-binge freak-out where he was convinced he was a Nam Vet himself despite never getting further East than the end of Mama Cass's fridge. Ohio always reminds me of the Cumberland boozer in town, a classic haunt of the pot smoking togger fan. One Monday night about 20 of us trogged down from the Yankee after scranning a load of mushrooms. Jimmy The Greek (ace covers band) were on, and when the mushies were properly kicking in they did a version of Ohio that caused a mini-outbreak of full-on loon dancing in our corner. Jimmy The Greek himself looked on, bemused.

Hendrix was yet another T-shirt at the match favourite. All his albums were de-rigueur, but If Six Was Nine had the added advantage of being on Easy Rider, as was Steppenwolf's The Pusher. Dennis Hopper out-cooled even Jack Nicholson, so much so, that you would occasionally see the odd match head sporting a Hopper-style suede 'fringie' jacket. Bummer, man.

The Bay Area psychedelic bands were all massive. Again, video played a big part in their appeal. Everyone had the Woodstock video, and at some point in the mid-Eighties Channel 4 screened Monterey Pop and everyone taped it. The Editor himself went one further and blew seven Memorex C90s (and his mind) on Radio One's 20th anniversary broadcast of the whole Monterey bash. Jorma Kaukonen (Airplane's virtuoso 3rd guitarist) was a style icon in Lee Park. The potheads round there were ringers for his all-denim and suede look (see also George Harrison on the cover of Abbey Road, that's 'the look' nailed). As well as the Neth-heads, this look was popular in the scally-hippy commune (serious) that was set up first by Garston Park and later moved to a flat by Penny Lane. If you ever went in there to score a quart, it was like going into that bunker in Apocalypse Now where Hendrix was blasting out the stezzer and the loon black GI shoots the gook on the wire.

The Dead were another T-shirt favourite, and hordes of lads made the trip to Wembley Arena to see them in '90/91ish. Section 43 was featured on Monterey Pop and as a result a few lads went out and bought The Fish's Electric Music For The Mind And Body, which along with Quicksilver Messenger Service's Happy

Trails and Airplane's After Bathing At Baxters were the essential San Fran sike albums.

The Hawks: If you ever wanted a snapshot of 'stoner scal', forget Floyd at Maine Road, and instead pick any mid-to-late Eighties Hawkwind show at Liverpool Empire. Whenever they were on, the Yankee Bar would be full beforehand as microdots were getting handed out, blue peters were getting bliffed up, mushies were being boiled, and Adidas trefoils were being stitched into lab coats... I made the last bit up. The Yankee Bar jukey used to have Silver Machine/Seven By Seven on it, but that was just a taste. Lads I know used to write fan mail to Dave Brock and get replies. Whole evenings were spent in darkened bedrooms trying to get our head round Michael Moorcock's rabbiting on The Chronicles Of The Black Sword while buzzing off reefer traces, and when the coast was clear the Hawkwind at Stonehenge video would get lobbed on, where you could get freaked out by the lead singer of support act The Enid and his litany of mad shouts – "I'd like to take you all home with me... you naughty naughty nor." To this day I don't know anyone other than togger heads who have even heard of The Enid. And if I had to nominate one tune as a 'Stoner Scal' anthem, it would be Hassan I Kaba.

Spirit's 12 Dreams Of Dr Sardonicus is another essential album and pretty much every tune on it is a killer. I've no idea how everyone got on it, but it does have a nutty psychedelic cover which always helped. Jethro Tull were always big, thanks in no small part to Groundpig doing covers of Tull's Skating Away and Living In The Past in the Bier Keller or Houlihans. I preferred Aqualung me-self, though. Years later everyone was gutted when the bass player had a sex change and the band started calling themselves Jethrene Tull. Sickener.

I'd wager that there are more copies of Love's Forever Changes knocking about in Liverpool households than there are copies of Sgt Pepper. One of the best concerts I ever went to was Arthur Lee's Forever Changes show at Liverpool Academy a few years ago. This album always used to be the last one on if you were about to get your head down, the perfect accompaniment to that last spliff. The mighty Shack used to be Arthur Lee's backing and as well, what more do you want.

Last but not least, my own personal favourite that you could throw in the hat if you wanted to 'out-obscure' someone in the Bier Keller: One of the lads had a older brother who was a 'proper' hippy and he had some great vinyl, including the first few Pentangle albums. We used to bladder them all and tape tunes off them for chonging all dayers in Sefton Park or down the Prom where, if you were lucky, you might even stumble onto a 'Peace Festival' with loads of arl hippies flogging "Psylocybin" T-shirts. Many years later, the Geordie biffa who does the Swine covers admitted that he secretly liked Pentangle.

Who's up for coming back to ours then?

Designer Scruffs

It wasn't only the scousers that went all scruffy, the Mancs did too. With flocks of Dolly's now swarming the length and breadth of the UK from every region before and after the match; or stood on concrete-cancer riddled terraces, or sat on rotten wooden benches in decrepit football grounds decked in a variety of sportswear during the 90 minutes come Saturday, or any day of the week, the Mancs wanted to stand out and distance themselves from the herd. Man United follower back then, Phil Thornton, had noticed this swagger of demeanour in Manchester and the rise of the scruff look which began to separate Mancs from the hoi polloi in 1983/84. Phil not only took the 'scruff' plunge which distanced himself from the national assemblage along with other likeminded Mancs, he created a singular remoteness in dress sense in his hometown with doing so too.

Phil: *One of the biggest fallacies about the whole 'casual' sub-culture was that it was reliant upon so-called 'designer' labels that became worshipped because of their aspirational kudos more than for the quality of the clothing itself. This was the 'top down' fashion that filtered through to the peasants via the nouveau riche and the ' jet set.' Nothing could be further from the truth.*

Long before the word 'casual' had even been coined circa 1983, there had been at least five years of scally evolution that went totally unreported by the mainstream fashion media or even those who felt they had their finger on the youth sub-cultural pulse. Such localised vagaries as baseball outfits, jogging suits, American football t-shirts, jockey jackets, Hunter leathers, sheepies, all manner of Adidas trainees and jean/cords label du jour went by long before the look became dominant enough to flicker on the radar of Ye Olde Soho Trendy Mafia. The look changed extremely quickly and at no point was the direction influenced by anybody other than those uber-scallies who got onto a look, a look that was then followed by the rest of the herd.

Whether this was ditching needle cords for jumbo cords or bleaching your jeans from a stripe pattern to a splashed pattern or jibbing Trimm Trab for Munchen, swapping Peter Storm for Berghaus, keeping a short back and sides or a crew cut when everyone was getting a wedge; walking with your hands behind your back or with a limp, wearing your tiny lapel badge in the middle of your crew neck Marks's jumper or just to the left, or having your jeans ruffled just right, not too long, not too short, or razzing about on a trials bike or matching your deerstalker with your Karmen Ghia jacket, or...

The list goes on and on and all this went totally undocumented, save for accidental crowd shots usually depicting pitch invasions or terrace aggro. The look that became most associated with 'casuals', the sportswear phase of 1982/83, was essentially only a slightly more exaggerated version of the dominant Adidas tracksuit and trainers look that diversified into previously unobtainable European labels. Even Nike, now so ubiquitous, was a rarity back in the early Eighties. I remember distinctly some bearded scally wearing a Nike sou'wester style cagoule whilst queuing up to get in our local club and wondering what that strange 'swoosh' logo was. The tribalism at the heart of British working class culture fed upon localised differences in style and fashion and whereas during 1982-83 most 'crews' or 'firms' were wearing more or less the same outfits, in the summer 1983 this all began to change.

I remember seeing these lads stood on the car park of Old Trafford cricket ground. They were all wearing full tracksuits by Ellesse, Tacchini and Fila which was peculiar because no-one really wore full trackies, usually only the top with jeans or cords. The tracksuit bottoms were flared in the style, the style worn by the Seventies' tennis players from the continent. These lads looked both faintly ridiculous and utterly cool. It was their air of confidence, however, that really struck me. A mutual defiance of fashion orthodoxies that declared flares a bygone relic of a much derided decade. It wasn't long before flared cords and jeans became standard fashion items on the terraces at Old Trafford and Maine Road and an idiosyncratic Mancunian version of the scally first became identified as something different to those of other cities.

Back in the early Eighties, Manchester was much of a mystery to us. Our mate Rossy drove us to Old Trafford and took us in the Brunswick and the Shakespeare pubs explaining who all the Seventies legends were; we were certain he'd made up the Viz-esque Paraffin Pete. But no, along with Sam Spade and Eddy Beef, there really was such a person. Rossy was four or five years older than us but dressed the part. He had a Jerry Dammers smile and an Arthur Albiston perm. He also had a Jack Russell named Jasper after Jesper Olsen, who he took to the pub with him. Shopping in Manchester meant a two bus trek over to Widnes to catch the Liverpool to Piccadilly train when we would then mooch down to Hurley's, the Arndale, Oasis and the Royal Exchange. Hurley's was the epicentre of the sportswear craze and like other shops suddenly found itself becoming a fashion Mecca by default. Their two stores by Piccadilly soon had the latest labels hooked up high on the walls to deter the sneaks. I remember buying a pair of Cerutti tracky bottoms with two weeks' worth of my meagre YTS wages. I was also determined to save up and come back for the top, but never succeeding.

When the flares/scruff look became big, it was the shop assistants at Hurleys who really led the way. I remember taking a few of my mates to the shop and them laughing at the kid behind the counter because he was wearing 26 inch flares. I thought he looked cool as fuck with his beard and simple crew neck, checked shirt, flares and Adidas Cord combo. But Runcorn was a backwater where such statements were deemed laughable more influenced by the conservative scouse look of semi-flares, Benetton or rugby jumpers and cord/tweed. The more outlandish Manc style never caught on round our way except for one other kid than me. My younger brother's mates were only 15 or so, but one of them walked up to me in a pair of massive flares, a beige golfing jacket and Marks's crewy one day.

What's more he had the outgrown cropped hair and goatee beard off to a tee. He ended up a goth within a few years and now lives a crusty existence on a narrow boat!

My favourite haunts of this era were the anti-fashion hotbeds of Greenwoods and Dunn & Co, as well as Phil Saxe's stalls in the Arndale and the Underground Shoes stall at the upper entrance to the Oasis. The lad who ran this stall selling the flat soled Adidas, suedies and cord shoes, that became the perfect accompaniment to the heavy duty flared jeans and cords, became a bit of a fashion icon to us out of town wannabe Mancs. He embodied all the traits that we admired in that era; the sloppy yet studied air of nonchalance that transcended mere pose. I copied the Manc styles so much that when I returned home after one shopping trip with some 26-inch Wrangler cords the rest of the lads at the Grangeway Unemployed Club paraded them around the pool room. The local scousers, it must be said, didn't take kindly to anyone gegging in on 'their' scene.

The very notion of Manc 'scallys' was something they just couldn't fathom and so they ridiculed what they couldn't understand. However, during 1984, the Manc look was copied by other firms and to be honest, reached a point where it was difficult to tell the difference between a top dresser and a care in the community case. Old skool blue snorkel parkas worn unzipped to show off a Marc O'Polo sweat became a big thing; I recall wearing this with my flares and Green Flash at a local shopping centre and getting confused looks of astonishment from the scousers. My own mates used to take the piss and said "If Mancs started wearing cornflake boxes on their heads you'd wear one too." And they were probably right.

Old Trafford at that time was perhaps at its zenith regarding the number of lads who'd turn out on the forecourt, all sporting the latest uniform. The team itself may have been underachieving as usual under Big Ron, but off the pitch the size and reputation of the United ' jibbers' was second to none. We stood in the United Road as close to the away fans as possible and at big games, the atmosphere inside a capacity OT even when the capacity was still only 54,000 or so, was electrifying. 'What's it like to see a crowd?' was a familiar chant and it was this triumphalism in numbers, if not trophies, that secured a sense of arrogance. It must be said that City had a pretty handy mob at the time, while me and Rossy spent an uncomfortable afternoon escaping City lads by paying into a Moss Side shebeen before their first home game since being promoted from the old Second Division.

Like all fashion crazes, the scruff phase petered out by the spring of 1985 to be replaced by an interim proto-Paninaro era, when Ball jeans and Timberland boots and Chevignon and Ciao jackets and jumpers began to make their way on to the terraces all across the land. It was an era of Ralph Lauren polo jumpers and pegged cords and chinos and Ocean Pacific and Pop 84 and Cecil Gee and Gee2 and various shops in the Royal Exchange selling big labels and patches and a phoney frontiersman Americana fetish. It also marked the launch of **Arena** *magazine and 'male grooming products' and affordable Armani and Next style high street appropriation and a general smartening up that carried on via places like Woodhouse and Phil Black. It carried on right up until the Madchester/acid house era when the scruff revival kicked-in.*

If one band epitomised the unique Manc scally style it was the Happy Mondays. When I first saw photos of the band in '86 on the cover of Melody Maker, there was no doubt even before reading the interview that these were Mancs. They'd remained true to that studied scruff aesthetic, so much so that many journalists refused to believe they had an image. And they didn't have an 'image'. For all image is a form of camouflage, just another way of selling product. The Mondays had a 'look' and it was the look of the streets, not one documented by the usual style press obsessed with hip-hop and other ghetto glamorous styles such as the 'Boy' look of MA-1's and DM's, or the preposterous Seventies revivalism of rare groove. This was a mostly white working class north-western sense of style that only those well versed in its nuances can truly appreciate. Take a mug shot, any mug shot; you can tell the scousers and the Mancs even by their faces, never mind their clothes.

The original ethos of scally/casual/Perry/dresser, call it what you like, was never about being dictated to; culturally, sartorially, politically, it was self-contained and self-determining and no-one could control or foresee what evolutionary mutations it would take. Perhaps that's why the self-appointed taste makers and opinion formers of the fashion press never gave it any credence and still malign or misconstrue its significance. Had they seen me in 1983 trying to perfect the 'half-in-half-out' shirt look for hours before leaving the house, or ensuring that the frayed edges of my 26 inch cords were just at the right length that they covered my cord shoes but didn't catch under the heel, they might understand to what lengths some of us went to achieve that ' just got out of jug' look.

A Right Good Flare Up

I'd also clocked this geographical Manc scruff look at the match, but not a North End game: With having a severe addiction to the 'adrenaline rush' of Saturdays, and a unstable craving for a pick-me-ups of midweek fixes too, my dependence and over reliance needed fulfilling one Tuesday night when North End hadn't a game. So what depths would I plunge to, for a fix.

'You have to balance reason with passion; reason keeps you open, passion keeps your adrenaline going.'

Burnley, our near neighbours and Division Three rivals in the 1984/85 season, had a game during the week in the Milk Cup at Turf Moor, to the illustrious 'Red Army', Manchester United, one chilly Tuesday night.

Preston were away on the Wednesday to Norwich City, only the long hike wasn't fancied even though PNE had held them to a thrilling 3-3 draw in the first leg. Norwich mauled North End the following night at Carrow Road 6-1, and then went on to lift the 1984/85 League Cup trophy at Wembley after beating Sunderland 1-0 in the final. But, due to the Heysel Stadium disaster on the 29th May 1985, English clubs were indefinitely banned from playing in Europe, so Norwich couldn't compete in next season's UEFA Cup.

Anyway, five of us had arranged on the Saturday, coming back from an away game at Lincoln, that we'd have a mooch over to the *Land that Time Forgot* for the Dingle v Man United match. We would have a double edged prospect of 'scoring' and, a chance to check out what the Mancs were layering themselves in, in the fall of 1984. Phil, a mate who had the only set of wheels between us, drove us there in his clapped out, shade of burgundy, Mark I Ford Escort. He did the rounds picking the other four of us up at our abodes, and then we headed over to Burnley via the A-roads, because there wasn't a motorway connecting our two lovely towns in '84. En route we stopped off for a couple of bevvies in Whalley, a quaint village set in the Ribble Valley, to whet our appetite.

On arrival in the stupendous, breathtaking town of Burnley around sevenish, we parked a 10 minute walk away from the ground in a bleak looking, stone terrace housed street. Kick-off was at 7.30pm, so we had a brief comb of the surrounding area for any potential traders of our requirements, claret or red, with none found. We then navigated our way down garbage strewn ginnels and back alleyways towards the floodlight beams. A circuit of the ground was undertaken to find either the weakness point of entry to scale or an unattended gate to boot open to jib in. Only there was a large police presence due to the Red Army having a rowdy reputation spanning back to the early Seventies. Times when they'd rampaged through towns and cities throughout Britain in their thousands. There would be just over 12,500 in attendance that night, including Burnley fans, but the Old Bill weren't to know that and they weren't taking any risks too. I suppose because of there being trouble week-in week-out at nearly every game in all four leagues in the Eighties, and the blood-chilling memories still somewhat fresh in the minds of the local authorities of a visit to Turf Moor by Celtic in the Anglo Scottish Cup in September 1978, this would deem a weighted amount of boys in blue making a show of strength that night.

Sidetracking: the night the Celtic hordes had flooded over the border to Lancashire had become instilled in Burnley folklore, forever. Not only did the marauding inebriated Celts paint the town green & white in IRA and Bhoys graffiti paraphernalia, they caused havoc smashing both the town centre and ground to pieces, leaving a trail of destruction in their wake similar to what a tsunami would; an emerald one, that is. Before and during the game they not only threw pies, piss and metal fence poles as spears over the separating no-man's-land divider from the away fans section of the Longside terracing into the home section, they fought with locals in all the other three stands on the ground. After the match had finished, the Gaelic barbarians also picked up a lone scarf-wearing Burnley supporter waiting for a bus and rammed him horizontally through the bus shelter he'd been standing at moments earlier. These and other acts of remorseless violence continued well into the wee hours. *No, nay, never, no, never no more, will they play the wild Celts at the Turf, no never no more.*

So, with the plod in numbers positioned everywhere and others on horseback milling around, the chances of nicking in were out of the window. We then approached a turnstile for entrance into the Bee Hole End which had an old bloke manning the grille for payment wearing a heavy tweed overcoat, crisp white shirt and old school military tie and a matching tweed flat cap. The Bee Hole end had been designated for the travelling Mancunians that evening; it was normally for home fans only, but not tonight. The entrance price was four or five quid but, as the mate, Chappie, went to hand over the fee as we queued behind him ready for a double click, the 70 plus year-old gadger gruffly informed him "Na then lad. If thee gives me two pound, and thee mates too, you can jump over the turnstile." He's the oldest entrepreneur I've ever come across, every credit, though.

"You're on." Came the reply. Only we soon gathered the last lad in the line, Wayne, hadn't quite heard the old bloke.

One by one four of us greased the leathery, furrowed palm of the grinning grey moustachioed chap with two pound notes each and vaulted over the turnstiles, whippet like. This apart from Micky who'd been the other side of 15 stone since his teens and struggled a bit. When it came to Wayne, he thought we were bunking in without paying. Halfway through his ascent of the wrought iron turnstile the old bloke was manning, the elderly chap somehow managed to slam the secondary wooden door right into Wayne's face, sending him reeling backwards. Us four were in stitches as we stood waiting inside.

The deep Burnley accent was once again detected after reopening the gate. "Come on sonny. Cough up thee you two pounds, and thee can jump over. Or would thee rather pay the full price?"

Sheepishly, Wayne coughed up, and we were all in. While he dusted himself off he bemoaned to us "Why didn't you tell us the craic with dropping him two nicker!" to more howls of laughter. Now the five of us were in, we made onto the open terracing just as the players ran out of the tunnel, *BANG!* All five of us seem to hit a transparent wall. We were wearing a salmagundi gamut of labels and styles: Adidas City range and their Leisure shoe series purchased from Topman were on our plates. Sergio Tacchini bottoms or Farah slacks, or varied shades, styles and brands of denim jeans concealed our sparrow like pins. Fila trackie tops, or Pierre Cardin and Gabicci jumpers covered our then slender Ned Kelly's. With Ellesse and Kappa ski coats, or Burberry golfing jackets accompanied by the obligatory Burberry scarf wrapped round the lower boat, protecting us from the rawness of the northern elements. The get-ups were a somewhat collaboration/commingle of the London look plucked off lads from Preston who followed Chelsea and West Ham for some unknown reason and, the clobber from others who'd jumped ship at North End and gone to the north-west's big four, the Red and Blues of both Manchester and Liverpool. I think I was strutting Hush Puppies desert boots, Levis cords, slightly flared, a V-neck Jaeger knit, C&A brown suede bomber jacket and, a back perm mullet hairdo. The C&A slick number jacket was a preference to the harlequin patchwork leathers with neckline bootlace drawer that were to be had from a leather shop in the centre of town – they were awful. Only what these Mancs were parading that night, stopped us in our tracks! They'd upped, or rather downed, the dressing stakes. Lads promiscuously promenaded new/old clobber to us as they ambled along the terracing towards the no-man's-land divider to taunt the local throwbacks. Once in position at the mesh fencing, they laughed out loud while holding their stomachs with one hand and pointing with the other at the Burnley contingent pressed tightly against the home side of the fence. The gap between was occupied by a sparse Old Bill presence keeping a stern eye on proceedings to make sure there wasn't a major 'flare-up' about to happen.

So what were the Mancs wearing? Mancs had gone all flared, with broad tones of flair. Flares were back and very salient. And not just semi-flares. These lads wore vast flared jeans and cords. Some were 18", 20" and 22", maybe even wider. Voluminous seemed fundamental. While the plethora of flares billowed in the breeze, their choice of footwear underneath these monster Seventies'-style flares that night couldn't really be clocked. Tops were M&S crewnecks in earthy tinge or dark blue. Small checked shirts hung over waistbands hiding their jeans labels, only not unkempt. Collars of shirts were either pulled high around the neck with the top button fastened and tucked inside the jumper or, flapped over, buttons on show. The odd skiing jacket was worn. And I'm sure one or two had Marc O'Polo sweats on. Hair, for most, was number-three or four crew-cuts, with the makings of goatee beards for some. *(Notes were jotted into our Filofaxes, for later reference.)*

Snapping out of our hypnotic stupor, and looking at each other without a word and at our dressage, we then turned our attentions towards the pitch. Witnessed that night was the Alan Brazil show: Man U ran out comfortable winners 3-0, Brazil notching 2 and Olsen t'other. Objects from both sets of supporters were exchanged during the 90 minutes, sporadically, over the dividing caging, many from where the vigorous, Manc scallies had massed in their hundreds. However, at no time did we really feel totally out of sorts and uncomfortable due to what we were wearing, 'cause there were still heaps of Mancs that hadn't gone through the transitional 'flare' phenomenon. But we did need to play catch-up with the ever weekly changing of the terrace uniform. We'd dilated our orbs to a whole new rage.

Spilling onto the cobbled streets after the final whistle, we made our way back to the motor, still on the lookout for a bit of fun. Then, when we made tracks down a darkened street, we audibly heard Burnley accents threatening Man U fans. Jogging in the direction of the vociferous commotion occurring some 50 yards ahead, we saw a dozen or lads pulling at a car's door handles while booting its side panels and pounding the windscreen with clenched fists shouting "Come on, you Manc bastards." There were two blokes sat in the front as far as I could see, and possible two/ three more crouched down in the back foot-wells of the car – who knows?

Anyway, the roar went up from us ("Come on then"), as we commenced bouncing on the spot 10 yards away like five Zebedees, arms outstretched, beckoning them on as we now caught their attention. Advancing towards us, forgetting about the car and its occupants, we took a couple of steps forwards with Chappie whipping out his comb from the back pocket of his Farahs like it was a knife. This due to being outnumbered more than two-to-one and to test Burnley's mettle.

"He's got a blade, he's got a blade" quickly changed to "Has he fuck, it's a comb. Come on then, you Manc cunts."

Now thinking we're up shit creek without a paddle, and it may come on top, a Burnley lad blurts "They're not Man U, they're Preston!" And for some bizarre reason they all spun on a sixpence and made rapid haste, leaving us momentarily in a state of bemusement. What happened next as they scarpered goes down in the lads' footy tales whenever recalling mischievous days.

One of the fleeing Burnley fans ran straight in to a lamppost, *KLUNK*. He plummeted backwards at break neck speed and hit the deck. He then rose to his feet even quicker than he'd hit the pavement, and 'did one' overtaking a few of his absconding mates in the process. This left us in bits nearly pissing ourselves and unable to pursue the skedaddled Burnley fans.

Giving up the ghost, we found our transport and mulled over why the Burnley didn't fancy a spot of dancing with five Preston lads, but they would have done if we were Mancs. We were also still creased up about the lad and the lamppost while wondering on the size of the egg-shaped lump he'd have on his deformed forehead in the morning. I bet he'd have had a headache for weeks. We then drove to Whalley again for a final ale before calling it a night.

Entering a boozer we were still boisterous and all chuckling about the events. The pub fell deadly silent in the best room, so we went through to the back room. Ordering a beer in the deserted vault, a Neanderthal chubby-faced skinhead, with 'tash and blackeye, popped his head round the door that led from the best room. This caused more chortling and suggestions that it might have been him that had kissed both the lamppost and the paving stones so swiftly earlier on. At a rate of knots, he then vaporised. Maybe he was wearing an original pair of half mast flares from the Seventies, and felt a tad embarrassed?

These Colors Don't Run

Rugby league is a simple game played by simple people, rugby union is a complex game played by wankers

Laurie Daley

The 'United Colours' of Benetton range became another in the long line of labels that lads latched onto in the mid-Eighties, especially their full chest, logo embossed rugby shirts. These classic garments came in an array of colours; the white cotton jersey version that had a single green, or blue, stripe with matching cuffs and collar that looped round the back of the top and arms was the most celebrated. I never owned one, though, but I had plenty of polos and T-shirts in the locker at home from a local store in Preston over this time frame (I still have a couple of items in the cupboard purchased during the World Cup in Germany, 2006). The 'Benny' shop had a wealth of vibrant stock neatly folded on its shelves. Many a time, following a visit by us footy lads, the aftermath looked like a tornado had hit the gaff. The store was situated in St George's Shopping Centre Bullring, in the centre of town, which was very convenient when strolling down to the train station on a scouting mission. The Benetton rugby tops still command extreme 'ackers on eBay, in this day and age.

Years later, thought-provoking, extreme Benetton ads were plastered onto billboards, without exception, or omission, throughout the world. These ads ranged from an AIDS activist in his last days on earth dying of the virus, right though to a nun and priest giving it tongues down each other's throats. All very controversial, in point of fact.

Around the same spell that 'dressing down' came in, in the back end of 1984/early 1985, mullets were once again sprouting at an alarming, rapid rate down the back of lads' necks. I'd also observed England rugby union shirts being worn under a nice cord or Harris tweed jacket with the English rose on the left breast poking out – every rose has its throne. I myself had began growing my locks in early 1984 and fancied an England union rugger top to partner a second-hand tweed number which had leather patches on the elbows plus a quality silk lining. I'd picked the jacket up in a charity shop for a fiver. The guise included flares, or semi-flares, from an old Army & Navy store opposite the boarded-up Public Hall/Corn Exchange listed building in Preston. I can remember going in the shop one Friday teatime after graft and asking if they had any Levi or Wrangler flared cords or jeans. "Bloody hell lad" said the elderly fella "I haven't been asked for a pair of them in donkeys!" The bloke disappeared into the stockroom, returning minutes later with an armful of Seventies-throwback flares and a price tag to match. Sorted. The said shop was paid quite a few more drop-ins on Fridays, but the coinage increased every time, even though I didn't let onto the lads where I'd acquired them from. Jumpers were M&S or my dad's cardies. And a favourite of mine to wear underneath a M&S jumper, was a Levi denim shirt with pearl push buttons that you left un-tucked. The shoes were Hush Puppies, desert boots, or various shades of brown, cheap-throwaway cord shoes from a basket outside Curtess shoe shop. I developed a ginger-ish tuftie on my chinny-chin-chin too. This 'look' being stolen from what I'd observed the Mancs were wearing at Burnley, with also a smattering of the Liverpool scally look.

Getting back on track; a car load of us drove to Preston Grasshoppers, on the outskirts of town – a leafy, posh part of Preston, if the truth be known – to procure an England rugby jersey. I'd played for Grasshoppers as a junior between 1975 and 1977, only it wasn't for me, even though they looked after you more than any football team I ever played for. You had pie, peas and gravy, and a real Coca Cola waiting for you in the club house once you'd showered and changed following the game. This compared to trying to get changed on a wind-swept field, pissing behind a bush and having a swig of water from a mangy plastic bottle, if you were lucky, at junior football. And, I didn't want to spoil my dashing good looks. If proof was needed on the looks front, I'd once bumped into Bill Beaumont – he lived locally – in PSD (Preston Sports Department) buying a squash racket. Not that you could avoid bumping into him, he was that wide. He'd also hit every branch when falling out of very lofty 'Ugly Tree', I tell you. Add to this an overhung brow with deep set eyes, a busted flat nose and a pair of cauliflower ears that green-fingered Percy Thrower would have been proud of. Beaumont had played for Fylde Rugby Club his entire career, having to retire prematurely due to sustained injuries. Facial injuries, me thinks. You get the picture? I'd also no intention of my dial ending up a clone of Mr. Potato Head.

Just as we pulled into the Grasshoppers car park, disappearing through the clubs entrance doors, nearly bent over double, was the ass-end of Wade Dooley hence his nickname, 'Blackpool Tower.' Standing at a colossal 6' 8", Mr Dooley played for the Grasshoppers and also represented England 55 times at lock-'you-up'-forward during his prosperous career. His day job, seeing players were semi-pro back then,

Old Bill. And if he was on duty when we played the Lashers, or were on a jolly to the wonderful seaside resort down the 11.4 mile long M55, you made sure you kept out of his way, for double sure. Anyway, four of us tried to gain entry into the club, only there was an old chap stood in the entrance hall wearing a pair of well shined Tuxan-red Royals, a neatly ironed pair of beige cords with turn-ups, a starched white shirt with club tie and tiepin and a tweed jacket. "Can I help you gentlemen?" This said with plums in his mouth, not like on our estate, cha.

"Yeah mate," (why is everyone your mate?) I replied. "You don't happen to sell England rugby tops, do you?"

"No," he replied as he drilled a profound stare my way that had obtuse written all over it.

"Do you know anywhere that does then, mate?" This second question was met with a second similar glare, that had "are-you-slow-on-the-uptake?" attached to it.

"No."

Now I understood. He didn't want the likes of us seen in the vicinity of the club, never mind step over the club's threshold. We were as welcome as dog shit wedged between the segs on his leather-soled Royals. The penny had dropped. I bet he was jealous of my jacket too. "OK, mate. Cheers for that anyway."

Nonchalantly we returned to car, glaring back occasionally, as Lord of Lightfoot Green kept an eye on us from behind the glass panelled doors. A brief wheel-spin in the car park, and we were gone. I nevertheless kept on with the hunt for an England top, for a month or so, but to no favourable outcome until other labels and matters beckoned my wad.

The Family Game

While on the subject of rugby shirts, here's a bit of an insight from a Wiganer called Dom, into the other game of rugby generally played in the north. Rugby league, the ostensible family game.

Rugby is a beastly game played by gentlemen; soccer is a gentleman's game played by beasts; rugby league is a beastly game played by beasts

Henry Blaha

Dom: *The history books show that the 'Northern Rugby Union' was formed in 1895 when RFU (Rugby Football Union) clubs based in the working class northern counties of Yorkshire and Lancashire became disillusioned with their middle-class southern counterparts for preventing the players (many of whom were miners) receiving payments for their exertions on the field of play. This despite the fact they often lost wages as a consequence of representing their town. However, a recently discovered document which was believed to have been lost suggests that the Northern Rugby Union, or 'rugby league' as it later became known, was formed when the lads from northern clubs like Rochdale Hornets and Leeds Athletic got sick of being served shandy when they played Harlequins. And having to watch Barnaby and Roderick sodomise one another in the shower after the game when they played at Bath.*

Anyway, rugby league, in itself, developed into a sport that had its stronghold in the north of England. This, you could probably argue, is concentrated along (although not entirely confined to) the M62 corridor, with the strongest teams of recent years being the likes of Leeds, Wigan, St Helens, Warrington, Bradford and so on.

If you grew up in Wigan, which I did, or St Helens, Warrington or Widnes the chances were you learned to pass a rugby ball long before you tried kicking a soccer ball. League was a man's game; football was for sunbed nancy boys with perms and homoerotic goal celebrations. If you'd walked down our street in 1978, you'd have seen me playing tick rugby with my mates, which was no different to other rugby towns. Although in the rest of Britain kids my age would have been playing soccer at that time. And so it was that naturally our childhood heroes were rugby players. Lads from Wigan would more often than not grow up following Wigan Rugby League, over and above the Latics, Wigan Athletic. You'd have a football team too who you supported like Liverpool or Man U, but your main interest was championing the cherry and white stripe.

People are surprised when you tell them it used to 'go off ' at the rugby in the Eighties, but why shouldn't it? Fighting at the time wasn't restricted just to football matches. Seaside towns had outbreaks of trouble on Bank Holidays. It happened in nightclubs on a regular basis. And in the Eighties – especially anywhere there were large gatherings of young men from more than one town – there was likely to be a casual element present; this usually veered towards some sort of standoff, confrontation or fight.

Through a lot of the Eighties I lived in a house not far from Central Park, near the old car park and practise pitch. My old boy had painted the sills, lintels and door on our house cherry red and the window frames white in support of Wigan. On Sundays there were always massive crowds walking down our street and sometimes it got a bit rowdy. I think one time against Warrington a window went through in our house, only I was too young to remember how or why. By the time I was 10 or 11, me and my guttersnipe mates knew all the ways of sneaking into the Central Park and a couple of times we had very minor scuffles with kids our own age. This got dealt with by a clip round the ear and a stern warning off a copper. This was around the same time that, at football matches, a casual element differentiated themselves from donkey-jacketed beer monsters scrapping on the terraces (the same thing started to happen at rugby league games too). If you read Cardiff City's Soul Crew *book by Tony Rivers, he talks about the same happenings at rugby union games they went to as well.*

Although I wasn't there, Wigan apparently took a huge mob to a cup semi-final against Warrington at St Helens in March 1986. Folklore says Wigan had about a thousand lads out that day and St Helens and Warrington joined forces but still didn't have enough manpower together to even have a look in. I believe (but will happily be corrected if I'm wrong) that was the day Wigan's name the 'Goon Squad' first started to be used too.

My first brawl was at a rugby match rather than at the football; Wigan versus Leigh at St Helens. The rugby didn't half throw up a good few local derbies every year which helped in building up something of a rapport with your opposition. There was one game in 1986 between Wigan and Leigh where according to the Bolton Evening News, there were 13 arrests and three policemen injured during a match – I was at the game myself. We'd filled two double decker buses from Wigan; downstairs and upstairs lads were cheek-by-jowl, stood and squashed into every corner. As we got near the ground we saw another firm of about a hundred strong and we got the drivers of the buses to pull over thinking we were in business. This was only to find out it was another firm of Wiganers from Hindley. It was mayhem inside the ground all through the match and there was a Charge of the Light Brigade after the game had finished. Three hundred triumphant Wiganers smashed the lowly Leigh to pieces all over their town. The Old Bill then refused to let us get back on any buses and made us walk all the way back home so we pillaged the shops en route of ice creams and cans of lager, because it was a scorching hot day.

Another, was a good old fashioned maraud through Bolton when we used Burnden Park to play Warrington in a semi-final in 1987. We got off the train to meet some of Bolton's firm going somewhere or other, and we made our opinions felt to them about their worthiness as human beings. We also left Yates' Wine Lodge in need of a touch of TLC, and broke a couple of noses in a pub that may have been called the Hope & Anchor on the way to the ground. On that particular day (according to the Bolton Evening News) a young gentleman from Orford, Warrington, was found to be brandishing a modelling knife as an offensive weapon and subsequently fined £350, plus costs. I remember that particular incident because it was me he was brandishing the knife at.

The rows at rugby were as frequent as they were at football. Leeds Service Crew once brought a coach load to Wigan one Sunday afternoon and we faced them down at the bottom of Scholes. Warrington fixtures were forever proving to be a highly charged too. And there were times that our love affair with Bolton spilled over to the point that some of their firm would check out when Wigan had a local derby and they'd barrel up with the opposition.

Their faces would be spotted in among St Helens or Warrington's firm on many occasions.

For whatever reasons the trouble at rugby didn't really get reported in the national press the way football did. Maybe it was because it was on a smaller scale. Maybe because it didn't happen on the international setting like at England games, or at the Euros and the World Cup where it brought shame on the country. Maybe because it happened 'up north' so parliament never got to hear about it? Or maybe the Rugby League did a better job of brushing it under the carpet to lower its negative PR impact on the sport. But yes, it did happen and on a regular basis. Perhaps not quite to the extent like it did at football because rugby wasn't always the be-all and end-all tense affair like football was back then. Also there was a lot more women and families attending, and most of the rough stuff was on the pitch. But if you talk to lads who went to rugby league, especially in the Eighties, they'll tell you just as much trouble took place around rugby matches as did the soccer back in the day.

9

RHAPSODIC TIMES

On Friday 29th March 1985, a band – sort of – played their first northern gig away from the city they were based in, this being at a Preston nightclub named Clouds: but they failed miserably to deliver; an understatement if ever there was one. Simply, the band just wanted to be adored; but they weren't – the concert concluding in mob violence.

Imagine the scene: it's a Friday night in Preston 1985, which meant 'Alternative Night' at Clouds. Loons, misfits and desperate Dans were in attendance. The band that was playing the nightclub that night had a tour manager, Steve Adge, who had rounded up a posse of his mates and followers of the band who loved a rumble. This following looked upon the local club-goers of Clouds as backward, white sock wearers. The locals were off their 'eads on cheap drink and cheap drugs. The atmosphere in the club was hostile and strained. Very strained. And during the band's set their equipment kept packing in; un-tuned tones of a Joy Division gig at Preston's Warehouse five years before. The crowd present were getting more and more agitated. Then, after three interrupted songs due to apparatus failure, the band had had enough. The drummer kicked over his drum kit, and the guitarist smashed his guitar up, and the gig was abandoned. Within seconds of these actions, the club descended into a warzone.

Later, the band's bassist told a reporter "... people started whacking each other with chairs and whatever else they could lay their hands on. It seemed like the entire town of Preston had turned up to have it with us."

And another writer for a music magazine said the band's performance was dire, with only a handful of diehard masochists showing any sort of appreciation, the majority of the attendees, being less than impressed.

The lead singer incoherently caterwauled through three songs drowned in feedback as he hurtled around the raised stage with the brief set being too aggressive, lacking coordination and without originality. They are meant to be the 'Mancunian Deviant Merseybeat'. It was a very pitiful exhibition.

Prestonians were less than impressed with the band that took the centre stage that night; would the rest of the world be shortly? However this band and a host of others from a bleak north-west city would soon make the nation, and beyond sit up, sit down and take notice, as well as digging the sui generis scene that these bands concocted in the years to come. The band in question were the Stone Roses, the scene 'Madchester.' Before dissecting the music tableau that the north-west crafted, and self-indulgent tales from this cycle too, let's see what other sub-cultural arts of melodic and rhythmic sounds were also out there.

Hip-hop had been evolving in parallel with the emergence of the casual/dresser, with its tubers in New York City's Bronx. Spoken-word poetry performances had been held in NY during the Fifties and Sixties, and were used to put across black civil rights issues and to help captivate listening audiences. Then in the early Seventies, Clive Campbell, aka DJ Kool Herc, introduced 'breaks', which are extended instrumental beats, scratching and loops of hard funk records, at venues while DJ-ing so dancers could dance longer on the dance floor; this was soon to be known as 'breakdancing'. Kool Herc began rhythmically talking over the tracks being spun too; this soon to be known as rapping/MC-ing. Though *Universal Zulu Nation* founder member Afrika Bambaataa is credited with first using the term 'hip-hop' to describe the new music and subculture with the first hip-hop recording widely regarded as The Sugarhill Gang's *'Rapper's Delight'* in 1979.

The social environment, poverty and drugs problems in the Bronx, in which hip-hop had developed, wasn't too dissimilar to the one that the casual/dresser had in the north-west, only the Bronx didn't have any football links. The Bronx ghetto surroundings were graffiti covered in 'crew' tags that saw nightly gang violence on its blocks and daily police harassment. In the UK, football lads would either hand-paint threats in white gloss, or spray, on rivals' grounds. Often these would be in the days leading up to derby games, and would include the name of the 'firms' as a forerunner to the fighting that would occur on the day of the match nearly every Saturday, or at midweek games, along with police harassment.

Youths heavily influenced by hip-hop would roll out an off-cut of lino, crank up the dial on their humongous boomboxes and commence popping and locking b-boy/breakdance moves on street corners to their hip-hop heroes on a regular basis. Urban street-cred kids would be decked out in full Adidas or other branded tracksuits and shell-toed, Adidas Superstar with added chunky shoelaces while floating, gliding or sliding. Or, they would pay homage to US sports labels and wear NFL jerseys or basketball vests over oversized white T-shirts along with baggy jeans and PRO-Keds or Converse Chuck Taylor All Star sneakers when busting a manoeuvre or two. Baseball caps would be worn back-to-front, hair shaved into patterns and 'massive', gaudy fake gold gangster chains hung around necks as a badge of pride and honour.

During the next couple of years house music had percolated to Britain from, once again, the land of the free and the home of the brave; more precisely, the underground gay discothèques of Chicago. DJs in clubs down London and the south were wise to the new style of dance music and began dropping in lengthy, mechanical electronic dance-based house music into their sets. House music is characterised by repetitive 4/4 beats and rhythms centred around drum machines, off-beat hi-hat cymbals and synthesised basslines. Then in January 1987, Chicago artist Steve 'Silk' Hurley's *Jack Your Body* reached number one in the UK pop charts. And within no time, other house tracks were weekly bestsellers. Maybe when DJ Paul Oakenfold went on his jollies to Ibiza with his buddies and drank in a bar run by Trevor Fung and Ian St Paul before heading on to the Amnesia club to hear the sounds of resident DJ Alfredo or, when a trio of Chicago DJs toured the UK , were climatic circumstances too.

Though Northern Soul audiences in the north seemingly embraced house music more than the south. Also, 1987 was the first year that the 'sexual stimulant', 3,4-methylenedioxy-N-methylamphetamine, more commonly known as ecstasy/'E', was seized by the Old Bill in London. There was also a dance scene morphing on the Balearic Island of Ibiza in 1987, that in no time at all would be the central point of something huge for those clubbers wanting to dance 24/7, seven days a week under a moonlit skies and to chill out in glorious sunshine. Also over a brief duration, experimental American DJs had federated the beats of Chicago house, Detroit techno, New York disco, European electro-pop and whatever other accoutrements leading to the formulation of acid house. Acid house was likened to what had happened in Sixties' San Francisco in a intermixture of compounds.

Back in Blighty, a new day was dawning, namely the 'Second Summer of

Love' – "Acieeeeeeeeeeeed". In and around London, acid house nights were beginning to be held every weekend, the youth demanding to dance all night long, aided by chemicals. This fledgling acid house scene took its name from the Chicago tune *'Acid Tracks'* by Phuture. Acid house parties – later on to be labelled 'raves' – rapidly needed bigger venues that would house thousands of punters wanting a good time. Warehouses and disused Victorian buildings were the urban solution; while open air events were held in fields in the countryside as well. The rest of the UK were soon *'on one'* too.

Footy lads were soon tripping the light fantastic at these crepuscule milestones. It became okay for casual/dresser lads to dance, which had been seen as 'puffy' before acid house came to the fore. Or, to put it bluntly, before lads had been introduced to and dropped 'E's'. Regardless of different club and firm turnouts, feelings of rivalry and any thoughts of kicking off were put aside. Either lads would be fuelled up and primed on the love drug and be hugging each other, or they would be making vast amounts of money supplying euphoria for those seeking such and sometimes staging these events. And it wasn't long before the underworld element were actively involved in *running* the show/shows too.

Though casuals/dressers were in attendance at raves in their Italian, 'Paninaro' togs, looser and baggier clobber was ideal to rave in. Relaxed attitudes led to lads having a more relaxed dress code. And in these dry-ice filled venues, laser lights would flicker at rapid rates, along with projected images bouncing off the walls, all of which enhanced the effects of additives consumed. The wild eyed champion gurners – without the braffin' – chewing on wasps danced in luminous, bright neon-coloured clothes or tie-dyed, smiley-faced or 'Where's the Acid House Party' T-shirts. Wearing dungarees or boiler suits, bucket hats or bandanas and white gloves, while mimicking an LA traffic cop on LSD during rush hour, was accepted as a new kind of 'norm.' Accessories included strapping on bum-bags to house any personal gear needed through the night, blowing whistles and horns that couldn't be heard above the bass-lines pumping out, flailing glow-sticks epileptically while suckling on fluorescent dummies and donning dust or gas masks with the filter smothered in Vick's Vapour Rub. This could all be classed as an icon, or a cliché, of ravers.

British politicians responded with a stiff upper lip to raves; they weren't for letting the youth have their fun and games come weekends, especially without their say-so. MPs, politicians and councillors sought laws to prevent, shutdown and fine anyone who held illegal parties and didn't hold the necessary licenses to hold legal ones too, which were soon brought in and enforced. To get round these new laws in the coming years, organisers of raves held 'free' parties but the Government acted in response with the *Criminal Justice and Public Order Act 1994* being passed.

Meanwhile, back up north in Manchester, the Haçienda, a late night club and live music venue, had been holding 'Nude' house nights since the mid-Eighties; then in 1988 it changed its Wednesday theme to 'Hot' acid nights. Bernard Manning, Madonna and Frank Sidebottom had taken to the stage earlier there too. But it was this underground scene that earned the Haçienda its later infamy as the most famous club in the world.

The Haçienda was previously a warehouse that had been modified in to a yacht builder's shop before becoming a Bollywood cinema in the Seventies. Then, in 1982, the Haçienda opened its doors to the public as a live locality, which had been financed by Factory Records and their associates. The Haç' had a industrial feel and echoing acoustics. A trio of clubs in New York, Danceteria, Fun House and Paradise Garage were the inspiration for the Haçienda house nights and its urban layout, with pioneering Northern DJs Mike Pickering, 'Little' Martin Prendergast and Graeme Park manning the decks. Freaky dancing attendees not only enthusiastically espoused the tunes being selected by the DJs with open arms, some of the lads at the Haç' had embryonic forms of bands that were soon to be hatched and unleashed on mankind too. The music domain had become stale and these radical, innovative evangelists would supersede the whole kit and caboodle out there. The inchoate formulate of 'Madchester' was taking symmetry with the groups that put the 'mad' in Manchester being at cultivation stage. The Happy Mondays 'Madchester Rave On' EP nailed it. This era and these seminal groups went on to have legendary status. The folk were cooler than cool, though they were higher than high. D'you know what I mean?

Manc, and Greater Manchester scallies, had been tinkering in bands mashing guitar music, psychedelic rock, indie, dance, goth and rock 'n' roll jointly, as well as letting their hair down on Fridays at the Haç' since, and before, the clubs genesis. James, The Stone Roses, Happy Mondays, Inspiral Carpets, Northside, 808 State, The Charlatans, Paris Angels among others became synonymous with Madchester. The coming-of-age of the band Happy Mondays, formed in 1980 (and for a time managed by ex-Twisted Wheel DJ Phil Saxe) was winning a 'fixed' Battle of the Bands in 1985 at the Haçienda, and being promptly signed to Factory Records by

Tony Wilson. Then there was The Stone Roses, formerly The Patrol and The Waterfront, with a monkey-faced lead singer, Ian Brown, which is no exaggeration to say, that they revolutionised the musical landscape forever, and were key to this eventuate. They meant business. Monkey business. Northern Monkey business.

Traits like Mark 'Bez' Berry, clambering on to the stage one night at the Haçienda to join the Mondays and dance, pre-maraca-shaking duties, on the request of his mate Mr Shaun William George Ryder to take the focus off his singing/wailing. Bez just kept on dancing like Forrest Gump kept on running. The Roses, vastly enhancing themselves by the late Eighties from their Clouds rendition, adopted a fifth member, former Mondays roadie Ste 'Cressa' Cresster to prance about on stage. Bez and Cressa made these two groups stand out from the throng. The lads had come good. The lads had purpose. Real purpose. The rest, as they say, is both a natural and synthetic substance insular haze. Though everyone and their mutt wanted a slice of the northern/Manc meat 'n' tattie pie! Include in this southerners: they were having it large; walking and jiving like Mancs had become voguish.

Hanging round in clubs, pubs and Dry Bar, these monkeyesque mad lads garrulously slagged and ostracised other braggadocio pretenders who dared to challenge their thing. A northern thing. An extensive proportion who were grooving and approving these Manc bands were northern footy lads. Fighting at the match on Saturday was put on the backburner; they were goosed after partying through the night – add 'E' to the balance too. Lads hung their battle armour up, and went shopping for hipper, baggier togs. Oversized hoodie tops, flares or baggies and Kickers or Clarks Wallabes with beanie/bucket hats were choice outfits.

Hair went thick, in pudding bowl or curtain shapes, or was left to grow long and worn in a ponytail when at a desirable length, or was left to flow loose when dancing. Most clothing, and hair shaping, were attainable from Affleck's Palace.

Affleck's Palace was an erstwhile department store until opening as a indoor market in 1981. Comprising of a labyrinthine layout of stalls and shops, Affleck's became a sanctum for pursuits of vintage clothing, bric-a-brac, salvaged jumble sale wares, hippy paraphernalia, flares and plain white T-shirts with a bold black typeface sold by DJ Leo Stanley from his unit proclaiming: Born In The North, Return To The North, Exist In The North, Die In The North; My England has a rose, wherein my heart it grows, Manchester my heartland; On The Seventh Day God Chilled Out; and, On The Sixth Day God Created MANchester. All sold like hotcakes.

And Affleck's was also home to the popular haunt 'Eastern Bloc' – owned by Martin Price of 808 State and also founder of the independent record label, Creed – that dealt in all the latest underground records and dance tunes of the time.

Due west, scousers mocked the flocks of Mancs by uttering that they'd championed the dressing down look years prior. Thus this look being passé. Only Phil Saxe and his kidder had been dealing in Seventies Levi and Wrangler flares since late 1983, and right through 1984 from a market stall, Gangway, situated in the Arndale shopping centre. Shaun Ryder and his chums were regular customers teaming their 'Lionel Blairs' with paisley or flowery shirts, rare Adidas trainers from the Oasis underground market or moccasins and grew goatee beards. It is also said that, with the city being split over their football club preferences, followers of City and United wore different width flares; the Guv'nors opted for 25-inch 'Cool Cat' prolific flares, the Red Army faction around the 20-inch mark. I don't think this was always the case, though.

Cressa the style guru, after jumping ship from the Mondays, had influenced the Roses image and wardrobe away from their resemble of another band, The Cult. Dropping the allied Goth costume, Ian Brown went for pant width, the rest of the band, going with parallel or baggy jeans with a medley of clobber. 'Baggies' were obtainable from a little shop called Somewear that opened in 1985, also in the Arndale, and also run by Saxe. Flares were eclipsed by baggy, 16" turned-up bottom jeans, that were slack and loose and rippled on the leg. General hippy stuff was the overall Mancunian Madchester look with also innuendos of casual/dresser. Manchester-based Joe Bloggs and Gio-Goi fashion labels specialised in catering for the Madchester look, both making themselves very affluent indeed. Thousands across the land soon aped the Mancs.

The year that was both the pinnacle and the watershed for the Manchester scene was 1990. This saw a mega turnout for the (acoustically disastrous) outdoor Spike Island gig in May, and the beginning of the end for the fundamental nucleus of the Madchester generation – they didn't want to suffer no fools. Door staff on rave clubs also began regularly looking down the barrels of guns every weekend as gun crime gripped the city that also created the next nickname of Manchester, 'Gunchester.' The Mondays imploded in 1993, and the Roses in 1996, following internal feuding. The Haçienda eventually bolted its doors for the last time in 1997 after being rinsed and in a great, financial crisis. The end of an era. Madchester seems to be the last of the underground subculture eras too.

Blackburn. The Haçienda did more than any other club in Britain to cultivate the house sounds, but in and around bleak Blackburn, among the wastelands of dark satanic mills, warehouses and pleasant pastures, Lancashire lads and lasses caught a high on wave after wave of raves. As bizarre as it is, Blackburn was a focal point for DIY dance parties; and did those feet and arms move at these raves in ancient times. These Blackburn warehouse parties were historical working-class cultural accidents, that took place before the global, mass appeal of acid house.

During the Eighties and early Nineties, the north, and more so, the north-west of England, was better known for its dole queues, strikes and protest marches. The north once had thriving mill industries and highly productive factories, but these industries had all but disappeared in the modern day working environment, with buildings left derelict and decaying. The north-west had nowt of worth to offer; incorporate in this northern nights out and nightspots compared to the south, and principally, London Town's highlife and 'loads a money' excess. Only between 1989 and 1991 the north-west began to host raves in the unconventional settings of disused abattoirs and failed business park units, and shone forth from the top of clouded hills. If there was any musical style to the Blackburn parties, it was kinda Balearic.

Re-enactments of catch the pigeon developed between the 'dibble' and the party animals wanting to attend illegal raves. After meeting at service stations, convoys became commonplace on Lancashire motorways come weekends. Lancashire Constabulary would position themselves on motorway bridges near to Blackburn, monitoring fleets of vehicles with their headlights on full beam, crawling along at a snail's pace underneath, sometimes on the opposite side of the motorway, going the wrong way.

They would be waiting on information, and directions, or a signal, to the whereabouts of that night's party location. Both parties would be high on hope. The Old Bill hoping to stop the party, the party-goers being high. These party people often physically dismantled barricades and broke through road blocks erected by the police, the force being powerless to stop the would-be ravers due to their sheer volume. Or, simply, the party-goers would outwit the rozzers. Ravers wouldn't cease from their mental fight even when a five-mile exclusion zone was brought in, because ravers had a great big convoy rockin' through the night and nothin' was gonna get in their way. And when ravers eventually arrived at that night's all night party, and paid one's dues of a couple of quid to enter, their countenance beamed divinely. All these components were essential; which amplified *the rush*.

These illegal raves were basic, raw and had minimum lighting and backdrops; with organisers (such as the charismatic duo Tommy 'Scotch' Smith and Tony Creft, plus DJs alike) involved for a good time just as the urban kids were, more so than earning a decent wedge out of the events. Electricity sources would be tapped into either inside the buildings or next door, the nearest lamppost or, power would be obtained from robbed generators juiced with siphoned diesel. Health and safety also wasn't on the agenda. With exits chained and locked from the inside till at least daybreak once double the capacity was crammed in. Thousands of Lancastrians tuned in and chilled out while letting loose at grassroot, outdoor parties too.

"These illegal raves were basic,
raw and had minimum lighting and backdrops;
with the organisers, (such as the charismatic duo
Tommy 'Scotch' Smith and Tony Creft, plus DJs alike)
involved for a good time just as the urban kids were,
more so than earning a decent wedge
out of the events."

Because of these gatherings, a series of large scale disorders resulted when helicopter spotlights focused on venues while commands were barked over the copter's loudhailer as fully kitted-out riot cops prepared for action. Rabid, snarling dogs, along with their handlers, as well as mounted police, were ready to mop up the leftovers that their colleagues hadn't dispatched, arrested or introduced themselves to at underground parties where there hadn't been one gram of trouble. This was until the boys in blue turned up to put an end to the 'party party' atmosphere by seizing the decks and PA system. In return for spoiling the partygoers' 'fun', panda cars were upturned and burnt-out with police lines attacked. If only they'd left them alone...

All these bittersweet happenings and locations were filmed by 'Preston Bob' on his video recorder. And many moons later, hours upon hours of footage were made into a film documentary by Piers Sanderson aptly named, 'High on Hope.'

From 1989, handfuls, then hundreds, then thousands, then tens of thousands, danced the night away at titled nights such as Live the Dream, Hardcore Uproar, Revenge and Joy parties at whereabouts such as Sett End, Bubble Factory, Unit 7, Pump and other once abstract localities until tit-for-tat actions by scouse and Mancs bullies, wannabe villains and the organised criminal element muscled in on the act. Anthony and Christopher Donnelly, promoters of the legendary Joy party in the Lancashire hills, went on to found the Gio-Goi clothing label and several Blackburn DJs still guest at raves nowadays. By the time the infamous Blackburn parties had run their course, nigh on four years later, their legacy continued at the ART LAB, a dance and art collective down the road in Preston.

'The light that burns twice as bright, will always burn half as long. ART LAB we salute you' – No Damn Cat (graffiti following police raid at the ART LAB).

Entrance to the ART LAB was by invitation only, so it avoided licensing regulations because it was someone's home. Allan Deaves converted the building where he lived, near the University of Central Lancashire on the outskirts of Preston town centre, into a party zone come weekends. The LAB's rustic walls had computer monitors tuned in to constant static, fixed to the brickwork alongside other technological components with rusty pipes intensifying its neoteric urban feel. The outside of the rendered Victorian warehouse also had metal artwork attached to it and a large fabricated 'ART LAB' sign. Every week artists would paint different logos on the dance floor that would be worn off come daylight by lads and girls dancing. The top floor a medley of settees, chairs and beds with tea, coffee and cold drinks and fruit on offer – donations were welcome. The LAB was a new emotional abode for northerners who craved rave partying.

For nearly a year the LAB lasted until its cast-iron doors were forcibly opened by a hydraulic battering ram and robo-cops steamed the gaff. Equipment was seized, court orders handed out and the free partying was over once again. But in its short existence, the ART LAB and its fun-loving consortium had achieved what they had felt a need for. This being a good time for all who wanted to party away from the non-understanding mainstream Joe Public, who just didn't have a clue.

Pills and Thrills

I wasn't one for raving; I was more into my misbehaving. I wasn't one for stopping up all Friday night and being unfit for Saturday's frolics at the match. And I wasn't one for the repetitive banging house sounds too. I did grow my mane shoulder length, purchase a pair of red Kickers and had a few 'out there' T-shirts and shirts. One shirt was a belting hallucinogenic black, white and orange florid number by Ciao. Amassing Massimo Osti garments and venturing aboard with English lads against acid following the national football team had become a chief profligacy for me rather than raving.

I had been asked to help with security at events in Lancashire on more than one occasion though, but I declined following advice from a mate's uncle who'd worked the raves. He'd had advice too, in the form of a 'piece', that his services were no longer required from now on at the parties one night. Also the ceiling was blown out with a sawn-off shotgun at a rave club, Lord Byrons, in Preston that I frequented. While a local boozer of mine, The Bees Knees, that held house all-nighters, once had a 'visit' in the early hours from folk wearing balaclavas and in possession of an assortment of weaponry. There was only the Back Street rave club, behind Clouds nightclub, in Preston town centre that seemed to have any karma with a 'lover not fighter' presence. But the alleyway that led to the Back Street saw much chemical warfare, intoxicated brawls and divvies in white shirts, black slacks and slip on black shoes wanting to fight you. Just what was the attraction?

Some of the lads from the match that I knocked around with started wearing two completely different coloured Kickers i.e. a blue left foot shoe and a white right foot. They also filled the laces of their Kickers with a rainbow of the Kicker 'fleurette' flower lace tabs. And add to this oddball appearance, baggy sweatshirts and baggy jeans. Only when one lad turned up for an away day wearing a multicoloured stripy poncho, I began to wonder if the potency of the drugs being consumed was too concentrated and had scrambled their tiny minds.

The after effects of raving and 'E' are still being felt to this day...

Northern lads and lasses just wanted be free, to do whatever they wanted to do, and have a good time, that's all they wanted to do. And that's what they did, baby, they had a good time and partied. These north-west phenomena are books and films in their own right, but let's have a brief supernova trilogy of accounts from folk who experienced pills, thrills and rhapsodic times.

Raving Mad

Now then, this mad-head who I urged to commit a tale or two towards raving and the 'Madchester' scene was Cyril. Mad Cyril. A reply to my request was forthcoming within hours, never mind days or weeks. He ploughed through the insanity of his mad goings-on in the Eighties and Nineties like he wasn't of sound of mind, or he was tripping – he seemed on one, matey. Really, what he wanted to do was convey a true adore on the frenzied era and he just couldn't wait to do so.

So, here goes; a breakneck trip through Madchester. 'Hooligans Against Acid!'

Cyril: *On leaving school in 1984, I started an apprenticeship with a local firm as a joiner, so I'd money to splash on clobber and follow my team, Man City. During these times I was good friends with Denis Law's sons, who were mad for their clobber too. Ian, one of the sons, once turned up one Saturday in some green, Adidas Gazelles, which were really cool in my eyes. I will also never forget a lad called Nicky H, he was the first casual lad that I took ideas off and kind of copied, as you do when you're 16. Labels like Pierre Sangan, New Man and Farah slacks were the ones to be seen in. And there was a shop in Altrincham called Elite which sold all the stuff, albeit slight seconds.*

Anyway, skipping through the years and casual/raving clobber – I could go on forever about it – I was always mad on my music as well. From Bowie to Duran Duran and most of the New Romantic bands. But then something different was bubbling on the music front. My first taste of change was the Stone Roses; now this stuff was different. I also went on to see the Roses at various venues over the years including Alexandra Palace in London, and Spike Island, which wasn't their best gig but a great day out. Then came the Happy Mondays, a more 'laddish' group of football lads than the Roses. After games at Maine Road we were knocking round in the Cyprus Tavern, and going to clubs to listen to remixes of Mondays tunes like the 'Wrote For Luck' dance version.

I'd also begun going raving outdoors through the night with dance and acid house beats becoming more and more popular. But I was into bands like The High and Paris Angels which were indie/dance crossover. One club that spun both tunes was called Konspiracy. This is where I met my future missus, of now 25 years plus. And this club is where I had my first encounter of Ecstasy. I'll never forget seeing lads from the match tripping their tits off dancing while others shook every fucker's hand then hugged them. I hadn't taken 'E' before that night, but I had some young lad ask the missus loudly 'if I was straight or what?' I didn't take kindly to him asking that sort of question and we ended up scuffling. I didn't know he meant had I taken anything!

By now I was buying acid house compilations instead of indie records, which I still have to this day. We were going to Thunderdome and Konspiracy and clubbing every week with Manchester being all over the news, claiming that it was the place to be and it was the centre of the universe. In the daytime, Affleck's Palace was something of a hub too, while clothes shops like Zico or Phil Black's or Hurley's had always been the shops for smart togs, Affleck's was the place to be seen in, while the bar of the moment was Dry101, where the Mondays and Roses drank. God had created Manchester/Madchester!

We then began going the Haçienda and regularly saw the Mondays and Northside while enjoying the new and illegal buzz. Also, Richfields on Deansgate was a top club that banged out indie and dance 'Madchester' tunes. This was until half of Salford took it over, as they did with the Haç', and anywhere else that was decent. I would be in Eastern Bloc Records most Saturdays stocking up on vinyl collection. I wore footwear ranging from red Kickers, Reebok boots or Nike Pegasus, paired with semi-flares, shell suits and bright T-shirts – the brighter and louder the better. Transport back then was a primed-up Ford Fiesta 1.1, in undercoat grey. And if you ever required a lift, I advised that you brought a brolly along 'cause it leaked in like mad when it rained (like it does all the time in Manchester).

One day I sprayed 'The High' on the side of this road-monster. Even when we went on holidays in Europe everyone wanted to hang around with you because you were from Manchester, that's how it felt anyway. Clubs in Tenerife were pumping out tunes like Kariya's 'Let Me Love For You Tonight.' That tune still sticks in my head to this day. Mad days. Raving mad days.

I stopped going to the footy, I'd jacked it in. Illegal raves were where it was at, and Blackburn was the place to dance the night away. Sure enough, the lads who punted out tickets at the match were there too, making good money from the scene. Manchester bands were still coming through trying to be the next big thing. Some failed miserably; others should have been bigger than the Mondays. The likes of The High and Paris Angels, who I've mentioned, were way ahead of their time.

As things started to fade, as they do, I bought my own gaff and got back in touch with my footy-going mates and began going the match again in 1992. I was soon hooked again. The clothes the lads wore were Paul & Shark, CP Company and Stone Island, although they cost a packet; it was always expensive to dress the part. I was going home and away and getting more and more involved with the violence side too. To cut a long story short, it kicked-off at Maine Road against Spurs in the FA Cup in '93. There was a pitch invasion. My mug shot was on the front of the Manchester Evening News, and, following several court appearances, I received a six-year ban.

But trying to cling onto the music buzz I began DJing, spinning drum 'n' bass. My DJ days were influenced by my best mate at the time, Gee Money, from Old Trafford. We use to play at Music Box and Planet K, all strictly drum 'n' bass venues. My first set of decks were purchased in 1994, and were Technics 1210s. I didn't mess about buying cheap, nasty shite, I dived in head first. DJing in Manchester was about who you knew, really, promoters and the likes, so I found it quite hard to gain spots, even though I considered myself good enough to get 'the break.' I ended up playing on pirate stations such as Buzz FM, which kept getting busted.

Clothes-wise I went through a Stussy and DC shoe stage when I was heavily into D&B, only because I wanted a change and the lads I was chilling with were into similar clothes. Clothes wore were hoodies and baseball caps, with trainers being Nike Air Force. To be honest, it was a dramatic change, but that was what D&B lads chose to wear.

I kept banging away with the D&B scene until around 2000, when it had just got harder and harder to get anywhere to gig. Gee Money was by now producing some groundbreaking tracks and getting them cut onto dubplate in London. But he was struggling to get the big break too, so I threw the towel in. The main tunes being played at clubs were too dark for me, and attracting the wrong sort of crowds. I thought they needed some nice vocals to freshen things up. So, for me, it was back to guitar bands.

It was a refreshing change to get back at the football when my ban was up and match going attire after a while. Once, when I was on the Crooked Tongues forum, a lad calling himself Barrington Smash got chatting about Eighties clobber and that he was thinking about setting up a forum on the subject, which he did. The forum is called Eighties Casuals, which I joined in 2005, and it is still going strong. I also joined the Casual Connoisseur forum, and the three lads involved began producing quality T-shirts that struck a chord. Today, t'CC have a cult following and their products are snapped up in minutes when limited runs are released.

Recently I bumped into a lad at a 40th, and he said he always regarded me as one of the best dressed lads in Sale, clocking what I was wearing. This was from leaving school to present day. I was flattered to say the least. I'm not saying Sale is the place to be at but, it's nice to know I didn't look a complete twat in my raving gear. Well, he thought so anyway.

I still long and look out for Madchester nights to this day, and rave like I did in the past.

Rave On Baby

The next person to inscribe into Northern Monkeys doesn't want to divulge their name due to diverse elements – I have to respect their desire not to do so. They will call themselves Nova, for the record. Only they would like to throw a kaleidoscopic light on the rave scene in and around the north, through their spacious eyes. Also, the effects and feelings of raving; the euphoria, the enhancement, the clarity of emotion, the clubs, the music and the buzz. And has we say up north, "Eeeee. It were bloody good!"

Nova: a star that undergoes a cataclysmic eruption,
which produces an outburst of radiant energy and an
increase in luminosity, many thousands of times greater
than its original brightness, before subsequently
declining to its former state of body.

Nova: *Being born into a family full of fanatical Preston North End FC supporters, there was only one place I would spend most of my free time at weekends: Deepdale. Also, I've always thought that football, fashion and music have had some sort of allegiance with each other. In my case all three had a significant impact in my years as a teenager, and subsequently in my twenties, even possibly into my thirties too.*

My first match was as a seven year old in 1977; I remember being sat on the wooden seats of the 'Pavilion' and was amazed at the amount of people all in one place to watch a game of football. From that point onwards I was hooked. I also began to understand why the adults in the family would descend back to my grandparents house after a home game either euphoric or totally pissed off – no change there then, even today.

It was only really when I became a teenager that the 'terrace fashion' was something I started to fully notice. This would be around 1985. At the same time I finally managed to earn enough money (or blag my parents) to be able to buy some of the labels I'd either read about, seen at the match or heard through the terrace grapevine. I remember being at school sporting the only pair of single bar Pods and thinking I was the bee's knees, this shortly followed by a pair of double T-Bar design. God, what kudos, I tell you! I remember back then the well known, not so secretive, warehouse over in Blackburn, just off Hayes Lane – the Kappa warehouse as it was known. Cheap Kickers and Kappa at knock down prices were the pickings.

Those items were teamed with Farahs, C17 jeans, Benetton rugby shirts and Ocean Pacific, Marc O'Polo, Fila, Sergio Tacchini, to name a few. My word, you weren't half labelled as a football casual. A label that was worn with pride, by many.

Along with this came the music. At first I tended to jump on the bandwagon and listen to the music I knew others were into because that's what people who were part of 'scene' did. The Housemartins were a firm favourite in the local pubs. I always remember a night in the Grey Horse pub on Fishergate, in Preston, that ended in Newcastle Brown Ale being thrown everywhere whilst a large group of revellers bounced around the top bar to one of The Housemartin's songs.

It was towards the end of the Eighties, 1988/89, that I got into the up-and-coming rave scene, a part of my life which was dysfunctional, manic and fucking brilliant. I'd got in with a crowd from Lancashire through a YTS I was on; they were from the areas of Accrington and Rishton, near Blackburn. One of the lads had an older brother who was into setting up venues for people to go to, playing music which wasn't readily available in shops and wasn't played in the pubs and clubs. Sett End was one such venue in the Shadsworth area of Blackburn. It was a large room set up with some decks and huge speakers; the noise was phenomenal, as were the sounds that would belt out of them. There were people from all over the county, all crammed into one small building, enjoying the sounds and socialising in a way I'd never experienced before.

But this was just the tip of the iceberg. We'd gone to Sett End a few times but never stayed until the end – that was until we'd been tipped off about an 'illegal' rave in the Tockholes area of the town. I knew where this place was because of the not-so-secret Kappa warehouse. So off we went along with hundreds of other ravers looking for the venue, who were already causing havoc in the surrounding areas of Blackburn. There were traffic jams everywhere, with coppers flying around not being able to cope with the sheer weight of traffic, or people. We ended up abandoning the car and going on foot through fields to get to the rave. I'd got this far so there was no way I was going to turn back. First you could hear the bass in the distance – it got louder and louder the nearer you got – which was a rush in itself. There were people everywhere; they were coming from all directions. Those people who had completed the journey were already dancing to the tunes oblivious to what was happening in the town behind them. We hitched up with some familiar faces, and listened to a few tunes.

We'd been there for about an hour when all of a sudden the boys in blue raided the place – that meant run, and run as fast as you can. They were mainly interested in seizing the electrical gear that was being used like the generator, speakers and decks, and the 'odd' bit of substances that were knocking around the venue. Hot-footing it back through the fields was as exciting in itself; the coppers were chasing everyone, including us, so we ended up hiding near a school just off Rock Lane. We must have been there for an hour before we decided to run as fast as we could back to the car and leave the area as quickly as possible. What a night. And what a rush. I was definitely going to do it again, and again, and again, as it happened.

During my exploration of East Lancs I'd met up with fellow Prestonians, one of whom was a hairdresser. I'd gone to her shop to say hello one Saturday, when she said they were off to Blackpool that night to a club that had newly opened, called Hacketts. This a club that was situated in the Palatine Buildings, just by the car parks off Yeadon Way. This place was awesome – people from all over the north-west descending to the club ' just' to dance the night away. We went there week after week to listen to the likes of Dave Charnley, who played Italian/piano house music, what you would class as your 'old skool' music nowadays. Blackpool ended up being the real hotspot for clubs, with the likes of Oz and Sequins opening, another couple of clubs which we decided to frequent as a change to Hacketts. Sequins was probably my favourite of the Blackpool clubs – it had a resident DJs mix factory. One of the DJs descended from Greater Manchester (Oldham if my memory serves me correct) and had a spot on one of the commercial radio stations in the Manchester district and a bar in the Oldham area too.

By this point it was 1990, and there were clubs popping up everywhere. We'd got bored with the Blackpool scene and decided to go and explore other venues. I remember a memorable night at Quadrant Park in Liverpool. I saw people in terrible states and things that would make your hair curl. I recall one clear incident with a lad upstairs; it was a big venue and a few of us were sat down taking a breather when this long haired lad stopped right in front of us. He then asked for a swig of my water, which I duly obliged. We then witnessed him put some LSD in his eye! Oh my God! Within minutes he was completely off his box.

We then ventured further afield, down south, travelling to Coventry and the club Eclipse; we'd heard really good things about this place and wanted to give it a try. Pure shite, that was our opinion of the place, and we left after about an hour. The music was more techno, which was the way lots of clubs were going, and it wasn't my/our scene. We then stumbled across this club in Coventry that had been visited by a friend of one of our gang. This place was run by Rastas; and I had one of the scariest experiences of my life on our visit. It didn't cost much to get in and the music was purely Rastafarian, but I felt totally out of my depth from the minute we walked in. There was an equal mix of whites and blacks, and I got chatting to a few different people inside. After the experience of our scouse friend putting LSD in his eye, and other aspects of additives, happenings in this place made him and others look like pussy cats. This place and the folk there were a real eye-opener. There were people jacking up behind the speakers happily sharing needles, crack pipes being offered round, and any kind of drug you could have *cared for or wanted to try. Hence our night in the midlands came to an abrupt end.*

Thursday nights were always good nights to go out. We sometimes went to Manhattan Heights in Blackburn, or Park Hall in Chorley, but one Thursday we decided to try a place called the Pleasure Dome in Bolton. It was here that I was to meet a group of fellow ravers; from that point onwards I was to spend a lot of time with them for the next few years.

I travelled over with just one another friend, and it wasn't very busy in the club, but I spotted another group whom I thought I recognised. They came from Salford and Swinton – my God, what a fun time was in store for us in the not too distant future. We arranged to meet up on the Saturday at the same place when it was supposed to be busier.

We went as planned and met up with some of the old Hacketts crowd too. DJ Wellie and Green Bins were DJ-ing that night and we had a fantastic time; in fact I didn't want the night to end. At this point many of the illegal raves were fading out, you would only find one if you dropped lucky, because the hassle involved didn't make it worthwhile. One of the lads from Salford had a mate who was the manager of a bar in the Castlefield part of Manchester, so we decided to go back there later. He had a free rein and I even got to spin a few records on the old Technics 12/10s. Also after going to the Pleasure Dome a few times, the gang from Salford mentioned about going to the Haçienda – a place which was to become 'home' for many, many months.

I'd been to the Haçienda before in the late Eighties, to watch some bands that had been signed to Factory Records. Little did I know at the time who exactly these bands were and how big they would become. One was The Happy Mondays, and I was really into them; they were an alternative to the house scene, but still had tracks used by DJs in some of the clubs.

The night I returned to the Haçienda, with the mates, was a Saturday; it was warm outside and we went to Dry Bar which was in the city centre further up Oldham Street from Affleck's Palace. It was full of very groovy people, to coin a phrase. We had a few beers and then ventured down to Whitworth Street to the club. There were queues right round the block; one side of the queue was for the VIP entrance, the other for us common people. After approaching the ticket booth you were welcomed by a huge picture of Anthony Wilson (RIP) and bouncers that looked like they ate bricks for breakfast, dinner, and tea. Inside you were overwhelmed by the bass, in fact, it made your chest pound it was so powerful. This old warehouse was simple and rustic, and the best club I've ever been to.

Week after week we would travel down to Manchester, drop off at one of the lads' houses in Salford, then head into town to Dry Bar and then on to the Haç. On one occasion we headed into town and met up with a friend of the Mancs who'd just come back from doing a Kibbutz. He introduced himself to us and we had a good chat about his travels and how humbling he'd found his experience. He also said he was waiting for a friend to arrive.

After about half-an-hour there was this almighty commotion in the bar; towards our group swaggered in Bez, the freaky dancer from the Mondays. Here I was in Manchester, with one of my heroes in Dry Bar making small talk – small world isn't it? It turned out the lad whom we'd come to meet was an ex-roadie for the Mondays and was still good friends with them all. That night we went to the Haç, with Bez in tow, and wait for it, we entered into the best club in England, maybe the world at that time, through the VIP entrance. Oh, what kudos that was, I tell you. This became a regular occurrence for us, as the lads knew most of the bouncers, and the ex-roadie had put us down as guests as he was still very much in with management.

"I'd been to the haçienda before in the late eighties
to watch some bands that had been signed onto
factory records, little did I know at the time who exactly
these bands were and how big they would become."

I spent much of my time in Manchester from then on. Especially with my good friend Mr B, mainly in Salford and Swinton, and got to know the Mondays quite well. That meant more mayhem and dysfunction, but it was well worth it. One of the best nights I had was a New Year's Eve party that the Haçienda held, which was probably in 1991/92. It was rammed with local celebs and some pretty well known Mancunian band members. The resident DJ at the time was a Scottish DJ called Graeme Park. He, along with Mike Pickering and John Dasilva, had made the Haçienda famous throughout the land, if not the world. Odyssey were headlining, and came on around midnight after we welcomed in New Year. As they played 'Native New Yorker', I had a sudden urge to clamber up on stage. I was holding hands with the female singer, with the bouncers turning a blind eye. In front of hundreds of people I was dancing with a top American disco group; my five minutes of fame, something which will live with me for forever.

Another night that sticks in my mind is the 10th birthday party. For anyone who is familiar with the club – if not, you missed out – they opened the doors from the upstairs seating area across the canal; there were fairground rides, games and all sorts of ridiculous things to keep young-at-heart adults occupied. Again the club was awash with different musicians. I decided to go on the big wheel and climbed into a carriage to be joined by Tim Burgess, the lead singer of The Charlatans and a ' friend!' It was just that type of club, and that sort of era, where fame and popularity didn't matter. You were all the same – no big deal really.

It was round this time that 'Revenge', 'Upfront' and various other all-nighters were popping up around the region. We'd been to a few of the Upfront ones – Stalybridge springs to mind – and once I started dancing, perched high up, on a speaker without a care in the world at about 5am. I've no idea what made me do that! Many of these venues were running to stop the illegal ones continuing. The authorities could keep their eye on you, and basically, contain you.

I remember once heading to the Lake District with the gang from Salford to a rave near Ulverston, in a disused quarry. It was staged in a huge tent with fairground attractions in the venue and a huge chill out area. What a buzz that was – I spent most of the time either dancing on the railings in the main tent or twizzing around on the bucking bronco. In fact, the security kept paying me back on every time I came off – I must have been entertainment for the night.

On the way back home we stopped off and went to visit 'Rave in t'Cave'; what a surreal experience that was. It was a right trek from the car park; it was literally a generator and some decks set up in a cut out of the rocks. I believe Bob Greaves from Granada Reports paid the place a visit the week after doing a report. Thank God it was the week after is all I can say!

The last all-nighter I ever went to was organised by the Wigan based 'Revenge' lads. This group of lads had been on the scene at the same time, and mainly in the same clubs as me, only it was sometimes hard remembering names and faces because you were having that much fun. I'd been to several of the other nights they'd arranged, but this was a big one that the authorities had worked with them to organise it. You could travel over to different parts of Wigan and get bussed into the venue. It was a huge tent set up on the outskirts of town. Here were the likes of Wellie, Green Bins and other local DJs spinning all the favourites from the era that was sadly starting to come to an end. I saw many familiar faces that night, and had a great time with the old Blackburn, Preston and Manchester crews.

There are still many other clubs, too numerous to mention, that we went to on our five year mission, so here's just a few: I've got to give a special mention to Angels in Burnley, and a local DJ called Mark Freejack who was resident there, and is still spinning the wheels of steel to this day.

Renaissance in Nottingham; this is where I saw Alison Limerick with my good friend Mr B from Manchester. Monroe's in Blackburn, which I sadly only went to a couple of times. Also, of course, good old home grown venues in Preston like

Byron's; it were small place, but bloody rocking. And of course, UCLAN's very own Feel.

Nowadays it's a good old, old-skool iPod party in the conservatory which invites very strange stares off the kids. But looking back, it wasn't half a buzz having a bit of chaos and mayhem, plus other 'stuff', in my life. Not half bad for a Northern Monkey from the back of beyond. These were times that will unfortunately never be experienced, or repeated, ever again. Rave on baby!

We Danced With The Devil In A Haze Of Moonlight

The next injection into the main artery of Northern Monkeys, with a pulsating veined account of the agony and ecstasy of raving and misbehaving and Class A drugs, especially heroin, is from a bloke called Ja'. Ja' tells his hard-hitting story in three poignant chapters of his life to date. A very heartrending story it is too. From the highs of 'E', to the lows of smack, he bears his soul. He tells just how heroin and other drugs left him a broken man on more than one occasion, and how he stared at the Grim Reaper face-to-face in his retreatism. I know only too well how 'H' can takeover someone's life having witnessed the drug ravage a best mate, who's still in its grasp to this day, and how it has also tragically taken other close friends' lives.

Fortunately, due to a combination of a strong state of mind and will power, dedicated doctors' medical skills, and sheer luck, Ja', has lived to tell his obsessive rollercoaster tale. Because if you dance with the devil, sometimes the devil takes the hindmost.

I guess happiness is not a state you want to be in all the time

John Belushi.

Ja': *You could ask me a thousand times if I would change my life and regret my actions; would I have been a different person? Could I have done better? Achieved much more? The answer is NO! There are some things that cannot be replicated and I consider myself very lucky to have lived and experienced an era which I hold close to my heart.*

It all began around a time when I had met a certain chap from Leeds, attending Hull College. He was much older than me. Carried himself with a swagger and wore his clobber with style; Aquascutum long mac, cords and Clarks Wallabies. He was an avid follower of Leeds Utd too. The laughs I had and the things I learned were to shape my life forever. We would smoke spliffs in between lessons and pop ohms (acid) when we didn't attend college. My diploma in Construction Engineering was going downhill, it was losing its edge, but I was having the time of my life. Dancing between pavement cracks, watching the clouds turn into demons, and been chased around college for skinning up in the toilets. It didn't last long for my counterpart to be excluded from education, and for the first time, I felt alone. I had a void, and I needed to fill it,

Long gone are the days of euphoric nights and hazy days; the stories are embedded deep in my memory of my experience of the rave culture in the north, though. I grew up on, which is open to debate, the largest council estate in Hull, Bransholme. This was a place where you didn't just grow up; you battled with turmoil, egos and status; all of which either destroyed your soul or took you to places not many would want to experience.

For me it was a pleasure coupled with fear; learning how to be streetwise from an early age. I always seemed to hang around with the generation above me; I would look at lads earning good money on the estate and wanting some of these riches too. Dressing in SPW, Chipie and Chevignon, these guys would travel around the UK and come back looking smart as fuck. They participated in the football culture; fanatical about Hull City.

I aspired to be like them, like many a teenager growing up in the culture.I had nothing else in my life. To make my own statement I decided to get a swallow tattooed on my hand and England on my forearm. It's funny when you look back and see the error of your ways. But just by doing this, I seemed to be accepted and was about to experience gang culture.

This was a world I never knew existed, and it was harsh. There were two main areas on the estate, north and south. I was South Bransholme. My outspoken confidence as a young gun had been noticed and I soon became part of Swallow's Barmy Army. We would hang around a local pub and venture into South Bransholme looking for a rumble with the enemy. It soon became apparent where this hostility was coming from. Club culture was its excuse; a battle for territory – more of which I will mention later. One thing I remember well was a cold winter's night and being confronted by a gang of about 20 lads who stood across what we called 'the divide' on the estate. No-one was prepared to make the first move. There was lots of shouting and bravado. This was my opportunity, I thought. If I was going to survive on this estate of high unemployment and uninspired ideas I needed to make a name for myself. I was 17, wearing the clobber, feeling cool. But I wanted more. Here I go.

Walking over to the divide in front of our enemy, North Bransholme, I stood there, knees trembling, and asked who wanted it. The fuse paper was lit. A traffic cone *was launched at me and I was pulled back. This resulted unfortunately in one of their lot being stabbed and everybody running around like headless chickens. I had gained kudos. I had earned respect. And from here on in my rave experience began.*

By now I was dressing in Berghaus, looking the part. Every weekend started on a Thursday; Juliets, the birthplace for Hull raving, alongside Welly Club. I was moving in circles with lads twenty years older than me. I felt on top of the world. Mind you, I felt so sorry for people paying £15-£20 for a California or Yellow (E's) because I wasn't.

Rave culture is something that you cannot explain. Everybody has their own interpretation of the cult.

Throughout the years, I've been lucky enough to witness grown men cry to certain records, and been involved in after-parties with the infamous Larry Heard. I've also been handed carrier bags full of magic mushrooms. It's an amazing sight to physically see what I would explain as raining indoors.

Through sheer sweat and debauchery the ceiling of Welly Club began to drip. Smoke machines, a sweet smell fills the room; darkness engulfs you, and your acid trip took you places your mind never knew possible. I would stand and observe lads echoing E's, whizz, trips. By now I had been stupid to move up the ladder and knock out drugs, only to close friends at this stage, though.

There are no happy endings in drugs unless you finally realise the error of your ways, or if you let your ego manifest into the underworld where it takes you. You either end up dead, stitched up or serving time at Her Majesty's Pleasure.

From the humble beginnings of entering this world I had experienced and witnessed all three of the above. Fortunately I am still here to tell the tale.

Life was becoming increasingly difficult come the early Nineties. Football was at the forefront of my mind – Hull City a passion. An adventure and a lesson learned all too quickly. You soon begin to realise the error of your ways due to harsh experiencing which either you learn to deal with quickly, or you'll sink fast.

I was still dressing in all the nice gear and partying from Thursday 'till Sunday. Attending the footy, travelling with the lads and lapping up what life had not yet offered me. I was hanging around with folk a lot older than me and began to notice a rapid decline in quite a few. These were smart gents; bringing in clobber from Manchester and people I aspired to. I remember paying £180 for a Chipie jumper which was a pure hand-knitted wool with a speckled cable knit pattern, and was two-tone too, and smart as fuck. Again, this gave me kudos and was the start of a long standing obsession.

The lads I moved around with used to be in the clubs running the show, standing their ground and enticing me further into their world. But there was something going very wrong too. Jellies (liquid temazepam) were on the scene in Hull by now and the perfect comedown after a hard session. But these came at a price; and I'm not talking money. Close friends began to do stupid things which they couldn't remember after abusing the wobblies; accusations of double crossing, ripping each other off and unprovoked attacks were the order of the day. The Hull mentality is very slow; and we soon found our solace in downers. Hull has always been known for its abuse of these. And for me, these moreish tablets ended in my first prison sentence – three months for kicking somebody's front door in under the influence, and not even knowing I had done this!

I was released six weeks later to nothing. My dad had kicked me out after finding me asleep with a bag of downers in my bedroom. I had decided to neck 10 while counting them out. So, I walked straight back into what I knew best, clothes, football and drugs. Lesson learned – not.

I remember going straight to Prem Clothing shop and buying a full velour Fila tracksuit. And once again my ego kicked in. When and wherever you grew up, or whatever society you were born into, one thing that's very apparent is that you will always be judged on your appearance looking back. Prison taught me nothing constructive, though. Hedon Road was like the council estate I grew up on, only with a roof on – home-from-home.

I tried to get myself into employment, but failed miserably. So, I chose the next best option, drugs. Temgesic was the drug of choice on the streets and I began to get involved with this. It soon spiralled out of control and I was soon to be faced with one of those moments in life where whichever decision you make, you know that it is going to shape your life forever.

Me and a pal couldn't get hold of any Tems, so he mentioned heroin, manipulating me into thinking they have exactly the same effect. I took him up on his offer and it didn't disappoint – my naivety showed. The damage I had seen from heroin in my youth was not enough to put me off. I was on the cloud, in the bubble, as soon as the poison hit my veins. Life was now beautiful. I had no worries.

Heroin puts you on the ever turning monotonous wheel, each day the same. Your focus is on one thing and one thing only. And once hooked, there is only one way 'it' takes you: down. I was addicted for eight years with my health deteriorating and body packing up. I was making rash decisions; getting involved in major situations, seeing people around me overdose and serving ridiculous amounts of time inside. I never learned. I'd be inside, then out for a while, then back in – with another habit to rattle from. Methadone was now my medicine and I used to travel around North Yorkshire using the six week temporary doctor technique asking for benzos, Nitrazepam and Diazepam. Coupled with heroin this was a deadly concoction. I ventured back into clubbing for a while but folk were not what they once were. I would watch the people I looked up to, playing imaginary cricket on the dance floor and other daft stuff. I'd also be ejected from clubs for suspicion of robbing places in and around the city to fund my habit.

Life was tough. Alone and afraid, but still masking my vulnerability, I had an ego built from my roots to uphold, too, I used to tell myself. This ego kicked in again on a day out in a nicked car, this after ransacking a village, the local shops and getting banged up over the weekend. Now I was with a well respected lad who knew nothing else but prison. We ended up in the dock praying for bail, because we'd had no methadone all weekend. Both of us were very fragile. P, the lad I was with, was remanded in custody and taken away. I awaited my decision and was given bail. Now just stop for a minute and look at the predicament that I am in here.

My pal, the co-accused, is remanded and I've been given bail. How did this look? Not a chance he was going on his own, the street rule kicked in and after a 'Fuck you' to the judge, I'd made my stance. I then began kicking off and abusing whoever I could. I got my warped wish. I was remanded too.

You can imagine the cheers under the courts as I walked back into the holding cells. I felt boss, on top of the world! P, and other lads, couldn't believe it and this news spread like wildfire around C wing once we were banged up. Again through my actions I was considered a geezer. In all honesty, and once behind my cell door, I knew I had made the wrong decision when the stomach withdrawal cramps kicked in. I ended up serving nine month and shanghaied from Hull via Oldbury to Armley, Leeds.

Upon my release, I continued with the wheel of addiction. Why the fuck did I do it; get banged up, endure the pain of withdrawal, only to come back out and go straight back on it? I did it because I was an addict. I was now beginning to overdose quite regularly too. But I never learned. Close pals were also dying through their additions. Why wasn't I, I began to think? I was going nowhere fast and the edge of no return. There are many stories I could reel off and hopefully people who fall into the perils of addiction would learn and realise, but in all honesty an addict will not listen until he is ready or has no other option left in his armour.

There was a culmination of events which changed my mind-set, and made me really think about what was happening with my life. There were two serious shootings on the estate and it wasn't nice. I had been stopped in the street unawares by plain clothes while doing my thing, and been questioned about certain people. I was also visited by police unannounced at my flat and had to sit on an ounce of heroin so it wasn't spotted. Not bagged up either, so I wasted a good chunk. So imagine explaining that to the geezer who laid out the money. And I knew I had lost total control when I made probably the worst decision ever. I was chasing my tail playing catch up on the money front too.

One of the local dealers got locked up and I ended up with his missus one night. The morning after I took his phone and carried on his trade, only this time I didn't have heroin, it was QT (instant tea) I was selling. It looks very similar. I ran around with another lad doing this for a few days before the word got out. Eventually I heard the guy I ran with was set upon in the city centre in daylight with iron bars and beat to within an inch of his life. And the word was I was next. I lived in fear and was on self destruct. Luckily for me I was offered a life line – rehab. I grabbed it, and off I went within four weeks. My mother played a big part in my great escape, and for that I thank her dearly.

To rehabilitate yourself successfully you have to be prepared to give your soul and share your deepest fears. Was I ready for this? I didn't really have a choice. If I were a cat then, my nine lives were well and truly up. This was my chance to echo what everybody had said to me in the past. "Bellie, you're too good for all that" I arrived at rehab in a haze. On the train up I had taken to many benzos. I didn't have a clue what I was doing and only made it to rehab late in the evening where straight away the senior residents segregated me to an annexe, away from the rest of the community. I now know this was to keep them safe and not have me set them up. It was a community-run rehab, whereby the residents ran the house and you would be given more responsibility the longer you were there. I can't remember much else during my segregation apart from the unthinkable happening. That night I must have been that out of it that I pissed the bed, in a room that I was sharing with another newbie. What an embarrassment. I was placed in with rest of the community, 36 in total, the next day amidst the whispers that I wet the bed. This could have destroyed me and I really didn't want to just leave there and then, because I'd nowhere to go. I couldn't go back to Hull, and I needed the rehab to save my life.

Luckily over time I blagged the other residents and I even joked about my so-called incident. Life in there became a little easier. Rehab is very structured but everything you do while there is for a purpose. At first when I saw other residents standing up after the morning meeting singing songs and dancing, it freaked me out. There was a lot of hugging and positive vibes though. We all mentored each other and I learned, that is what it was all about, helping each other. It was hard at first, don't get me wrong. I suffered for three weeks withdrawing off methadone. But the moment I knew that I was normal, life was quite beautiful again. I was sweeping the drive, with it being quite a warm day, and all of a sudden I heard a chainsaw in the background. Somebody nearby was cutting the hedge, and then I heard birds singing in the trees. This might seem a little strange, but when you are *on gear, you don't really notice anything other than your focus on your next hit. Life just revolves around your next fix. No natural sounds even enter your head. Well mine anyway. And at that moment I knew I had a chance to do the programme.*

Over time I had delivered my life story to the community, shared my fears and got to know some really good people who would remain my friends.

I laughed so hard during the 12 months, and shed many a tear too. My confidence was back. I had my swagger again. The thing with rehab is you see many people come and go; statistically only three percent stay clean out of a peer group. My time flew pretty fast once I had started to unravel all the pain inside me. A lot of my addiction was identified from the painful breakup of my parents and how I had never confronted them or asked them for answers. I had an addictive personality, and devoured anything I put my mind too until it offered no more. Then I tossed it aside and moved onto the next thing.

I graduated from rehab in 1999, was given a tenancy and left to take on what this world now had to offer me. I met my partner not long after rehab, and within four months we were living together. She was slightly older than me and worked in the social care field. She kept me safe, I was still vulnerable. I use to get anxious around people or in town. Kind of like when you come out of prison, they open the gates and everything is moving too fast for you to take in.

I soldiered on with my partner building up a nice little flat and I seemed to progress through life as any normal folk would. The only problem was, I didn't feel normal. There was something missing in my life and I identified that my addictive behaviour of searching for a buzz needed a direction. I then managed to get my foot in a door. I volunteered to help with student film crews and worked my way up to focus puller on 35mm cameras (cinema standard). Only it was never really what I enjoyed, but it was something to keep me occupied. From this form of volunteering I started getting invited to parties with my partner. Life seemed good again.

Then one Christmas I managed to get hold of some Ecstasy tabs from one of my film buds, and put them in a little box for my partner – she had been the same as me in her past and enjoyed the acid house era – thinking it would be a nice little New Year's tickle for us both. Her face lit up and we went out, found a club and danced the night away. This club was to become our institution for the next 3/4 years. Had I found my sanctuary again?

We partied hard every weekend; I was clean from hard drugs and loving the buzz of going out again. I got into the party scene in a big way, even having a moment on the dance floor one night, thinking to myself 'I can do what they do' – what the DJs doing, that is. So in between partying and working all week I would get myself some decks, CD mixers and practise away the night. By now I had fucked the film stuff off around 2001 after breaking my hand dry slope skiing. Once you're out the loop in that industry, you are almost forgotten about. It wasn't any skin off my nose; I didn't really like all the arse licking anyway. So I went back to the only thing I knew, UPVC Fabrication/window fitting. I earned good money and, with the missus working we continued to party hard.

I had broken into a nice little underground scene and started to play with what music I'd amassed. I became obsessive, buying and hunting records. I wanted all the obscure tunes and could see my addictive nature taking hold. But this was my drive; it was how I had always succeeded in life. By now we were travelling to Manchester for the infamous Electric Chair and taking more and more drugs. I had discovered truffles too – 'philosopher's stone', small walnut-esque treats which gave you a very nice buzz. I was also importing grow kits from Holland around the time when there was no classification on them. I gradually got to know who was who and started putting my own nights on, while enjoying some pretty crazy parties.

With DJing came cocaine, and I wasn't strong enough to turn it down. With all the knowledge in the world of where this kind of drug could take me I still got involved. And slowly I felt the decline again. I was now suffering from severe urine infections which hospitalised me up to three times a year. My kidneys were packing up, but I continued partying until I got septicaemia which nearly killed me. I was in hospital for eight weeks and came out so weak that I had to learn to walk again.

My partner and I had bought our first house and we were living a great life, doing normal things. We went away twice a year and bought a new car. We had responsibility in our lives. We had tried for kids for the last few years, but just put it not happening down to the drugs we were taking. So,

I got myself fit again and took up the gym. Again I became obsessive, this time with training and I started taking supplements and creatine to aid my goals. I was well aware of my personality destroying me again only with a different vice. I couldn't miss training, I had to go and pound my body at least five times a week.

By this time I was unhappy with window fitting and felt I needed to do something more. So being as erratic as I am, I packed the job in and miraculously one week later I saw an advert for a Substance Misuse Worker for a male homeless hostel. This was an opportunity for me to give something back to society, repay my dues. With my life experience I felt sure I could achieve this.

It didn't quite go according to plan; I got an interview but was offered a casual position with the hostel. I took this on and slowly worked my way up to a senior member of staff. This is still what I do today alongside another little venture I sunk my teeth into along the way. I am also instructing physical intervention techniques to external agencies who work with challenging behaviour. But for the first time in my life I feel pretty complete, there is no void inside me. I am not trying to deflect my own behaviour or mask my insecurities though. Granted, I still had a very healthy appetite for very nice clobber, but I'd now earned that right to do so and continued with my passion which has been evident throughout my life and I still do. And I still go out and party, when the likes of The Idjuts/Theo Parrish or Rahaan are playing nearby and love to let loose. I think a blowout is required every once in a while.

Do I have any regrets when thinking back? I said no at the beginning of my life changing experiences, but the main thing I feel guilty about is the painful split from my missus in 2007. I took 20 grand off her and walked away from our home with just a bag over my shoulder.

Within 18 months I was penniless; I had relapsed big time, spiralling out of control, wasting money on stupid fast cars, thinking I was somebody. I clearly wasn't. And I was back in hospital with embolism and clots in my legs with also a nasty infection on my lung. It wasn't looking good at one stage. The doctors battled for three months trying to fight the infection, which they finally did and I was nursed back to health. During this period I realised I wanted, and needed, my partner back in my life. I had stupidly lost the one person in my life who understood me as myself, no mask, just me.

I remember being sat on the end of my bed after four months in hospital and hearing footsteps on the ward. I didn't even have to turn to look it was. I knew who this was. It was my partner. She'd heard the news about my condition and decided to come and see me. We didn't say anything to each other. It was one of those moments where you just have to look into each other's eyes and you both just know what it is your both thinking. My angel was back.

And that is where I am at today. Find the balance and we can succeed.

A typical Friday night/Saturday morning somewhere in or around Blackburn.

'Are you on one, matey?'

Phil Thornton, author of the casuals bible, Casuals. Phil
Thornton, old skool tweed and man's best friend. The Farm:
dressing & tunes, but not for the Dolly's.

Pink Adidas Gazelle 'wheels'.

Proper mags, for proper dressers.

Setting new standards, Casual Connoisseur.

High Kicks in rhapsodic times.

| Stone Island, ultra-light reversible jacket and vintage Izod Lacoste ski hat.

| Immortal Massimo Osti, Left Hand Thermojoint jacket.

The streets and clubs of Manchester where the last subculture, Madchester, was spawned.

A quintessential Benetton rugby shirt from yesteryear; but still a much sought after item to this day.

It's still Grim up North!

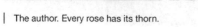

The author. Every rose has its thorn.

Stepping for forwarded; Stansfield, classic modern-day threads. Jonny the Mod; suave and sophisticated.

Always the ones up for making a buck, casuals/dressers, especially to fund their clobber needs, 'booze cruises' and 'fag & baccy runs' abroad became instrumental in the Eighties and Nineties. A casual/dresser in France 1986 donning a dapper New Man waterproof jacket in the pouring rain looking rather pissed-off.

| Scooter Boys: The second coming of mod/scooter boys.

| The evolving, primordial casuals.

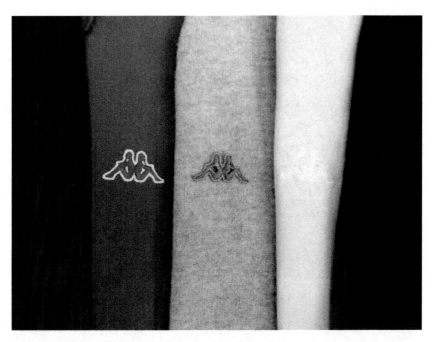

Robe di Kappa, and the Omini logo; Kappa's beautiful symbolic emblem is both eye catching, and a masterpiece work of art. Kappa was a staple label with northern casuals in the early Eighties too.

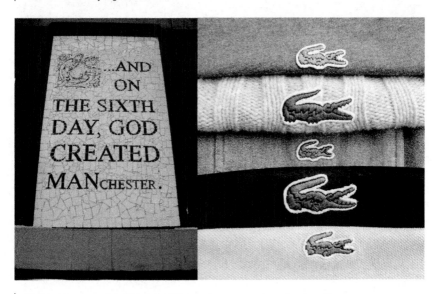

Madchester, so much to answer for? The ageless, snappy Lacoste crocodile.

345

Even in rhapsodic times some hoolies weren't 'on one'. Boneville, another label by the main man, Massimo Osti.

Adidas Bermuda leisure shoes.

In 1977, about to witness the upsurge of scooter riders during the second coming of mod.

Our Culture: the stand against modern football.

| Wade Smith: the original store in Liverpool. Feast your eyes.

| A shop to get your mitts, and feet, on your Adidas Holy Grails.

Gary Aspden, Adidas global brand guru, everything can be traced back to Darwen, Lancs.

Barry Bown, keeping the flame of quality burning bright at JD Sports.

10

HEALTHY OBSESSION

Being a casual/dresser is not *all* about appearance and labels but, the *look* and certain trademark brands do play a major part in the cult. So in this section lads illustrate the irony and influence of what the casual/dresser culture is about for them, and the laborious lengths they've gone to in order to obtain their Grails. The perseverance and continuing aim of sourcing that next essential label amongst a select number of forward thinking individuals has brought a manifold of labels to the attention of the masses that designers and marketers would never have thought possible when they initially commenced in the trade. Though in some cases, to the annoyance of the designer, that he never ever wanted to be associated with. They even won't serve certain 'types' of lads in their boutiques. Also some designers only tailor their range sizes to fit wafer-thin, anorexic skinny sorts, not your BIG-boned lads.

Along with designers not wanting their threads worn by casuals/dressers, specific branded attire is frowned upon by many sections of society and tarnished with the hooligan-brush, even though the casual/dresser labels and look have long influenced the styles and trends of the High Street too. Owners of mega capacity sportswear outlets, which are situated on retail parks and in city centres, sell to the commonalty, which claws in large-scale wealth, as you would have read in the 'Social Entrepreneurship' chapter. Though certain conglomerates spew out crappy substandard, time-honoured old-school terrace faves in every colour way imaginable, which is *oh so wrong*. And some designers churn out heaps of second rate clobber for the 'blinded by the label' brainwashed consumers who just want the brand cos it's worn by the masses. Small independent brands are where it's at nowadays; for me, that is.

But lads do love a label, with some casuals/dressers having an obsessive-compulsive disorder for togs, as in, compulsive buying and obsessive hoarding. And I'm as guilty as anyone; I've the other side of 50 coats in my closet. Not ever casual/dresser has a form of neurotic-chronic malady, though.

The following articles are from authoritative, aplomb and panache lads.

The Osti Influence

One in the know lad, Marc, indicates that apart from cleaves of northern outposts dressing down, others stepped it up a gear. He also tells of the shops that these lads shopped at. Marc also heaps preponderance laudation on a certain man's goals on producing outwear that would give results just as the label stated and, looked the dogs dangly bits too.

Marc: *If Adidas had best represented the sportswear origins of the casual as a movement in the late 1970s and early 1980s, then Stone Island and the brands of Massimo Osti would best represent the next evolution of casual/dresser and become what was almost a uniform for the terrace dwelling dressers of the north. Expensive sportswear had whetted appetites for looking better than the next man, for travelling to European countries and paying (or not paying in the case of some gentlemen with particular skills) for brands like Adidas, Fila, and Sergio Tacchini. Sports shops on the continent had access to brands and pieces that were not commonly available, or even available at all in the UK. Exclusivity had been a key factor, with some stores still only selling certain goods in cases where proof of membership of an athletic or sporting organisation could be presented, a practice found widely in America for anyone trying to buy Nike or Adidas products.*

"If Adidas had best represented the sportswear origins
of the casual as a movement in the late 1970s and early 1980s,
then stone island and the brands of Massimo Osti would best represent the
next evolution of casual/ dresser and become what was almost a uniform
for the terrace dwelling dressers of the north."

Sportswear was, in the Seventies, reserved for those competing in sport, and arguably the journeys by football fans from the UK in the late Seventies to mainland Europe were as important as the dress code of the hip-hop community on the east coast of America in starting one of the widest common practices in the world for clothing today – wearing trainers when not doing sports. Finding unusual colour-ways in trainers such as Adidas Trimm Trab and Gazelle, or the rare sightings of three strap Adidas Stan Smith, might have been the highlight of those times, but the search for something smarter was the next step, and no matter how poor your wages may have been – that is if you had a job up north at the time – you had to find a way of looking better than the next man. Brands like Armani, Cerrutti, and Valentino began making appearances on the terraces with some, like Missoni, being more sought after than others. Knitwear was a particular item where a man would have to invest carefully. The right logo, such as the ubiquitous Armani eagle, became a signal of status. It showed that someone had knowledge of how to dress well, had either spent money or time getting the item, and had probably travelled some distance to at least London or further afield to France, Spain, Switzerland or Italy to obtain the garment.

It was about this time during the very start of the crossover that an Italian designer by the name of Massimo Osti was starting production of garments which took the best functional elements of sportswear but combined them with the cut and cloth associated with the premium Italian brands. Osti had been producing CP Company as a menswear collection for five years when he produced his first garments under the name Stone Island. The ethos was to push the use of fabrics with science more than fashion, and to add further elements of sportswear, and workwear, to create unique individual raiments. The name was arrived at when Massimo consulted his wife about some of the ideas for the brand. Massimo had a love of sailing and many say the brand was named after his boat. One of his first creations was a stonewashed cape with waterproof qualities which had a distinctive removable button on the badge on the mid chest area. For later creations, this badge would be moved to several locations before finally ending up on the left sleeve of the garments, in the process becoming one of the most identifiable logos in men's fashion.

The mid-Eighties would see Osti's penchant for experimenting with fabrics that set out the stall for the brand in years to come. Creations such as Raso Gommato (also known as raso ray) as a fabric meant you could have a natural fabric on the outside of a item of clothing or jacket with a rubber inside, making them largely waterproof and wind proof. He had already set out a standard for the company of using garment dying procedures – Stone Island apparel would typically start off as a cloth developed with scientific methods, then the cloth would be constructed *into vestments, and finally the colour would be decided upon and sprayed to the desired colour on to it.*

It's impossible to identify who did what first in bringing the brand to the UK, but as with sportswear, no retailers readily had the brand on their radar. Sightings of the brand at matches in the 1980s have caused much discussion. Early pictures of clubs involved heavily in Europe in the mid-Eighties throw up the earliest images of the brand's association with the continually evolving casual culture – a well known picture of some Aberdeen fans around 1985 is possibly the earliest available sighting of someone wearing the brand.

A few clued-up casuals experimenting with different brands caught on and clubs in London seemed to lead the first wave of Stone Island interest. Harrods had a renowned casual menswear designer section, located on its fourth floor and named 'Way In', which was possibly the first location within the UK to sell the brand, along with other stores in London like Jones, Quincy, Woodhouse, John Anthony, and Pie.

Massimo Osti spent some time developing colour changing fabric which was dependent on temperature. Inspired by his love of military uniforms, he spent time testing the fabric on beaches in cold waters to ensure the fabrics would change colour as designed – a picture released in recent years shows the designer pacing the beach, smoking what could well be Benson & Hedges and braving the elements in the name of good clothing. The fabric, once developed, was made in treated cotton cloth in camouflage colours, which is most commonly seen in a short Harrington jacket style. A much rarer form is the long parka coat with rabbit fur hood; as if colour changing camouflage wasn't enough to cope with wearing at one time. The fabric was also developed in synthetic, water resistant form; in half-zip padded cagoules which really kept out the elements. Shop 70, on Lamb's Conduit Street, near Holborn, became a destination for a select number of casuals and Stone Island fans in the early Nineties as they were able to source past seasons and sample clothing at ridiculously low prices. Stone Island Ice Jackets in both parka and Harrington styles were available at a fraction of their original prices at times, a huge difference to men who had been prepared to shell out £500 for these items. For some Stone Island fans in the north, the existence of Shop 70 came to them through word of mouth, a rumour which might not have been true. Those who made the journey to London on faith to find the store were rewarded with a great price on some classic pieces. And in the early Nineties, £500 still was considered a lot of money to spend on a jacket, even if it had become the norm to do so for so many.

Into the Nineties, as Stone Island grew, agents were needed to control distribution of the brand. The best known of these would be Fourmarketing in the UK, formed by four ex-employees of Gruppo GFT, who ensured their portfolio of brands appeared together where possible. An extremely tight rein was used to see that only certain stores with a good profile, and good adjacencies (retail term for brands which you see your brand sitting alongside) would be present in stores which were authorised Stone Island stockists. Popular Italian brands such as outerwear manufacturer Napapijri and a then cult (and quite small) jeans manufacturer called Replay, would have been seen alongside the brand.

During this time, some stores were allowed to purchase more of the product than anyone else. One of the best known stores in the south was Woodhouse in London. Woodhouse, as a chain of stores, built its success around the Stone Island brand. In the north, some locations were more prestigious than others when it came to a place to view Stone Island products.

***Flannels, Manchester**: When Flannels expanded to its Manchester city centre store in the 1980s, Stone Island became a key brand which added a more technical dimension to the traditional European high end designers carried by Neil Prosser, founder of the Flannels group, in his original store in Knutsford, Cheshire. The Flannels association with the brand was such that no other retailer was viewed as such an important destination for the brand in the north of England with close runners being Strand in Newcastle and Autograph in Birmingham. In its bigger cities, Flannels opened a slightly more casual-orientated shop named Life. Indeed the Life stores in Leeds and Manchester were great places to go for Stone Island with Life's staff in the Leeds store in particular being very knowledgeable about the brand.*

Brands that Life introduced as northern delicacies, such as Napapijri and Paul & Shark, sat very well alongside Stone Island as technical brands with superior fabric technologies, but the ultimate destination within the group remained the Manchester Flannels store, located off St Ann's Square. A small selection of men would have in depth knowledge on the brand. The director, Neil, is rumoured to have an encyclopaedia of knowledge on the brand, having worked with it for the best part of the 30 years. But if that wasn't enough, the store was for a time the working home of the country's biggest collector of Stone Island pieces.

The Keyzer Soze of Stone Island obsessives, this man was something of an urban legend until he surfaced on internet message boards in the late 2000s. Rumours had long been doing the rounds of a Lancashire-based man with a coat collection of 300, or even as many as 500 pieces. While he may have never had time to count them, it was said to be into the hundreds at the very least, and that was just outerwear. A healthy store discount can be very tempting it would seem.

***Cruise, Glasgow:** Cruise began as a store in Newcastle operated by Jim Gibson, a modest affair selling clothing aimed at men for nights out and in particular, gaining them access to night clubs. It was Jim's move further north to Edinburgh* *that led him to open a store with a serious list of brands, but it was his opening in Glasgow that gave a store with a legendary selection of Stone Island and CP Company products.*

Cruise became the biggest account for Stone Island in the UK for a time, and much of that was directed at the Glasgow store. The deceptive space was like a reverse of the Flannels store in Manchester, with a small street level area descending into a vast basement. Indeed the two were very similar concepts selling brands that were high end either from a designer or product orientated focus. The Glasgow store kept on for a number of years a glass cabinet which was used to house the original Stone Island ice jackets in their first release, a nice touch where other retailers might have ditched such items. It would house many highlight outerwear pieces over the years.

The benefit of having an extremely knowledgeable, hands on and fashion obsessive owner such as Jim Gibson, meant that Cruise went from strength to strength until he left the company following a buyout in 2006.

The Bureau, Belfast: *Michael Hamilton and Paul Craig opened The Bureau in Belfast in 1989 in a small shop in a city centre alleyway. Belfast had traditionally been a city that did not keep up with clothing trends, particularly at the high end happening in the other big cities in the north of the UK. Opening the store was a big risk, but a selection of brands unseen in the city expertly bought from the available seasons collections ensured an immediate dedicated following from men who cared about what they wore.*

Initial success with the Stone Island brand for the Bureau came in the Nineties where it sat alongside brands such as Paul Smith, Dries Van Noten, and other technical brands such as Napapijri. The smaller nature of the shop and the keen eye for the best pieces of the owners ensured that the selection available in the Bureau was very impressive. The Nineties would typically see a scramble as soon as the items arrived, with sell outs typical of most of the collection year on year. The store expanded to larger premises but continued with good collections of Stone Island alongside other premium brands from a product focused background.

Today the store remains as a quality independent with a huge reputation for stocking the best brands and being ahead of its time with bringing in largely unheard of brands before they make it big in the UK. Many people, including Paul Smith, continue to see it as one of the best independent clothing retailers in Europe.

A key incident in the brand's association with football related violence came in 1995 when England visited Dublin for a ' friendly' match with the Republic of Ireland. Thousands of English fans descended on the capital for what was initially a good humoured *build up to the game, with no problems reported in the city centre. The problems came as the match began shortly after the singing of the British national anthem. Some items were thrown between opposing fans with England fans being particularly aggrieved in the aftermath that these had included cans filled with urine. Alleged pro-IRA chants could not be heard on the television coverage, but when the Republic of Ireland scored, the worst stadium violence seen in years erupted on the biggest stage possible. England fans fought with police and ripped up the stadium using whatever was possible – huge planks of wood and seats – to throw into opposition fans and onto the pitch below.*

A few made Nazi salutes, and many more goaded everyone around them. And as the cameras zoomed in on the away section, massive amounts of England fans with Stone Island knits and jackets could be seen, easily identifiable from the Stone Island badge.

From The Old Smoke, To One's Own Back Yard, In Search Of 'The' Grail.

As you have just read, Massimo Osti was the Italian goose who laid golden eggs and had the Midas touch plus many "Eureka" moments, too. His conventional formulaic styles and scientifically advanced brands are time-honoured classics that have standout masterpieces from each and every season. Trademark brands such as Chester Perry, CP Company, Stone Island, Boneville, Left Hand and WWW are all seen worn still today and Osti also lent his ideas and golden touches to many more products and labels. His timeless, iconic jackets are the Mille Miglia,

Ice Jacket and Metropolis, to name just three of several. And someone who sought out, and still does, such jackets and other classic items is Adil Hoxha.

Adil: *During the European Football Championships in 1992, any 'attendees' of a certain ilk will remember the shop (whose name escapes me) with branches in Denmark – Copenhagen – and Sweden – Malmo and Stockholm – which had untold Osti dead stock gear. Not just the past season, we're talking about Eighties specials such as jeans with the rubber pads on the knees (like the jackets of the same era which had them on the elbows), Ice Jackets, CP under 16 (very rare at the time, in the UK), you name it, they probably had it... but not for long. As in repayment for the Viking invasions of the UK, it was decided that the stock in these shops needed to be pillaged. That is with the exception of one lad (I think he was from Gloucester) who was caught bragging about how he'd had it away with a Stone Island coat he was wearing, only for his pals to arrive on the scene and say he'd bought it!*

It was that good a find that further visits were made by some lads over the next few months. I don't know what happened to the shop in the end but, I went to Gothenburg in 1995 and in conversation with an English lad living over in Sweden, I found it had long since gone.

At the same time, 1992, London had its own version initially known as Walker & Webster, this before changing its name to Shop 70. I first heard about the shop at some point in early 1991 though. A couple of lads I knew had seen a lad wearing a rare Stone Island scarf and he'd told them it was from a shop near Holborn. I then met someone sporting a black Stone Island bubble jacket who told me about a shop called Walker & Webster on Grays Inn Road. So off I went to London with my pal and his then girlfriend.

On arriving in London, we walked the length of Grays Inn Road twice, in desperation, to no avail. We were about to give up when one of us suggested we call directory enquiries from a phone box and see if they have a listing (to any of the younger readers, I know it's hard to believe but, this was before mobile phones, we had to use phone boxes). Anyway, success, and we knew where we're going. So off we head to Lamb's Conduit Street. And upon our arrival, we find we're in an Aladdin's cave of classic Osti gear: blue to pink Ice Jackets from, I think, summer 1989 or 1990, Stone Island cycling goggles, and Boneville driving goggles too, plus an array of sought-after wares – it was like being a kid let loose in a sweetshop. We must've been in there for about three hours just touching and admiring the stuff. I really wanted one of those blue to pink Ice Jackets, a bit like a cagoule, which were a snip at £119. But for some reason I let my pal and his girlfriend persuade me to buy a pinkish purple see-through sample Stone Island jacket for £79 – I must say it was a nice jacket though. Only one of my biggest regrets is that I didn't purchase the Ice Jacket instead.

I went back to the shop a few times when I was in London, only as with any bargain shop, it was one of those hit-and-miss places, a case of being in the right place at the right time. I picked up a nice sample CP jacket once from the 994 season range in late 1995 for £125, one that Woodhouse on Oxford Street tried to sell me for £400 the previous year! And at the same time they had 994 brown Mille Miglia, the lined version, at the same price.

My last visit was on the eve of France '98: the company I worked for at the time merged with one based near London Bridge, and everything was to be moved up to our offices in Cheshire. A handful of us were sent down for a couple of days to help the transition to our department, and for some reason whoever had made the travel arrangements decided to put us in some hotel fleapit near Euston – there wasn't even a bar, you had to use the one at their 'sister' hotel over the road, but that's another story. Anyway, on the first night we went for some scran down by Russell Square, headed up towards Holborn for a few beers, and we ended up drinking on

Lamb's Conduit Street. As we walked past Walker & Webster, I spotted what appeared to be a vintage three-quarter length, cream Stone Island mac in the window.

Next day I decided to clock-off at around 3pm and get back to the shop and possibly make a purchase. And If I remember correctly, they had two in there, at £175 each. They had brown rubber pads on the elbows, and in the centre of the back, a matching rubber rectangle embossed with the words 'Stone Island' – typical features from that era. I must've spent a good hour in the shop deliberating on whether or not to buy it. Would I dare wear it when out with the lads? Would I look like a member of the James gang on a bank job? Would I look like a flasher... and other such thoughts?

Eventually I decided against a purchase on the basis that I really wouldn't wear such a mac, and the cash would be better spent on a forthcoming holiday to Portugal. Not a great regret, although come the middle of the Noughties when you could get top dollar for stuff on eBay, I'm sure I would've got a good return on the purchase.

I did venture back down to Lamb's Conduit Street a couple of years later in the hope that it was still going to be rammed to the rafters with goodies – but sadly it was no more. It had been replaced by French shirt maker Café Coton, and is sadly now a Starbucks!

One final point on Walker & Webster; there was a stunning 'mature' woman (I was in my early to mid-20s at the time) who worked in there – I don't know if she was the owner's wife, or one of the staff's mothers, but I challenge you to find someone who went in the shop and didn't have the hots for her following their visit.

Other notable mentions for establishments with excellent shelves of Osti deadstock gear include; Tissoti in Knutsford, circa 1997. They had a small shop back in 1997, this prior to becoming a haunt of footballers' wives and 'lads' who look like they've had half their hair cut off by their pals when they've fallen asleep after a drunken night out. Someone who I knew picked up a 995 brick red, Mille Miglia in there for the extortionate price of £35. It had £70 on the label but by arrival at the till, the shop assistant revealed that the half price sale was still on. I kid you not.

Massimo in Manchester, the original shop on Dale Street, where I once spotted a vintage small Stone Island Marina denim jacket from circa 1987, that I later saw a few months later being sported by a small lad shopping in Life on Old Bank Street.

And last, but not least, TK Maxx, who picked up a huge amount of Osti deadstock attire in 2007 – predominantly his Boneville label, but with a bit of Navy Arctic and CP Company thrown in the mix. The items ranged from the early 80's right up to the mid-Nineties – what a find indeed. A real snowball effect then happened. A handful of Boneville cagoules and T-shirts began appearing on the rails, then an avalanche of stock followed. There were stories of people travelling within a two hour radius in order to get themselves a bargain or an odd rare piece that they would be able to make a good profit on, following a listing on eBay.

From times of rummaging for one-off in a shop down The Old Smoke, to delving in to a chain store, bargain basket, in one's own back yard, the hunt for 'the' Grail, goes on...

A Proper Lad

The next contribution is from Mark Smith, the co-editor of a magazine that was born out of the casual/dresser scene, but isn't a 'casual' mag. Having started the project in his bedroom, he and Neil, his partner in crime, now publish a genuine magazine version, *Proper Magazine*, twice a year, sending copies to every corner of the globe. The dual editors met over a decade ago in a dead-end job and within a year the old 'Propertop' website had been launched. When that began to run out of steam, a fanzine version was born. Making more of an effort to write about clothes, it was well received and each subsequent issue is an improvement on the last. It has evolved way beyond the realms of casual/dresser, while still retaining the same personality and points of reference. *Proper Magazine* is primarily a publication which centres on clothes, not fashion. Though the magazine is acknowledged and championed by not only stripling and mature casuals/dressers alike due to the detailed well-informed articles featured in the mag, but also innovative designers within the rag trade and multi-brand retailers. From observing, to setting the pace, Mark tells of his passions.

Mark: *I find it hard to talk about football culture these days without ending up sounding bitter and twisted. I was born in 1978 so the Nineties were the era I have committed to the part of my brain marked 'The Golden Age'. Coincidentally, I grew up during the best decade of my club's life. I'm a Stockport County fan and the era that began with Danny Bergara's appointment in 1989 saw our crowds treble, our team visit Wembley four times and the club climb two leagues higher up the pyramid. What has happened since then has perhaps sullied my view of what I once thought was the beautiful game, but I'll not go into that.*

I've always been an actual football fan. I played the game growing up and still dust off my 1995 Predators when the call comes, though my knees creak somewhat. Unlike many of my friends, the green bit in the middle was my initial focus. Players like big Kevin Francis, Mike Flynn, Andy Preece and Lee Todd were my heroes. Anyone reading this as a follower of a club with genuine superstar players may find it hard to believe I view these moderately successful Nineties footballers with such reverence, but to me, they were giants. Toddy still lives in Stockport and I recently enjoyed his company. I was still star struck.

But it was the culture surrounding the game that became more and more important to me as I headed towards my twenties. I became more conscious of terrace trends and the characters that conveyed.

I've always lived in Stockport but as a kid, Saturday afternoons were spent in Levenshulme, Manchester, where my mum had grown up. County played home games on a Friday night you see. It was hardly Moss Side but it was still much rougher than the streets of Stockport, and a world away from my secondary school in the Cheshire town of Macclesfield. With the benefit of hindsight, I'd say that odd cocktail of influences afforded me an uncommon insight into how people from different areas and backgrounds would dress and act. Music, clothes and hairstyles would all radiate from Manchester and into the suburbs and beyond. I distinctly remember my first weekend finding my feet with new friends in Macclesfield and noticing a marked difference in the clothes people wore. Remember, this was pre-internet and before most people had mobile phones. Sky TV was still a novelty and Macclesfield still had punk rockers.

The fact Macc was at least six months behind my hometown when it came to fashions and trends made it easier to exercise a bit of sartorial superiority, although I cringe at most of the stuff I sported. Most of the lads I knocked about with came from Stockport or Handforth. The latter was largely an overspill for relocated Mancunians and it was no surprise that they were a bit more clued up than the children of Bollington, Prestbury and Congleton. The school dress code was strict, but scope for individuality came in footwear. Most of what we called the 'Moshers' would wear Doc Martens and not wash their hair while we'd try and pass off black trainers from brands like Travel Fox as school shoes, often just about getting away with it. The regulation haircut for us seemed to be curtains though the more daring would risk suspension by going the whole hog and having a flat top. I'm not sure whether it does me any favours to admit this but on the first day of summer holidays, aged just 12, I asked my dad for a fiver as I needed a trim and promptly went and got my ear pierced. It was my attempt at staying ahead as many of my mates had spoken of their uncharacteristically lenient parents' attitudes towards piercings and I wanted to be first. Needless to say I was. Though my dad's assertion that I was "a big bloody puff", not to mention the horror followed by laughter I got from my mum made me think I'd made a mistake.

Meanwhile at the football, my mid-teens saw the end of my football shirt-wearing days. I still can't get my head around grown men wearing replica shirts, but each to their own, I suppose. For me, perhaps the seeds of oneupmanship and individuality were sown by those early years spent alternating between such disparate backgrounds.

With the turn of the millennium looming I was going to football with mates and, for want of a better phrase ,'wearing the gear'. It was terrible gear though. The presence of the Adidas UK HQ in Stockport and a friendly staff member meant we had a route to some of the best footwear and my obsession for three stripes began in earnest. And yet at that time truly credible Adidas were thin on the ground. Campus, Gazelle, Stan Smith and even Superstars were my footwear of choice. Bootcut denims and jackets by brands like Sonetti were my slightly un-clued up choice.

Away games on the train were always more enjoyable and through that I gradually started to get to know a different circle of friends. I'd been on nodding terms with many of them for a long while anyway; you know how it is at smaller clubs. It helped that this period coincided with the end County's five years in the Championship. We were getting decent crowds and there was a whole raft of lads who had come of age during that period. As for stories of overcoming the odds, I'll leave that to others. Their stories are probably better than mine.

What stands out more than the various 'on top' situations I experienced in that era was how valuable a Saturday afternoon became to me. I became a father aged 24 and again four years later. And having chosen to stay at home so the missus could further her career, the weekend represented a total contrast to the CBeebies and rusks existence during the week. It was my outlet, my 'me time'. During the week, the spare time and an internet connection also afforded me the opportunity to consider what on earth I wanted out of my work life. I'd briefly done boring admin jobs and stuff vaguely related to the internet and IT. But most of my work choices were flawed. That period at home changing nappies led me down a path I didn't ever consider, but one I now really value. Having edited a County fanzine for a short time I found there was an appetite for a so-called casual fanzine too. This was the start of Proper Magazine. *In partnership with my mate Neil, I printed the first issue on a £40 printer in my loft. It wasn't very good, and yet I've seen original copies go for silly money on eBay.*

Six years and 10 issues later and we found ourselves sitting in a garden in north London with a very influential publisher who now helps us produce two magazines a year that truly befit the title 'Proper'. We send hundreds of copies all over the world, with prestigious retailers stocking the magazine and things continuing to build. We've forged relationships with some of the brands we've grown up wearing. I've also snagged various writing work for brands like Levi's, not to mention my work for Oi Polloi, the shop that perhaps influenced the casual movement most throughout the Noughties without ever consciously trying to.

Oi Polloi introduced Fjall Raven to the UK having recalled friends wearing it two decades earlier. While neither of the owners were football nutters, both came from those streets and that background and as a result they had their own take on stealing a look or label from a different arena and making it their own. Along with the likes of Fjall and Norrona, walking shoes like Mephisto were dragged from old men's shops to a younger audience of appreciative lads. The amount of brands they broke at Oi Polloi led to a whole raft of retailers who saw their formula and twisted it to create their own take. As the consumer became more sophisticated so did the retailers, and simply selling a nice jacket wasn't enough anymore.

It needed to have a story, an ethos, a hook. This is where the heritage trend took hold, and brands would fine tune their history books and convince people to buy into what they were about. Contemporary brands would counter this by getting their clothing made in the US or UK.

"As the consumer became more sophisticated
so did the retailers, and simply selling a nice jacket
wasn't enough anymore. It needed to have a story, an ethos,
a hook. This is where the heritage trend took hold, and brands
would fine tune their history books and convince people to buy into what
they were about. Contemporary brands would counter this
by getting their clothing made in the US or UK."

What will probably go down in history as the heritage era was what dominated the Noughties. Checked shirts, selvedge denims, the understandably ubiquitous mountain parka and mostly suede shoes were what I rounded off the decade in and yet the signal to move on has come in the shape of high street appropriations of that same look. I'm finding more and more I'll up the dose of 'timeless' while trying still to remain slightly contemporary. As I get older, I find myself observing trends more acutely but participating in them less.

From Country Estate To Council Estate

Next up is a very informative and cognisant chap, Richard, who has an invigorating enthusiasm for casual/dresser labels and their social aspect.

· · ·

Richard: *One of the most important aspects of casual/dresser culture is the labels considered to be essentials in forming that much sought after look. The dictionary definition of 'casual' is noun: "clothes or shoes suitable for informal everyday wear" and whilst that description does go some way to understanding just what a casual/dresser is in the sense of popular male culture, it doesn't touch upon the notion that a casual/dresser should be striving towards being an individual and that can often mean being brave in his selection of attire, whether that be for a day out at the football, attending gig, or night out with his mates. The idea of informal wear is correct, but one key component to the casual/dresser is the idea of being smart at the same time and taking pride in his appearance.*

Like many social groups, a true casual/dresser can make a statement to his peers and the rest of the world via his style. Social individualism theory suggests that "there is no society, only individuals" and this could not be more apt to the casual/dresser who knows what he is doing and boasts a diverse wardrobe of various labels and style.

When actually considering some of the most popular labels within the portfolio of lads brands, it is fascinating to realise that over the years, many have been hijacked from other social groups and walks of life, the majority of which could not be any further removed from a football stadium on a Saturday afternoon.

Take Hackett for example, a brand whose origins are firmly rooted on the polo fields of upper class England and intended to be worn by members of the high society. Upon the label's launch in 1983, founder of the brand, Jeremy Hackett, stated his intentions for the brand were to "cater for the head to toe needs of gentlemen who wish to dress stylishly and to whom quality is more important than the vagaries of fashion" and whilst that may strike a chord with lads up and down the country, it is safe to assume that they certainly weren't his intended target audience. Hackett said of his first store's location that it was "the wrong end of the New King's Road", probably a little too close to Stamford Bridge for the label's kudos, but in an ironic twist, those Chelsea regulars together with casual/dressers the country over, have probably lined his pockets as much, if not more, than any pony rider or City banker over the past couple of decades.

Hackett really does satisfy the 'smart but casual' mantra and its signature polo shirts complete with large branding on the chest and numbers on the sleeves were both ground breaking and iconic during the Nineties and still remain popular today.

The most publicised incident of brand hijacking by casual/dressers came with the resurgence of Burberry in the 1990s which culminated in front-page headlines during Euro 2000 about 'middle class yobs' who were captured battling on the streets of Charleroi wearing Burberry's signature checked shirts and baseball caps.

For over a century Burberry has been one of the most prestigious labels in Britain, tailoring members of high society from famous explorer Ernest Shackleton to members of the royal family with the finest clothing and accessories and was for many years inaccessible to the majority of people. That changed during the Eighties and Nineties when the brand diversified and started to manufacture products sporting the famous tartan check and whilst still expensive, it was much more affordable, especially to the discerning casual/dresser eager to satisfy his need for expensive and unique items. So when items such as check scarves, baseball caps and the classic golf jacket with the check under the collar started appear on shelves of more mainstream stockists in the bigger cities, it was a lad's wet dream.

The thought of wearing a check cap and matching shirt was alien to many and turned many a head during the Nineties, but it was what it was all about – a hard-to-source table, expensive and one that set you out as an individual. It may be a fashion crime looking back but it was the Nineties, pretty much anything went.

Sadly, Burberry has become a victim of its own success since the turn of the millennium and has become one of the most counterfeited trademarks in the world and can only blame itself by opting to prostitute itself through increased distribution channels. Much like Adidas has with its many re-releases of classic trainers under the 'originals' brand in recent years. A result of suffering from brand imitations, Burberry is now synonymous with the 'chav' faction of society and the casual/dressers must shoulder some responsibility, given their status as national trend setters.

Unlike Burberry, the distinctive plaid of Aquascutum never caught on in main stream society and remained fairly exclusive to the terraces and high society. Somewhat underground within the movement of the Eighties and early Nineties, Aquascutum, named after the somewhat appropriate Latin for 'watershield', exploded on to the terraces on the back of Burberry's success as lads looked for an alternative check pattern to finish their outfits, and to a much lesser extent, Daks too. Aqua' was much more popular in some geographic locations around the UK than others but has been in decline in recent times. But like Burberry, and many other labels on the 'casual/dresser carousel' it is sure to have second/third coming.

One of the most popular labels of the last couple of years has been Barbour. The famous outdoor clothing company, which for the majority of its 115 year history has been the outfitter of men, and women, of a rural disposition. Their trademark use of materials such as tweed, moleskin, corduroy and wax have long kitted out farmers, huntsmen or just about any activity which required exposure to the elements – football excluded! That is until the signature Barbour piece, the diamond quilted jacket, started to creep on to the scene during the mid-Noughties. Like many labels to be worn down the years, the quilted jacket soon went mainstream and could be seen sported by everyone from rock stars to gang members on inner city council estates, via the royal family whom continue to wear it whilst passing time on their Sandringham Estate, much to the delight of J. Barbour & Sons and their expanding balance sheet.

The Barbour example epitomises the influence that the casual/dresser scene has had on fashion in the UK down the years. I am sure that I'm not alone in being referred to as Elmer Fudd of Looney Tunes fame when first donning my Polarquilt for the match several years ago only for those who found much amusement in my appearance to be seen wearing the same piece further down the line after Pete Doherty and Kate Moss had been spotted in a tabloid wearing the latest must have 'rural chic' attire whilst on a cocaine bender.

Barbour currently remains one of the most popular labels, and whilst the diamond quilts have been hung up by the more astute, the more expensive and understated technical items from the north east based firm are becoming increasingly popular together with the more daring accessories such as trapper and hunting hats that have become a statement of confidence for lads down the years.

Remaining on the theme of how famous clothing brands can cross a broad demographic within its wearers and become so far removed from its intended audience largely thanks to the casual/dresser scene, Ralph Lauren is possibly one of the best examples of all. Founded in the late Sixties by Ralph Lauren, the label was intended to appeal to a niche the New York designer had identified for high end smart/casual (sound familiar) wear.

He added the pre-fix 'Polo' to this casual line in order to become associated with the upper class sport of the same name and the now renowned logo is that of a man on horseback, playing the sport. Instant success amongst the fashion conscious in the States saw the chain expand to target the very same members of high society in the UK with the opening of its London store in 1981, which at the same time, unbeknown to Ralph, was to open the door for a whole new breed of people who would be seen wearing his apparel. Whilst the famous Polo motif could be seen on the intended wearers throughout the Eighties at exclusive polo clubs around the south of England or tailoring the image hungry students of Britain's 'red brick' universities, it was also a must have amongst lads who were quick to cotton on to the smart but casual ethos of this brand. The polo shirt was born.

However, whilst Ralph Lauren grew in popularity into the Nineties, very much like Burberry, it became a victim of its own success and counterfeits become all too common and eventually the label declined with it is only in the last couple of years that Ralph Lauren has once again become popular Saturday wear. Tommy Hilfiger arrived in the UK during the Nineties, just as Ralph was on the way out, and whilst popular with many lads for a very short time, it too suffered the same fate as its American rival and has yet to recover its status amongst Britain's best dressed.

The polo shirt, however, has remained strong for three decades now and whilst Ralph Lauren can lay claim to being one of the daddies of the 'polo', just every brand in the casual/dresser 'hall of fame' has knocked out polo shirts at some stage or another. With special mentions for Lacoste, Robe di Kappa, Hackett, Sergio Tacchini and Fred Perry down the years, all have catered for that smart look that this trademark piece provides. For the record, Argentine polo brands, La Martina and Polistas, are the two labels currently vying for exposure amongst the 'to be seen in' and, which could well be the next must have in the near future.

Like many of the great labels that hang in the wardrobe of your typical football casual/dresser, Paul & Shark is a label with a rich heritage firmly associated with yachting. Its style is that of your typical nautical and maritime influenced apparel; good quality, hard wearing, congruous fabrics in understated colours. You will rarely see a Paul & Shark piece that isn't one of in a combination of navy, red, white or yellow and either solid in colour or incorporating the cornerstone of all nautical garments, and a favourite of the casual/dresser down the years, the stripe.

Like many other labels that make up the portfolio of brand that is casual/dresser culture, the original design objective of Paul & Shark clothing is to provide the necessary protection to yachtsman experiencing the extreme weather conditions of the high seas. P&S is a label that's more at home on the decks of challengers in the America's Cup than 'wannabe' challengers of the terraces for close on 20 years; Paul & Shark has more than served its purpose to loyal fans of the brand. The closest any casual/dresser has probably come to testing a jacket capable of repelling 20,000mm of water, just one of the many unique selling points of the famous Paul & Shark Typhoon 20000 series, is on a stormy winter's night on the open terrace at Bournemouth's Dean Court Stadium when 10mm of rain fell – this putting the game in doubt. Add to this, the Typhoon jacket is also oil proof and has an advanced temperature control system that manages sudden changes in temperature so your football casual/dresser has nothing to worry about when he breaks down on his road trip across Russia for a UEFA Cup tie in Moscow, in December.

It's no surprise that the said jacket first retailed at over £500 back in the late Nineties, and still remains similarly priced over 10 years later. It's not that fact that this label demonstrates cutting edge technology in its fabrics and designs that appeal to the casual/dresser; it's merely the innovative features adding a premium to the price, thus eliminating the possibility of others on your next away trip owning the same jacket that appeals, and if it comes at a cost, you are willing to pay that. It's all about the pursuit of being an individual and making that all-important statement.

The signature piece from the Paul & Shark back catalogue is undoubtedly the four-button shoulder fastening jumper, which has been re-issued, like so many other P&S staples, as part of their winter range for years now. For anyone who has ever owned the said item will confirm they will never need to replace it unless, they find themselves struggling with the tribulations of weight gain that advancing years often presents, or it gets 'accidentally' damaged! Featuring the famous Paul & Shark logo, the very subtle yet stylish anchor on the upper left sleeve, the knit has become a timeless classic for any casual/dresser and will be still going strong in years to come.

It's also probably worth giving a token mention to the now famed add-ons that you used to get when purchasing Paul & Shark items, namely the tins, duffel bags, stickers and posters. Whilst no self-respecting casual/dresser would ever admit to such gimmicks influencing their purchase, I, for one, am not ashamed to say that I have over 10 years' worth of copper amassed in a rather fine looking Paul & Shark tin.

In recent years, the label has begun to sell out to the commercial demands of the less affluent and ever-emerging 'chav' element of society. And with this they have sacrificed the cutting-edge look, introducing items such as trainers, tracksuits and multicoloured jumpers and polo shirts through outlets such as Ath Leisure, which is part of the JD Sports Group. However, stick with the high end understated pieces from this label and you won't go far wrong.

The beauty of casual/dresser attire is that you could wear certain labels in the Eighties, or even nowadays, and they would still look as good, and Paul & Shark firmly fits in to that category.

Down the years many nautical and yachting influenced labels have come and gone from the casual/dresser scene. Most still exist in some form or other and many still remain popular with certain individuals while the quality often remains uncompromised. However, like many other casual/dresser labels, the likes of Helly Hansen and Henri Lloyd, both of which were cutting edge in the early Nineties have since been hijacked by chavs and become mainstream, removing all appeal to the casual/dresser.

Luckily the latter is slowly beginning to make a return to its original ethos, dropping the large logos and multicoloured designs to return to its nautical influenced roots, underpinned by quality. The same as it was when it first caught my eye in Manchester's famous Affleck's Palace around 1992 in a shop owned by Nigel Lawson, pioneer of so many casual/dresser labels around the epicentre of the casual/dresser movement, England's north-west, and now of the casual/dresser Mecca that is Oi Polloi; a man who also lays claim to introducing Henri Lloyd to the UK casual/dresser market. More recently he has reintroduced Fjall Raven to the casual/dresser by being the only stockist of this Swedish brand in the country from 2002 to 2006, when it started to become more popular again.

To this day, Paul & Shark has remained very much a label exclusive to England's north-west, most popular with casual/dressers from Manchester, Liverpool and surrounding towns and cities. That's not to say it is uncommon elsewhere in the country, but it has not exploded on a national scale as most labels have and does highlight that geographical location does bear influence on the scene, especially when closest to its roots.

Some of the other labels in this nautical casual/dresser genre worth a mention include North Sails, Murphy & Nye, Gill, Musto and one of the most underrated, yet excellent quality brands currently around, French sailing label, Saint.

Adidas V Puma: A Dassling Take On The One-Upmanship Of Sibling Rivalry

Trainers have played a major part in the casual/dresser evolvement, especially in the early formation period – I've been through hundreds of pairs of trainers over the years myself, the majority being Adidas. And one of the most annoying things was when you turned out for the match and someone else turned up in the same top or trainers. But one time I was glad to see another pair of Adi TRX Comps, which I'd had on – this from the hatch of a cell door. I'd been absolutely gutted in the morning when a mate, Chappie, had made an entrance onto the platform of Preston train station wearing a pair TRX's too. This because I thought I would be the only one who'd hunted them down in Manchester the previous week, but I wasn't. The same pair Chappie had proudly appeared in were now positioned outside a cell door opposite where I had taken up residence in, come teatime. At least I had someone to banter with over the weekend through the hatch until we appeared in court on Monday.

I've umpteen slapstick tales connected to trainers too. Tales like ruining a brand new pair of Adidas Samba the first day I wore them; this after running through dirty puddles all day, chasing Dingles. I couldn't get rid of the filthy marks and the efflorescence stains that kept forming on them. Also, when being sat on a cable car in San Fran when, before the car began its descent downhill, the Gripman glanced down at my Nike Wimbledons and declared "Fuck me man. I had a pair of those when I was in school!" I chatted to the bloke for the next 20 minutes about Nikes before I reached my destination. He nearly forgot to put the brakes on, on more than one instance – folk were jerking backwards and forwards at rapid rates. And, following a fracas against Derby's lunatic fringe once, on the stairs of the old Pavilion Paddock at Deepdale, in my promptitude, I left behind one of my Puma California. It was returned by a Fringe member a short while later with the strategic, pinpoint accuracy of a V-1 flying bomb, hitting me right between the eyes.

The true king-of-kings of athletic shoes are Adidas, though. And Adi Dassler, the crowned head of the three stripe German company, and his brother, Rudi, the head of Puma, fell out during the Second World War; a feud they would take to their graves. Only the 60-year old feud between the two sportswear and training shoe companies, Adidas and Puma, ended in September 2009, when they held a friendly football match. The two manufactures well and truly buried the *'beil.'* Tom will now explain in more detail.

Tom: *When Adolf Dassler invented the football boot, and lent the first syllables of his names to create Adidas in 1949 in Herzogenaurach in southern Germany, his brother Rudolf moved across town and set up Puma. It seems unlikely that a town, to which just 23,000 people called home, could produce two of the biggest sportswear giants the world has seen.*

It did though, and not only does the town house those two brands it also plays host to one of the fiercest rivalries. Forget your local derby match, how far does a rivalry have to develop before the mayor of the place has to defend his town with a statement that reads; "It is not true to say families of Puma employees and Adidas employees do not mix socially and that marriages between the two firms are forbidden!"

It wasn't always like that: In the 1920s, Rudi and Adi (as they were better known) were quite happy working together side-by-side for the family cobbling business – Dassler Brothers Shoe Factory (or 'Gebrüder Dassler Schuhfabrik' as they say in downtown Herzogenaurach). Adolf developed some studs, and business boomed under the Nazis. And by the 1936 Olympics some of the top athletes were wearing Dassler spikes.

The reasons behind the family feud are shrouded in mystery, though, it seems. The Herzogenaurach rumour-mill churned out stories of Adi sleeping with Rudi's missus, their respective wives hated each other, that Rudi fathered Adi's son and that Rudi, the less successful entrepreneur of the pair, had his hands in the petty-cash box. But until Jeremy Kyle gets involved we'll probably never know the real reasons that are all alleged and unfounded.

Certainly the final nail in the coffin might have been when, one night in 1943 in the bomb shelter, Adi remarked, seemingly talking about the RAF bombers overhead, "There come those pig dogs again!" However Rudi was convinced that his brother was talking about him and his family! Rudi's bitterness increased when he was shipped off to an American prisoner of war camp and Adi carried on running the family business without him. Rudi returned in 1948 and set up his own factory on the other side of the river, taking loyal employees with him, and Puma was born.

Before the 1970 World Cup kicked-off, Adidas and Puma agreed that Pelé was such a huge star that a bidding war to recruit him to wear their gear would get out of hand so they made a pact to stay away from the legend. Puma, however, had different ideas and offered the star $120,000 to wear their shoes. When Pelé had finished chewing over the offer (more like after biting Puma's hands off!) he agreed to wear Puma. Just before the opening whistle of a Brazil game in the World Cup finals, he requested to the referee that he could tie his bootlaces, which the ref granted. He then knelt down to give millions of people watching a close up of his Puma's.

This was the genius idea of Hans Henningsen, a Puma representative, and proved to be a huge triumph over Adidas, and others, in the early days of market supremacy in sports merchandising.

Not to be outdone, during the 1972 Olympic Games in Germany, Mark Spitz, the American swimmer, was on course to win an unprecedented seven gold medals when he was approached by Horst Dassler, son of Adi Dassler and Adidas chief at the time, in the Munich Olympic village.

Dassler asked Spitz to wear Adidas at the medal ceremonies, but this would've led to the medals being covered up by the loose fitting warm-up gear. So Dassler, ever so determined to get his way, asked Spitz to carry a pair of trainers in his hand instead. I'm not sure what words of encouragement, or dollars, Dassler gave to Spitz, but Spitz got a bit carried away and actually held up a pair of Adidas Gazelles as he waved to the crowd instead of his medals! This left Spitz with some explaining to do to the International Olympic Committee. But you just can't buy that sort of endorsement, can you?

This isn't a normal battle between two rival businesses; this is the petty point-scoring battle that only two siblings could throw up. In the early 1980s, a young, pre-pubescent Boris Becker turned up at the front door of Adidas with his manager hoping for a sponsorship deal only to sent packing by Adidas boss, Horst Dassler. But Ion Tiriac, Becker's Romanian manager, drove them straight over the river to Puma's HQ and demanded a meeting.

"Go on," he said to Rudi's son, Armin Dassler, who was the Puma chief at the time. "Take our Boris on. That'll really piss your cousin off." And it seemed that

that was all Armin needed to hear. Boris Becker went onto sign a £100,000 advertising contract with Puma. Tiriac earned his commission that day.

Another example of this tit-for-tat ethic, and someone taking advantage of the situation, was when some painters who were commissioned to paint the outside of the Puma building turned up wearing Adidas footwear. Within literally minutes, the Puma boss had 'em kitted out with new Pumas to wear for their work. It worked so well that they turned up at Adidas to carry out similar work only a month later, and where no doubt the same trick worked again.

It's apparent now, however, at managerial levels at least, that the rivalry has relaxed a little. One of Rudi Dassler's grandsons, for instance, now works as a legal consultant for Adidas. Something like that a decade or two ago would have been unthinkable. Although the rivalries do seem to have diluted somewhat in recent years, the mayor was forced to admit recently that the defection of Frank Dassler, Rudolf's grandson, from Puma to the management board of Adidas 'caused waves in Herzogenaurach!'

Puma is the smaller of the two companies with about 4,000 employees worldwide, compared to Adidas's 17,000, and Adidas's sales dwarf Puma's too, although Puma's profit margins are superior. Adidas also have a monopoly on the main European markets with sponsorship of many of the top football teams, and notably the German national side. Puma, though, interestingly, have invested heavily in African football and now supply the kit to at least eight African national teams.

Now I'm not gonna to lie to you, I'm a three-stripe man, and I'm not sure I actually own anything with the single Puma 'Formstripe' on it. But you've got to admire the spirit behind each brand and the fraternal battle that still goes on which ultimately runs a lot deeper than how many stripes people are wearing. It'll be interesting to see if Puma can claw back any ground on their rivals, or if Adidas' magnificent legacy of footwear will always keep them ahead.

I purchased a pair of Adidas Rekord – blue suede with light blue stripe and a caramel soul, they're the dog's bollocks – a few years back because I'd wanted a blue pair of trainers for while to match up with a 'Stoney' jacket from a couple of summers ago and had never seen a pair that was right. Although purchasing a pair of trainers these days definitely isn't the enjoyable experience it might once have been.

Saturday morning: JD Sports, Manchester Arndale, mid-January 2010, and its looks like the Green Room at The Jeremy Kyle show. Pikeys, gangsters, rude boys all arguing and shouting with kids running about. Now I'm no angel, but this isn't my sort of crowd. I've darted for the Rekord sitting resplendent on the shelf and grabbed the nearest shop assistant to sort me my size out sharpish. I get like this whenever I enter shopping centres and supermarkets, all I want to do is get what I came in for and leave as soon as possible.

Anyway, as I'm waiting for the spotty, teenage lad to get the trainers, this little pikey kid comes right up next to me and starts looking at me. (This is just the sort of thing that I'm on about!) I just said to him "What you looking at little man?" Fairly innocently I thought. But to my surprise the little bastard gives me the 'V's' and runs off.

My first thought is, 'this could end in tears, and they won't be mine.' But also, what is he going to be like when he's 10 years older and knows how to swing a baseball bat? A right little... I bet! But as I looked round to see where he's run off to, I notice that he's stood just behind me, still giving me the 'V's.' Remaining cool, I told him, with an air of discipline, "Piss off and go and play with your mates." And to be fair, he turned away looking a little bit startled, and buggered off round the corner, to the other side of the shop.

The shop was busy, in fact it was full, but how long does it take to go and get one pair of trainers out of the stock room? I'm starting to get a little hot and bothered by this point; I've got pikey kids running round my ankles, domestics left, right and centre, and all I want is to get out of the place.

Trying to avoid looking like I'm loitering, I'm doing all the time killing tricks like making sure my jeans are nice and neat on top of my Clarks, my jacket collar is straight and checking the time on my phone only to look up to see the aforementioned little hell-raiser come back round the corner with his big hell-raiser dad, and his big hell-raiser dad's mate – and they don't look like they're coming to ask me for my opinion on the shoes they've been trying on. One of 'em is the size of a single mattress stood on its end, and the other has got a token young offender's tear under his eye and scar that a Roman would've been proud of.

I uncomfortably made one last look round for the dawdling shop assistant – who's still nowhere to be seen – and think, 'there could actually be some tears here now, and they might end up being mine!' I've had a ruck or two over the years but, I'm not stupid, I wasn't about to take on two of Kersal's finest on my own in fuckin' JD Sports. So I just looked at them as if to say, 'What's the problem?' when the little devil runs up and kicks me on the shin. In disbelief I just turned round and walked out of the shop.

I later bought the trainers online, and I will never step foot in similar sports shop again.

11

THE YOUTH OF TODAY

With the casual/dresser scene being over 30 years old, a scene created by lads from the streets and council estates of the UK, who hadn't a inkling what chain of events and occurrences they'd kick started, and who hadn't given a second thought to if there be future for the cult in decades to come, and more so, would it keep developing and progressing with the times, what are the youth of today's thoughts on the cult?

Yes, the casual/dresser baton has been taken up by today's youth. The longest, ongoing evolving 'fad' has been adopted in some guise by each and every generation. But, with films connected to the rise and early origins of the casual/dresser hitting the big screen of late like *Awaydays*, and the woefully shite remake of *The Firm*, has the movement continued to make strides or stagnated? Some of the clobber the younger element I've borne witness to wearing at football stadiums up and down the country (i.e. 'authentic' sportswear in abundance, reissues of the last reissued trainers in a different colourway and baseball caps galore) , leads me to think that the youth haven't got their own mindset. And when the riots and looting took place in the UK during August 2011, JD Sports was one of *the* main targets to be ransacked and pilfered, with £700,000 worth of stock taken. Even though it is cited, by some, that the plundering of booty from shops and outlets was just 'opportunism.'

Also, in 2012, each town, city and stadia, I'm sure, is plagued by a variation of *faux pas*, facsimile flocks of youths assembled in either Barbour quilts, G-Star jeans and Adidas reissue trainers with a half stuck-to-the-pillow, half gelled–up electric shock hairstyles. Or black North Face, Lowe Alpine or Berghaus jackets accompanied by black Nike hoodies, black Nike trackies, black Nike Airs or white Reebok Classics and a shaved to the bone bonehead. There is also the odd £1,000+ jacket/ piece on show by the try too hard Hipsters. Spending just for the sake of spending on some designers' pieces ain't what it has been about, *ever*. There is even a new breed called 'moduals' – nowt new there though.

So, what do two of the more clued-up 'yoof' of today think of the cult, and where do they think it's *at*?

On the northern take of matters is Paul:

Paul: *Football, music and fashion have always been big things to me. Some of my earliest memories are asking my older sisters why I couldn't have a pair of Nikes instead of Nicky's from the market (does anybody else remember them or did I imagined it?). I would write down a list of songs for them to put on a compilation tape for me too. And, of course, memories of standing down the front of the Bee Hole End at Turf Moor whilst my dad went and stood with his mates, come flooding back. Thankfully my dad never listened to 'dad' music, and as me and my sisters were growing up we were spoilt on that front. We were brought up listening to good music from The Smiths, The Clash, James, Joy Division and New Order, The Roses, Manics, The Happy Mondays and so on. As I got older it was Oasis, Ash, Beck, Eels; you name it and I was sublimely a fan. The first gig I went to was Suede at Manchester Academy. I had some time to kill before I met my dad and popped into the Size? concession in Selfridges and splurged £85 on a pair of Adidas Italia II, those soft leather ones. I tried them on, loved them, asked the price and bought them. Anyway, fuck knows where I got that kind of cash from seeing as I was on £3.50 an hour as a glass collector, but I told my dad they were £40 when he asked how much they were just to save myself from a lecture. Money well spent though, as I still have them now. Only I must have bought them a size too big at least because they still fit today.*

Musically I've gone through obsessions: The Clash for example, which included buying each album in chronological order when they re-released them on CD with original artwork in the early Noughties, and playing them each to death, especially London Calling, until I could afford the next one. Then New Order, whose gig at Blackpool on their tour a couple of years ago was undoubtedly the best gig I've been too. Also since they arrived on the scene, I've had, to be honest, an unhealthy/geeky obsession with the Arctic Monkeys. For me they have got better and better with each record they've released and have grown from a band of lads singing about going out getting pissed, chasing girls and fighting (albeit very skilfully as opposed to the obnoxious 'Everybody's 'aving it!' style of someone like The Twang) to the deeper Nick Cave influenced sound they have nowadays. Obviously all fuelled by Turner's way with words. The man is a poet.

Looking back, high school is a big thing for everyone, and luckily I loved it. I was finally old enough to have a my own mind when it came to choosing and buying my clothes. I used to love going into Wade Smith JNR in the Trafford Centre, and briefly Originals Kids plus Originals in Burnley. I would usually go once in the summer before start of school term, around my birthday time, and as much as I could in the Christmas holidays, when the sales were on. One item I've kept from this time just for the sake of it is a Hackett crew neck jumper which I absolutely wore to death. It's now all faded to a purple colour and the sleeves are really baggy and pulled, but I definitely got my £55 pounds worth – so my mum can eat her words on that one. Other favourite labels at this time (early Noughties) were Puma trainers, Diesel and French Connection, mainly because my sisters' boyfriend, who was about 20 at the time, was wearing these items that I could afford and I thought he dressed 'cool as fuck.' But I couldn't dream of affording a £100+ Stone Island jumper, or Evisu jeans that all the older lads were wearing, which was perhaps a good thing, actually, when you look back at Evisu jeans styles! Fake London was another favourite; I still occasionally wear a couple of T-shirts from the label which I've looked after, from their Tour De Britannia collection. The label to me was good because it offered something a little different and not everybody liked it. Paul Smith Jeans T-shirts were always a big hit for the same reasons. (I've just remembered a white one with an X-Ray of somebody's skull been electrocuted. I'll have to search for that and see if it's still wearable.)

My mates who went the football and were well into their music and clobber were largely in a slightly different mould to myself – in the later years of school, Lacoste tracksuits and Nike Air Max were everywhere. Personally I stuck to polos and jeans, unless we were just 'dossing' up in the woods drinking when trackies were preferable, even to myself at times. They weren't for wearing to the match, but our social scene was dominated by Bounce and Donk dance music. I thought the sound was alright, but seeing as I was never into pills, and I could never see the fun in bouncing round a club in a tracksuit while having to watch your back from gypos and older lads from other areas of town who were drugged up and carrying knives. Although, I've tried and failed miserably DJing on a mates decks a few times.

My mates understood my tastes in music so always stuck on some indie or Northern Soul at house parties as they were into that as well. Now the dance thing has largely been knocked on the head, bar the odd big night, everyone seems to be into your usual 'lad' bands; Arctic Monkeys, Ian Brown, Kasabian, The

Courteeners, and obviously Oasis, plus the recently reformed Stone Roses. This trend has followed in mine and their tastes in clothes after leaving school in 2005. It was Armani, Levi's or Henri Lloyd jeans – which label you bought depending on if it was the January sales or not. Ralph Lauren and Lacoste polos, Aqua' and Henri Lloyd shirts. It was nearing the end of school, during Sixth Form, that I became obsessed with Adidas trainers. Until then, I'd still been a bit trainer happy – I'd get anything which was in my budget and looked good. From then on though, pretty much all footwear I bought for two years had to have three stripes.

These passions for clothes, as well as music, became the link between my mates and a gang of older lads who we'd always known to let on to, but had never hung around with all through school. It's funny how on all those none-uniform days at school when all the older 'peacocks' couldn't wait until dinner time to strut around the yard in their best gear. We would look at these lads and think what they were wearing was smart, but we didn't dare compliment them or ask where they'd got it from for fear of looking soft arses. Now, though, we're best of mates because of the same tastes and interests.

A lot is made of the 'one-up-manship' element to this 'casual' thing, but for me, if you're after a quality pair of trainers or a nice as fuck jacket in order to look better than other people, then I'm sorry that's not a love of what you're wearing! It's some sort of inferiority complex which you should probably seek help about. That's why I've no qualms with discussing what labels or bands I'm into at the minute – 2010/11 – with like minded people. So, if you're wondering right now, it's anything from Twisted Wheel to weekly dub step podcasts on the music front and lots of YMC, TukTuk shirts, Superga footwear and if Stansfield ever release a new collection of clothing again. I'd rather those who have the same interests as me know about what I'm into, too. And hopefully a 'share-and-share alike mentality' from them, by putting me onto some band that I'll want to see live over and over again or some label that's going to make me skint next payday, again.

And from the south, Matt:

Matt: *Since the late Seventies casual has always been about constant evolution. Starting with the influx of continental sportswear and rare (at least in the UK) footwear, it was a look that never stood still, never became stagnant. What was 'in' one moment, was 'out' the next. It was a constant search for new labels and looks all fuelled by a desire to be 'one-up' from your mates – to stand out from the crowd. But what is it nowadays?*

I believe that the casual, perhaps more so than any other British subculture, is impossible to define. At least that's how it was initially. Nowadays you have the 'Green Street Brigade' – Stone Island clad louts who hold a misguided view that amassing a collection of the perceived correct labels makes them a casual. It doesn't. They don't have a clue. You can't pinpoint this look. I think there was an Eighties casuals slogan which said "Those who know, know". That sums it up quite nicely for me. Some have a natural flair for dressing, others simply don't. Donning a Stone Island jumper, Burberry scarf and any old pair of Adidas trainers doesn't make you a casual. You can't dress by numbers. (You can, but you'll stick out like a sore thumb!).

The saturation of the casual look can be linked to a number of factors. Recent films like the 'Football Factory', 'Green Street' and anything Nick Love puts his name to have in part caused the whole look to become more and more mainstream and commercialised. Now teenagers up and down the country are buying into the whole sportswear look, something they have no real link to.

The internet has also no doubt played its role in the increased stagnation of the look. It's all a bit too easy in all honesty. You don't even need to leave your house to buy your clobber anymore; it's all just a click away. While this has its benefits the downsides are also clear for all to see. Whereas a special journey may have been required to get that jacket, that label or that trainer all you now need do is fire up your computer and you're away (provided you have the means, of course). Maybe that's why there's not really a north/south divide when it comes to dressing these days. There have always been certain labels that you were more likely to spot in certain corners of the country. One True Saxon was always thought as being a bit more of a northern brand but these days it's sold widely in the south as well.

Despite this, I don't think dressing is a thing of the past. It's a lot more commercialised these days. You only need to look at the number of big brands trying to cash in on the market to see this. Fila have revisited some of their retro designs recently and Adidas seem to want to reissue every trainer in their back catalogue – even if it means putting them out in a completely different (and wrong!) colour. But for every whopper and JCL who jumps on that bandwagon there are a few who will try and seek out new things. Labels like 6876, Albam, Engineered Garments, Folk and Universal Works have all become favourites for lads up and down the country who were wanting to look a little different. I still, sad as it sounds, get a bit of a buzz when I latch onto something before my mates do. I'm not trying to sound like some ultra-progressive style icon either, but I still like to look smart and a little different. I'm sure that I speak for a great number of young lads from all corners of the country when I say that.

There's always been other elements to the scene as well as the clothes. Music, football and violence have all played their part in this great scene's history. I've never been into the violence side of things and I'd be lying if I claimed to have burning desire to be involved with it, so that's a story for someone else to tell!

As for the football, I think that many now feel a growing frustration with the way our game is heading. Increasingly big finance plays far too big a role in English, and indeed global, football and it just isn't right. It's a sad sight to see any football club, big or small, suffer because of financial mismanagement. After all no matter how big your fan base is you're still a fan and it's still your team, so for someone to come and take that away from you for their own personal gain isn't something that sits right.

Many older people I know have stopped going on a match day for these exact reasons. The whole experience of going to a match has probably changed somewhat as well. I guess we have the prawn sandwich brigade and Sky television to blame for that. There's nothing quite as irritating as kick-offs being rearranged to some shit time just so someone can sit on their arse at home and half-heartedly watch the game. There are other reasons as well I guess. I never experienced terraced stadiums and have grown up going to the game in all-seater stadiums so perhaps I can't judge but others have claimed the atmosphere at matches is dying. Unfortunately, so is a significant minority's interest.

If you'd have told me a year or two ago that I would have only gone to 10 or so games last season then I'd have laughed in your face. But my interests have changed slightly too. I'd sooner spend a decent wedge of cash on travelling a bit or on a good gig/night out than I would sitting still in a sanitised atmosphere. I want to remember my teenage years by the places I've seen and the people I've met. At the end of the day, there's more to life than football and clothes, isn't there?

EPILOGUE

So, there you have it. Or do you?

On the football front: Since the summer of 1977, the year when youthful, straight jean wearing scallywags circuited Wembley Stadium, the League 1/Premiership title has been won by north-west teams a great deal more times compared to the title heading down south, past Birmingham. The FA Cup has had divided ownership, so we'll call that a score draw. I won't even go there on the European Cups that have been won by northern clubs in weight and balance, facts and figures, and if you know your history. We are superior. I would also like to mention for the record that Preston North End, one of the 12 founder members of the Football League, were the first ever Double Winners, while remaining unbeaten all season in 1888-9, and they didn't even concede a goal in the FA Cup too. A feat never bettered, and I doubt it ever will be.

Music and bands: Mersey Beat and the world dominance of the Beatles may have happened many sunsets ago but 'Beatlemanics' still pilgrimage from around our earthly sphere to Liverpool to pay homage to the Fab Four. The scousers came good once more at the beginning of 1984; there were seven Merseyside artists in the Top Twenty of the charts come one Sunday in January, which is quite a major accomplishment indeed. The iconic psychedelic, Madchester scene and bands created in those *dolce vita*, loved-up times, by Mancs, Salfordians and the confines of Greater Manchester alike, in the mid-to-late Eighties, will never be recaptured or superseded again. We did have the Oasis v Blur (north v south) saga in 1995, though – yawn. And there has been nothing of worth, or of note, to date since, aside from the resurrection of the Stone Roses, that is.

And on the casual/dresser forefront: Well, stone the crows. The southerners of late think they've invented the Bakers Boy/flat cap! I'll have you know us northerners have worn flat caps/bonnets since the 14th Century, and southerners have ripped us for many years for wearing such titfers – as well as braces and thick-knit woolly scarves. So, you urban chic chappies that are claiming bragging rights, I can't doff my cloth cap on this one either.

In Garry, 'the Godfather of Oi!' Bushell's book *Hoolies*, his closing lines seem to evaluate what's occurring on the new, and, the up and coming cult and sub-culture front – nothing. He also declares that music isn't the prerequisite of 'yoof' anymore – which I agree with. But, do cockneys/southerners really believe that they were the vanguards and trailblazers on all of Britain's cults since the teddy boys; or that they created the last big cultural explosion, the casual/dresser? I guess they think an anticrepuscular ray/Jacob's Ladder does beam outwards from their hotbed of all things hot, and they lead the way on 'all' forefronts. I, and other northerners, beg to differ, because we are in the know, and we know not. We're very clever-clogged, too. Also, if you are not aware of it, planet earths stratospheric ozone shield is goosed, and at some stage cockneys/southerners may have had a touch of thermoplegia, that caused a tad of genetic damage from ultraviolet radiation. Which in turn, confused them when stating they were 'the' 100 per cent maiden casuals/dressers. Thus, these sort of hallucinations made cockneys/southerners hostile towards everyone and everything north of Watford Gap, and those who question such things too.

You lot down south wanna get your Uncle Neds out of the smog and polluted stormy petrels down in The Smoke, and get your plates of meat well and truly back down on terra firma – sorry, I meant, your golden cobbled lined streets. We up in the north-west haven't suffered from sunstroke, see. This due to us living in, very grim, sullen climes I'll have you know. We're also not inflicted with any lack of co-ordination, or under any illusions who were *the* first casuals/dressers, so there!

Right then, Mr Bushell, and the rest of you southerners reading this, let's draw a line under it: us up north have just put our four toed feet up for a while, and we're having a siesta, in a splendid seasoned, grand old oak tree, for the mo. Because one day, we Northern Monkeys WILL rise again...

It is not the strongest of the species that survive, nor the most intelligent, but the one most responsive to change Charles Darwin

REFERENCES

Dave Hewitson: *The Liverpool Boys are in Town*

Ronnie Sharpe: *Sharpe as a Blade & Sharpe as a Blade 2*

Phil Eaves: *Xtrbop & Amethyst Nights*

David Nowell: *Too Darn Soulful*. Co-author: *Soul Survivors*

Cass Pennant: *Cass, Congratulations You Have Just Met the ICF &Top Boys: True Stories of Football's Hardest Men*. Co-author: *Rolling with the*

6.57 Crew, Terrace Legends, Good Afternoon, Gentlemen, the Name's Bill Gardner, 30 Years of Hurt & *Want Some Aggro?*

Les Fowler: *Dry Powder*

Ian Hough: *Perry Boys & Perry Boys Abroad*

Steve Cowens: *Blades Business Crew & Blades Business Crew 2.*

Co-author: *Divide of the Steel City*

Phil Thornton: *Casuals*

Dominic Lavin: *Last Seen in Bangkok*

William Routledge: *Oh Yes, Oh Yes, We are the PPS*

Printed in Great Britain
by Amazon

16119351R00224